The Book in the Islamic World

83237

D1507632

The Book in the Islamic World

The Written Word and Communication in the Middle East

edited by
George N. Atiyeh

State University of New York Press
The Library of Congress

Published by
State University of New York Press, Albany

©1995 State University of New York

All rights reserved

Printed in the United States of America

No part of this book may be used or reproduced
in any manner whatsoever without written permission
except in the case of brief quotations embodied in
critical articles and reviews.

For information, address the State University of New York Press,
State University Plaza, Albany, NY 12246

Production by Christine Lynch
Marketing by Dana E. Yanulavich

Library of Congress Cataloging-in-Publication Data

The book in the Islamic world : the written word and communication in the Middle East / edited by George N. Atiyeh.
p. cm.
Consists of papers presented at a conference held November 8-9, 1989 at the Library of Congress, Washington, D.C.
Includes bibliographical references and index.
ISBN 0-7914-2473-1 (alk. paper). — ISBN 0-7914-2474-X (pbk. : alk. paper).
1. Books—Middle East—History—Congresses. 2. Middle East—Intellectual life—Congresses. 3. Manuscripts, Islamic—History—Congresses. 4. Printing—Middle East—History—Congresses.
I. Atiyeh, George N. (George Nicholas), 1923-
Z8.M63B66 1995
002'.0956—dc20 94-29487
CIP

10 9 8 7 6 5 4 3 2 1

Contents

Figures

9.10 On the left, the Ka'bah is depicted—appropriately inclined to the meridian—on a crude cartographic grid from which one can determine the *qiblah* very approximately by joining one's city to the Ka'bah (here Bursa is shown connected to the Ka'bah [via Medina]). On the right is a diagram of sacred geography, showing various areas around the Ka'bah and indicating the astronomical horizon phenomena which define their *qiblah*s.

9.11 A *qiblah*-indicator from Isfahan, ca. 1710, unique of its genre. The *qiblah*s and distances from Mecca of 150 localities marked on the cartographic grid—which can be read from the circumferential scale when the diametral rule, centered at Mecca, is laid on the marker for the locality in question—are given accurately for all practical purposes.

9.12 An eleven-sector scheme of sacred geography from a manuscript of al-Qazwīnī's *Āthār al-bilād* (Iraq and Syria, ca. 1250). The information on the *qiblah* in each sector has been suppressed. Also one of the sectors in the original scheme has been omitted by mistake.

9.13 An eight-division scheme of sacred geography from a manuscript of the treatise on cosmogrphy by Pseudo-Ibn an-Wardī (Aleppo, ca. 1420). There are several different traditions of sacred geography in the numerous manuscripts of his treatise; the illustration in the published text shows two of these but are hopelessly corrupt.

9.14 Two different twelve-sector schemes of sacred geography with associated astronomical horizon phenomena for finding the *qiblah*, as found in a manuscript of a thirteenth-century Yemeni treatise on folk astronomy.

9.15 An Ottoman scheme of sacred geography with 72 divisions of the world around the Ka'bah, suitable for marking on a horizontal *qiblah*-indicator—see figure 9.17.

9.16 An Ottoman sundial cum *qiblah*-indicator on which a scheme of sacred geography has been included on the circular base.

9.17 The imposing ventilator on the Musāfirkhāne in Cairo, one of the few surviving examples. In medieval times, most buildings in Cairo were fitted with such ventilators, all astronomically oriented.

9.18 A diagram showing the orientation of ventilators in medieval Cairo, found in the treatise on astronomical instruments of Ibn al-Sarrāj (Aleppo, ca. 1325).

9.19 The different *qiblah*s accepted in medieval Cairo. In the case of the southerly *qiblah*s, any direction between the rising and setting of Canopus would have been considered acceptable.

9.20 On the left is a ground-plan of the Ka'bah (the rectangular shape is here exaggerated) and on the right a diagram which associated the edifice—incorrectly oriented—with the cardinal directions and their intermediaries,the winds, and the *qiblah*s of various localities.

9.21 The basic orientation of the Kaʿbah and the directions of the four "cardinal" winds as recorded in various medieval texts. Actually, the minor axis is aligned with the most southerly setting point of the moon.

9.22 The basic information on the Kaʿbah contained in figure 9.20 (r.h.s.). The orientation of the Kaʿbah has been "corrected"—in fact (see figure 9.10 (l.h.s.) and figure 9.21), its major axis is at about 30° E. of S.

9.23 A diagram showing 28 traditional divisions of the world, from a manuscript of the geographical treatise of Abū al-Fidā' (Hama, ca. 1320) which never made it into the published text.

10.1 Topkapi Sarayi Müzesi, Hazine 1510, fol. 775b, Colophon of Niẓāmī *Khamsah*.

10.2 Topkapi Sarayi Müzesi, Hazine 1510, fol. 484b, Colophon of Firdawsī *Shāh-nāmah*.

10.3 Turk ve Islam Eserleri Müzesi, T. 1950 fol. 464b, Colophon of Khusraw Dihlavī, *ʿAīnah-i Iskandarī*.

10.4 Topkapi Sarayi Mžesi, Hazine 1510, fol. 1510, fol. 7a, "Colophon Signed by Warqah ibn ʿUmar Samarqandī".

10.5 Topkapi Sarayi Müzesi, Hazine 1510, fol. 498a, "Firman in the Name of Ḥusayn Bāyqarā".

10.6 Topkapi Sarayi Müzesi, Hazine 1510, fol. la, Dedication medallion in the name of Ḥusayn Bāyqarā.

10.7 Topkapi Sarayi Müzesi, Hazine 1510, fol. 499a, Dedication medallion in the name of Shāh Rukh.

10.8 Topkapi Sarayi Müzesi, Hazine 1510, fol. 682b, "In Praise of Spring."

10.9 Topkapi Sarayi Müzesi, Hazine 1510, fol. 13b, "Ḍaḥḥāk Enthroned."

10.10 Topkapi Sarayi Müzesi, Hazine 1510, fol. 502b, "In Praise of His Patron: A Prince Enthroned."

11.1 The back page of al-Shidyāq's newspaper, *al-Jawā'ib, no. 1017, Istanbul, 19 Ramaḍān* 1298/25 August 1880. The right-hand column gives a price list of al-Jawā'ib Press books available from the newspaper offices, starting with al-Shidyāq's own works, including the original Paris edition of his *al-Sāq ʿalá al-sāq*—"of alien appearance" (*ʿalá shakl gharīb*). On the left are other Arabic and Turkish books which can be supplied, including some from "Syrian," that is, Lebanese, presses, followed by a list of those available from the Egyptian agent of *al-Jawā'ib*.

11.2 Two pages from al-Shidyāq's *al-Lafīf fī kull maʿnā ṭarīf*, Malta, 1839, showing his use of punctuation marks: dash, comma, question mark, and colon. The typeface, which has been admired for its beauty, was specially cut and cast in Malta, almost certainly to his designs. The only incongruous feature is the use of Western numerals for the page signature.

Abbreviations

ALECSO	=	Arab League Educational Cultural Scientific Organization
BRISMES	=	British Society for Middle Eastern Studies
CMS	=	Chruch Missionary Society
ENAL	=	Enterprise Nationale du Livre (Algeria)
GEBO	=	General Egyptian Book Organization
IBLA	=	Institut des Belles Lettres Arabes (Tunis)
MELA	=	Middle East Librarians Association
IRCICA	=	Research Centre for Islamic History Art and Culture (Istanbul)
SI	=	Studia Islamica
TKD	=	Türk Kütüphaneci Derenği

Encouraging the study of books in society is one of the purposes of the Center for the Book in the Library of Congress, which exists "to heighten public interest in the role of books and printing in the diffusion of knowledge." Drawing on the rich resources of the Library of Congress, the conference on which this volume is based brought scholars, librarians, diplomats, and other public officials together to examine the Islamic book and its influence. An exhibition of Islamic books and printed materials prepared by the Library's Interpretive Programs Office enhanced conference discussions and informed the general public about the role of the book in Islamic civilization. The conference and exhibition demonstrated the special significance of the Library of Congress as a center for the study of the history of the book and the printed word.

The Center for the Book in the Library of Congress was established by law in 1977 to stimulate public interest in books, reading, and libraries and to encourage the study of books. Its projects and publications are supported primarily by contributions from individuals, corporations, and foundations. The Near East Section and the Center for the Book are pleased to present this volume as a contribution to the study of the history of the book.

John Y. Cole
Director
The Center for the Book in the
Library of Congress

Introduction

A book is obviously not simply a physical thing. It is a living entity. People's lives are definitely influenced by this old and basic vehicle of communication. Our planet's civilizations and cultures, one may safely state, did not begin to flourish and expand until the book was invented. Books have become so general and extensive that we need not emphasize what is manifestly plain.

In the West, the study of the book as a vehicle of culture has been common and fruitful, but is not so in the world of Islam. There, the book, so much esteemed and cherished, has not been the subject of many serious studies as an entity and as a vehicle of cultural development. Aware of the need for further studies on the subject, the Library of Congress, which holds one of the largest collections in the world of books and other materials from the Islamic countries, convened an international conference on 8–9 November 1990, and mounted an exhibit in order to discuss and display the role of the book in the development of civilization in the Islamic world. It thus provided an opportunity for a number of distinguished scholars to examine and reflect upon this very important aspect of Islamic civilization, and it is hoped that this would open the doors for further studies. All the papers in this volume, except for my own, were read and discussed, and sometimes debated, by the scholars who wrote them and the scholarly public who attended the conference.

The study of "the book" as an entity is complex and multifaceted. Any such study embraces the origins, production, content, use, and role of books in culture, education, and society in general. The production of books involves materials, formats, script, typography, and illustration, among other things. As an instrument of communication, the book in its many forms has been and still is the greatest factor in the growth, development, and preservation of culture, inasmuch as it carries the knowledge, the ideas, and the messages without which an advanced culture cannot exist. Whether in the form of clay tablet, scroll, codex, or volume, the book remains central to culture. In the words of Dr. Guy Story Brown, Director of the Bureau of Educational and Cultural Affairs at the United States Information Agency, "the idea of *culture* itself originally emerged in connection with cultivation of learning through the written word. . . . The idea of *the book* or centrality of writing as a universal human inheritance in a sense involves a fundamental change in the idea of culture, a change that itself is characteristic of modernity, and underlies the ubiquity of books."

Although the development of the book, from its rudimentary form into the codex, and later the book manuscript, owes much to Christian scholarship in the Roman and Byzantine periods, the book in the Islamic world was more fundamentally integrated with Islam as a religion and with the Arabic language and script, which were the early means of communication in the Islamic world. Scarcely has the literary life of any other culture played such a role as in Islam. The Koran, referred to as the Book or *al-Kitāb*, has a privileged place in Islam in that it is considered to be the word of God and in that it is inimitable (*mu'jizah*). It was only natural that The Book affect greatly the course of Arabic and Islamic culture. Under its stimulus, the various sciences (*'ulūm*, plural of *'ilm*) developed. Science, or learning (*'ilm*), by which is meant the whole world of the intellect, engaged the interest of the Muslims more than anything else except perhaps politics during the golden age of Islam, that is, the early part of the Abbasid period. It was a period that saw the elaboration of methods of publication, transcription, bookbinding, and book selling to a great degree. The circulation of books was greatly assisted by the introduction of paper in the eighth century. Literature and the art of the book received a great impetus from the manufacture of paper. The Muslims developed paper manufacturing through the employment of new materials and the discovery of new methods. This was as much a revolution as the one achieved in the fifteenth century by Gutenberg. As Professor Irfan Shahid says, "Neither parchment nor papyrus was able to bring about such a revolution." The extraordinary efflorescence of book making is reflected in the large number of repositories, or libraries (*maktabāt*), and the large number of manuscripts that have reached us. Once the printed book came into being and the process of dethroning the manuscript began, opposition to the new technology by the Islamic *'ulamā'* grew. The *'ulamā'*, until the invention and spread of printing, monopolized the transmission of knowledge. The manuscript, moreover, represented for the Muslims an historic and cultural value. This remains so until today. Most of the Muslim scholars who visit me at the Library of Congress begin their questioning by asking how many Arabic or Islamic manuscripts the Library holds. Printing meant a new cultural direction. The manuscript, which represented the old culture, became the center of controversy between the old and the new. Although it is presented in different forms and on many levels, this controversy remains with us today.

The rise of *al-warrāq*, a person who made a profession out of transcribing books, was a high point in the "Civilization of the Book." The *warrāqūn* (plural of *warrāq*) were the link between men of letters and the general public. They were interested not only in beautiful calligraphy, but also in reproducing correctly and exactly the text. They were not only copyists, but also booksellers, and oftentimes they were men of letters themselves. al-Jạhiẓ (d.255/868), who was a versatile author and a great bookworm, hit upon the idea of hiring booths from the *warrāqūn* and spending the nights in their shops reading. In his famous book, *Kitāb al-ḥayawān* (The Book of Animals), al-Jāḥiẓ dedicates a lengthy section to the topic of "the book". In it he responds to a critic of books by describing the value of the book as a companion, a vehicle of learning, and a versatile tool for the success of all human endeavors. He recites stories about book collecting, calligraphy, ancient writing, the preservation of cultural heritage, translation in general and translation of religious books, book editing, and the conflict between the written and oral traditions. Throughout the history of Islam, oral transmission of "the book" proceeded alongside the written. Many considered the written as merely a corroboration of and complement to the memory.

There is indeed a great need to look into the role of the book in the development of the Islamic world and its culture. The history of the book, not only as an artifact, but also in terms of intellectual content and physical properties, needs to be seriously explored. An investigation into the creation, manufacture, and use of the book in its written and printed forms has not been systematically approached, although there have been several attempts to do so. The kinship between the book and civilization is obvious yet understudied. Investigating it, as far as the Islamic world is concerned, can offer many insights into the nature and characteristics of that world.

The term "Islamic world" should be clarified. We don't mean by it the *ummah*, or community of believers, rather the countries that became mostly Muslim by religion and contributed to the growth and characterization of the widely spread Islamic civilization. The essays and studies in the present volume are, however, concerned only with what might be called the core of the Islamic world, namely, the Middle East.

The distinguished professors and scholars who participated in the conference expounded on many aspects and problems related to the book and its study in the Islamic world. Professor Muhsin Mahdi, in his issue-raising paper, confirms the need for more information on the history of books in the Islamic world. He explains the reasons why the printing of religious books by Muslims came late, as late as the nineteenth century, and wonders why the excellent scribal traditions of dictation, collation, and illustration have not been applied to the exigencies of modern book production. He systematically raises many issues resulting from the introduction of printing, such as the impact of translations on the development of the sciences, languages, and even orthography. Furthermore, he calls for the preservation and sustenance of scholarly traditions and systems while looking forward to the new technologies in the editing and preservation of the great wealth of manuscripts remaining in the Islamic world. Jacques Berque elaborates more abundantly on the meaning of the term *al-Kitāb* (the Book) and the methods used in compiling the text of the Koran in its final form, looking at the early conditions under which the task of compilation was initiated. Looking at the properties having to do with the Koran, Professor Berque discerns a structure of type strongly akin to the synchronal and concludes that the Koranic "edition" attests to a reflective and orderly character and is not a miscellany of disorganidation and arbitrariness. The text of the Koran was the outcome of a laborious effort and is laden with potentialities that have stood the test of time well.

Professor Franz Rosenthal discusses Muslim attitudes toward books and the dilemma caused by the abundance of books in terms of quantity and quality. Books were often so plentiful that one could think of discarding some, but this was generally considered wrong. The destruction of books is discussed, when and why it occurred, the meaning and scope of originality, and the relationship between knowledge and books. Rosenthal points out the persistent distinction between oral and written information, a theme that appears in several papers and is effectively handled by Professor Seyyed Hossein Nasr, who discusses the great significance throughout Islamic history of oral transmission in education and the spoken word as compliment to the written text. The Islamic intellectual tradition itself has functioned with the belief that oral tradition is of central importance. Oral teaching always accompanied the written text.

Professor Annemarie Schimmel considers the metaphor connected with the book in Islamic literature. After discussing the great love Muslims have for books, she deals with the figurative language in which books are used as metaphors in the works of the Persian and Persianate poets, showing the central role the imagery of the book played in Islamic poetry.

Biographical books are among the earliest and most extensive genres of Arabic literature. Professor Wadād al-Qāḍī believes that biographical dictionaries are not only indispensable tools of research, but also a mirror in which are reflected important aspects of the intellectual and cultural development of the Islamic community. A study of the inner structure of biographical dictionaries produced during the first nine centuries of Islam reveals that development. Professor Ramzi Baalbaki traces the development of the grammatical book by examining three stages in the history of Arabic grammar, based on Sībawayhi's book (*Kitāb*) as the focal point in this development. He concludes that Sībawayhi's originality was not to be matched by any of the later grammarians. Professor Salāḥ al-Dīn al-Munajjid discusses the role of Muslim women in learning, and after explaining the position of calligraphy in Islam, he investigates women's role in the copying of Korans and narrates the achievements of several women who distinguished themselves in that field. Professor David King considers the significance of certain categories of book illustrations, especially in works on astronomical instruments, and concludes that there are numerous illustrations in Islamic scientific books which further our understanding of different aspects of Islamic science, and even aspects of Islam and Islamic civilization.

Illuminated and illustrated books in the Islamic world were sought after diligently by kings, princes, and scholars. The special prestige attached to books with a royal or princely provenance appears to have encouraged another method of book collection used by rulers, that of appropriating volumes from each other's libraries. Professor Priscilla Soucek and Dr. Filiz Çağman follow the path of such a volume now kept in the Topkapi Saray in Istanbul.

The transition from scribal to print culture, as exemplified by Aḥmad Fāris al-Shidyāq, is ably presented by Dr. Geoffrey Roper, who has shown that al-Shidyāq personifies in his career, as well as in his attitudes, the dawn of a new cultural era for the Arab and Islamic worlds, an era in which the communications revolution caused by the printing press brought radical changes to intellectual, political, and social life. In my article on the book in the Arab world, I survey the history of book publishing in the modern Arab world, describing the general attributes of book production and dissemination, and the prevalent trends that characterized the different periods of the last two centuries. Professor Eickelman's work, although it does not seem to be related to the history of the book as a cultural vehicle, is indirectly related in that it attempts, in a new approach, to show the impact of new means of communication in the field of education, a field that used to be associated almost exclusively with the book.

One can see from the sum total of the studies in this volume that we have only touched upon the surface of a whole new multifaceted discipline, the history of the book as a cultural vehicle. We hope that our efforts will lead to and point the way for further studies on this important and serious subject.

In the editorial work we have sought uniformity but not conformity. We adopted the Library of Congress' transliteration system and one style for the annotations. All foreign words found in *Webster's Third New International Dictionary* are not italicized. Some proper names are written as they have been commonly used by the press or as they have been established by their owners. Names of cities are transliterated only when there is no English equivalent. The dates appear according to the *Hijrī* as well as Gregorian calendars. Whenever the solar instead of the lunar system is used for the *Hijrī* year, this is indicated. The words Koran and *tārīkh* are transliterated as Qur'ān and *ta'rīkh* whenever the author has requested it.

The editor wishes to thank a great number of colleagues and friends for their most valuable assistance. A special mention, however, should be made of Michael Albin, who did not spare any time or effort in making the conference "The Book in the Islamic World" the success it was, and to John Cole, the director of the Center for the Book at the Library of Congress, who co-sponsored the conference and supported it morally, administratively, and financially.

The editor also wishes to take this opportunity to express his gratitude to Shaykh Aḥmad Zaki Yamani, the Institute of Turkish Studies, Saudi ARAMCO, the United States Information Agency, and the Embassy of the Kingdom of Saudi Arabia for their financial and moral support, which made holding the conference possible. He also wishes to thank all those staff members in the Near East

Section and the Library of Congress whose help was crucial in organizing the conference and the exhibit that accompanied it, in particular Christopher Murphy, Anne Boni, Doris Hamburg, and Carol Ido.

George N. Atiyeh

1

From the Manuscript Age to the Age of Printed Books

Muhsin Mahdi

The period of transition from the manuscript age to the age of printed books is the second and less important transitional epoch in the history of the book in the Islamic world. The first and more important epoch was the initial emergence of the book during the first two centuries of the Islamic era, the seventh and eighth centuries of the common era. The seriousness and persistence with which scribes and scholars in the Islamic world were able during that period to preserve and transmit the text of the most important of all books in that world, the Koran, and, next, the traditional collections of the sayings and deeds of the Prophet of Islam, meant that, once codified, their preservation and transmission could remain free of the many problems besetting the preservation and transmission of most other books, both religious and secular, during the transition from the manuscript age to the age of printed books.

In contrast, the disturbing manner in which European printers took liberties with the text of the Koran (when compared to the care taken in printing the Gutenberg Bible, for instance) could not but raise doubts among Muslims regarding the virtues of printing when they first came into contact with the new technology. One look at the title page of the Koran printed in Hamburg in 1694 (figure 1.1) must have made Muslim readers of the Koran think that only the Devil himself could have produced such an ugly and faulty version of their Holy Book; and the same must have been the impression made on them by Alessandro de Paganino's Venice Koran printed in the 1530s, where the printer, perhaps following some contemporary Arabic vernacular, did not distinguish between certain letters of the alphabet, such as the *dāl* and the *dhāl* (figure 1.2). One would expect a handbook on medicine and medicaments, such as the Arabic text of Avicenna's *Canon*, to be free of printing errors, since errors in a book of this nature can easily lead to unfortunate results. Yet the Medici edition (Rome, 1593) of this work commits a serious grammatical fault, to say nothing of the syntactical infelicities, on the title page itself (figure 1.3). Unlike

Fig. 1.1. The Koran printed in Hamburg, Germany in 1694 by Officina Schultzio-Schilleriana. Copy in Library of Congress.

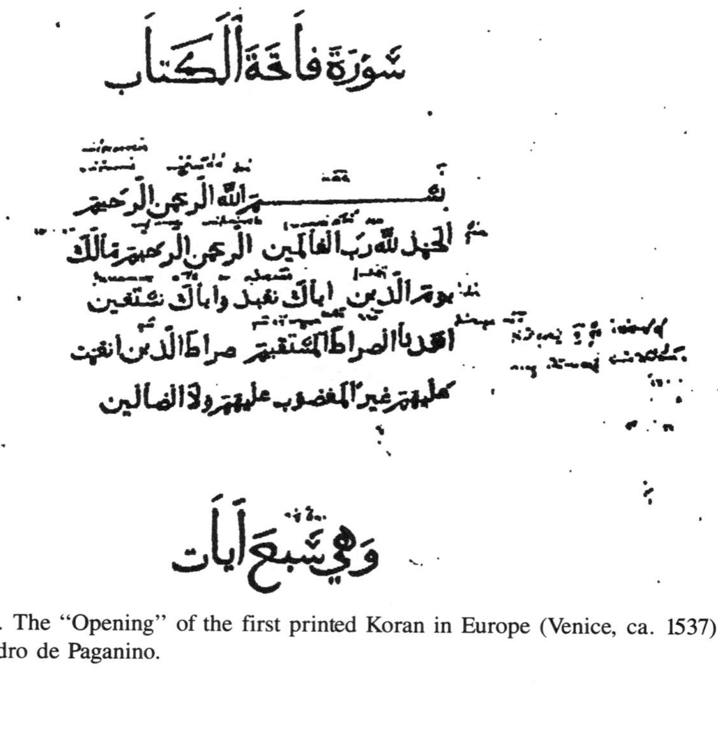

Fig. 1.2. The "Opening" of the first printed Koran in Europe (Venice, ca. 1537) by Alessandro de Paganino.

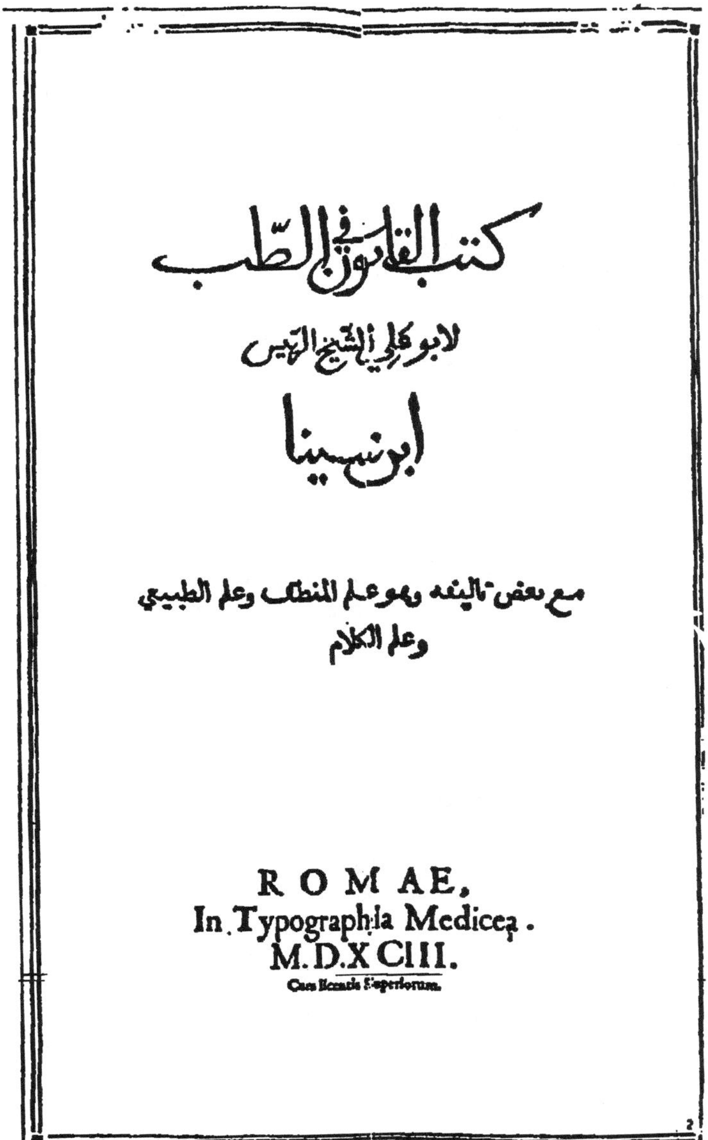

كتب القانون في الطب

لابو علي الشيخ الرئيس

ابن سينا

مع بعض تاليفه وهو علم المنطق وعلم الطبيعي

وعلم الكلام

ROMAE,

In Typographia Medicea.

M.D.XCIII.

Cum licentia Superiorum.

Fig. 1.3. Title page of Avicenna's *Canon of Medicine* printed in Rome, 1593, by the Medici Press.

a faulty manuscript copy by some ignorant scribe, such printed books involve an orderly organization, extensive financing, and the distribution of a large number of copies with the same errors, making it less easy to dismiss them as unimportant or inconsequential incidents.[1]

This brings us to the frequently cited objections made in the Islamic world to printing when it was first introduced, delays in introducing the printing of books dealing with religious subjects, and the strictures against printing religious works.[2] Were the initial fears of the dangers of printing books on religious subjects justified? Yes, if we recall the examples just cited. But why were no ways found to overcome such problems before the nineteenth century? Various economic or doctrinal hypotheses have been presented to explain this phenomenon. What is clear is that in many cultural centers in the Islamic world a scribal tradition flourished with standards of accuracy that could not be assured in printed books, especially when the printing was done outside the Islamic world by printers with limited knowledge of the languages involved; and many of the early printers both outside and inside the Islamic world were not Muslims and not well versed in Islamic religious sciences. These strictures did not last; ways were found around them, primarily in the control of standards that made it possible to print books in all religious subjects, starting with the Koran.

But the expertise shown in the printing of the Koran and the ḥadīth was a carryover from the expertise developed during the manuscript age in the strict disciplines associated with these highly specialized texts. There was, on the other hand, a more general scribal tradition specializing in the transmission of books in the manuscript age and which, depending on the field it was in, had developed specialized techniques and methods of dictation, collation, and illustration that seem to have deteriorated with the advent of printing. Why were those techniques of editing not transferred in an orderly fashion to the exigencies of book production when using movable type? What was the extent of the effort to recover, systematize, improve upon, and make use of the old scribal art in the new conditions? Why was the printed book treated as though it were a manuscript copy, with printed comments placed or variants noted on the margin of the text? The art of textual criticism developed in Europe during the second half of the nineteenth century does not seem to have reached the Islamic world, and the beginnings made in introducing it during the present century remain limited and partial. The result has been the loss of knowledge of the techniques and approaches of earlier Islamic scholarship, now replaced by only an incomplete and imperfect knowledge of the new European tradition. A number of works were no doubt edited and printed in an exemplary manner in the Islamic world. It is equally true, nevertheless, that on the whole printing has simply fixed and diffused many books that are hardly superior to any stray manuscript copy untouched by a careful scholarly hand, and others whose scholarly form is mere pretension.

The period of transition from the manuscript age to the age of printed books in the Islamic world was long and tortuous, extending over centuries and presenting the student of the history of the book with different sorts of problems from one century to another and from one region of the Islamic world to another. Then, after it largely came to an end sometime during the last half of the nineteenth century and the beginning of the twentieth, a new problem arose: the Islamic world slowly forgot what it meant to depend on scribes and manuscript copies for the creation, diffusion, and transmission of knowledge. In the mind of the vast public at least, printed books came to represent a degree of solidity and authority that went far beyond the solidity and authority of the manuscript copy or copies of the same book. Not only has the manuscript age by now come to an end in the mind of the public—hardly anyone copies an entire manuscript by hand anymore (unless it is in preparation for printing it, and photographic reproduction and printing have in some cases made even this effort unnecessary)—the manuscript tradition has for all intents and purposes ceased to be alive and to develop as it had done for more than a millennium.

It is impossible, of course, to cover, or even touch upon, all the problems arising from every aspect of the period of transition from the manuscript age to the age of printed books. Indeed, it is foolish even to try to do so, given how much remains unknown about the cultural, social, and economic history of the period and how risky it is to establish any causal relation between the introduction and spread of printed books in the Islamic world and particular social, economic, and cultural factors that may have interacted with the introduction of printing and the spread of printed books. Nevertheless, it may be useful to raise some of the questions that need to be answered if one is to gain a fuller picture of what happened during the period of transition and learn about the issues involved in the transformation of books already there in manuscript form into printed books in particular.

There are, to begin with, the numerous cultural and social implications of the transition from the manuscript age to the age of printed books: the spread of printing in the second half of the nineteenth century went hand in hand with the rise of national sentiment among the various Muslim peoples and, as happened in Europe earlier, Muslims became less and less likely to speak or be able to read more than their own national language and had to have translations from other Islamic languages in order to preserve some of the cultural homogeneity of the Islamic world. There is the role of the state in encouraging translations and the spread of secular culture through control of some of the early presses. There are the new cultural vistas and literary forms opened up through printing. And there is the role of non-Muslim communities in spreading the printing of books, first in Europe and then inside the Islamic world.

Then there are the authors (leaders of mystical fraternities, leading thinkers, reformers, and pamphleteers) who wrote original works during the nineteenth century and made a massive contribution to cultural change through printed books. There are a number of interesting questions to be asked about the diffusion of the works of those contemporary authors. How many of the original works printed during the period of transition survive today? How did the transition help create a new profession, that of the author engaged not merely in writing or dictating an original copy of his work and presenting it to a prince in the hope of financial reward and otherwise hoping for the best as to its survival and diffusion in manuscript form, but the author who could see his work printed, corrected, published, diffused in many copies, and sold, establishing himself slowly as a professional writer whose works are read immediately upon their publication by wider circles of readers?

To what extent and how fast did such contemporary works, be they literary, scientific, or religious, replace older ones? Who were the authors who commanded large audiences? When did the reading public become so large that only printing could satisfy it? Did printed books create the mass culture and the standardization of reading habits, or was it the emergence of a mass of educated readers that led to the spread of printing? Who was buying or reading the newly printed books? Did the transition merely expand readership or did it change its character as well? How was the expansion of readership connected with the change in the educational system and the emergence of new classes of professionals and educated people, the change from the time students of religion and bureaucrats were the main readers to the time after the emergence of new free professions—teachers and students of the new secular schools, new types of lawyers, doctors, engineers—who began increasingly to collect and read printed books?

Then there is the impact of translations and the role of printing in encouraging the paraphrase and translation of foreign books, especially those from European languages, which were instrumental in introducing modern science and technology to the Islamic world. Finally, one needs to consider such questions as the importance of the press in the diffusion of scientific literature, whether ancient or contemporary and Western, and of technical manuals of medicine, military science and strategy engineering, and so forth.

Then there are the political and economic aspects of the production of printed books. It was precisely that so many identical copies could be made of printed books which made printing into a mass medium, drew the attention of public authorities, religious and secular, and made it possible to exploit printed books as instruments of state policy, to censor them, or to forbid their diffusion when they were thought not to agree with, or to run counter to, the policy of the state, something not easy to accomplish in the manuscript age. But the state also came to own presses; it was able to distribute copies of printed books free of charge; and it acquired the authority to decide which books should be printed for use in its educational system. The state and the mystical fraternities seem to have been the initial sponsors of the printed book in secular and religious fields, respectively. In the case of the state, a ready clientele, consisting of functionaries and students of technical and generally of secular schools, and government subsidies, made the printing of books on non-religious subjects economically feasible. But the role of the mystical orders in spreading the printing of religious books is a subject that is well worth investigating also. Like the state, they had a ready market in their membership, which made it less risky to undertake the printing of books. Some mystical fraternities had vast memberships spreading out in many countries of the Islamic world, a readership that made the printing of literature of interest to these mystical fraternities economically feasible. When and to what extent did printed religious books begin to compete with printed secular literature, both ancient and contemporary? How did the proportion of the latter grow relative to the total?

To answer such questions, it is important to collect, preserve, and study the archives of publishers wherever they can still be found in the Islamic world, but especially in major centers of printing such as Istanbul, Cairo, and Teheran. One needs to study not only the fact of a book's publication, but how many editions and printings there were, the size of each, and the pricing of copies. We may even learn from these archives how slow or rapid the transition was from the manuscript age to the age of printed books in each major center. In general, one expects the new technologies to have exceeded by far the old in making books both widely accessible and accessible at greatly reduced prices, and to have penetrated new markets and social and economic strata of society. But did any of this happen? To what extent and at what point? What was the weight of the role of the state as against such private institutions as religious fraternities or private commercial enterprises? Which books were promoted by which sector? Which books were in demand by which sector of the reading public? What proportion of printed books were read by members of each of the two educational systems, the religious and the scientific or secular, after they parted company, and what portion by the wider public?

Then there is the impact of printing on the development of language. At the beginning of the transition from the manuscript age to the age of printed books in the Islamic world, the Arabic language was still the international Islamic language in the religious and secular sciences, even though works on modern European science and technology were translated into national languages other than Arabic, such as Turkish and Persian as well. What happened after the introduction of printing? To what extend did Arabic maintain its position? Was Arabic gradually replaced by the other national languages? When did this take place in the case of each nation with a native tongue other than Arabic, and in what fields? That is to say, when and how did languages like Persian, Turkish, and Urdu, in the main vehicles of literary culture and of the administration, become vehicles of modern scientific disciplines as well? How is it that even today, in matters of common concern to the Islamic world, works are written in Arabic by writers from countries such as Iran, India, and Pakistan?[3]

Then there is the impact of printing on the orthography, structure, and vocabulary of each of the languages of the Islamic world. To what extent did printing contribute to simplification and uniformity in any of these aspects of each of these languages? Would the problem of orthography have come to the fore in Turkey without the spread of printing? Would the problem of orthography in Arabic, that is, the unsuccessful campaign for the use of Latin characters, have been even thinkable without the spread of printing? How did printing contribute to the spread and use of punctuation, and why is it that the only strict punctuation system remains the one employed in printing the Koran, while one faces utter confusion, in Arabic at least, in the punctuation of books printed with movable type? Similar questions need to be asked regarding other aspects of scholarly form and techniques, such as the use of abbreviations. What explains the rise and decline of strict standards of typography, of orthography, punctuation, and design?

Then there is the role of linguistic and literary renaissance in the case of each of the national languages during the nineteenth century in the recovery and diffusion of older works of prose, poetry, narrative—in some cases recovered from rare manuscript collections or libraries not accessible beyond small circles of owners and scholars who happened to be in, or to have traveled to, the place where the collection or library was located. To what extent did printing contribute to the resurrection of works forgotten for a long time and made for another age, with its own taste and preoccupations? How was the development of printing related to the development of language education and literacy? And how important was government intervention in the spread of printing (e.g., the availability of printed readers, grammars, dictionaries)? Above all, to what extent was the diffusion of older works through printing a sign that these works were being read, not merely acquired as collectibles?

It is characteristic of the transformation for the manuscript age to the age of printed books in the Islamic world that it was a continuous process rather than a violent turning point. Originally, the book in the Islamic world had co-existed with an oral tradition in which memory played an important role and writing was intended as an aid to memory. Yet writing is supposed to decrease reliance on memory. The question is the extent to which printing may have accelerated this trend. Apart from the question of memory, however, the writing of books itself underwent many changes as to organization, the materials on and with which books were written, and the techniques used by scribes and readers to assure the book's integrity and correctness. This scribal and scholarly tradition underwent certain changes over time in the material it used, in the scripts it developed, and in the organization of book production; and local sub-traditions developed in various parts of the Islamic world, in different languages, and in different disciplines. By the time printing had become more than a curiosity in the Islamic world, a strong scribal and scholarly tradition was in place which was devoted to the book in manuscript form; and one of the most urgent tasks of the students of the transition from the manuscript age to the age of printed books in the Islamic world is to find out precisely what this scribal and scholarly tradition consisted of in the main centers of Islamic civilization during the eighteenth century its transformation during, the nineteenth, and its role in the introduction of printing. For it is that tradition which was instrumental initially in making the transition to the age of printed books.

One needs to ask, therefore, what were the technical and organizational features of the book reproduction industry, not during the manuscript age in general, but at the end of the manuscript age in particular: who engaged in it, patronized it, subsidized it, helped sell the scribes' works, and supplied the materials necessary for the exercise of the profession? Were they merchants, technicians, learned men, calligraphers? Were there *scriptoria* for the mass production of manuscript copies? What was the market for manuscript copies like in places such as Istanbul, Cairo, or Isfahan? How far did manuscript copies travel, and in which direction? Was the trade confined to the Islamic world? Did the manuscript copies of certain books tend to remain in certain localities and not cross certain borders? For instance, to what extent was the experience of the Ottoman statesman and man of letters Rāgib Mehmed Paşa (1699–1763), in looking for Mullā Sadrā's *Asfār*, unique? Rāgib Paşa was a voracious book collector who travelled through the Ottoman Empire and occupied important political positions in Syria, Egypt, and Iraq. Yet he tells us that this comprehensive work of illuminationist philosophy and mysticism was not well known in Anatolia and that he had to bring a copy from Iraq, from which then one or two copies were made.[4] Since it is known that a vast number of manuscript copies produced in the Safavid Empire reached Constantinople, and that this particular work was well known throughout the Safavid Empire and the Indian subcontinent, was the absence of this particular book from the book market in Istanbul and the libraries of Anatolia due to its subject matter and doctrinal content? And why even now can one hardly find a lithographic copy of it in Egypt, for instance, when it had served as the basic textbook of philosophy in many schools in Iran and India?[5]

Let us turn to the printing and diffusion of books surviving from the manuscript age. Of the millions of manuscript copies existing at the time when printing began to spread in the Islamic world, not all could be printed; a selection had to be made. By whom and on what basis was this selection made? By the political authority aiming to spread knowledge of the practical arts necessary for building a modern state? By booksellers with a view to large printings and profit? What works and what literary forms disappeared from view without being remembered except by a new generation of specialists? Were the books most widely diffused in the Islamic world in manuscript form at the time printing was introduced the ones printed? That is, did printing simply continue to feed people's interest in books that were the most widely read before? Who were the ancient Muslim authors selected and printed? How did the ancient Muslim authors not usually read at the end of the manuscript age fare with their new audiences? One could learn a great deal about such questions from studying the holdings of libraries in Istanbul, Cairo, and Teheran that ceased to grow as printing became widespread, provided one realizes that most of the mosque and school libraries did not contain many types of books—popular literature, practical disciplines, astrology, forbidden things—that were diffused and tended to be widely read outside the schools and scholarly circles, and that such books were also the ones more likely to perish. In general, then, one needs to find out what the impact of printing was on the literary culture of the time. To what extent did printing change the type of books available to readers, as compared to before the introduction of printing? How and why did this change take place? What kinds of books were involved? How much of the earlier literature became more widely available? Was this partly due to the ease with which the text of rare manuscript copies of a book could now be multiplied, to access to libraries and collections in places that had been inaccessible before, or to the printing and diffusion of information about manuscript copies through printing in general and manuscript catalogues in particular?

It is a mistake to think that the scribal and scholarly tradition still alive when the transition to printed books was taking place in the Islamic world was as competent or achieved the same high standard when transcribing *every* kind of book. In addition to the text of the Koran and the Traditions of the Prophet, there were certain disciplines in which accurate and correct transmission was essential. This was largely true of manuscript copies of books in scientific fields, such as astronomy, medicine, and mathematics, where mistakes and corruption could be easily detected by experts and render the manuscript copy almost worthless as far as they were concerned. Many scribes copying manuscripts in these disciplines were themselves experts to some extent or had developed a method of copying that reproduced the exemplar with an unusual degree of precision. In other fields (a vast majority of manuscript copies are in literary fields, such as narratives, history, and geography) the language and sometimes even the content of the work was consciously or unconsciously modernized as manuscripts were copied from one generation to another. Much of the so-called Middle Arabic features found in manuscript copies of books by early authors can be attributed to this tendency.

In the age of printed books, the *muṣaḥḥiḥ*—literally the person in charge of producing a "correct" printed version—performed a task similar to that of the scribe in the manuscript age, that is, he corrected and sometimes revised the language of the manuscript copy before it was sent to the printer, and the same person contributed to assuring that the proofs were properly corrected and a list of errata was appended to the printed book. Especially during the period of the renaissance of linguistic learning (of the *fuṣḥá* in Arabic, for instance), it was the function of the *muṣaḥḥiḥ* to make sure that the language of the manuscript copy prepared for the printer was free of grammatical mistakes and stylistic blunders. But by "good" Arabic during the eighteenth and nineteenth centuries one did not mean the stage the language had reached in the eighth or ninth under the Umayyad or Abbasid dynasties; it was already a neoclassical Arabic with its own features.[6] Thus, while the attempt was made to stem the tide of so-called Middle Arabic, and in most cases much of this kind of Arabic was eliminated, there was no assurance that it was replaced by the Arabic current during the second or third century of the Islamic era. And sometimes the attempt to reverse the evolution of the language led to making the printed book more archaic than its author had meant it to be. The revision of the language of all the first four printed versions of *The Thousand and One Nights* is quite instructive in this respect.

It is therefore also important to trace the fortunes of this scribal and scholarly tradition as printing came to be widespread in the Islamic world; study the role of its representatives as publishers, editors, and proofreaders in printing establishments; and learn about their educational background, first in the religious institutions and then as part of the new Europeanized educational system, where as scholars, teachers, and students they continued to play a significant role in transforming the culture of the manuscript age into the culture of printed books. This will require careful study of the techniques used in preparing the manuscript for the printer; what manuscript material was reproduced and what manuscript material was not reproduced (the fate of marginal corrections, conjectures, variant readings, and comments) when a manuscript was copied and corrected in preparation for being printed; the extent to which these were reproduced or suppressed or placed in a different position on the page; and whether dispensing with variant readings and the comments in printed books was due to technical or economic reasons.

A systematic study of early printings can instruct us on whether and to what extent the printed text was a better or worse scientific instrument that a manuscript copy of the same book current before the introduction of printing.[7] Yet the printed copy, which may not have been better than an imperfect manuscript copy, was now published in hundreds if not thousands of copies, sought by everyone interested in that book, and taken by the public to represent *the* book itself, the book to which reference is made and from which quotations are reproduced. It came to have the authority and finality only the author's copy could have claimed in the manuscript age. It is therefore important to find out when and to what extent printed books relegated manuscripts to a secondary position so that readers came to be psychologically oriented to look for, and expect to read, a printed book rather than a manuscript copy; and when and to what extent the habit of reading a manuscript copy—the ability to handle a manuscript copy with ease, interact with it, and learn from it—disappeared from the reading public and became a specialty confined to a few scholars and to those planning to transform the book from manuscript to print. Here again, a study of libraries, public and private, and their use over time, especially those that froze at a particular point in time, could help clarify such questions.[8]

Nevertheless, the transition from the manuscript age to the age of printed books in the Islamic world is not something that took place in the past only. Even though a lot has happened during the past two centuries or so, in certain respects the transition is still with us. Books in manuscript form continue to be transformed into printed books, and this process will continue for the foreseeable future, since a vast number of books produced during the manuscript age in the Islamic world remain in manuscript form and their transformation, by way of printing, editing, and re-editing, is not likely to come to an end very soon. Indeed, it is hard to conceive of a future date when the Islamic world will cease to be concerned with the question of the transition from the manuscript age to the age of printed books and with the many problems connected with the transformation of its heritage at the hand of printers and editors. One can only hope that, slowly, the transition will be controlled by scholars with increasingly better knowledge of the scribal and scholarly tradition that produced the books in the manuscript age, rather than by predators in search of gain or fame.

Nor has the transformation always been directly from the book in manuscript form to the printed book. We recall, for instance, the continuous role played in the transformation of manuscript copies into printed books by photography, microfilming, xeroxing, and, more recently, word processing. Think, for instance, of the accuracy and ease with which photographic reproductions of manuscript copies are now being printed. Is the product of this process a manuscript copy or a printed book? Then there are other techniques, some of which once played a significant intermediary role between the book in manuscript form and books printed with movable type: lithography, xylography, metal plates—processes that were once current in India, Iran, Egypt, and Morocco. Their use in printing books of common prayers, the Koran, religious tracts of all sorts, and secular books as well, is known.

Just at a time when the Islamic world seems to be reaping the benefits of the technological and cultural revolution brought about by printing, that revolution is being increasingly superseded by another revolution, one that is replacing both the manuscript book and the printed book with the electronic, machine-readable book. This is perhaps the most significant question we must keep in mind as we look at the transition from the manuscript age to that of printed books. But we need to remember also that, even without this recent technological revolution, at least since the beginning of this century the printed book began to lose some of its hold on the human race. One could say that until about 1914 there was no other "mass" communication medium (apart from the human voice of narrators, teachers, and preachers) besides the book, the pamphlet, or the flier. There was no radio or television, no record or tape, no film, to compete to any significant extent with printed matter. Pictures played only a limited role, and illustrations were rather rare and expensive. The printed/written word held a preeminent position; there were as yet no serious competitors to reckon with. Whenever a serious question was disputed in the Islamic community—Wahhābism, coffee drinking, smoking—the dispute was enshrined in printed books, pamphlets, and fliers.

In some respects, the book in electronic, machine-readable form will mean a return to one of the main features of the manuscript age: copies can be made and subjected to continuous change and improvement, free of the fixed form introduced by printing and movable type. With the use of various means of communication, it will be possible to make what is initially a single copy available immediately across the globe and as far as humans can reach beyond this globe, with the possibility that, from one copy, an infinite number of copies can be made, used, and disposed of.

The potential of this revolution is, or should be, of particular interest to those engaged in the effort to collect and organize information about the enormous surviving manuscript heritage of the Islamic world in all Islamic languages. This potential extends far beyond the use currently made of it in cataloging books and manuscripts. Sooner or later, the electronic, machine-readable book—consisting of digitized text, digitized graphics, or a mixture of digitized text and graphics—is likely to replace both the book as it was known in the manuscript age and the book in print; for it will be the most convenient way to access the content of books, including books that exist already in manuscript form or in print. And the electronic, machine-readable form will in turn determine the most convenient ways of packaging the book, just as it was the manuscript and printing that determined its characteristic material components.

Given the speed with which the technology is changing, however, it remains to be seen how many forms the new electronic, machine-readable book will take. It seems certain that the main advantages of the printed book, wide diffusion and an affordable price, will continue to favor certain types of printed books, perhaps those that are popular. Otherwise, many scholarly works, and generally all works of specialized interest, including illustrations, will be available in electronic form, more easily accessible across the globe, not requiring the publication of a large number of hard copies. The other function of the printed book, that of reproducing the content of books existing in manuscript form, and certainly much of the body of books produced in the manuscript age on which scholars are likely to be working in the future, will be transferred directly from the original manuscript form to electronic, machine-readable form, rather than going through the printing stage, which can now clearly be seen to have been yet another intermediate stage. But whether this transition is carried out successfully or we end up with another mess on our hands depends on how willing we are to learn more about the book in the manuscript age, how willing we are to learn the lessons of the delays and problems encountered during the transition from the manuscript age to the age of printed books, and how determined we are to face and overcome the difficulties encountered during the transition to the age of the electronic, machine-readable book.

NOTES

1. To see that such problems can arise in books edited in more recent times by authors who could not be accused of ignorance or malice, one can consult the edition of the work on the proof of prophecies by the tenth-century Isma'īlī thinker Abū Ya'qūb al-Sijistānī, *Ithbāt al-nubūwāt*, ed. 'Ārif Tāmir (Beirut, 1966), p.76, where the editor took the liberty of rewriting a paragraph of the original text in twentieth-century Arabic.

2. The relevant decrees, legal opinions, and related documents have been discussed recently by Wahid Gdoura, *Le Début de l'imprimerie arabe à Istanbul et en Syrie* (Tunis, 1985), pt. 1, ch. 2, pt. 2, ch. 2; and Fawzi Abdulrazak, "The Kingdom of the Book," PhD Dissertation, Boston University, 1990, ch. 4.

3. Consider, for instance, the Arabic writings of thinkers like Khomeini, Mawdūdī and S.S. Nadvi.

4. Rāgib Paşa, *Safinat al-Rāghib* (Bulaq, 1282/1865 or 66), p. 322.

5. The single lithographic copy of the work I came across in Egypt had been brought there by an Indian scholar and reached the marketplace when his library was sold after his death.

6. Once, in the manuscript reading room of the old Dār al-Kutub Library building in the Bāb al-Khalq, in Cairo, I saw across the table a blind Azharite scholar with a youngster next to him reading from an old manuscript copy and holding a ballpoint pen in his hand to transcribe the text of the manuscript in

a notebook. The youngster read aloud as he transcribed the manuscript while the scholar listened, sometimes nodding in approval but frequently instructing the youngster not to transcribe what was in the manuscript copy but what was to the scholar's mind a more correct version of the text. Worse than this, he seems to have arranged with the youngster that the latter should also correct the text of the manuscript itself with his ballpoint pen. Whether because the scholar was eminent or influential, I do not know, but the keeper of manuscripts at Dār al-Kutub, the late Fuʿād Sayyid, did not dare protest the practice.

7. Modern editors treat printed books of which they cannot find the manuscript source as just another manuscript copy, with all the potential virtues and defects of a manuscript copy.

8. I recall, for instance, having to consult some Arabic manuscript copies in the Küprülü Library in Istanbul, where the only other users of the tables and chairs in the reading room. were high school students reading (modern Turkish) school books they had brought with them rather than any of the manuscript copies for which that library is known to users like myself.

2

The Koranic Text: From Revelation to Compilation

Jacques Berque

Nowadays, the term that springs immediately to mind, and that is also commonly used in discourse to designate the Koran, is the word "Book" with a capital letter, that is, "*Kitābun*" in the indefinite, and "*al-Kitābu*" with the definite article. Such a designation, however, is not helpful in specifying its subject. In itself, "*kitāb*" is generic rather than specific and, per se, it means nothing more than "written." It is context alone that can determine precisely whether the designation is of a simple inscription, of a holy writ, of fate as pre-ordained by God, of the roll that those called to justice in the Last Judgment shall wear around their necks, or else of the Koran proper, as is the case here. It should be noted here that the Koranic message, when first revealed to mankind, was not delivered in written form, but rather in the form of intermittent vocal communications, which varied widely in length.

It should also be noted that, according to dominant tradition, the opening word of the Revelation consisted of the well-known injunction "*Iqra'*," of Surah 96. This term, however, is one that we often find a problem with: What does it really mean?

If we take "*Iqra'*" to mean simply "Read," as is often done, then what text could the imperative "*Iqra'*" be referring to? Could it be the standard archetypal codex, "*al-Imām*," of which the Koran presents itself as an extract? On the other hand, the communication initiated from God to the Prophet had taken, as it has always done, the auditory medium as well as the mediation of the Archangel Gabriel. For a more accurate reflection of this aspect, "Chant or Psalmody" is perhaps a more appropriate translation than simply "Read."

A third option which should not be excluded out of hand is the translation "assemble or compile." One reservation, however, is that it references an ulterior operation, now already completed, namely, the collection or recension of all revealed messages. Admittedly, from the point of view of faith, this ordering (sequencing) partakes of divine inspiration, hence of the atemporal and the pre-ordained. Human logic, nonetheless, is liable to be confounded and puzzled by seeing reference to the collected message at the very opening of the revelation.

In this, indeed, the main psychological and didactic dynamic is not so much to anticipate, but to recollect. Hence there is all the richness that we find in the uses of the root "*dh•k•r*." Even the Koran qualifies itself as *dhikr*, "recall," inasmuch as it calls up from, the depths of human memory truths long thought obliterated. It also endows upon itself credibility for all time.

Certain listeners even go so far as to claim a special faculty for "re-saying" the revealed message. The function of those "keepers by heart," or "*ḥuffāẓ*," is not to be confounded with that of *qurrā* and *muqri'īn*, "readers and reciters." The astounding reliability of the *ḥuffāẓ*'s memory, not uncommon in this type of society, did provide a link between the transcendental communication operating through the voice of the Prophet, and deep resonances evoked in the primary consciousness and discourse of the people.[1]

Shortly after the death of the Prophet, there appeared other modes of preservation. Followers of the faith, according to tradition, began to inscribe the message in segments, more or less long ones; they even attempted to bring the text together as it was being revealed. They used any materials available to them, for instance, scraps of parchments, shoulder blades, palm leaves cut lengthwise, and so on. These picturesque inscriptions, however, provided only limited guarantees of reliability. Apart from discrepancies or inconsistencies, they risked omission. By definition, these fragments were disconnected. Besides, there was no way the followers could have given consideration to the elaborate taxonomy which, starting from a certain date, guided the compiling of the pieces into graduated surahs.

It was the Prophet himself, we are told, who assumed the task of compiling the Koran in written form. His actions were guided by inspiration, though he was aided by secretaries and experts. To one of the most active among them, Zayd ibn Thābit, is attributed the statement: "We were at the Messenger of God's [house] to collate the Koran from disparate scraps," or "*nu'allifu al-Qur'ān min al-riqā'.*"[2]

Hence, the setting of the revelation into written form, defective as it was, was nonetheless not wanting for a base in dogma, at least provisional, considering that the order in which the pieces were to be fitted together was in a large measure contingent upon the course of revelation that the Prophet alone could foresee in advance.

In two surahs, 27, *The Ant*, and 15, *Hijr*, the opening verses juxtapose the appellations "Koran" and "*Kitāb*", inverting the order from the one to the other, respectively: "ayātu *al-kitābi* wa-qurā'nin mubīnin" and "ayātu *al-qurā'ni* wa-kitābin mubīnin." Shaykh T. Ibn 'Āshūr underlines this chiasmic structure, which puts the stress alternately on revelation as an ongoing process and on the objective entity which it now constitutes. In fact, the two formulations concerned, being close in date of revelation (48th and 54th, respectively), do not allow for the hypothesis of a change in intent from one formulation to the other. It allows for the differentiation to me made between two referents which have come to be generally confounded in subsequent usage. And thus it is all the more reason to question the hypothesis of Bell, whereby a "Koran Period" is to have preceded a "Book Period" at about the time of the Battle of Badr.[3]

Furthermore, it is of interest to note the passages that have to do with putting the revelation "in lines", *masṭūran*, in 17, *The Night Journey*: 58; and 33, *The Clans*: 6. These texts are classified as 50th and 90th in order of revelation by tradition, and 67th and 103rd according to Nöldeke, Theodor that is, for the first surah, long before the Hijrah. Inasmuch as the revelation of the text, as is often the case, keeps referring to temporal data (*asbāb*), the written recording had not only begun, but also was taken into consideration in the revelation itself, along with an indication we ought not to forget, that of lines being drawn in ink on a surface.

If we are to believe al-Bukhārī, the Prophet at his death could not have left a Koran that was fully inscribed, and only four of his Companions then knew the full text of the message by heart.[4] The precariousness of a method of preservation that was fully entrusted to memory naturally gave cause for concern to those responsible. The very concern for the preservation and protection of so sacred a heritage from the hazards of segmented transcriptions or of memories subject to the risks of negligence, oblivion, or death—this is what later on led the caliph ʿUmar ibn ʿAbd al-ʿAzīz to compile the *ḥadīth*—prompted a first attempt at systematic compilation under the caliph Abū Bakr. It was done on unbound sheets, *qarāṭīs*. The effort was renewed in a more systematic way at the time of the caliph ʿUthmān. It succeeded. The text then acquired, in physical appearance and layout, the form that we currently know, that is, that of a coherent text made up of divisions (surahs) and subdivisions (verses). It was Zayd ibn Thābit who presided over this accomplishment.[5]

It was expected, both in establishing the corpus of content, as well as the organization, to follow unswervingly the tradition of the Prophet. The Prophet, we should again emphasize, had himself set this arrangement. The tradition, however, is not so explicit with regard to the comprehensiveness of the initial organization. Reliable sources limit it to the long surahs, the *Hawāmīm*, surahs that begin with the two initials H. M. (*hā'mīm*), and the *Mufaṣṣal*, commonly understood as the totality of the smaller text placed at the end of the collection.

Such, at least, is the traditional view, one that we have no way of contesting. To do so, like some others have, would trigger endless controversies. We would even be running the risk of endangering any attempt at a scientific approach to the subject. On the other hand, what we can do, and ought to do, is look into the early circumstances of an effort initiated while the revelation was still in progress, and sustained throughout the period of delivery of the message; we could thus cover the whole set of texts throughout its growth. It goes without saying that a chronological sequence of individualized surahs such as we would be able to reconstruct could not have been proven to be so until a sufficient quantity of verbal material had been amassed in the memories of the reciters. What classification were we to follow, or what order to establish, if, first of all, there had been no identifiable units to be distinguished from one another and placed in a serial order? This, at least, is what common sense would suggest.

A first step was perhaps illustrated in the words of surah 11, *Hūd*: 13; "Produce ten surahs like it (this one)." But if the said surah fell in the eleventh place in the sequence of the material collected, it would rank, in the sequence of revelation, 52nd (or even 75th, according to Nöldeke). Such a start is troubling indeed.

One should take special note of this remarkable aspect, that the tradition has kept no record of any substantial disagreements over the text. We only know that the Caliph gave orders to burn the already existing codices, just to avert all debate. Was it to avert it or to close it, or both at the same time? In a community so prone to argument of a subject held close to heart by all, one wonders whether or not to attribute the silence of the sources, just as the latter themselves do, to the unanimous consensus of the multiple witnesses (*tawātur*) (except for slight phonic variations on a text so collated, and eventually on the details of the layout). Once more, we have no grounds to doubt that. But unanimity on such a scale as the believers claim is owing to divine grace rather than to sociological laws of transmission.

Another form of silence that impresses us is one that concerns the reactions that were likely to be stirred up in the process of compiling the Koran, as a result of the shift from the vocal to the visual medium. Obviously, the functions of *ḥuffāẓ* and *muqri'īn* were only partially replaced by reading, a skill of little currency at the time. Surely, their ritualistic, psychological and social roles persist up to the present. This fact, however, has not prevented the "written" to assume a certain halo of dignity which it did not possess initially. In matters of religious texts, the transition from the spoken word, a carrier of a breath of life, into signs restorable in resonant equivalents would not generally occur gratuitously. The Bible becomes the echo of a "passion" which affects the word of God when put in script. Such a *kenosis* does not usually occur without risks.[6] An affective reaction by some might sanction the despoiling of an original fullness inherent in the breath and voice. A tradition, actually quite isolated, has it that Ummayah ibn Abī al-Ṣalt was the first to have read the written Koran. In no way will this eliminate all adjudication in this case. The association with this suspect poet, envious of prophetism, should it have happened, would not be comfortably accepted.[7]

Still, at the time of the Umayyad caliph ʿUmar ibn ʿAbd al-ʿAzīz, who presided over the compilation of ḥadīth, divergences in approach were noted regarding the issue of the relative suitability of writing as opposed to memory for the preservation of the *Sunnah*. In this connection, Mālik mentions a question put by the Prince to *faqīh* and the reassuring answer of the latter: "There is no objection to the recording of science." This was, after all, the opinion of Abū Ḥanīfah.[8] It is true that this consultation applied to Sunnah and not to the Koran; a question of principle was nevertheless raised.

We must also stress that in Islam the transcription of the Koran into written form did not in any way substitute completely the use of "live and permanent voice." In the absence of more positive evidence to invalidate our observation, we consider the reticence of the sources with regard to such a development as somewhat amazing.

At the time and in the region, writing was *scriptio defectiva*, that is, lacking periods and diacritical marks. The writing medium remained primitive, obviously closer to an elliptical epigraphy than to a genuine form of transcription. The successors of Muḥammad, no less than Muḥammad himself, could not have ignored the existence of more advanced forms of writing, for instance, Hebrew, Syriac, Greek, and Latin. This is especially true since the Prophet had frequently visited the markets of Byzantine Syria. He must also have seen the scrolls of the Torah in Mecca. He had them presented to him several times. His Companion, Warqah ibn Nawfal, once a Christian, is believed to have transcribed the Gospels in Hebraic characters.

The Koran refers to these works with the ancient biblical term of *safr*, plural *asfār*.[9] The ironic anecdote of the donkey laden with books, carrying with solemn compunction his precious load, conveys a perhaps all too familiar image (62, *The Day of Congregation*: 5). There were, moreover, other words available to translate a message into conventional signs, using any procedure of stable encoding (tattooing, inscription). Let us recall a verse by Labīd: "The flood channels of al-Rayyān, their traces are laid bare, worn smooth, just like writing on the rocks" (*kamā ḍamina al-wuḥiyā' silāmuhā*). Thus goes the *muʿallaqah*. The critics analyze *al-wuḥiyā'* as a plural form, and the term has more than one appeal to it, especially since it was the one retained for "revelation". Several examples of *Lisān al-ʿArab* attach to the meaning of the term many suggestive undertones, especially those of a secret language, not easily accessible to others, just as we would imagine it was initially done for writing. Let us also cite in this connection the verse of Abū Wajzah al-Saʿdī: "O dwelling of Asma, which the rippled streams reduced to a wasteland, just like the writing, or the original that the scribe spells."

As for the material surfaces on which they wrote, we have already mentioned a variety of surfaces utilized by the early reciters of the Koran. For ancient scriptures, for instance, the Torah, which was preserved in *volumina* which could be unrolled, animal parchment, *al-riqq*, was used (52, *The Mount*: 2).

Poetry, furthermore, uses another vocable, *qiṭṭ*, which we can construe as an abbreviation of *qiṭʿah*, "a piece of parchment or paper." This was indeed a "perfidious scriptum" *qiṭṭ muḍallil*, that al-Mutalammis threw into a river when he read into it his own loss. Obviously, the writing was hastily done and "antlike," *munmal*, or *munammal*, a figure of speech used in this context by Abū al-ʿIyāl al-Hudhalī.

It is also true that in other periods of paganism. namely, at the time of the letters of Ṭarafah and al-Mutalammis (*Ṣaḥīfat al-Mutalammis*), as well as the imprecatory writings and vows that people used to throw at the Kaʿbah at that time, it was the term *ṣaḥīfah*, "surface," hence, "sheet", that came to prevail.

When the Koran was finally collated in a systematic way into an official manual, and in order to designate the edited volume, a term with the same root was resorted to, following the two pronunciations of *muṣḥaf* and *miṣḥaf*. The first is deemed to be the older one, unless this has to do with a tribal inflection of the *m*, Tamīm being inclined towards a vocalization with *i*, while Qays leaned towards *u*. This noun, being still currently in use, was supposed to have been derived from the preterit *uṣḥifa*, indicating the setting together of a manuscript into leaves, *ṣuḥuf*, the plural of *ṣaḥīfah*. This original term was commonly used to designate a plate made out of wood provided for feeding about five persons. The diminutive *ṣaḥīfah* has long been given the special meaning that concerns us here, namely, "page, sheet, folio."[10] Since then and until the present, the book wherein the Islamic revelation has been collected was to carry three names:

- *al-Kitāb*, where the dominant connotation seems to refer, in the absence of contextual precision, to the archetype held by God;
- Koran (*Qur'ān*), which was a phonic unit subject to a repetitive, continuous psalmody; and
- *Muṣḥaf*, as a visual object, an assembly of sheets, a "book," as we now say, which brought among the Arabs the revolution of the book, a revolution that followed, other things being equal, the revolution of *tanzīl*, or revelation.

Let us compare this second stage with the stage when the message was being communicated at the time of the Prophet. This communication unfolded over a period of about twenty years. It was delivered in successive fragments, in a scattered order. Regrouping it into sets of surahs could not normally be achieved without a certain maturing in the memory of the Prophet, and of some of his close affiliates, just as the *individuatio* (to borrow a medieval term) of these future chapters were shaping up. This quality, we shall so call it for the moment, was not to crystallize for the large surahs, such as the surah of *al-Baqarah* (The Cow) (we are informed of when its revelation started but never when it was completed), before several months, or even years, had elapsed. Inevitably, the dictation of the surahs would interfere with the dictation of other texts.

It is true, some would retort, that this argument will not hold as long as we cannot attribute human normality to a process marked by divine intervention. But the *Sunnah*, concerned with preserving the strictly human attributes of the Prophet that the Koran explicitly assigned to him, allows for an interpretation along the lines of human normality. Allow me, in a witticism, to help illustrate the notion by which we can come to conceive of so complex a process. This whole process could be visualized as though the Messenger had gradually solved a crossword puzzle, as the letters and boxes were revealed to him in successive and partial strokes. Let us, however, draw away from this playful analogy. What really matters is the inchoate and reflective characteristic of an operation that is essentially diachronic, just like the revelation itself, a characteristic sharply in contrast with the final collection that henceforth we have before our eyes.

This question has to do, let us repeat, with a book that was indeed put out in a rudimentary form; but in spite of this, or rather in spite of the many ways of reading it—eventually reduced to seven—it maintains through recitation, whether individually or collectively, a stable and practically permanent constitution which has endured since then, up to the present.

This book, on which the believers began to meditate, possesses features particular to it alone, when compared to other monotheistic messages to which it refers, that is, the Torah, the Psalms of David, and the Gospels. And if we are to extend the comparison to approximately contemporary works, be it Latin (*Digesta*), or Greek, Maximus the Confessor, Romanos Melodos, and, more pertinently, *The Fount of Wisdom* of John the Damascene, there is no doubt the Koran would present a more vivid contrast. The originality that astounded the Arabs and, soon after, even the Byzantine polemicists, will not but gain in intensity if submitted to a probe of its intrinsic properties, properties of which we are most assured. Being inherent to the Koran, these properties owe nothing to the speculation of others, not to a tradition that we can easily deem as broken, nor to methods anachronic to such things.

Let us turn once more to those properties having to do with the composition of the Koran, for they address best of all its quality as a book. It is exactly here that the majority of Westerners will see nothing more than a miscellany of disorganization and arbitrariness. We believe, however, that we can discern a structure of a type strongly akin to the synchronal. There, for instance, is a didactic recurrence of themes and the proliferation of alliterations, and also the frequent overlapping and merging of motives.

The argument for a synchronal structure suffers, nonetheless, from a central shortcoming. The traditional sequence of the revelation is maintained for eleven surahs, numbered 31 to 51, and these alternately enclose ten non-successive units. Within this entire group stand out such radiant texts as 36, *Yāsīn* and 40, *The Believers*; we could perhaps talk here of a central reinforcing support where the two dimensions, the chronological and the synchronal, would converge.

This would be even so much more convincing, since with surah 52, *The Mount*, begins the second half of the Book, as it is commonly accepted. A change of tone occurs then and there. The short surahs, which have an apocalyptic ring to them. and which proceed from the first Meccan period, pile up in the second part, while the homilies of the third period are symmetrically paralleled in the first part. On the other hand, the surahs of Medina, generally focusing on social matters (organizational and legislative), are strewn among surahs 49 to 110, over almost the totality of the collected work. All this cannot be due to mere chance.

Many other features of what we ought to call, rightly, the Koranic edition attest to the same reflective, orderly character (even deliberative, I daresay). I pass over the many mutations of the metatext, or the contents bearing on the discourse itself; the significance of the role given in many surahs to the median verse; the presence of rhythmic expressions, often decimal; in sum, a number of facts bearing on form as well as content which we stressed elsewhere.[11]

The rejection of a classification of surahs in terms of the sequence of their revelation was an option carrying a crucial demarcation value. The Koranic discourse was thus destined to leave the domain of metahistory in order to enter, as an object of culture, the history of man. Was it not, after all, complete, and did it not, at the same time, close the era of revelation? By the very movement with which it closed up itself, it made room for human ritualistic and repetitive practices, psalmody, exegesis, and a model; it returned to sacred history its own revelation, along with the prophetic dictums which have accompanied it.

There is, moreover, an additional aspect which we have not touched upon yet, that is, its potential as an art form. Writing, in Islam, was not to remain a minor art confined only to the pages of a manuscript, nor even a social art, similar to Roman epigraphy. Rather, it was to assume the proportions of a major art, plastic as well as spiritual, embodied in the superb mural works in stucco, plaster, and so on, which were to succeed one another over the centuries in a manner that has no analogy in the West.[12]

Another development, no less rich in cultural value, is the importance ascribed by Islamic tradition to the "science of letters," *ʿilm al-ḥurūf*. Esoterism, Hermetism, and cosmogony all combined with phonetics and calligraphy in a manner little intelligible to moderns. We cannot but refer in this connection to the analysis recently made in relation to a work by Ibn ʿArabī.[13] But even though this may be no more than very old speculation, in part preceding Islam, the elaboration of the letters into proper Arabic characters does not seem to have occurred before the third/ninth century.[14]

The final form of the Koran certainly had not been reached by the time the first copies of the Koran were made on parchment, and later on papyrus and paper were made. The caliph ʿUthmān, if we are to believe the tradition, was to have been the first among the copyists. He is said to have been assassinated while holding in his hand a copy of the Koran that he himself had written.[15] His assassin, al-Ghafīqī, is said to have kicked the venerable volume wirh his foot.[16] For what reason? A few years later, the calligrapher Zayd ibn Aslān made a copy of the Koran for ʿĀ'ishah and another for Ḥafṣah, both widows of the Prophet.[17]

In his comments on the renowned calligraphy of Ibn al-Bawwāb (d.413/1022), D S. Rice brings into focus the evolution of styles of writing,[18] starting from the most ancient, the angular, through Kufic, and up to the cursive *Naskhī*, which prevailed toward the end of the fourth/tenth century. Many of these styles, illustrated with rich colors, were the object of study in a number of scholarly monographs.

For our part, our attention will turn to a Koran, printed in color in Italy by the Tunisian publisher A. Ben ʿAbdallah, based on a photocopy of a text calligraphed by Bach Mamlūk Ḥajj Zuhayr, who had died, almost a centenarian, in 1904. This copy, dating from 1275/1858, was revised by Shaykh Muḥammad ʿAlī al-Dallāʿ.[19] The 619-page volume, ornate with delicate colorings, presents a distinctive peculiarity. On each page, at the rate of one to three times per page, certain words or clusters of words are colored in red. The words affected consist in all grammatical forms,—substantives, pronouns, adjectives, verbs, and so on. The referents did not seem to present any special character. The only oddity is that every time we open the volume flat, these words or clusters of words written in red on the right-hand page, the even-numbered page, also appear exactly at the corresponding place on the left-hand page, the odd-numbered page.

Coincidence, we might say? Impossible, since the same arrangement recurs from one end of the book to the other, or just about. It all begins with the *Fātiḥah*, hence to the right, the word *al-dīn* of *yawm al-dīn, wa* of *wa-iyyāka, alladhīna* of *ṣirāt alladhīna* parallel to the left of the words *ladhīna* of *alladhīna yu'minūna*, of *wa* of *wa-mimmā razaqnāhum, alladhīna* of *alladhīna yu'minūna*. Now, is this graphic tour de force due to a judicious prolongation of horizontal features in the body or writing? Undoubtedly, at times, it is. But coincidences or unusual tours de force are both apt to lead to perplexity, then stupor, when, we become aware that those symmetries, no matter how artificial they may be, persist from the beginning of the book to page 600.

There is even more. In surah 26, *The Poets*, symmetry brings back, and recrossing them, nine lines of writing from page 378 to page 381. Translators are well aware of the refrain that recurs, with its own sameness, v. 103 and 104, on pages 121–122, 132–140, and 174–175. We had to have, however, the all too special configuration of this manuscript for these four distichs to overlap respectively two by two, from odd-numbered page to page.

For these regular visual patterns to stand out in 300 other interfaces of the volume, one would need to allow each of the recurrences to be lodged in its proper place through the transcription of fifteen lines on a page and the exact positioning of horizontal pot-hooks and intervals. This is quite strange, since the verbal material which is spread out over the sheets of our volume, as we all know, first appeared in a vocal and discursive manner in a sequence completely different from that of the manuscript.

The Koranic text has always been the focus of research, from philological investigation to numerical speculation. Nowadays, with the aid of computers, the focus has turned to the study of frequency patterns. This is how many features peculiar to the Book are now surfacing. To mention only one, the frequency of the letter *qāf* in the two Medinan Surahs, *Qāf* and *al-Shūra*, was 57 in each, totalling 114 times. This number, curiously, matches the number of surahs in the Book. Based on features of this kind, believers are apt to keep entertaining new arguments in support of the miraculous nature of the Koran. The secular researcher, rightly or wrongly, would see no more into it than an extreme case of internal regularity such as we often detect in the core of a poetic text, like the phonic symmetry noted by H. Meschonic in Victor Hugo, or the anagram of "spleen" only recently noted by Roman Jacobson in the poem carrying the same title by Baudelaire, and so on.

However, let us suspend the discussion at this point. What matters is to end with a conclusion based on hard evidence, and include a question for a further investigation.

1. The conclusion: The symmetries of the two-color manuscript described above do indeed confirm the highly analytical character of Koranic recension dating from the time of ʿUthmān. This is a conclusion we have reached through methods of internal textual criticism.

By becoming "foliar," *muṣḥaf*, the message had found a concrete visual form, quite at variance with its initial rhythm. One is now bound to view it as a "single composition," *jumlah wāḥidah* (25, *al-Furqān*: 30), or as "unrolled sheets," *ṣuḥufun munashsharah* (84, *al-Mudaththar*: 52). These definitions, however, were once disclaimed, and indeed they did not fit into the early stages of the message.

We must bear in mind, though, that it was through organized recitation that the Koranic message sustained its phonic power, connected with a remembrance, with a breath, with a voice, all so linked together as to evoke the image of the collectivity, rather than mere individuality.

Reading, *tilāwah*, in fact, is different from a psalmody, *qirā'ah*, and, a fortiori, from intonation, *taghannī*, and from chanting, *tartīl*. Reading calls for exegesis and for tradition, and it seeks an intellectual, in-depth grasp of the text, by meditating on it, and pursuing the analysis of its contents through the appropriate methods of exegesis or hermeneutics.

Materially, as already seen, this process has led to the development of several arts, including calligraphy, illumination, binding, gilding, and so on.

2. As to the question called up earlier, we still uphold the skepticism and doubt underlying the search we are venturing on.

The text of *tanzīl*, "revelation," turned into a book under 'Uthmān, was the outcome of an elaboration so rich in possibilities that throughout the centuries. it has held fast. What strikes us most in the present study is the active involvement, just less than one generation after the death of the Prophet, of an entire task force of experts designated by the Caliph himself, and apparently not without the full consensus of the Companions.

Yet again, how can we help being intrigued by the complete silence kept by the sources? This feeling will continue to live with us so long as there is no new evidence available to break this silence.

We can ill imagine, indeed, how an attempt at putting the Koran into shape, critical as it was, could have ever happened without arousing some opposition! Given the high stakes involved, one assumes there must have been some reaction, including some reactions that would qualify as hostile, if not even frightening. Is it not likely that some such reaction may well have initiated the uprising that finally took the life of the Caliph who had inaugurated the *Muṣḥaf*?[20] Perhaps the relatively flimsy excuses invoked by the conspirators in vindication of such an outrageous action could well offer, a contrario, a clue to this action's motive? This is an assumption that has yet to be, and perhaps never will be, sustained.

Translated by
Dr. Naim N. Atiyeh
American University of Beirut

NOTES

1. The data summarized below are made explicit in all works dealing with Koranic Islamology, especially R. Blachère, *Introduction au Coran*, 2nd ed. (Paris, 1959); W. Montgomery Watt, *Bell's Introduction to the Qur'an* (Edinburgh, 1970); and the introduction of the great commentator Shaykh Muḥammad al-Ṭāhir ibn 'Āshūr, *al-Taḥrīr wa-al-tanwīr* (Tunis, 1984), vol. 1.

2. Ibn ʿĀshūr, op. cit., 1: 86.

3. Montgomery Watt, op. cit., pp. 137 ff.

4. El-Bokhari, *Les traditions Islamiques*, trans. O. Houdas (Paris, 1908), 3. 527 (Ḥadīth Anas).

5. El-Bokhari op. cit., 3: title 66, ch. 3 and r.

6. See Eugen Biser, "God's Word," in *Dictionnaire de théologie*, 1988 ed., p. 511ff.

7. Abū al-Faraj al-Isbahānī, *Kitāb al-aghānī*, ed. Ibrāhīm al-Abyārī, 31 vols. (Cairo, 1969), 4: 1335.

8. Mālik ibn Anas (al-Imām), *al-Muwaṭṭa'*, ed. ʿAbd al-Wahhāb ʿAbd al-Laṭīf (Beirut, 1981), p. 330.

9. Where another term comes close, phonetically, is in *zabr*, plural *zubūr*. See Koran, 27: 192: *Zubūr awwalīna*. The term *zabūr* is particularly related to the Psalms of David.

10. Ibn Manẓūr, *Lisān al-ʿArab* (Cairo, 1966).

11. Reference here is made to the exegetical study which follows the introduction to my translation of the Koran into French (Paris, 1990).

12. The monumental role of writing is made the subject of a study by Armando Petrucci, *La Scrittura ideologia e rappresentazione* (Turin, 1986). Emile Male had already brought out the relations between the ornamentation of cathedrals and the illumination of manuscripts. About the calligraphy of the Koran as a strictly regulated art, see Abū ʿAmr ʿUthmān ibn Saʿīd al-Dānī, *al-Muqniʿ fī rasm maṣāḥif al-amṣār maʿa kitāb al-naqaṭ*, ed. M. Ṣādiq Qamḥāwī (Cairo, 1978).

13. See Denis Gril, "La science des lettres," in Ibn ʿArabī, *Les illuminations de la Mecque*, ed. Michel Chodkiewicz (Paris, 1988), p. 385ff.

14. According to Sahl al-Tustarī (d.283/896) and Ibn Masarrah (d.319/931), for example.

15. al-Ṭabarī, *Les quatre premiers califes*, trans. Hermann Zotenberg (Paris, 1981), p. 325.

16. Manuscript no. 14,246 of the National Library of Tunis. Also, M. Hamidullah, *The Prophet's Establishing a State and His Succession* (Islamabad, 1988), p. 147.

17. Ibn Anas, *Muwaṭṭa'*, p. 344.

18. D.S. Rice, *L'unique manuscrit d'Ibn al-Bawwab*, trans. from English, Club de Livre, Philiippe Leband, 1972.

19. Manuscript no. 14,246 of the National Library of Tunis.

20. There are indications given by Hichem Djait regarding the participation of the *Qurrā'*, especially those of Kufah, in the rebellion against the Caliph. See his *La grande discorde* (1988), p. 125ff. and passim. According to ʿAbd Allah ibn al-Ashʿath al-Sijistānī, in his *Kitāb al-maṣāḥif* (Cairo, 1985), p. 20ff., the conflict of the Companion ʿAbd Allah ibn Masʿūd with the Caliph and with Zayd ibn Thābit on the question of the Koran has left aside the case of transcription.

هو الذي خلقكم من تراب ثم من نطفة ثم من علقة
ثم يخرجكم طفلا ثم لتبلغوا أشدكم ثم
لتكونوا شيوخا ومنكم من يتوفى من قبل
ولتبلغوا أجلا مسمى ولعلكم تعقلون ۝ هو الذي
يحيي ويميت فإذا قضى أمرا فإنما يقول له كن فيكون
۝ ألم تر إلى الذين يجادلون في
آيات الله أنى يصرفون ۝ الذين كذبوا بالكتاب
وبما أرسلنا به رسلنا فسوف يعلمون ۝ إذ الأغلال في
أعناقهم والسلاسل يسحبون ۝ في الحميم ثم في النار يسجرون ۝
ثم قيل لهم أين ما كنتم تشركون ۝ من دون الله قالوا ضلوا عنا بل
لم نكن ندعوا من قبل شيئا كذلك يضل الله الكافرين ۝ ذلكم بما
كنتم تفرحون في الأرض بغير الحق وبما كنتم تمرحون ۝ ادخلوا
أبواب جهنم خالدين فيها فبئس مثوى المتكبرين ۝
فاصبر إن وعد الله حق فإما نرينك بعض الذي
نعدهم أو نتوفينك فإلينا يرجعون ۝

ولقد أرسلنا رسلا من قبلك منهم من قصصنا
عليك ومنهم من لم نقصص عليك وما كان لرسول أن
يأتي بآية إلا بإذن الله فإذا جاء أمر الله قضي بالحق وخسر
هنالك المبطلون ۝ الله الذي جعل لكم الأنعام لتركبوا
منها ومنها تأكلون ۝ ولكم فيها منافع ولتبلغوا
عليها حاجة في صدوركم وعليها وعلى الفلك تحملون
۝ ويريكم آياته فأي آيات الله
تنكرون ۝ أفلم يسيروا في الأرض فينظروا كيف كان
عاقبة الذين من قبلهم كانوا أكثر منهم وأشد قوة
وآثارا في الأرض فما أغنى عنهم ما كانوا يكسبون ۝
فلما جاءتهم رسلهم بالبينات فرحوا بما عندهم من العلم
وحاق بهم ما كانوا به يستهزئون ۝ فلما رأوا بأسنا
قالوا آمنا بالله وحده وكفرنا بما كنا به مشركين ۝
فلم يك ينفعهم إيمانهم لما رأوا بأسنا سنت الله التي قد
خلت في عباده وخسر هنالك الكافرون ۝

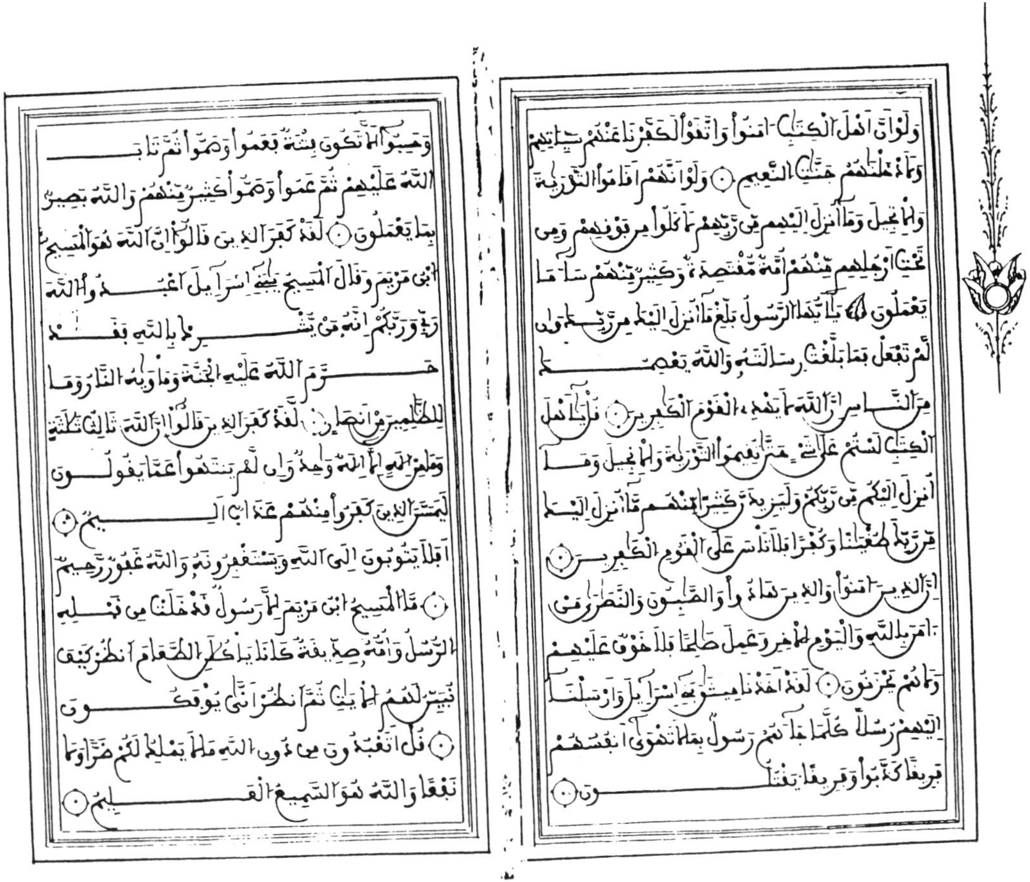
ولو ان اهل الكتاب امنوا واتقوا لكفرنا عنهم سيئاتهم
ولادخلناهم جنات النعيم ۝ ولو انهم اقاموا التوراة
والانجيل وما انزل اليهم من ربهم لاكلوا من فوقهم ومن
تحت ارجلهم منهم امة مقتصدة وكثير منهم ساء ما
يعملون ۝ يا ايها الرسول بلغ ما انزل اليك من ربك وان
لم تفعل فما بلغت رسالته والله يعصمك
من الناس ان الله لا يهدي القوم الكافرين ۝ قل يا اهل
الكتاب لستم على شيء حتى تقيموا التوراة والانجيل وما
انزل اليكم من ربكم وليزيدن كثيرا منهم ما انزل اليك
من ربك طغيانا وكفرا فلا تاس على القوم الكافرين
۝ ان الذين امنوا والذين هادوا والصابون والنصارى من
امن بالله واليوم الاخر وعمل صالحا فلا خوف عليهم
ولا هم يحزنون ۝ لقد اخذنا ميثاق بني اسرائيل وارسلنا
اليهم رسلا كلما جاءهم رسول بما لا تهوى انفسهم
فريقا كذبوا وفريقا يقتلون ۝

وحسبوا الا تكون فتنة فعموا وصموا ثم تاب
الله عليهم ثم عموا وصموا كثير منهم والله بصير
بما يعملون ۝ لقد كفر الذين قالوا ان الله هو المسيح
ابن مريم وقال المسيح يا بني اسرائيل اعبدوا الله
ربي وربكم انه من يشرك بالله فقد
حرم الله عليه الجنة وماواه النار وما
للظالمين من انصار ۝ لقد كفر الذين قالوا ان الله ثالث ثلاثة
وما من اله الا اله واحد وان لم ينتهوا عما يقولون
ليمسن الذين كفروا منهم عذاب اليم ۝
افلا يتوبون الى الله ويستغفرونه والله غفور رحيم
۝ ما المسيح ابن مريم الا رسول قد خلت من قبله
الرسل وامه صديقة كانا ياكلان الطعام انظر كيف
نبين لهم الايات ثم انظر انى يؤفكون
۝ قل اتعبدون من دون الله ما لا يملك لكم ضرا ولا
نفعا والله هو السميع العليم ۝

Sample pages of the Bach Mamluk Hajj Zuhayr Koran (Tunisia, 1858)

قالوا آمنا برب العالمين ۝ رب
موسى وهارون ۝ قال فرعون آمنتم به قبل أن آذن
لكم إن هذا لمكر مكرتموه في المدينة لتخرجوا
منها أهلها فسوف تعلمون ۝ لأقطعن أيديكم
وأرجلكم من خلاف ثم لأصلبنكم أجمعين ۝ قالوا إنا
إلى ربنا منقلبون ۝ وما تنقم منا إلا أن آمنا بآيات ربنا
لما جاءتنا ربنا أفرغ علينا صبرا وتوفنا مسلمين ۝
وقال الملأ من قوم فرعون أتذر موسى وقومه
ليفسدوا في الأرض ويذرك وآلهتك قال سنقتل أبناءهم
ونستحيي نساءهم وإنا فوقهم قاهرون ۝ قال موسى
لقومه استعينوا بالله واصبروا إن الأرض لله يورثها من
يشاء من عباده والعاقبة للمتقين ۝ قالوا أوذينا من قبل أن
تأتينا ومن بعد ما جئتنا قال عسى ربكم أن يهلك عدوكم
ويستخلفكم في الأرض فينظر كيف تعملون ۝ ولقد أخذنا
آل فرعون بالسنين ونقص من الثمرات لعلهم يذكرون ۝

فإذا جاءتهم الحسنة قالوا
لنا هذه وإن تصبهم سيئة يطيروا بموسى
ومن معه ألا إنما طائرهم عند الله
ولكن أكثرهم لا يعلمون ۝ وقالوا مهما تأتنا
به من آية لتسحرنا بها فما نحن لك بمؤمنين ۝ فأرسلنا
عليهم الطوفان والجراد والقمل والضفادع والدم آيات
مفصلات فاستكبروا وكانوا قوما مجرمين ۝ ولما وقع عليهم
الرجز قالوا يا موسى ادع لنا ربك بما عهد عندك لئن
كشفت عنا الرجز لنؤمنن لك ولنرسلن معك بني إسرائيل
۝ فلما كشفنا عنهم الرجز إلى أجل هم بالغوه إذا هم
ينكثون ۝ فانتقمنا منهم فأغرقناهم في اليم بأنهم كذبوا
بآياتنا وكانوا عنها غافلين ۝ وأورثنا القوم الذين
كانوا يستضعفون مشارق الأرض ومغاربها التي باركنا فيها وتمت
كلمت ربك الحسنى على بني إسرائيل بما صبروا ودمرنا ما كان
يصنع فرعون وقومه وما كانوا يعرشون ۝

3

"Of Making Many Books There Is No End:" The Classical Muslim View

Franz Rosenthal

In our time, we seem to have reached the point where we may well ask ourselves whether the incessant production of books might not be too much of a good thing. The more books we throw away (actually or figuratively), the more there are to take their place. It is no longer unjustified to hope against hope that book production could be limited, even if, on the face of it, it clearly involves an uphill battle comparable to the limitation of population growth. Of course, those in the book business, whether out in front or in the rear echelons, do not welcome the prospect of reduced production and consider the idea as anything from eccentric to scurrilous to outright dangerous.

Books have been valuable and cherished possessions all through history. For the first time, their devaluation as material objects could possibly have occurred in medieval Islam, what with the introduction of a rather cheap, yet durable, writing material and the feverish and almost global activity in science and scholarship.[1] This could conceivably have happened, but it did not. Before the Muslim era, no realistic opportunity existed for the feeling to arise that just too many books might be around. The famous verse of Ecclesiastes 12:12: "Of making many books there is no end, and much study is a weariness of flesh," at the most expresses a tentative apprehension as to theoretically uncontrollable quantities of books, and so do other putative complaints about the vastness of existing knowledge.[2] The biblical verse presents many difficulties for the understanding and lends itself to various interpretations. To the best of my—admittedly very limited—knowledge, no unanimity has as yet been reached as to what it really meant in its historical context. Whatever it did mean originally, it does not contain evidence that already in ancient times, people complained about too many books as physical objects being around. There were not, and could not have been.

The fact that Eccl. 12:12 is widely considered a later addition poses a further problem,[3] but this is a minor matter. Among the principal difficulties is, for one, the great variety of meanings of the Hebrew verb "to make" and, in the second colon, the meaning of the hapax legomenon *lahag*. Recent translations include a conservative "book learning" for "to make=to use,"[4] or "a thing of no purpose" for "no end,"[5] as well as more radical suggestions such as assuming that *lahag* is in fact parallel to "no end"[6] or re-interpreting the entire passage as "Und lass dich, mein Sohn, von ihnen gut belehren, viele Bücher ohne Unterlass zu benutzen und viel zu meditieren bis zur Körpermüdigkeit."[7] The question of the applicability of "to make" to "books" appears to have been settled by the existence of an equivalent idiom in Aramaic meaning "producing. . .a document (spr znh zy 'nh ʿbdt)" and the Akkadian usage of *enněsu* as a stage in the bookmaking process.[8] The possibility that "making" here might mean "collecting" (with reference to Eccl. 2:8 "I got me singers")[9] must be put on hold for the time being, although it would go well with the Arabic idiom of *ikthār min al-kutub* for collecting many books.[10] However, the production or overproduction of books would seem to be connected in Eccl. 12:12 to the physical process of writing rather than the intellectual task of composing works.

Lahag, translated traditionally as "study" reflecting the Greek translation and a combination with Arabic *lahija* "to be deeply engaged in something" (preferably, in study)[11] remains uncertain. The derivation from the root *hāgāh* (or a Ugaritic *hg*)[12] cannot be dismissed offhand but leaves room for doubt. Rabbinical associations of *lahag* with *l-ʿ-g* and *h-g-wy* are as much guesswork as modern theories. It should, however, be noted that both *l-ʿ-g* and *h-g-wy* are based upon the uttering of sounds, such as stammering or scoffing. The Targum speaks of "(making) books of wisdom" as parallel to "(the occupation with and understanding of) the *words* of the Torah."[13] More to the point, the Syriac translation has *man(l)la* which is most readily understood as "speech." Following this lead, a Syriac commentary of Ecclesiastes used "words (*melle*)."[14] And Arabic knows a noun *lahjah* in the meaning of "tongue, speech, dialect," whose history, however, is not quite clear.[15] It is thus possible that *lahag*, whatever its derivation, refers to some sort of oral expression. This was suspected also by M. V. Fox who states that "either 'study' or 'utter' would make sense here, because study in the ancient world was essentially oral recitation."[16] Taking it all together, we may conclude that Eccl. 12:12 indeed referred originally to the combination of two modes of study, the reading and reproduction of written materials and oral discussion. Whatever mode was used committed, in the eyes of the author, the student to an endless and painful task.

It may be worth noting that Eccl. 12:12 seems to be more famous now than it was in premodern times. Generally speaking, the verse was not much discussed and, again speaking generally, it was not frequently cited. From the medieval Muslim environment, we have a comment by the tenth-century Karaite Salmon ibn Yeruham, paraphrased by G. Vajda: "Et garde-toi encore des livres innombrables qui ont été faits." Man must not attempt to become too wise.

Nobody should make the rounds of cities and markets to search for philosophical and heretical works.[17] Reflecting further the attitude of certain segments of Muslim scholarship, Abū al-Barakāt al-Baghdādī (d. ca. 547/1166) interprets Eccl. 12:12 as a warning against wasting time on books that are an outgrowth of the human imagination, whose study could take up more than a human lifetime. Abū al-Barakāt translates *lahag* as *hadhayān* "talking nonsense."[18]

It was too much knowledge, not too many books, that was complained about in ancient times and continued to be complained about through medieval Islam. Knowledge, especially in certain fields, could not be mastered in its entirety; of books there were, in a way, never enough. In the course of time, we often hear it said that works in a given discipline were "many." For example, Ibn Khallikān (d. 682/1282) said that he did not intend to include caliphs among his biographees, because "the many works on them are sufficient."[19] Works on history were so many that they obviously could not all be listed.[20] And, in particular, anything connected with ḥadīth and other religious subjects produced an enormous literature.[21] When an eighth/fourteenth-century scholar wrote a commentary of al-Bukhārī's *Ṣaḥīh*, he was able to draw on 300 earlier commentaries;[22] for him, this was a boast rather than a complaint. This superabundance of specialized works also led to an unwholesome restriction to standard works.[23]

Despair in the face of an overwhelming amount of existing knowledge was the almost universal complaint and the situation most generally referred to. The physical problem of the multitude of books was much less obvious. There were many reasons for this state of affairs. In the first place, it has to do with the character of our sources. They were the work of authors who naturally would not wish to play down the desirability of making more books—preferably, of course, their own. Like ourselves, they would rarely be willing to admit that anything of theirs could be superfluous, let alone harmful. In their forewords, the one thing they generally avoided was referring to an existing glut of other works on the subject.[24] A second, more objective reason was the frequent lack of books in a given environment and the constant need to replenish the stock. In an area as vast and diversified as the Muslim world, imbalances in the supply of books were unavoidable. Books that were plentiful in one place were hardly known and accessible in another.[25] Since books were expensive, scholars, with rare exceptions, had to build up their libraries by copying materials with their own hands; this was so not only at the beginning of their careers, but usually continued throughout their lives. Not many were so fortunate as to be able to buy (or inherit) books or have others do the copying for them as a favor or inexpensively, and it was probably quite unique for a scholar to have a wife whom he could train in proper copying.[26]

A third reason is peculiar to Muslim civilization and of great import for the attitude toward books. It resulted from the never abandoned fiction—very soon to be enshrined in the very center of Muslim intellectual activity, the science of ḥadīth—of the primacy of the spoken word. Books were seen as innovations that came about only after the year 120/738 when the true models of scholarship, the men around Muḥammad and most men of the second generation, were dead,[27] and so on. In fact, of course, written books were indispensable almost from the outset, as was admitted in various ways, for instance, by claiming that memory had been good enough among the ancient Arabs to suffice for preserving and safely transmitting all knowledge; among later generations, this was no longer the case.[28] It became a matter of pride to own, or, at least, have access to, as many books as possible. Yet the deep conviction lingered that there was, in addition, something else that was essential for civilization, no matter how many, or how few, books were around. As a result, their numbers were basically inconsequential. Yet even in this climate, subdued feelings not only about the very existence of books but also about their numbers can be observed on occasion. Religious scholars would complain that once knowledge was committed to writing, there developed an unending process of writing "book after book after book,"[29] the implication being that oral transmission was more restricted and thus less contaminated and more reliable than the endless array of written material. Even for secular scholars, the great increase in books (*al-kutub wa-al-taṣānīf*) made it possible for ignoramuses to infiltrate the ranks of qualified intellectuals, and actually diminish the quality of books.[30] In a way, this can be read, as another faint complaint about the proliferation of literature.

There were other ways in which feelings of this sort tried sporadically to work their way to the surface. This is the subject of the following pages.

The formation of large libraries which was eagerly pursued inevitably led to problems caused by quantity and variety. Selectivity in forming a library, be it that of a private individual or one of semi-public character, was indicated.[31] It was an occasional problem then and, needless to say, has remained one to this day. Not discarding any book was considered the better part of wisdom, even if it was a book on a subject beyond the owner's interest and competence. The brief chapter on "the amassing of books (*al-ikthār min al-kutub*)" in the Khaṭīb al-Baghdādī's (d. 464/1071) *Taqyīd al-ʿilm* "The written fixation of knowledge" contains the essence of medieval thought on the importance of each single book for the educated. As the title suggests, the *Taqyīd* ultimately comes out in favor of the written word but balances and, in a way, conceals the message by first presenting a full array of negative attitudes toward books. The chapter in question deals with three considerations that work against selling any of the books in one's library or not buying books one has the opportunity of buying. Anecdotal as it is, it is best reported in the Khaṭīb's own words.[32]

The first of the three considerations is that a book deemed disposable may later on turn out to be badly needed: "As remarked by some scholar, a person must hoard all kinds of subjects, even subjects he does not know. He must amass works on very many subjects. He must not believe that he can dispense with any subject. If he can dispense with some books on one occasion, he may need them on another. If he is unhappy with them at one time, he may enjoy them at another. If he has no time for them on a given day, he may have time for them on another day. He must not act in a hurry (to sell a book or pass up the opportunity to buy one), lest he later regret very much to have done so. It could happen that someone discards a book and then wants it badly but cannot get hold of it. This may cause him great trouble and many sleepless nights. We have a story about a certain scholar who said: 'Once I sold a book thinking that I did not need it. Then I thought of some matter that was dealt with in that book. I looked for it among all my books but could not find it. I decided to ask some scholar about it the next morning, and I stayed up on my feet all night.' When he was asked why he did not sit down rather than stand, he replied: 'I was so perturbed that I could not get a wink of sleep.' "

This scholar only lost a night's sleep and apparently was able to find a replacement in a colleague's library. But it could also be terribly frustrating and expensive to sell or discard a book, as described by the Khaṭīb in the following two stories: "Someone sold a book thinking that he did not need it. Then he needed and looked for a copy but could not find any either to loan or to buy. The man to whom he had sold his copy had left for his place of residence. He went to him and told him that he would like to cancel the sale and return the purchase price. When the man refused, he asked him to lend him the book, so that he could copy the passage he was interested in. Again, he received a negative response, so he went home frustrated and swore that he would never again sell a book. There was someone else who sold a book which he thought he did not need, but later he did need a passage from it. He went to the new owner and asked him to let him copy the passage in question but was told: 'You won't copy it unless you pav me the price of the entire book.' So he had no choice but to return the price of the book, in order to copy the passage he wanted."[33] The words of someone who was asked why he did not sell the books he did not need sums it all up: "If I do not need them today, I may need them the next day."

The second consideration is that books in fields with which their owner is unfamiliar at the moment may give him the opportunity to familiarize himself with that field. Of course, any field of scholarship has its special interest: "When someone bought a book outside his own special field and asked why he did that, he replied: 'When I buy a book outside my own field of learning, I do it in order to make that particular field part of my knowledge.' And when someone else was asked why he did not buy books to have them in his house, he replied that it was his lack of knowledge that prevented him from building up a library. He was told that one who does not know buys books in order to know. Again, someone else who used to buy every book he saw replied to the question why he bought books he did not need: 'I may need (at some time) what I don't need (now).' "[34] We may add here that the Khaṭīb's chapter ends with an anecdote about the great bibliophile al-Jāḥiẓ (d. 255/868) to the same effect, with the stress on the idea that all written materials should be investigated as to whether they contain information not found elsewhere. Nothing should ever be dismissed offhand.[35]

The third consideration concerns books as a scholar's indispensable tools. He should therefore have them handy at all times: "A judge," the story goes, "used to go into debt to buy books. Questioned about it he replied: 'Should I not buy something that has taken me so far (in the world, i.e., to a judgeship)?' "[36] Further in the same vein: "A carpenter had to sell his ax and saw. He was sad about it and regretted having sold his tools, until one day he saw a scholar, a neighbor of his, in the booksellers' market selling a book. Now he was consoled. He remarked: 'If a scholar can sell his tools, a craftsman is certainly excusable, or even more so, when he sells his.' "

We may conclude from this discourse in praise of books—which is one among many—that books were often so plentiful that one could think of discarding some, but this was generally considered wrong and something one was not supposed to do. There was, however, a dissenting voice if a rather lonely one according to our knowledge. The well-known physician and scientist in eleventh-century Egypt, Ibn Riḍwān, tells us that he either sold the books for which he had no use or stored them away in chests. Selling them, he contends, was preferable to storing them.[37] It is not quite clear whether he meant that it was better to put unneeded books back into circulation rather than keeping them out of sight. It is, however, more likely given, Ibn Riḍwān's great concern with his finances, that he was unwilling to pass up an opportunity to make some more money. He was well known as the champion of the hotly debated view that learning from books was better than by means of oral instruction. It does not seem that he was complaining about owning too many books, or more than he was able to cope with, although this could have easily been the case.

Large semi-public libraries faced a bigger problem as to what to do with their holdings when they grew too large. Books being valuable, the most common danger for libraries, not the least the libraries of which every college had one with a scholarly librarian, was frequent inroads into their holdings by neglect and theft (the always present danger of accidental destruction by fire or water damage does not concern us here). When large libraries were dissolved, it proved a bonanza for scholars who could acquire or appropriate books cheap or sell worthless or made to appear worthless, library books for their own benefit.[38] The failure to return books borrowed from libraries or individuals was often bemoaned in verse and prose. It was thus probably much more difficult to hold together large libraries than trying to weed out unwanted materials. However, we also hear about an author's hesitancy as to whether his works would be accepted for incorporation into a large library.[39] Selectivity was always practiced by collectors and was required in forming a *waqf* library.[40]

The deliberate destruction by fire or other means such as erasing (*maḥā*), washing off (*ghasala*), tearing up (*kharraqa*), or burying (*dafana*) should be mentioned here, even if it had other motives than the weeding out of books when they had become too many. Regrettably, as elsewhere in the world, book burnings were not unheard of in Islam. They affected principally books adjudged heretical or otherwise religiously objectionable.[41] This contributed to the virtual disappearance of manuscripts of such works over the centuries. Where there were both fervent partisans and violent opponents in substantial numbers, of course, the situation was different. This, for instance, is shown by Ibn 'Arabī's (d. 638/1240) voluminous corpus. Even if there were those who wrote *fatwā*s permitting the destruction of all books by him,[42] or who went to such scurrilous lengths as tying the *Kitāb al-Fuṣūṣ* to the tail of a dog,[43] his innumerable followers saw to it that copies of his works survived. An instructive story on the destruction of a work of presumably literary merit is reported in connection with a book by the blind poet al-Ma'arrī (d. 449/1057) which supposedly criticized the Qur'ān. A librarian, of all people, destroyed it. He was challenged by al-Wajīh al-Naḥwī (532–612/1137[8]–1215) with a witty argument: If the work was indeed equal to, or better than, the Qur'ān, it would be untouchable; on the other hand, if it was, as there could be no doubt, inferior to it, it ought to be preserved as a witness to the inimitability of the Holy Book.[44] Perhaps, the underlying and unexpressed moral of the al-Wajīh's remark was disapproval of the destruction of books in general.

The destruction of valuable property such as books expectedly found the attention of jurists. Strict Hanbalite opinion, for instance, was expressed by a scholar of the stature of Ibn Qayyim al-Jawzīyah (d. 751/1350). Other schools and individuals saw the matter differently.[45] Ibn Qayyim al-Jawzīyah held that no financial responsibility resulted from the destruction of books. It was as legal and free from liability as the destruction of everything connected with wine. Ibn Qayyim al-Jawzīyah's basic tradition is one of Abū Bakr al-Marrūdhī (al-Marwazī) (d. 275/888) who consulted Ibn Ḥanbal (d. 241/855) on whether he thought that he could burn or tear up a book he had borrowed that contained objectionable matters. Ibn Ḥanbal expressed the view that it was permissible, quoting a tradition to the effect that the Messenger of God once saw a book in 'Umar's hand in which 'Umar had written down material from the Torah that had pleased him because it agreed with the Qur'ān. The Prophet's face showed such anger that 'Umar rushed to the furnace and threw the book into it. How then, Ibn Qayyim al-Jawzīyah continued, would the Prophet have felt had he been able to see books which contradicted the Qur'ān and his Sunnah as were published later. Only the Qur'ān and the ḥadīth were permitted to be put down in writing, and this is presented as the view of Ibn Ḥanbal himself.

All books on *ra'y*—here, approximately, dogmatic and juridical speculation—and all the more so, all books on other subjects were anathema as leading to error. To err is human, Ibn Ḥanbal is said to have opined, but the most prone to error are those who write books. While the composition of books was seen as a complicated legal problem, Ibn Ḥanbal and his followers were adamantly opposed to books that were in conflict with the Qur'ān and the Sunnah. It was, however, different with works written against those books; they could fall into any of the positive legal classifications as necessary, preferable, or permitted.[46] It does not take much to realize that we have here a good example of the eternal problem of censorship. Once set in motion, does it have proper limits, and can they be observed without detriment to intellectual life and growth? We do not know the answer.

Another common theme is that of an author himself burning his books or ordering their destructions. Among littérateurs, Abū Ḥayyān al-Tawḥīdī (d. after 400/1009) is famous or infamous for having "burned his books at the end of his life because they served no longer any purpose and he did not want those who did not appreciate their worth to have them after his death." In a letter, in which he defends his action, he speaks of burning his valuable books or washing them off. Having lost everybody near and dear to him, he says, "I found it difficult to leave them to people who would play around with them, besmirch my honor when looking into them, gloat over my oversights and mistakes when studying them more closely, and look at each other (and say how) incompetent I am."[47] This makes it clear that al-Tawḥīdī speaks about his own books and not about books by others in his library. It would seem a bit curious that he would burn his own works when they included books that had been published and had been in general circulation for a long time. Therefore, speaking about his own "books," there can be no doubt that he had in mind his unpublished manuscripts and, in particular, his notebooks and drafts.[48] This also applies to, and is confirmed by, his list of those early Muslims who served as model and excuse for his action. The earliest name in al-Tawḥīdī's list is Abū ʿAmr ibn al-ʿAlā' who buried his books. A Ṣūfī, Dāwūd al-Ṭā'ī (d. 205/821), threw his books into the river,[49] while Yūsuf ibn Asbāṭ locked his away in a mountain cave.[50] Another Ṣūfī, Abū Sulaymān al-Dārānī, burned his books in a furnace.[51] The great Sufyān al-Thawrī (d. 161/778) tore his manuscripts to pieces and scattered the pieces in the wind.[52] The last name in the list is that of a teacher of al-Tawḥīdī' Abū Saʿīd al-Sīrāfī (d. 369/979), who exhorted his son (Abū) Muḥammad[53] to burn his books if they turned out to play him and others false and distract them from acquiring religious merit; as in the numerous examples from modern times for requests to destroy the literary Nachlass of famous men, this request, of course, may or may not have been honored. The variety of ways for the disposal of books we find in al-Tawḥīdī's list is owed to his sense of style, and not necessarily to the sources from which he derived his information.

With the possible exception of Abū Saʿīd al-Sīrāfī who, however, was highly praised for his asceticism, all these men were famous exemplars of Muslim piety and religious commitment. Their alleged actions expressed their suspicion of the written word in general. But they hardly were appropriate models for al-Tawḥīdī who, in spite of pietistic episodes in his life, produced mainly works that were quite worldly in character. As other sources make abundantly clear, the destruction of one's written materials is a topos of the science of ḥadīth and of mysticism. How much reality was connected with the topos, we cannot judge. Later biographers showed a certain lack of enthusiasm for reporting these data.

We thus hear it said already about the first/seventh-century ʿAbīdah al-Salmānī that he called for his "books" and erased them when he lay on his deathbed. Asked for his reason, he replied that he feared that some people might get hold of them who would not treat them properly (*yaḍaʿūnahā ghayr mawāḍīʿihā*).[54] This seems to be the earliest and, superfluous to say, fictitious example within the tradition of ḥadīth scholarship. The Khaṭīb al-Baghdādī mentions already Ibn Masʿūd among his many examples of men who erased written ḥadīth material.[55] He tells of Abū Qilābah that he willed his "books" to another scholar if the latter survived him; if not, they were to be burned or, according to another recension, torn up.[56] A certain Yūnus ibnʿĪsá meant to burn his books.[57] Shuʿbah ibn al-Ḥajjāj (d. 160/777) directed his son Saʿd to wash off and bury his "books" after his death, which was done.[58] Others buried eighteen chests and baskets of books for Bishr al-Ḥāfī. It is to the credit of Ibn Ḥanbal that he could not see any sense in burning books.[60]

These and similar data continued to have a long life. The seventeenth-century Ḥājjī Khalīfah has a list that includes al-Tawḥīdī's Abū ʿAmr ibn al-ʿAlā', Dāwūd al-Ṭā'ī, and Sufyān al-Thawrīi. He took their names not from al-Tawḥīdī but from other sources which he indicates, but which I have been unable to check. He added the Ṣūfī Ibn Abū al-Ḥawārī (6th/12th century) from the *Ḥilyah* of Abū Nuʿaym al-Iṣfahānī (d. 430/103Q). The *Ḥilyah* presents different recensions, all of which agree that Ibn Abī al-Ḥawārī was motivated by his conviction that books may serve as guides to gnosis but become superfluous as soon as a person attains gnosis and reaches the Lord.[61]

It is to Ḥājjī Khalīfah's credit that he clearly distinguished between the two strands that defined all the statements about the destruction of "books." One of them, he realized, was the need of ḥadīth theoreticians to produce telling evidence for the alleged superiority of oral over written transmission. The other was the persistent claim of pious individuals and devoted mystics to have direct access to the divine which made any material medium such as books altogether unnecessary and undesirable.[62] Ḥājjī Khalīfh considers the view expressed by Ibn Ḥajar in connection with Dāwūd al-Ṭā'ī that the motivation for the destruction of their books by men like him was the prevention of their transmission in a way that might lead to their being branded as "weak transmitters." On his part, Ḥājjī Khalīfah realized that more was involved here: "This explanation," he says, "would not hold for the destruction of their notebooks (*dafātir*) by Ibn Abī al-Ḥawārī and his ilk. Dāwūd al-Ṭā'ī did what he did because he was concerned about the resulting weakness of his *isnād*. On the other hand, Ibn Abī al-Ḥawārī did it because of his asceticism and devotion to God. The explanation why he (and others like him) chose to destroy (their books, instead of selling them or giving them away) might perhaps be (sought in their fear) that, if they had divested themselves of the possession of their *dafātir* through gift or sale, their emotional (*qalbī*) attachment to them would not have been severed completely and they could not be sure that they might not at some time get the urge to go back to them and study them, thereby occupying themselves with something other than God."[63]

In historical cases, the evidence for such destruction is occasionally ambiguous. Thus, we hear that Aḥmad ibn Ismā'īl ibn Abī al-Su'ūd (814–870/1412–66) reached the point, probably because of religious scruples (?), where he wanted to give up all his literary activities, and he washed off all his poetical and prose writings, so that only his previously published works survived. However, another source maintains that this did not happen intentionally. When Ibn Abī al-Su'ūd was in the process of sorting out the poems he did not like in order to destroy them, a colleague appeared unexpectedly and he went out to meet him. Meanwhile, he ordered someone to destroy the papers on the right in his study. That individual became confused and destroyed the papers which Ibn Abī al-Su'ūd wanted to keep. When Ibn Abī al-Su'ūd came back and saw what had happened, he was very dismayed (*suqiṭa fī yadihi*) and destroyed the rest.[64]

Such destruction of papers and notes, or books in our sense, whether historical or not, did not reflect on the size of book production. This, I feel, probably also applies to a statement telling us that, at the time it was made, there were people who disapproved of all authorship (*al-taṣnīf wa-al-ta'līf*), even of those who were qualified and knowledgeable enough to write books. So far, I have been unable to trace this statement to any source earlier than Badr al-Dīn ibn Jamā'ah (639–733/1241–1333) who mentions it in his well-known treatise on education, entitled *Tadhkirat al-sāmi' wa-al-mutakallim*[65] Ibn Jamā'ah strongly disapproves of this attitude. If, he argues, there is no legal disapproval of the written fixation of poetry and entertaining stories, provided no indecency is involved, why, then, should the writing of books on useful religious subjects be disapproved? It is obvious that unqualified people should never be allowed to write books on any subject. As Ibn Jamā'ah sees it, the only possible explanation for the disapproval of authoring books is the constant envy and competitiveness among generations (*al-taḥāsud bayna ahl al-a'ṣār*).[66] Quoting Ibn Jamā'ah's view, Ḥājjī Khalīfah then goes on to criticize it as a reflection of the popular attitude that considers only the achievements of earlier generations as important and routinely holds contemporary scholars in low esteem, and he treats his readers to the verses:

> You who think nothing of contemporaries,
> considering the ancients to be out in front:
> The ancients were once young/new,
> And the young/new will stay on and become ancient.[67]

Neither Ibn Jamā'ah nor Ḥājjī Khalīfah seem to be correct. The disapproval of composing books may also here be rooted rather in the pietistic/mystic attitude and the long tradition of philosophers (such as Socrates) and, above all, mystics who feel revulsion at the thought of profaning their insights. It is not impossible that the expression could be explained as a complaint about the proliferation of books, but this does not really seem plausible.

The problem of overproduction is more directly addressed in the strong sentiment in favor of abridgements and brief handbooks as against long, comprehensive, and scholarly works. The latter were, of course, always produced in large numbers. They were, in fact, quite characteristic products of medieval Muslim civilization. However, the attitude, serious in part and in part a snobbish pretense, that big books are a nuisance was old and deeply engrained. al-Tawḥīdī put it succinctly: "Big books are boring *(al-kutub al-ṭiwāl mus'imah)*.[68] As A. Mez stressed long ago, writers of Muslim civilization's so-called golden age feared nothing more than boring the reader.[69] This fear persisted through the centuries and found expression in the frequently professed aversion to unnecessary length and the claim of having exercised restraint for the sake of brevity. While conciseness had special meaning for the entertaining literature, it soon invaded the scholarly and scientific community where it led to the popularity of compendia. Resistance to the trend never faltered entirely. For instance, in the introduction of his long geographical dictionary, Yāqūt (d. 627/1229) expressed himself with strong emotion against any attempt to shorten his work, quoting al-Jāḥiẓ as having been of the same mind when he stated forcefully that an author is "like a painter; his work is a painting representing its subject perfectly, and the idea of abridging it means atrocious mutilation.[70] The practice (often also indulged in by us) of exploiting large works for educational and/or commercial reasons by compiling shortened versions, which, as noted by Yāqūt, stood a better chance of achieving wide dissemination, was part and parcel of medieval Muslim life.

It was recognized that progress dictated the creation of larger and better works. Treatments of new and as yet unexplored subjects tended to start out small and then grow to ever larger size in the course of time.[71] Originality was stressed as the fundamental purpose of and justification for writing and was one of the guiding principles of research.[72] The remark, already used by Abū

Tammām (d. 231/846) the poet as a cento,[73] was constantly repeated: "How much did the ancients leave for later generations (*kam taraka al-awwalu lil-ākhiri*)." al-Jāḥiẓ is quoted again by Yāqūt as having stated that nothing is more harmful to science and scholarship than the opposite contention that the ancients did not leave anything for later generations, as this had a discouraging and debilitating effect.[74] The consequence, however, was the constant creation of new disciplines and subdisciplines, small at first and then often expanding to barely manageable proportions. With the technical means then available, they were probably unmanageable and required forgetting and discarding. More, and better, techniques are available now and offer a certain, possibly deceptive, measure of hope that we shall be able to keep up with the accumulation of knowledge and of books.

The theoretical approach of philosophers to the overwhelming mass and variety of knowledge put into writing was to suggest, as did al-Tawḥīdī and al-Miskawayh (d. 422/1030), that "since the particulars (*juz'īyāt*) are infinite, and whatever is infinite cannot achieve existence, it is the generalities of each discipline, which comprise all its particulars *in potentia*, that should be aimed at."[75] Deprived of its technical philosophical trimmings, the idea also lived on and found expression, for instance, in al-Zarkashī's (d. 794/1391) detailed elaboration of the different Qur'ānic sciences. Since, he claims, "the *'ulūm al-Qur'ān* are innumerable and the Qur'ān's meanings are inexhaustible, one must deal with them (not exhaustively but) to the degree possible." And "since earlier scholars composed no work comprising the different topics (*anwā'*) of Qur'ānic science in the way it was done in relation to the science of ḥadīth," he wrote his comprehensive work covering forty-six topics, but, he says,

> I am aware that every one of these topics cannot be dealt with exhaustively by any human being. If anyone tried, the whole of his life would be spent, and yet, he would not accomplish his task. Therefore, we have restricted ourselves to the principles (*uṣūl*) of each topic, with (only) occasional hints at the details (*fuṣūl*), for—quoting Hippocrates without naming him—"the craft is long and life is short."[76] We have dealt with as much as can possibly be achieved by imperfect speech, in accordance with the verse:
>
>> They said: Take the essence/eye (*'ayn*) of everything! I replied: There is excellence in the essence/eye, but the beholder of the essence/the glance of the eye (is imperfect).[77]

In the popular and entertaining literature, a simpler analogy was proposed in a saying which, like the philosophical approach, also had its roots in classical antiquity: Like a bee, an author should select the best flower. A more direct version of the same idea was attributed to ancient Muslims such as 'Abd Allah ibn 'Abbās (d. 68/686) and Ibn Sīrīn (d. 110/728): "Knowledge is too much for being comprehended in its entirety. Thus, take the best of every knowledge!"[78]

The statement of Ibn ʿAbbās was combined later with another one attributed to al-Shaʿbī who, like Ibn Sīrīn, lived a generation after Ibn ʿAbbās. al-Shaʿbī (d. 105/723) supposedly also alluded to Hippocrates without naming him. As he phrased it: "Knowledge is much, and life is little. Thus, take of knowledge the variety of its inner spirit (*arwāḥ*)—that is, its essences (*ʿuyūn*)—and leave alone its outward expression (*ḥurūf*)!"[79]

This advice was meant for the creative scholar and intellectual. For the mass of the educated, the compendium, the short exposition of the essentials or high points of a subject or the selective presentation of details, promised a better approach toward the elusive mastery of knowledge in its infinite variety. Another approach was for an author to justify writing a book by suggesting that his work, being an original product, would serve to replace all other works in the field[80]—this, we might say, being one way of dealing with the avalanche of books. In writing his great chronological work, al-Bīrūnī (d. 440/1048), for instance, claimed that the highly educated person who asked him to compose such a work did so in order to have a book that would make it superfluous for him to consult a large number of sources.[81] More commonly, authors expressed on their own the hope or conviction that they were about to replace any need to consult all the earlier works that had dealt with their subject. The large number of titles such as *al-Mughnī*, it may be noted, also attests to this motivation. On the other hand, it could also happen that a would-be author originally thought that the existing literature was exhaustive and made another work on the same subject unnecessary. After much research, however, he discovered that this was not the case, and he was justified in going ahead with his project and compose a more complete work likely to supplant all his predecessors' efforts. He reflected, at the end, "how much the ancients had left for later generations to do."[82]

The production of compendia in order to cope with the great amount of material to be read and digested and to make the acquisition of knowledge easier for the student eventually found full discussion in both its positive and its negative aspects in Ibn Khaldūn's *Muqaddimah*.[83] As Ibn Khaldūn (d. 808/1406) saw it, the great number of scholarly works, coupled with the refinement and sophistication reached in many fields, is an obstacle to scholarship, while the great number of brief handbooks is detrimental to the formation of a sound scholarly habit and thus of outstanding scholars. In many disciplines such as grammar[84] the literature is too vast for everything to be perused. More recently, says Ibn Khaldūn, this has also come to apply to the many writings on literary criticism which were produced in addition to the four standard works on the subject.[85] An even more crowded field, the science of ḥadīth, had developed an enormous amount of books and this had the consequence that a limited number of basic works was exclusively used for reference.[86] Ibn Khaldūn, it seems, considered this a rather dubious development. He did not go as far as to suggest that there were too many books on the market, but he clearly intimated that something was wrong with the prevailing situation and called for remedies if such could be found. Focusing his attention on the handbooks, abridgements, and compendia, he acknowledged that one of the legitimate purposes of authorship was generally recognized the production of brief and succinct abridgements.[87] The custom, he said, had become popular in his time (although it was, of course, widely practiced in preceding centuries). He considered such abridgements as often awkward but did not object to them as such. He pointed out that on the one hand, they tended to be too succinct and complicated for beginners, while, on the other, they were likely to stultify genuine scholarly minds, for true scholarship, he argued, required the painstaking study of long and detailed works over a considerable extent of time. It is clsar that for Ibn Khaldūn and those who followed him, the issue was not seen simply as the superabundance of books, although he realized that it caused a problem. It was rather a question of the proper methods and goals of scholarly and literary activity which were appropriate for a highly developed civilization such as his. These methods and goals, however, happened unavoidably to be dependent on the relentless production and wide availability of books. By his time and very probably much earlier, their numbers had come to seem threatening.

Ibn Khaldūn's discussion greatly impressed Ḥājjī Khalīfah who utilized it in the introduction of his large catalogue of Arabic books in Istanbul or otherwise known in his time.[88] In his capacity as a bibliographer, Ḥājjī Khalīfah might well have had special feelings about the cultural significance of the riches of book production in Islam. About seven centuries earlier, the situation was different. In his famous *Fihrist*, Ibn al-Nadīm (d. 380/990) had already vast numbers of titles to report on, but there was no real reason for him to sense, let alone comment on, too many books. So he concerned himself in his opening pages with the technical aspects of bookmaking which to him meant handwriting and scripts in their various forms and historical development. In the century before Ḥājjī Khalīfah, Ṭāshköprüzādeh produced a mammoth catalogue of the sciences, entitled *Miftāḥ al-sa'ādah*. His interest lay in the enormous amount of what he classified as special disciplines that together constituted the sum total of written knowledge no longer to be mastered in its entirety; he had occasion to mention only a limited number of standard works. It is due to Ṭāshköprüzādeh's influence that Ḥājjī Khalīfah in his introduction discourses lengthily on knowledge and its multiple disciplines, instead of book production as would have been logical. Thus, he misses out on the opportunity to speculate on the subiect that interests us here most. He remarks, however, in the beginning that an exhaustive bibliography such as his had become finally necessary, "because the scholarly disciplines *and books are many*, and the lives of individuals are preciously short."[89]

In conclusion, let me state that the feeling that there are simply too many books in the world remains a present-day phenomenon and is left to us not only to ponder but also to try to do something about it, if this is in our power. Possibly the fate of our civilization depends on it. In medieval Islam, books as physical objects were valuable since, for the ordinary individual, they were difficult to obtain and to amass; although plentiful in some locations, they could be scarce in others. The censorial destruction of books for one reason or another did occur at times, to the detriment of modern scholarship, but contributed little to limiting the constant increase in the number of books. The relationship between knowledge and books remained determined by a fictitious and, from our point of view, unfortunate distinction between oral and written information. Again, this did not contribute much to diminishing book production. It did, however, give some slight encouragement to the age-old tradition that some type of special secret or sacred knowledge was better left unwritten. Still, in the face of the pretended belief in the superiority of oral transmission, it was generally recognized that all knowledge was important and would disappear without books. This recognition often extended to the realization that all written materials were valuable and required preservation. The only practical attempts, however, to regulate, if modestly, the flood of books consisted of the production of works that were supposed to take the place of all the previous publications in a given field, and of the composition of handbooks and compendia, but the value and efficacy of these procedures did not remain unquestioned. Before the age of printing and modern technology, this was probably the most that could be done. The Muslim scholars cited here deserve credit for having been aware, if ever so dimly, of the problems resulting from the overproduction of books as an unintended by-product of the intellectual flourishing of their civilization. As it turned out, of making many books there was no end in medieval Islam, and we have every reason to be glad that this was so.

Notes

1. A good brief survey of contemporary scholarship on all aspects of bookmaking is by G. Endress, in *Grundriss der arabischen Philologie*, ed. by Wolfdietrich Fischer (Wiesbaden, 1983), 1:271ff.

2. While I was working on this paper, the Book Review section of the *New York Times* of 20 March 1989 published an essay by Arthur Krystal, "On Writing: Let There Be Less," dealing interestingly with our subject as reflected through the ages. Krystal mentions the Ancient Egyptian statement of Khakheperre-sonbe, which reads in the translation of W.K. Simpson: "He said: Would that I had unknown speeches, erudite phrases in new language which has not yet been used, free from the usual repetitions, not the phrases of past speech which (our) forefathers spoke." See W.K. Simpson (ed.), *The Literature of Ancient Egypt* (New Haven and London, 1972, 1973), pp. 230–33. This should

not be understood as a complaint about the existence of too much literature. Rather, it is an expression of the author's desire to be original. Expectedly, the modern plea for fewer books elicited heated responses among the essay's readers, as shown by letters to the *Book Review* of 30 April 1989, p. 5.

3. An exception is Michael V. Fox, *Qohelet and his Contradictions* (Sheffield, 1989. Bible and Literature Series 18), p. 311. I am grateful to Robert R. Wilson for bibliographical guidance through the vast ocean of biblical studies.

4. Cf. R.B.Y. Scott's commentary on Ecclesiastes in the Anchor Bible (Garden City, NY, 1963).

5. Fox, op. cit., 237.

6. According to M. Dahood, cf. H.L. Ginsberg, *Koheleth* (Tel Aviv 1961), p. 139.

7. Osweld Loretz, *Qohelet und der Alte Orient* (Freiburg-Basel-Wien, 1964), p. 139.

8. Cf. Ginsberg, loc. cit.; Michael Fishbane, *Biblical Interpretation in Ancient Israel* (Oxford, 1985), pp. 30–32; Fox, op. cit., p. 328f.

9. The presence of a possessive pronoun, which strengthens the meaning of collecting, would hardly be needed or fit into the syntax of Eccles. 12:12.

10. It seems as yet undecided whether *harbeh* (=Aram. Saggi) is used here as an adjective or as an adverb (cf. J. Goldin, "The end of Ecclesiastes," in A. Altmann, ed., *Biblical Motifs* [Cambridge, 1966], pp. 135–58.) The adverbial combination, lit., "the much making of books," appears preferable. In Semitic languages there is no easy distinction between "much" and "too much." Thus, *harbeh* in Eccles. 7:16 is translated by Ginsberg "don't overdo," cf. his *The Five Megilloth* (Philadelphia,1969), p. 68.

11. Cf. for instance Muḥammad ibn al-Raḥmān al-Sakhāwī, *al-Ḍaw' al-lāmiʿ li-ahl al-Qarn al-Tāsiʿ*, 12 vols. (Cairo, 1353–55/1934–36), 9:259, "*lahija bi-ṭalab al-ḥadīth wa-al-qirā'ah*."

12. See above, n. 6, and M. Dahood, "Canaanite-Phoenician influence in Qoheleth," in *Biblica* 33 (1952), p. 219.

13. According to the publication of A. Sperber, *The Bible in Aramaic*, 4 vols. in 5, (Leiden. 1968), 5:167.

14. Cf. W. Strothmann (ed.), *Kohelet-Kommentar des Johannes von Apamea* (Wiesbaden, 1988. Gottinger Orientforschungen, I Reihe: Syriaca, Band 30), p. 182. It is, however, not surprising to find *huggaya* "meditation" as a translation of *lahag*, cf. W. Strothmann, *Kohelet-Kommentar des Dionvsius bār Ṣalībī* (Wiesbaden, 1988, Band 31).

15. I am greatly obligated to M. Ullmann for communicating to me his Wörterbuch entries for *lahjah*. They seem to leave doubts in his mind as to the relationship between the root *l-h-j* and *lahjah*.

16. Fox, op. cit., p. 328.

17. Cf. G. Vajda, *Deux Commentaires Karaïtes sur l'Ecclesiaste* (Leiden, 1971), pp. 61, 75.

18. Abū al-Barakāt Hibat Allah al-Baghdādī, *al-Muʿtabar*, 3 vols. (Hyderabad, 1357–58/1938–39), 2:347, line 12ff. I owe this reference to Moshe Perlmann.

In the following generation, Moses Maimonides interpreted the Mishnaic expression "heretical books (*sefarim hitsonim*) as including books on history and *adab* which constitute a waste of time, cf. his commentary on the Mishna Sanhedrin, X, 1, ed. J. Qafih (Jerusalem, 1934), p. 210.

19. Ibn Khallikān, *Wafayāt al-a ʿyān*, 8 vols., ed. Iḥsān ʿAbbās (Beirut, 1968–72), 1:20.

20. Cf. al-Ījī and al-Sakhāwī as quoted in F. Rosenthal, *A History of Muslim Historiography*[2] (Leiden. 1968), pp. 242ff., 388.

21. Cf. Murtaḍā al-Zabīdī, *Itḥāf al-Sādah*, 10 vols. (Cairo, 1311/1893). Reprinted in Beirut, 1:273, line 14ff.

22. Cf. al-Sakhāwī, *Ḍaw'*, 10:21. The number 300 appears again in connection with al-Khirāqī's *Mukhtaṣar*. See *The Encyclopedia of Islam*, 2nd ed. (EI[2]), s.v Hanabila, 3:159, col. 1, line 30 and again s.v. al-Khiraki (H. Laoust), 5:10, col. 1, line 23, but, of course, other figures appear as well. In all cases, it can be assumed to have been a boast about the large number of sources consudted.

23. Cf. Ibn Khaldūn, *Muqaddimah*, tr. by F. Rosenthal, 3 vols. (New York, 1958; Princeton, 1967), 2:455. See below, p. 43.

24. See the most useful dissertation by Peter Freimark on *Das Vorwort als literarische Form in der arabischen Literatur* (Münster, 1967). Writing on *Latin Prose Prefaces* (Stockholm, 1964, *Acta Universitatis Stockholmianiae, Studia Latina Stockholmiana* 13), Toe Janson apparently found nothing in his material on the overwhelming amount of available books on a given subject, nor did Freimark in Arabic.

25. Murtaḍā al-Zabīdī, *Itḥāf*, 1:274, line 12f.

26. Al-Sakhāwī, *Ḍaw'*, 2:180, line 4 from bottom.

27. Al-Ghazzālī, *Iḥyā' 'ulūm al-dīn*, 4 vols. in 2 (Cairo, 1372/1953), 1:70, line 4ff., from Abū Ṭālib al-Makkī, *Qūt al-qulūb*, 2 vols. (Cairo, 1310/1892), 1:159; 4 vols. in 2 (Cairo, 1351/1932), 2:37.

28. See, for instance, Ibn 'Abd al-Barr, *Jāmi' bayān al-'ilm*, 2 vols., (Cairo, n.d.), 1:69f.

29. Ibn Qayyim al-Jawzīyah, *al-Ṭurūq al-ḥukmīyah* (Cairo, 1372/1953), p. 277.

30. Abū al-Barakāt Hibat Allah al-Baghdādī, *al-Mu'tabar fī al-ḥikmah*, 3 vols., (Hyderabad, 1938–39), 1:3.

31. See below p. 000.

32. al-Khaṭīb al-Baghdādī, *Taqyīd al-'ilm*, ed. Youssef Eche (Yūsuf al-'Ishsh) (Damascus, 1949, reprint 1975), pp. 136–38.

33. Some trickery might be used by a rare book dealer, in order to raise the fee for lending a book to what the price of the entire book should have been, cf. al-Sakhāwī, *Ḍaw'*, 9:148. The owners of lending libraries as a rule would seem to have been honest and often generous.

34. Here follow verses attributed to al-Sārī ibn Aḥmad al-Kindī, i.e., al-Sārī al-Raffā'. They are not included in the 1355/1936 and 1981 editions of his *dīwān* They deal with the widespread topos of the lasting value of all knowledge and have little to do directly with the subject of books.

35. Cf. also, for instance, Ibn Ḥazm, *Marātib al-'ul*ūm, in Anwar Chejne, *Ibn Hazm* (Chicago, 1982), text, 234, trans., p. 202f. Ibn Ḥazm also called it an error to decry the amassing of books.

36. Al-Jāḥiẓ already discussed at length the "pleasure" of spending money on books, if it was done for the sake of scholarship and not for purposes of religious ostentation as, he claims, was done by the Manichaeans. Cf. *Kitāb al-Ḥayawān*, 7 vols., ed. ʿAbd al-Salām M. Hārūn (Cairo, 1938–45), 1:56. See also Ibn Ḥazm, loc. cit.

37. Cf. J. Schacht and M. Meyerhof, *The Medico-Philosophical Controversy between Ibn Butlan and Ibn Ridwan of Cairo*, Arabic text 5 (Cairo, 1937), p. 38, from Ibn Abī Uṣaybiʿah; F. Rosenthal, "Die arabische Autobiographie," *Studia Arabica* I (Rome, 1937, Analecta Orientalia 14), p. 22, from the manuscript of Ibn Riḍwān's autobiography. The eighteenth-century Murtaḍá al-Zabīdī, *Itḥāf*, 1:66, lines 15–67, line 11, still found the passage interesting enough to quote it.

38. Cf. Youssef Eche, *Les Bibliothèques arabes* (Damascus, 1967), p. 250. Selling books "by the lot *(bi-al-ʿadad)*" from a bookseller's estate might have been necessitated by their large numbers but, above all, indicated general ignorance and a lack of discrimination by potential buyers, cf. al-Sakhāwī, *Ḍaw'*, 3:150, line 6. An ignorant (*mutakhallif*?) son of Ibn Yūnus would sell the books and works of his father left to him "by the pound *(bi-al-arṭāl)*," cf. Al-Ṣafadī, *Wāfī* (Stuttgart, 1988. Bibliotheca Islamica 6u) 21:226, line 8.

39. Cf. Eche, op. cit., 104 from Yāqūt, *Irshād al-arīb*, ed. D.S. Margoliouth, 7 vols. (Leiden-London, 1907–27), 1:242; ed. A.F. Rifāʿī, 20 vols. (Cairo, 1355–57/1936–1938), 4:6.

40. Eche, op. cit., 198, from al-Qifṭī, *Ikhbār al-ʿulamā' bi-akhbār al-ḥukamā'*, ed. J. Lippert (Leipzig, 1903), p. 269.

41. The justification for book burnings was probably always sought in lèse-religion. The sad case of a grandson of ʿAbd al-Qādir al-Jīlānī, ʿAbd al-Salām ibn ʿAbd al-Wahhāb (548–611/1154–1214), whose books on magic and star worship were publicly burned, illustrates the blend of personal, academic, and religious politics with suspicions of heresy that could lead to legal proceedings and autodafés, cf. Ibn al-ʿImad, *Shadharāt al-Dhahab*, 8 vols. (Cairo, 1350–51/1931–32), 5:45f.

42. Cf. al-Sakhāwī, *Ḍaw'*, 3:32, line 17.

43. Cf. Ibn Ḥajar, *Inbā'*, 9 vols, (Hyderabad, 1387–96/1967–76), 7:394, anno 823, quoted by al-Sakhāwī, *Ḍaw'*, 3:31.

44. Cf. Eche, op. cit., 188, following Yāqūt, *Irshād*, ed. Margoliouth, 6:235; ed. Rifāʿī, 27:59f.

45. See ibn al-Jamāʿah, below, p. 42. (regarding the attitude towards the disapproval of writing books.)

46. Cf. Ibn Qayyim al-Jawzīyah, *al-Ṭurūq al-ḥukmīyah*, pp. 275–77.

47. Cf. Yāqūt, *Irshād*, ed. Margoulіouth, 5:386ff.; ed. Rifāʿī, 15:16, 9:21ff.

48. Ḥājjī Khalīfah, *Kashf al-Ẓunūn*, ed. Serefettin Yaltkaya, 2 vols. (Istanbul, 1945–47), vol. 1, intro., col. 52b, quotes the section of *Kunā* from Ibn ʿAsākir's *History of Damascus* as using *dafātir* in connection with Sufyān al-Thawrī (below no. 52). Although historically, *daftar* had different meanings (see EI², s.v. "Daftar" [B. Lewis]), in our context "notebooks" is intended. It need hardly be stated expressly that the range of meanings of Arabic *Kitāb* is not coextensive with our "book."

49. According to al-Khaṭīb al-Baghdādī, *Tārīkh Baghdād*, 14 vols., (Cairo, 1349/1931), 8:348, line 2f., Dāwūd al-Ṭāʾī did so after he felt sure that he no longer needed the books and was ready to devote himself conclusively to solitary divine worship.

50. Mention of the mountain cave is not found in the biographical notices. They say that he buried his books, with unhappy results for the reliability of his traditions. See al-Bukhārī, *Tārīkh*, 8 vols. (Hyderabad,1360–78/1941–58), 4 pt. 2:385; Ibn Abī Ḥātim al-Rāzī, *Jarh* (Hyderabad, 1941–53), 4 pt. 2:218 on the authority of his father Abū Ḥātim al-Rāzī; al-Dhahabī, *Mīzān al-Iʿtidāl*, 4 vols. (Cairo, 1382/1963), 4:162; Ibn Ḥajar, *Tahdhīb al-tahdhīb*, 12 vols. (Hyderabad, 1325–27/1907–9), 11:408. This does not necessarily indicate that al-Tawḥīdī invented the mountain cave for artistic effect—he could have found it in some other source—but it is quite likely.

51. Abū Sulaymān al-Dārānī was an authority of Ibn Abī al-Ḥawārī (below, no. 61), who was a contemporary of Sufyān al-Thawrī.

52. I have not gone through the large literature on Sufyān to find out whether this information is repeated elsewhere.

53. The text has Muḥammad, but he is presumably Abū Saʿīd's son Abū Muḥammad ibn al-Ḥasan (whose name is occasionally distorted), see Ibn al-Nadīm, *al-Fihrist*, p. 62f., also 31, line 23, as well as Bayard Dodge's English

translation, 2 vols. (New York, 1970), 1:136, and the Persian translation by M. Riḍā Tajaddud (Teheran, 1343/1965), p. 106; ʿAlī ibn Yūsuf al-Qifṭī *Inbāh al-rūwāh*, ed. M. Abū al-Fadl Ibrāhīm, 4 vols. (Cairo, 1369–93/1950–73), 1:314; Ibn Khallikān, *Wafayāt*, ed. Iḥsān ʿAbbās, 2:79; Sezgin, *GAS*, 9:98; al-Sīrāfī's long biography in Yāqūt, *Irshād*, ed. Margoliouth, 3:48–125; ed Rifāʿī, 8:142–232, draws on al-Tawḥīdī's works, but the request to have his books burned is not mentioned there. On Abū Saʿīd al-Sīrāfī, see also, more recently, G. Endress, "Grammatik und Logik" in Burkhard Moisisch (ed.), *Sprachphilosophie in Antike und Mittelalter* (Amsterdam, 1987, Bochumer Studien zurr Philosophie 3).

54. Ibn Saʿd, *Ṭabaqāt*, ed. E. Sachau and others, 9 vols. (Leiden, 1904–40), 4:63, lines 17ff.; al-Khaṭīb al-Baghdādī, *Taqyīd*, p. 61; Ibn ʿAbd al-Barr, *Jāmiʿ bayān al-ʿilm*, 1:67, etc.

55. *Taqyīd*, p. 39, line 11f. Ibn Masʿūd was put on the spot for transmitting a ḥadīth differently from what his son had written down.

56. *Taqyīd*, p.62.

57. Ibid. Yūnus ibn ʿĪsā was an authority on Bishr al-Ḥāfī.

58. Ibid.

59. *Taqyīd*, p. 63. According to Ibn Ḥajar, *Tahdhīb*, 1:445, Bishr disliked the transmission of ḥadīth and therefore buried his books. Abū Nuʿaym has nothing on the subject.

60. Ibid.

61. Abū Nuʿaym, *Ḥilyat al-awliyāʾ*, 10 vols. (Reprint Beirut, 1387/1967), 10:6f.

62. On the other hand, scholars were considered foolish to brag about composing works without recourse to relevant literature. Such disregard of their predecessors meant that they would not know what distinguished their works from those of others, cf. al-Zarkashī, *al-Burhān fī ʿulūm al-Qurʾan*, 4 vols. (Cairo, 1376/1957), 1:16.

63. Cf. Ḥājjī Khalīfah, *Kashf*, 1:intro., col. 32f. The wish to approach God (*qaṣd wajh Allah*) was generally accepted goal and precondition for any successful study. Without it, collecting books would be useless, see, for instance, Yūsuf al-Balāwī, *Kitāb alif bāʾ*, 2 vols. (Būlāq, 1287/1870), 1:17, line 2f.

64. See al-Sakhāwī, *Ḍaw'*, 1:232f.

65. See Ibn Jamā'ah, *Tadhkirah* (Hyderabad, 1953), p. 30. In the context, Ibn Jamā'ah mentions al-Khaṭīb al-Baghdādī, but the quoted statement is apparently not included in the reference. In a somewhat shortened form, with the omission of the qualified and knowledgeable persons, the statement is quoted by Ḥājjī Khalīifah, 1:intro., col. 39. On his own, it seems Ḥājjī Khalīfah adds *muṭlaqan* "absolutely (disapproved)." *Taṣnīf* usually referred to the original composition of books. Cf., for instance, al-Sakhāwī, *Ḍaw'*, 1:46, line 19ff., on the very learned Ibrāhīm ibn Khiḍr: "In spite of his learning, he did not occupy himself with *taṣnīf*, although he made valuable notes on many books." Cf. also Ibn Ḥajar, *al-Durar al-kāminah*, 1st ed., 4 vols. (Hyderabad, 1348–50/1929–31), 3:490; idem, *Inbā'*, 1:184, or al-Sakhāwī, *Ḍaw'*, 2:79.

66. One may compare, from a different time and situation, al-Jāḥiẓ's remark about an ignoramus who progressed from finding fault with al-Jāḥiẓ's works to condemning the writing of books in general (*Kitāb al-Ḥayawān*, ed. Hārūn, 1:19, 37–38).

67. See also below, p. 44.

68. Cf. al-Tawḥīdī, *al-Imtā' wa-al-mu'ānasah*, ed. Aḥmad Amīn and Aḥmad al-Zayn, 3 vols. (Cairo, 1939–44), 2:194, line 6.

69. Cf. Mez's introduction to his edition of *Abulḳāsim, ein bagdäder Sittenbild* (Heidleberg, 1902), viii f.

70. Cf. Yāqūt, *Mu'jam al-buldān*, ed. F. Wüstenfeld (Göttingen, 1866–73), 1:11f., trans. Wadie Jwaideh, *The Introductory Chapters of Yāqūt's Mu'jam al-Buldan* (Leiden, 1959), p. 16.

71. Cf. F. Rosenthal, *The Technique and Approach of Muslim Scholarship* (Rome, 1947. Analecta Orientalia 24), p. 43a, and idem, *A History of Muslim Historiography*[2], p. 71, n.3.

72. As indicated in the enumeration of items that justify the writing of books, see below, n. 87.

73. See Yāqūt, trans. Jwaideh, p. 9, n. 4.

74. See Yāqūt, *Mu'jam*, 1:6, trans. Jwaideh, p. 9. Jwaideh notes that the statement recurs in the biography of al-Jāḥiẓ in Yāqūt, *Irshād*, ed. Margoliouth, 6:58, ed. Rifā'ī, 16:78.

75. Al-Tawḥīdī and Miskawayh, *al-Ḥawāmil wa-al-shawāmil*, ed. Aḥmad Amīn and al-Sayyid Aḥmad Ṣaqr (Cairo, 1370/1951), p. 268f.

76. Below, in the reference by al-Sha'bi to the common idea that human life is all too short to know everything, it is not as certain as it is here and elsewhere that the first aphorism is indeed the inspiration, but it seems highly probable.

77. This appears to be the correct interpretation of the verse to be read: . . .*wa-lakin nāẓiru al-'ayni*. See al-Zarkashī, *Burhān*, 1:9, 12, quoted in part by al-Suyūṭī, *Itqān*, 2 vols. in 1 (Cairo, 1317/1899), 1:5.

78. Cf. Freimark, p. 64, referring to al-Washshā', *Muwashshá*, for Ibn 'Abbās, and to Ibn 'Abd Rabbih, *'Iqd*, for Ibn Sīrīn. This latter ascription appears also in al-Balāwī, *Kitāb alif bā'*, 1:14, line 19.

79. See 'Alī al-Ghuzūlī, *Maṭāli' al-budūr*, 2 vols. in 1 (Cairo, 1299–1300/1881) 1:7.

80. Cf. Freimark, pp. 40ff., 164.

81. Cf. al-Bīrūnī, *al-Athār al-bāqiyah*, ed. Sachau (Leipzig, 1878), p. 4, line 5 quoted by Freimark, p. 142.

82. Cf. Ibn al-Athīr, *al-Nihāyah fī gharīb al-ḥadīth*, 5 vols. (Cairo, 1322/1904), 1:15, line 15f.; 6, line 18; 8, line 15ff.; 9, line 17.

83. Ibn Khaldūn, *Muqaddimah*, trans., F. Rosenthal, 3:288–91.

84. Op. cit., 3:324.

85. Op. cit., 3:340f.

86. Op. cit., 2:455.

87. Op. cit., 3:287. See 284, n. 1123, for parallels. Ibn Khaldūn mentions the writing of abridgements as the last of the seven justifications for authorship. Al-Maqarrī, *Azhār al-riyāḍ*, 3 vols. (Cairo, 1358/1939), 3:34, puts abridgements in the sixth place. They were promoted to fourth place in Ḥājjī Khalīfah, 1:intro., col. 35.

88. Ḥājjī Khalīfah, *Kashf*, 1:intro., col. 43f.

89. Op. cit., 1:intro., col. 1. For the allusion to Hippocrates, see above, n. 76.

4

Oral Transmission and the Book in Islamic Education: The Spoken and the Written Word

Seyyed Hossein Nasr

The revelation of the Qur'ān was auditory before becoming crystallized in a written text. The Prophet first heard the term *iqra'* and only later recited the first revealed verses on the basis of their audition. The whole experience of the Qur'ān for Muslims remains to this day first of all an auditory experience and is only later associated with reading in the ordinary sense of the word. There is an ever present, orally heard, and memorized Qur'ān in addition to the written version of the Sacred Text, an auditory reality which touches the deepest chords in the souls of the faithful, even if they are unable to read the Arabic text.

Since it is the "Mother of Books" and also the prototype of the written word in Islam, the oral dimension of the Qur'ānic reality, combined with the traditional significance of memory in the transmission of knowledge, could not but affect the whole of the Islamic intellectual tradition and educational system. It could not but enliven both the poetic and the prose memory of the Islamic peoples, strengthen the significance of oral transmission, and leave something of its impact upon the very understanding of the book in the context of traditional Islamic culture. As a result of the influence of the Qur'ānic revelation and also other factors related to the rise of the whole Islamic educational system, the significance of the oral tradition and memory as a vehicle for the transmission of knowledge came to complement the written word contained in books, especially those books which became central texts for the teaching of various schools of thought and which figured prominently in the relationship between the traditional master (*al-ustādh*) and the students (*ṭullāb*).[1] Such books became more than simply the written text. Rather, they came to accompany and in a sense became immersed in the spoken word, through an oral teaching transmitted from master to student and stored in the memory of those destined to be the recipients of the knowledge in question. Such books were not exclusively written texts whose reality was exhausted by the words inscribed in ink upon parchment.

The oral tradition also played a cultural role in determining which book or books of a particular master would become texts to be discussed in study circles and would act as a vehicle for the transmission of the teachings of the master in question. The oral transmission helped to establish the authority of teachers who were to follow and it served as the criterion with the aid of which one could distinguish one student from another as far as his closeness to the master and understanding of the latter's message were concerned, although naturally debates often ensued.

This paper seeks to pursue this theme in one field, namely Islamic philosophy (*al-falsafah*), and its close ally in later centuries, theoretical gnosis (*al-ma'rifah* or *al-'irfān*), with which it merged especially in Persia and the other eastern lands of the Islamic world. Our analysis is based not so much upon scholarly research, as upon over twenty years of continuous study with traditional masters in Persia in the field of Islamic philosophy and gnosis, masters who would mention at the beginning of their instruction that the good student must learn not only to read correctly the black lines of the text in Arabic or Persian but that he must also be able to read what they would call "the white parts" of the page or what in English would be called reading between the lines.[2] But this reading of the "unwritten" text had to be carried out not according to the student's individual whim and fancy, but in accordance with the oral transmission stored in the memory of the master and going back through generations of teachers to the original author of the text and ultimately to the founders and major figures of the school in question—figures who also possessed a "vertical" and non-historical relation with the source of that traditional school.

As far as philosophy and gnosis are concerned, there is also a factor of a more external order to consider. In order to avoid the criticism and condemnation of certain exoteric '*ulamā*' and also the uneducated who might misconstrue their teachings, most philosophers couched their ideas in deliberately difficult language whose meaning they then taught orally to their chosen students. Although there are exceptions in this matter, as one sees in the case of Mullā Ṣadrā, the majority of the masters of Islamic philosophy practiced this art of dissimulation through a deliberately complicated language, the key to whose understanding remained in the hands of those well acquainted with the oral tradition which alone could elucidate the meaning or the levels of meaning of the technical vocabulary (*al-iṣṭilāḥāt*).[3] The significance of the oral transmission was by no means limited to this function, but this role is also of some importance in the total understanding of the oral tradition and the spoken word in Islamic intellectual history and education.

Before turning to an examination of the works of individual authors, we should note that, in the context of the traditional educational system, knowledge of a particular figure meant and still means a penetration in depth into the thought of the author in question rather than a study of his thought in breadth. Today, in the modern Western method of study, if a person wishes to master the thought of let us say a St. Thomas or for that matter Kant, he goes back to their original writings in Latin or German and examines all their work. In fact one would not dream of writing a serious book on a particular philosopher before reading all his writing. In the traditional Islamic context, on the contrary, the greatest interpreters of Ibn Sīnā, whose knowledge of Avicennan metaphysics could not be matched by anyone in the West, would probably have cast no more than a cursory eye over his metaphysical works beyond the *Ilāhiyāt* of the *Shifā'*, the *Najāt*, and the *Ishārāt*, not to speak of the *mashshā'ī* master's numerous other writings. We have seen traditional masters who have spent fifty years studying the *Shifā'* and the *Ishārāt*, often along with numerous commentaries, and who have had an incredible understanding of Ibn Sīnā's ontology without having delved into the many other works of the master dealing with the subject.

In this context it is important also to mention how in a manner that is often mysterious, if viewed from the outside, one or two works of a master survive and become a main text in the teaching of a particular school accompanied by the oral transmission of his teachings, while other works do not enjoy such a status. The reason in certain cases such as that of Ibn Sīnā are easy to understand while other instances are much more difficult to explain. What distinguished the *Tamhīd al-qawā'id* of Ibn Turkah or the *Kitāb al-hidāyah* of Athīr al-Dīn Abharī from other highly qualified available texts and made the former main items in the traditional curriculum?[4] Must not the answer be sought in the spoken word, the oral transmission which accompanied such texts, and the reception of these teachings by immediate students of the authors in question, students who then propagated these teachings and established the "privileged position" of the works in question? Surely the oral tradition along with the special master-disciple relationship must be considered, not to speak of intellectual and spiritual links between scholars and philosophers of different generations and the existence of affinities among various figures in the non-historical and atemporal dimensions of reality which remain outside of the framework of intellectual history as understood in the West today.

With these brief comments in mind, let us turn to a few of the outstanding Islamic intellectual figures. The first major Islamic philosopher, al-Kindī, certainly left his mark upon later Peripatetics but left no work behind which came to be established as a text in the traditional curriculum of Islamic philosophy. The towering figure of Ibn Sīnā in a sense eclipsed such earlier figures as al-Kindī and Abū al-Ḥasan al-'Āmirī, although al-Kindī continued to be honored in later centuries as a great philosopher. The type of studies devoted to his writings by both West and modern Muslim scholars, especially since the discovery of the manuscripts of a large number of his works in Istanbul half a century ago,[5] did not exist among those who kept the torch of *mashshā'ī* philosophy alive in the Islamic world itself, and in fact his particular interpretation of *mashshā'ī* philosophy did not gain acceptance among later members of this school, namely al-Fārābī, Ibn Sīnā, and Ibn Rushd.

Turning to the towering figure of al-Fārābī, again one notes that such major works of his as the *Kitāb al-ḥurūf* remained peripheral to the development of most of later Islamic philosophy and its significance has only recently been discovered as a result of the publication of its Arabic text by M. Mahdi.[6] Even al-Fārābī's greatest masterpiece of political philosophy, *Ārā' ahl al-madīnah al-fāḍilah*, although very influential in the genesis and growth of Islamic political thought, did not become a main text in the later phases of development of the Islamic philosophical tradition. It was only his somewhat enigmatic work, the *Fuṣūṣ al-ḥikmah*, considered by a number of modern scholars to be not by him but by Ibn Sīnā,[7] that has continued to be studied and taught over the centuries, accompanied by an oral as well as a written tradition of commentaries. It was enough to attend the teaching sessions of Mahdī Ilāhī Qumsha'ī, one of the outstanding traditional masters of *ḥikmah* in Persia in recent times who translated this work into Persian,[8] to realize the vast "unwritten philosophy" and the spoken word which have accompanied the written text attributed to al-Fārābī.

With Ibn Sīnā the presence of the oral transmission, which has survived for a thousand years, becomes felt more than before for anyone who experiences the teachings of the traditional masters of *mashshā'ī* philosophy. It is in fact a profound lesson in comparative philosophy to juxtapose the understanding of Avicennan ontology by such traditional masters of the subject during this century as 'Allāmah Ḥā'irī Yazdī Mazandarānī, author of *Ḥikmat-i Bū 'Alī*, or Mahdi Hairi,[9] and such Western masters of medieval philosophy as E. Gilson and H. Wolfson.[10] The difference in their treatment of the subject emanates not only from different methodologies, but also from the existing oral transmission in the one case and the simply written text in the other. The oral transmission did not certainly prevent different interpretations from being made in the Islamic world itself as one sees in the case of Naṣīr al-Dīn Ṭūsī and Mīr Dāmād, or the Ṣadrian interpretation of Ibn Sīnā made by certain followers of the school of Mullā Ṣadrā in the Qajar Period as against the views of a Mirzā Abū al-Ḥasan Jilwah.[11] But all of these differences remained within the matrix of the traditional world with the presence of the oral or spoken word as well as the written text and therefore differ from the understanding of Ibn Sīnā emanating from the study of only his written words.

There is no doubt that there have been scholars in the West such as Wolfson or Corbin who had read more of Ibn Sīnā than most of the traditional Persian masters whom we came to know personally. But the latter, who usually limited their study in depth to the *Shifā'* and *Ishārāt*, with an occasional interest in the *Najāt*, had an understanding of Ibn Sīnā of a different order resulting from being immersed in an Avicennan world in which the written and the spoken word were combined in a unity that transcended the simply literal, historical, and grammatical understanding of the written text. It is important to note in this context that even the brilliant reconstruction of Ibn Sīnā's "Oriental Philosophy" by Corbin,[12] based so much on the understanding of the later Islamic philosophical tradition, must be seen as a part of the vaster world of Avicennan ontology and cosmology dominated during later centuries by the two basic texts of the *Shifā'* and the *Ishārāt* and not in isolation from them.

Nowhere in the history of Islamic philosophy is the significance of the oral transmission and the spoken word more evident than in the case of Suhrawardī, the Master of Illumination (*Shaykh al-ishrāq*), whose masterpiece *Ḥikmat al-ishrāq*[13] is itself the crystallization in written form of the spoken word received orally both "horizontally" and "vertically", that is both through unspecified historical sources and the angelic pleroma of which Suhrawardi wrote so vividly.[14] Later Islamic intellectual history knew him primarily through the *Ḥikmat al-ishrāq* and to some extent the *Hayākil al-nūr* while, in comparison, his other writings, especially the doctrinal works *al-Talwīḥāt, al-Muqāwamāt*, and *al-Mashāri' wa-al-mutāraḥāt*,[15] remained more or less neglected by most later philosophers, Mullā Ṣadrā again being an important exception.

The whole nexus between the *Ḥikmat al-ishrāq*, written so rapidly towards the end of its author's tragic life, and the later tradition of *ishrāqī* philosophy relies upon oral transmission and the spoken word. The figure who revived Suhrawardī's thought a generation later through his masterly commentary on the *Ḥikmat al-ishrāq*, namely Muḥammad Shahrazūrī, had not known Suhrawardī personally.[16] Yet he was bound to the master not only by the written text of his works, but also by a spiritual and intellectual bond which definitely must have issued from a living oral tradition. In reading Shahrazūrī's commentary on the *Ḥikmat al-ishrāq* as well as his own masterpiece, the as yet unpublished *al-Shajarat al-ilāhiyah*, one feels as if Shahrazūrī had sat at the feet of Suhrawardī for many years. What relates the two figures to each other is not only a written text, but also the spoken word or an "unwritten book" which delineated the universe of *ishrāqī* wisdom shared by both figures. There must have been a special oral teaching which accompanied the *Ḥikmat al-ishrāq* surviving Suhrawardī and surfacing later in the works of Shahrazūrī and Quṭb al-Dīn Shīrazī and even during later centuries in the writings of Jalāl al-Dīn Dawānī and Mullā Ṣadrā. How could Mullā Ṣadrā have written his glosses (*Hāshiyah*) on the *Ḥikmat al-ishrāq*[17] without an oral tradition which linked him beyond the written words of the text to the founder of the School of Illumination? This continuity is what in fact characterizes an intellectual tradition which unfolds over the centuries on the basis not only of what the founding figure has written but also of the oral tradition which he has left behind, a tradition which remains alive through both the "vertical" renewal of the tradition and the ever present oral transmission, which in turn makes possible successive crystallizations of the doctrines and teachings in question in written form.

The crucial role of oral tradition is also evident in the case of Ibn ʿArabī whose influence swept over the Islamic world shortly after Suhrawardī. How different the intellectual history of at least the eastern lands of Islam would have been if the Ibn ʿArabī of the *Futūḥāt al-makkiyah* had become better known than the Ibn ʿArabī of the *Fuṣūṣ al-ḥikam*, especially as interpreted by Ṣadr al-Dīn Qūnawī![18] Of course the *Futūḥāt* was known to many authors but not as a whole. Rather, to quote a leading authority on the *Futūḥāt*, M. Chodkiewicz, the work served "as an overflowing cornucopia of symbols, technical terms and ideas from which everyone picked his choice."[19] In any case it was providential that the *Fuṣūṣ* seen through Ṣadr al-Dīn's interpretation, itself based upon the closest intimacy with Ibn ʿArabī, became the central work associated with Ibn ʿArabī and seen primarily as a text of theoretical gnosis which had the profoundest influence upon not only Sufism but also later Islamic philosophy and even theology, as we see in the case of Shāh Walīallāh of Delhi. Outside the circle which became heir to the Akbarian current of Sufism, Ibn ʿArabī came to be viewed not so much as the master of practical Sufism and the *Sharīʿah* and *fiqh* interpreted esoterically in the *Futūḥāt*, but as the metaphysician of the *Fuṣūṣ* seen through the eyes of Qūnawī, Mu'ayyid al-Dīn Jandī, ʿAbd al-Razzāq Kāshānī, and others.[20] Even the most characteristic doctrine associated with Ibn ʿArabī, namely *waḥdat al-wujūd*, derives from the teachings of his disciples and the oral teachings which must have accompanied the *Fuṣūṣ* rather than from Ibn ʿArabī's own written works. We do not know what Ibn ʿArabī taught Ṣadr al-Dīn and others orally, but we do know how Ṣadr al-Dīn interpreted the written text of the master in the light of those oral teachings and it is this which is of significance as far as the oral teachings of Ibn ʿArabī are concerned.

The Ibn ʿArabī seen by centuries of Islamic metaphysicians and philosophers is not the same as the Ibn ʿArabī who emerges from a scholarly study of all his works put alongside each other and without recourse to the oral teachings received from a living master. The whole difference between the Ibn ʿArabī seen by Kāshānī, Mullā Ṣadrā, al-Nābulusī, or Ismāʿīl Ḥaqqī and the one seen by modern scholars, whether they be Westerners or Muslims, but basing themselves solely on the extant texts, is again the spoken word, the oral tradition as it has been transmitted over the centuries by generations of masters, some of whom have claimed direct contact with Ibn ʿArabī in the "invisible world" (*ʿālam al-ghayb*) besides being heirs to the historical oral tradition of his school.

Whether current Western scholarship accepts the authenticity of this oral tradition or not is of secondary significance. What is most important is that the Islamic intellectual tradition itself has functioned with the belief that the oral tradition is of central importance. In the case of Ibn ʿArabī, for example, such recent masters as ʿAllāmah Ṭabāṭabā'ī or Sayyid Muḥammad Kāẓim ʿAṣṣār, with both of whom we studied gnosis and philosophy for some twenty years,[21] would insist that it was of little use to simply read the text of the *Fuṣūṣ* and understand the Arabic by oneself. Rather, it was necessary to study it with a real teacher who could also impart to the qualified student the oral tradition which alone can clarify the meaning of the written word. That is why in gnosis, as in philosophy, a person who is said to have really studied the subject is called *ustād dīdah*, literally one who has "seen" a master, that is, one who has benefitted from the oral teachings and also the presence (*ḥuḍūr*) of the master who embodies those teachings and who renews and revives them through the very act of living their truths.

Turning to later Islamic philosophy, we see the same principles at work as in earlier centuries. The *Sharḥ al-ishārāt* of Naṣīr al-Dīn Ṭūsī caused the revival of the school of Ibn Sīnā. But later traditional philosophers did not consider this work to be solely the product of the exceptional intellectual powers of Naṣīr al-Dīn but also the result of the oral transmission of teachings which Ṭūsī received through several generations of masters stretching from Ibn Sīnā to himself. As for the *Sharḥ al-ishārāt*,[22] it in turn became a main item of the later philosophical curriculum taught by generations of teachers going back to Ṭūsī and his circle in Maraghah where he imparted oral teachings to accompany this exact and exacting philosophical text.

After Ṭūsī, numerous works inspired by the Avicennan or *mashshā'ī* school appeared in both Arabic and Persian including the encyclopedic work of Quṭb al-Dīn Shīrāzī, the *Durrat al-tāj*. But it was again one work, the *Kitāb al-hidāyah* of Athīr al-Dīn Abharī, which became a popular text in educational circles in Persia and was taught and commented upon by many teachers both orally and in writing. One needs only to recall the *Sharḥ al-hidāyah* of Mullā Ṣadrā which gained so much popularity in India that it became the main text for the teaching of *mashshā'ī* philosophy in the subcontinent and gradually came to be known as *Ṣadrā*. When students claimed to have studied *Ṣadrā*, they did not mean that they had studied the various works of Mullā Ṣadrā,[23] but the single text of the *Sharḥ al-hidāyah* which was again accompanied by an oral teaching. The selection of Abharī's original work in philosophical circles, as well as Mullā Ṣadrā's later commentary, was based not on the texts alone of these works, but on the accompanying oral teachings and the later masters who were well versed in those teachings and therefore chose to teach those texts rather than numerous other works which were also available.

The same truth holds for the writings of Mīr Dāmād, Mullā Ṣadrā, and later philosophers. Whether it was the *Qabasāt* of Mīr Dāmād or the *Asfār* of Mullā Ṣadrā, an oral teaching always accompanied the written text.[24] In the case of these later figures, the chain of transmission of the oral teachings is much better known. For example, such an undisputed master of the school of Mullā Ṣadrā as Sayyid Abū al-Ḥasan Qazwīnī, with whom we again had the privilege of studying the *Asfār* for many years, could trace his teachers back through the Qajar masters of this school to Mullā Ṣadrā himself and displayed an almost "personal" relation to him as if the two were not separated by four centuries of human history. In his presence one felt that his link with Mullā Ṣadrā was not only the lithographed edition of the *Asfār* which he would hold in his frail hands and read before expounding his commentary and explanation. It was also a common universe of discourse and a lived and experienced intellectual reality which he shared with the Safavid master through the unwritten yet very much alive word, through the spoken truth transmitted orally as well as the written text from which he read. That was why, when he held the book before his shining eyes and read it, the book revealed another dimension of its meaning, one which would remain hidden if one were to turn to the text oneself without the help of the oral teachings.[25]

The reality of the oral tradition constitutes the reason why the line of transmission of traditional Islamic philosophy is nearly as important as the *silsilahs* of the Sufis. In the latter case a *barakah* and initiatory power are transmitted which alone allow the soul to ascend to the higher levels of being, while in the former it is an oral teaching which is the necessary concomitant to the written text, a complement without which the text does not reveal all of its meaning save in exceptional cases. In both instances, there is a truth to be transmitted which is not simply discursive and which cannot be exhausted in letters and words written upon the page, a truth which must remain in part oral to be transmitted to those prepared to receive it.

Although the subject of this essay is limited to the field of Islamic philosophy, it is not possible to speak of the oral tradition and the spoken word without saying a few words about the distinctly Sufi view of the subject. This view was shared in part by many later Islamic philosophers (*falāsifah*) and by those whom we might call theosophers (*ḥukamāy-i ilāhī*) those thought to be distinguished from what philosophy has come to mean for the most part in the West today.

One cannot speak of the spoken word without mentioning that primordial "book" which is inscribed in the very substance of our being and with which the Sufis have dealt more directly than the Islamic philosophers. Jalāl al-Dīn Rūmī, whose *Mathnawī* alone consists of six long volumes of poetry, says:

> The book of the Sufi is not black lines and words,
> It is none other than the whitened heart which is like snow.

In the Islamic tradition the heart is the seat of the intellect and the instrument *par excellence* of original knowledge of which mental activity is a relatively externalized reflection. True knowledge is the knowledge of the heart, and it is here that man carries within himself the real "book" of knowledge. This "book" is composed of unwritten words. It is the inner chamber wherein the spoken word in the highest sense of the term, which means none other than the Word of God, reverberates. This inner "book" is not available for all to "read", for not everyone is able to penetrate into the inner chamber of his or her being, which is the heart, nor possesses a purified heart as white as the snow which has not as yet become sullied by the darkness of man's passionate soul.

Yet, this inner "book" has resonated and still resonates within the being of certain men and women and through them has left its deepest effect upon the intellectual life of Islam, not only in the domain of theoretical Sufism but also in later Islamic philosophy. It manifests itself directly in many illuminative passages of a philosopher such as Mullā Ṣadrā who often refers to such crucial pages of his works as *taḥqīq^{un} ʿarshī*, that is, "truth verified through the Throne", the Throne being not only the Transcendental Throne of God but also the heart which is *ʿarsh al-raḥmān* or Throne of the Compassionate.[27]

The significance of the oral tradition, its continuation over the centuries, its "vertical" renewal by certain masters of a particular school, and the emphasis upon the memory to preserve the oral tradition are all affected by the reality of that other inner "book" to which Rūmī refers, a "book" whose reality has always subsisted in the firmament of Islamic intellectual life at whose center stands *the* Book, namely the Qur'ān which is at once an oral and a written reality. One must never forget that to know something really well and to committ the spoken word to memory in an abiding manner is to know it by heart. It is this knowledge by heart[28] which has made possible, not only in Sufism but also in Islamic philosophy, the continuation of an ever-renewed oral tradition which has played such an important role in the Islamic education system and the modality of the transmission of knowledge from teacher to disciple over the centuries.

The oral tradition has affected the manner of reading and interpreting the written text, its teaching and transmission, and the role of certain texts and commentaries in the educational circles of the Islamic world. It is even significant in the correct reading of a particular manuscript and in the selection of manuscripts for establishing the text of a particular work. The spoken word is the key to the solution of many enigmas concerning the continuity of certain teachings as in the already mentioned cases of the *ishrāqī school and the predominance of a particular interpretation over others as in the case of* Ṣadr al-Dīn Qūnawī's interpretation of Ibn ʿArabī. The oral tradition also provides a direct link between the student and a master who might have lived generations ago, enabling the student to study the teachings in question in depth and to concentrate on one or two works which are then penetrated inwardly over a whole lifetime rather than to study horizontally the text of many works written by the same master. There have been exceptions such as Mullā Ṣadrā, who had, in addition to oral instruction, an encyclopedic knowledge of earlier philosophical, theological, and mystical works ranging from al-Fārābī, al-ʿĀmirī, and Ibn Sīnā to Shahrastānī, Fakhr al-Dīn Razī, al-Ghazzālī, and Ibn ʿArabī, a knowledge which he combined with the oral tradition.[29] But usually the oral tradition and the spoken word created a different type of intellectual ambience from the modern one, an ambience in which one or two works surrounded by a vast oral commentary came to constitute knowledge in depth of the teachings of the traditional authority.

The oral tradition transformed the written book from the definitive text which was the sole basis of the ideas to be understood to the gate to a whole living world for which the book became the point of departure. We recall once when studying *al-Insān al-kāmil* of ʿAbd al-Karīm al-Jīlī with the late Mahdī Ilāhī Qumsha'ī, he read the Arabic text and then gave a long discourse on divine love and its manifestations which seemed to have little connection with the outward meaning of al-Jīlī's words. When asked how these words conveyed such meanings, he answered that one should look at these words as signs to the spiritual world and not in their usual literal meaning and as concepts closed in upon themselves. He added that only by becoming familiar with these words through understanding the traditional oral commentary upon them would one be able to fly with their help from the earth of literalism to the heaven of symbolism. The nexus between oral tradition and esoteric interpretation of gnostic and philosophical texts must not, however, detract from the outward meaning and diminish the role of oral tradition in enabling the written text to be read correctly, albeit outwardly. The traditional masters insist that the major texts of Islamic thought such as the *Ishārāt* or *Asfār* cannot in fact be "read" correctly without the help of oral tradition, hence the central importance of having studied with a master. In a sense the spoken word makes possible the full understanding and correct "reading" of the written text.

Much of what has been said here is of course to be found *mutatis mutandis* in other traditions, such as the cabbala in Judaism, and is not exclusive to Islam. But in Islam the oral tradition and the spoken word have played and continue to play even to this day such a central role that their importance must be asserted in the face of all the historicism and positivism which have sought to reduce the reality of the Islamic intellectual tradition to written texts and historically established influences. Historical studies and careful attention paid to the written text do of course also possess their own validity and significance but they cannot become exclusive and totalitarian without destroying the integrity of the Islamic intellectual tradition.

Today not only are the physical remains of the Islamic book in the form of manuscripts being destroyed in many parts of the world, but also much of the oral tradition and the spoken word is being lost as a result of the destruction of the traditional methods of education and transmission. Paradoxically it is therefore necessary to put into writing for posterity and also for the present generation much that was transmitted until now only "from the breast" of one person to another. But in doing so, one should never lose sight of the great significance throughout Islamic history of oral transmission in education and of the spoken word as the complement of the written text. Even today, when due to exceptional historical conditions so much is being recorded and needs to be recorded and preserved in written form, the essence of the oral tradition continues to survive as oral tradition, especially that primordial Word which can only be heard and yet remains eternally inscribed upon the very substance of our soul as human beings.

NOTES

1. Concerning the texts used in traditional curricula of the *madrasahs* and in private circles, see, for example, S.H. Nasr, "The Traditional Texts Used in the Persian *Madrasahs*," in his *Islamic Life and Thought* (London, 1987), ch. 10; M.S. Khan, "The Teaching of Mathematics and Astronomy in the Educational Institutions of Medieval India," *Muslim Educational Quarterly* 6 (1989), no. 3: 7–15; and the major study of G. Makdisi, *The Rise of Colleges—Institutions of Learning in Islam and the West* (Edinburgh, 1981), which contains a wealth of information on the use of texts in Islamic *madrasahs* as well as an extensive bibliography on Islamic education including works on the use of texts in various schools.

2. On the living tradition of Islamic philosophy in Persia see H. Corbin, "The Force of Traditional Philosophy in Iran Today," *Studies in Comparative Religion* (Winter, 1968), pp. 12–26; S.H. Nasr, *Islamic Philosophy in Contemporary Persia* (Salt Lake City, 1972); and T. Izutsu's introduction to *The Metaphysics of Sabzavari*, trans. M. Mohaghegh and T. Izutsu (Delmar, NY, 1977).

3. Books dealing with these technical terms have therefore been always important and have served as a basis for the exposition of teachers or have complemented for the student the oral explanation of the master. That is why books such as the whole class of *al-Iṣṭilāḥāt al-ṣūfiyah* by ʿAbd al-Razzāq Kāshānī and others, *al-Taʿrīfāt* of Sayyid Sharīf al-Jurjānī, *Kashshāf iṣṭilāḥāt al-funūn* by al-Tuhāwī, and other works on terminology have been so important in the history of Sufism and Islamic philosophy. See the still valuable studies

of L. Massignon, especially his *Essais sur les origines du lexique technique de la mystique musulmane* (Paris, 1954); J.L. Michon, *Le Soufi marocain Aḥmad ibn ʿAjība et son miʿraj-Glossaire de la mystique musulmane* (Paris, 1973); P. Nwyia, *Exégèse coranique et langage mystique* (Beirut, 1970); J. Nurbakhsh, *Sufi Symbolism* (London, 1986-); and M. Horten, "Philogogische Untersuchungen zur islamischen Mystik," *Zeitschrift für Semitistik und verwandte Gebiete* 6 (1928), pp. 57–70. Concerning Jurjānī's *Taʿrīfāt* see G. Flügel (ed.), *Definitiones Sejjid Scherif Ali...* (Leipzig, 1845).

4. On these little-known figures, as far as the West is concerned, see H. Corbin (with the collaboration of S. H. Nasr and O. Yahya), *Histoire de la philosophie islamique* (Paris, 1986), pp. 365 ff.; Corbin, *En Islam iranien*' 3 (Paris, 1972) pp. 233 ff.; and S.H. Nasr, "Theology, Philosophy and Spirituality," in Nasr (ed.) *Islamic Spirituality—Manifestations* (New York, 1991), pp. 431 ff.

5. Discovered by Massignon and published later by M. Abū Rīdah as *Rasā'il al-Kindī al-falsafiyah*, 2 vols. (Cairo, 1950-1953).

6. See M. Mahdi, *Alfarabi's Book of Letters (Kitāb al-ḥurūf)* (Beirut, 1969).

7. See, for example, S. Pines, "Ibn Sīnā et l'auteur de la Risālat fuṣūṣ fi'l-ḥikma," *Revue des Études Islamiques* (1951), pp. 122–4.

8. See Ilāhī Qumsha'ī, *Ḥikmat-i ilāhī khāṣṣ wa ʿāmm*, vol. 2 (Tehran, A.H. solar 1345).

9. See, for example, his *Hiram-i hastī*, ("The Pyramid of Existence") (Tehran, 1983).

10. Both Gilson and Wolfson have dealt with Avicennan ontology as expounded by Ibn Sina himself or by later Peripatetics in several of their works, for example E. Gilson, *L'Etre et l'essence* (Paris, 1948); and his *Avicenne et le point de départ de Duns Scot* from *Extrait des Archives d'Histoire Doctrinale et Littéraire du Moyen Âge* 2 (1927). As for H.A. Wolfson, see his "Avicenna, Algazali, and Averroes on Divine Attributes," *Homenaje a Millás-Vallicrosa* 2 (Barcelona, 1956), pp. 545–71; and his "Goichon's Three Books on Avicenna's Philosophy," *Muslim World 31* (1941), pp. 11–39.

11. See S.H. Nasr, "The Metaphysics of Ṣadr al-Dīn Shīrazī and Islamic Philosophy in Qajar Iran," in C.E. Bosworth and C. Hillenbrand (eds.), *Qajar Iran—Political, Social and Cultural Change 1900–1925* (Edinburgh, 1983),

pp. 177–98; and S.J. Āshtiyānī's introduction to Mullā Muḥammad Ja'far Lāhījānī, *Sharḥ risālat al-mashā'ir of Mullā Ṣadrā* (Tehran, 1964).

12. See Corbin, *Avicenna and the Visionary Recital*, trans. W. Trask (Irving, TX, 1980).

13. See Suhrawardī, *Oeuvres philosophiques et mystiques*, vol. 2 ed. H. Corbin (Tehran, 1977); and H. Corbin, *Sohravardi, Le Livre de la sagesse orientale* (Paris, 1986).

14. See S.H. Nasr, *Three Muslim Sages* (Delmar, NY, 1975), ch. 2.

15. Even in contemporary scholarship these works have remained relatively neglected in comparison with the *Ḥikmat al-ishrāq*, edited in its entirety by Corbin, and his complete Persian works, edited by Nasr. Corbin edited the section of these works on metaphysics but not those on logic and natural philosophy. See Suhrawardī, *Oeuvres philosophiques et mystiques*, vols. 1 and 2 ed. Corbin (Tehran, 1976–7); vol. 3 ed. Nasr (Tehran, 1977). Recently H. Ziai has turned to the study of the logic of *al-Talwīḥāt* and other neglected doctrinal works of Suhrawardī in his *Knowledge and Illumination: A Study of Suhrawardi's Hikmat al-Ishraq* (Atlanta, GA, 1990).

16. See H. Ziai, "The Manuscript of *al-Shajara al-Ilahiyah*, A Philosophical Encyclopedia by Shams al-Din Muhammad Shahrazuri," (in Persian), *Iranshenasi* 2 (1990), no. 1: 89–108.

17. See H. Corbin, "Le thème de la résurrection chez Mollā Ṣadrā Shīrāzī (1050/1640) commentateur de Sohrawardī (587/1191)," in *Studies in Mysticism and Religion Presented to G. Scholem* (Jerusalem, 1967), pp. 71–115.

18. See J. Morris, "Ibn 'Arabī and His Interpreters," *Journal of the American Oriental Society* 106 (1986), pp. 539–51, 733–56; 107 (1987), pp. 101–19; M. Chodkiewicz, et al., *Les illuminations de la Mecque* (Paris, 1988); and the major new study of W. Chittick, *The Sufi Path of Knowledge* (Albany, NY, 1989).

19. From a paper delivered at the conference on Medieval Persian Sufi Literature at the University of London in November 1990.

20. See W. Chittick's several studies on Ṣadr al-Dīn al-Qūnawī and his students, e.g., "The Last Will and Testament of Ibn 'Arabī's Foremost Disciple and Some Notes on its Author," *Sophia Perennis*, 4 (1978), no. 1: 43–58;

and "Ṣadr al-Dīn Qūnawī on the Oneness of Being," *International Philosophical Quarterly* 21 (1981), pp. 171–84.

21. On ʿAllāmah Ṭabāṭabāʾī, whose writings are gradually becoming known in the West, see the introduction of S.H. Nasr to his *Shiʿite Islam*, trans. and ed. by S.H. Nasr (Albany, NY, 1975). As for ʿAṣṣār, unfortunately none of his works have as yet been translated, but some have been published in the original Persian and Arabic, for example, *Waḥdat-i wujūd wa badāʾ*, ed. with introduction on the author by S.J. Āshtiyānī (Tehran, AH solar 1350).

22. Printed in both Tehran and Cairo (the Cairo edition edited by S. Dunyá, 1960; and the Tehran edition without editor, 3 vols., AH 1378), this work has never been seriously studied by Western scholars of Islamic philosophy, although many have drawn attention to it.

23. See S.H. Nasr, *Maʿārif-i islāmī dar jahān-i muʿāṣir* (Tehran, AH solar 1348), ch. 8.

24. On the relation between Mullā Ṣadrā and Mīr Dāmād see S.H. Nasr, *The Transcendent Theosophy of Ṣadr al-Dīn Shīrāzī* (Tehran, 1977), pp. 32–3, 40, 41, and 45–46.

25. S.J. Āshtiyānī has traced the intellectual lineage of such figures and their link with the Safavid masters of the "School of Isfahan" in his already cited introduction to Lāhījānī and also in his introduction to Mullā Ṣadrā, *al-Shawāhid al-rubūbiyah* (Meshed, 1967).

26. *Mathnawī*, ed. R.A. Nicholson (London, 1925–40), ii. 159.

27. See, for example, his *Wisdom of the Throne*, trans. J. Morris (Princeton, NJ, 1981), where he refers to such crucial sections as *baṣīrah kashfiyah* (insight revealed to inner vision) or *qaʿīdah mashriqiyah* (principle from the source of illumination).

28. On the traditional significance of the heart as the seat of knowledge see F. Schuon, *L'Oeil du coeur* (Paris, 1974).

29. See Nasr, *The Transcendent Theosophy. . .*, pp. 69 ff.

5

The Book of Life-Metaphors Connected with the Book in Islamic Literatures

Annemarie Schimmel

"Man is mighty in volume, with him all things are written, but veils and darkness do not allow him to read that knowledge within himself."[1] This is not a quotation from John Donne's *Devotions*, where a similar comparison is used, but from Maulānā Jalāladdīn Rūmī's (d. 1273) prose works *Fīhi mā fīhi*.

The saying well reflects the close relationship between man and book, for as Frithjof Schuon once said with a daring comparison, "God became Book for man [i.e., in the Qur'ān] and man must become book for God"—a book in which the secrets of Divine creation can be recognized.[2] Thus, 'Ālī Khān, an officer and poet at the court of the Mughal emperor Aurangzēb, could describe himself:

> I am like a book, both silent and talking;
> The content of my question is hidden in my answer.[3]

The Muslims were great book lovers, and the history of libraries in the Muslim world, from the collections in medieval Baghdad to the famous library of Akbar's generalissimo 'Abd al-Raḥmān Khānkhānān (d. 1627), to mention only one major example, is well known. Public and private libraries all over the Muslim world, many of them still uncataloged, give witness to the bibliophilia of scholars and rulers in bygone times.[4] Most of the collectors would probably have agreed with Mollā Jāmī (d. 1492) of Herat:

> There is no better friend in the world than the book;
> In the house of grief in this time there is no better consoler,
> Every moment a hundred kinds of peace come from it
> In the corner of loneliness and it never hurts the heart.[5]

Classical Arabic literature contains numerous sayings and verses about books, some of which have been translated into German by J. Christoph Bürgel in his article "Von Freud und Leid mit Büchern" (About happiness and grief caused by books).[6] There, one hears the collectors' laments about the loss of books due to theft, to fire, or to "book loving" insects. I once found a long *maqāmah* in highly polished rhymed prose in praise of a glorious tomcat who deserved his master's eternal gratitude because he saved his master's library by catching the numerous mice that were interested in the manuscripts, for unscholarly purposes.[7] With a comparison that occurs rather frequently, an Ottoman poet of the sixteenth century sang of his joy in books:

> The heart of those who are narrow-hearted like the bud
> opens like the rose—
> It seems that the book is a hundred-petaled rose in spring![8]

Gēsū Darāz (d. 1422), the Chishti Sufi saint of Gulbarga in the Deccan, goes so far as to describe his book as his beloved:

> My book became my beloved —
> Thanks to it my pressed heart was opened.
> You say: "Lend it to me!"
> Has anyone ever lent his beloved [to someone else]?"[9]

However, allusions to the actual form of books, let alone descriptions of specific books, seem to be comparatively rare. One may think of allusions to Qur'ān manuscripts in comparison with beautiful human faces or bodies: Khāqānī (d. 1199) suggests to his beloved to wear red and yellow garments, as the Qur'ān is written in red and gold (for she is as flawless as a Qur'ān page).[10] Maulānā Rūmī tells in a delightful story how some ants walked across a beautifully illuminated manuscript and were wondering whether this was a garden with roses and herbs; then they learned that this "garden" was produced by the pen, which served the hand, which in turn was depending upon the arm; the arm, however, relied upon the spirit's command which was inspired by God—thus, every movement led back to the One and Unique Creator.[11]

Yet, in a small group of verses, Persian-writing poets from the fifteenth to the seventeenth century have composed verses in honor of actual manuscripts. It seems that such descriptions reflected the book culture at the Timurid and Mughal courts, and it is certainly no accident that book imagery became quite prominent during Mughal times. Jāmī sings of an album which was probably made for his patron, Sultan Ḥusain Baiqarā:

> Before this copy, which is the pleasure ground of intellect and soul,
> the eye of reason is bewildered.
> It is a cheerful garden filled with roses and odoriferous herbs;
> The pages are roses and the lines sweet basil, *rīḥān*.[12]

The last line plays on the double meaning of *rīḥān*, *rīḥānī*, which is not only "sweet basil", but also a calligraphic style which was used mainly in copies of the Qur'ān and important manuscripts. This pun appears in most Persian and Turkish writings from the Middle Ages onward.

Perhaps the finest description of an album is found in Abū Ṭālib Kalīm's (d. 1650) *Dīwān*. The poet, who lived in Shāhjahān's time, mainly in Kashmir, describes some albums which were collected by Jahāngīr and then arranged for his son Shāhjahān after 1628. Calligraphic pages with superbly illuminated borders alternate with fine miniatures, so that, as he claims, "the tress of the [long] letter *lām* in the calligraphy is combined with the tresses of the houri-like beauties" on the miniatures. It may well be that he speaks of one of the collections to which parts of the so-called Kevorkian Album in the Metropolitan Museum belonged.[13]

To understand the importance of the metaphors of the book or of writing in Persian and Persianate poetry, it suffices to look at the numerous poems with the *radīf* (recurrent rhyme) *nawīsand*, "they wrote" or *niwishta*, "written," or *radīfs* derived from the Turkish root *yazmaq*, "to write," in Ottoman poetry. As much as this imagery may appear repetitive, one can yet find delightful verses by some lesser-known authors, such as the clever comparisons that the south Indian polymath Āzād Bilgrāmī (d. 1784) used in his *Mir'āt al-jamāl*, "The Mirror of Beauty," to admire his beloved's tresses:

> Are these two locks of hair on the whiteness of her cheeks,
> Or two marginal columns on the book of beauty?
> Or two nights of the two *'īd* that came together,
> Or are these two of the seven *mu'allaqāt* hung on the Ka'bah[14]

Sometimes, poets offer the reader whole lists of books they had perused during their lifetimes, as did the fourteenth-century North Indian author Muṭahhar Karh (d. 1390), who speaks of Wāqidī's historical work, of Nāṣirī, that is, the ethical work, *Akhlāq-i Nāṣirī*, and of Abū Ḥafṣ 'Umar al-Suhriwardī's Sufi handbook, *'Awārif al-ma'ārif*, along with some others, which makes us understand what kind of material was used in medieval Indo-Muslim education.[15] Even more sophisticated is a poem by the Urdu poet Walī Deccani (d. after 1707), who describes his state of mind and the beauty of his beloved exclusively in words that are pen-names of poets such as *Firdūsī*, "paradisiacal," *Jāmī*, "cup-like," *Anvarī*, "most radiant," *Shauqī*, "longing," and so on.[16]

More frequent, however, are allusions to famous books whose titles can be used in puns: 'Aṭṭār's *Manṭiq al-ṭayr*, "The Birds' Language," and Sa'dī's *Gulistān*, "Rose Garden," appear, as is to be expected, mainly in poetry devoted to spring; Niẓāmī's *Khamsah*, the "Quintet," could be connected with the five senses; the *Kashf* (either Hujwīrī's *Kashf al-maḥjūb* or Maibudhī's *Kashf al-asrār*) appears now and then as opposed to the rational interpretation of the revelation as is found, according to poetic parlance, in Zamakhsharī's *Kashshāf*, the important commentary on the Qur'ān. Ḥāfiẓ offers a good example of this combination.[17] On the other hand, Ibn ʿArabī's (d. 1240) *Fuṣūṣ al-ḥikam*, "The Bezels of Wisdom," are used not only in strictly mystical context, but also in love poetry for the lip of the beloved is like *faṣṣ*, "bezel," of ruby. Thus, Jāmī, followed by many others, may claim that the life-bestowing lips of his beloved would be worthy of being described in the chapter about Jesus in Ibn ʿArabī's *Fuṣūṣ*, for the breath of Jesus quickens the dead as does the kiss of the beloved that quickens the near-dead lover.[18] Similarly, Jāmī can also see the dangerous, tempting eyes and sweetly smiling lips of his beloved as a commentary on the Qur'ānic verse, "He created death and life" (Surah 67, 2), for while the eyes kill with their glance, the sugar lips grant new life.[19]

It is not surprising that the imagery of the book plays such a central role in Islamic poetry. The Qur'ān itself uses this imagery frequently: We often hear of the "book of actions" and also of the "*kirām al-kātibīn*" (surah 82, 11), the noble scribe angels who note down man's actions in the books that will be shown at Doomsday and should therefore not be blackened by too many sins.

Nāṣir-i Khusrau, the great Ismaili philosopher and poet of the eleventh century, admonishes his readers:

> The soul is a book, thy deeds are like the writing.
> Write not in thy soul aught else than a fair inscription.
> Write what is wholly good in the book, brother,
> For the pen is in thine own hand.[20]

Much later, in the mid-eighteenth century, one finds in the *Nāda-i ʿAndalīb* of the Delhi mystic Nāṣir Muḥammad ʿAndalīb advice which he may have taken from some earlier Sufi poet, but which he may also have written himself:

> I want to correct the nine books
> and to select the manuscript of Existence,
> to empty the library of the heart
> line by line from unfitting letters,
> to purify the picture gallery of the body page by page
> from the pictures of eating and sleeping,
> to transform the black book of the crimes of the lower soul (*nafs*)
> into the first page of the exordium of good works.[21]

But how to perform such a purification?

The poets discovered that there is a way to clean the books blackened by sins, namely, weeping. Most oriental ink is soluble in water, hence, books could be and have been washed off comparatively easily—and what would be a better way than to weep so profusely that the tears of repentance wash off the black writing of the book of actions?

Poets liked this idea, and they often—especially in later times—combined it with the image of the tear as a child that runs away from the eyelashes. Thus, the Kashmiri poet Fānī (d. 1670), whose poetry contains a remarkably great number of writing metaphors, says:

> How many copies did our child see and wash off! But due to its confusion
> this child "Tear" has never become acquainted with the book.[22]

The same poet refers to emperor Akbar's device, "Peace with all", and applies it to the mystical intoxication which makes mankind forget the differences of religions and sects:

> When the old master of the tavern teaches the book "Peace with all!",
> One can wash off the pages of the different religious sects with the wine of *tawḥīd*, [declaration that God is One].[23]

One wonders whether his remark was an answer to Bābā Fighānī's (d. 1519) *ghazal* in which he had joked:

> Fighānī, the *safīnah*, [notebook, anthology], of your heart is polluted—
> Wash off the dust of griefs with wine from the book![24]

In connection, one should remember that the term "book", *kitāb*, is rarely used for anything but the Qur'ān, or at least a religious, important work, while books of poetry are referred to as *safīnah*, "boat," that is, a small book stitched together at the narrow end. Such *safīnah* became very popular as anthologies in Timurid times, and are usually written in delicate *nastaʿlīq* script. Often the designation of a book as *daftar* occurs, that is, a notebook bound only loosely or consisting of loose pages.[25]

The religious importance of books is reflected time and again in allusions to books by mystics and mystically inclined writers. The Prophet of Islam, being *ummī*, "illiterate," appears as the one who did not need any book knowledge but knew everything that had ever been written.[26] Thus, the mystics, too, tried to find access to the great book of creation and to discover and interpret its *āyāt*, its signs. Did not God Himself state that He had put His signs "in the horizons and in yourselves" (surah 41, 52)? Thus, the *magister magnus* of theosophical Sufism, the Andalusian Ibn ʿArabī, conceived of the whole cosmos as a book, readable to the understanding people, and his near-contemporary in Iran, ʿAzīzaddīn Nasafī, used the same image, as did many other thinkers and poets. An additional feature of this comparison was the fact that surah 68 begins with the words, *Nūn wa-al-qalam*, "*Nūn*, and By the Pen!," an expression that lead some Sufis in Ibn ʿArabī's tradition to speculate that the letter *nūn*, as suggested by its very shape, could be interpreted as the primordial inkwell that belongs with the primordial Pen that writes on the Well Preserved Tablet whatever is to happen.[27]

However, the idea that the cosmos or the universe is a book occurs long before Ibn ʿArabī. Sanāʾī of Ghazna (d. 1131) writes in his didactic epic, *Ḥadīqat al-ḥaqīqah*:

The form of the universe is like a book
in which advice and fetter (*pand u band*) are together.
Its form is a fetter for the body of the blameworthy,
its qualities are advice for the hearts of the wise.[28]

To have understood such advice in the book of the universe was a claim of numerous mystically inclined writers. Akbar's court poet, Faiẓī (d. 1595), boasted that he had seen:

One by one the details of the notebook, *daftar*, of existence and place, *kawn wa-makān*,
and table by table the pages of the calendar of the sky.[29]

That means, he was able to understand and interpret the astrological chart, *jadwal*, which shows how the sphere rules human life.

A century later, Fānī offered a fine comparison:

The world is like a book filled with knowledge and justice.
The bookbinder Fate made two volumes of it with two points of return.
The stitching at the back, *shirāzah*, is the *sharīʿah* and the different religions are the pages:
Tonight we are all disciples, and the Prophet is the teacher.[30]

Interestingly, most poets who used book imagery developed a rather pessimistic worldview, and one is pleasantly surprised when discovering the lines of one Ashraf, a little known Kashmiri poet in Mughal times:

Everyone who has seen the notebook of the days from top to bottom,
has seen the day between the lines of the nights,[31]

For the book does not only contain the dark and sometimes crooked script of fate, but also the white background, the days of happiness.

There are also other interpretations of the Book of the Universe. One pun that is found in hundreds of verses is that on *khaṭṭ*, which means both "line, script" and "down," the first black signs of a growing beard on the cheeks and upper lip of a teenage boy.[32] This pun makes it next to impossible to render into a Western language a great number of Persian and Turkish verses which are replete with plays on *khaṭṭ*. A fine example are the lines by Zēbun-Nisā (d. 1701), emperor Aurangzēb's gifted daughter, who writes:

I have seen the library of the world page by page—
I have seen your *khaṭṭ* and said: "That's the real purpose!"[33]

The punning with *khaṭṭ* goes back to much earlier days of Persian poetry and is used by Saʿdī (d. 1292), who addresses a beloved:

O you: from the booklet of your moral qualities, the *ḥusn-i khaṭṭ* ["beautiful script" or "lovely down"] is just one chapter,
and sweetness is just one letter from the book of your qualities.[34]

As the face was considered to be a book of loveliness, even in a veritable Qur'ān copy, the *khaṭṭ* plays a very special role:

> Due to the musk colored *khaṭṭ* his cheek appeared like the book of beauty,
> for the commentator himself has written carefully these marginal notes.[35]

The down sprouts by itself, and therefore the poet could think that the black lines of the down were nothing but the author's commentary of his own book which he wrote, as is customary, on the margins, that is, the cheeks.

Poets allude to the custom to put a dot on a certain place of a manuscript to indicate a verse or a single word or letter which should be chosen for its beauty or elegance:

> Sit like the point of selection in the margin of the books of the assembly.[36]

Thus Fānī admonishes someone who is very special. One often finds verses like the following one by Fārigh, another Kashmiri poet:

> My high nature has selected his stature from out the world;
> That means, it has selected the letter *alif* from this book.[37]

The combination of the straight, upright letter *alif* and the elegant, slender stature of the beloved is commonplace and can be easily combined with the religious interpretation of the *alif* as pointing to God's Unity and unicity, as its numerical value is One, and as all the other letters, according to the calligraphic rules of Ibn Muqlah (d. 940), are shaped by measuring the *alif*, just as Adam was created "according to His, God's form." Ḥāfiẓ's famous verse:

> There is nothing on the tablet of my heart but the *alif* of the friend's stature.
> What can I do? My teacher did not give me any other letter to remember,[38]

plays most skillfully on the double meaning of *alif* and has therefore been imitated by innumerable poets.

As already mentioned, the comparison of a beautiful face to a book, in particular to the Qur'ān, in whose copies not the smallest mistake must be seen, occurs often in poetry. That is not only the case in Ḥurūfī poetry, where comparisons of human limbs with letters and the idea of the entire human being as a divinely written book form the center of the worldview, but also in earlier and later poetry.[39] Writers who may never have heard of Ḥurūfī interpretations of the letters used such comparisons, for they seemed to be quite natural. Thus, a poet in the Indus valley, Ismā'il Bakhshī, is quoted as having written:

> Your face is like a Qur'ān copy without any mistake and flaw
> which the Pen of Destiny has written exclusively from musk.
> The eye and your mouth are verse. . .dots for stopping, the eye-brows
> a *maddah*,
> the eyelashes signs of declension, the mole and the down letters and dots.[40]

Such allusions, especially of the eyebrows to the *tughrā*, of eyes, nose, mouth, ears, and curls to the individual letters of the alphabet, abound in Arabic, Persian, and related poetry.

One aspect of the comparisons of beautiful, pure things with the Qur'ān is that the Holy Writ was used for prognostication. Poets made use of this quality of the Qur'ān, too, and could compare Love to a Qur'ān from which one might be able to receive some information about the future. But, as Amīr Khusrau Dihlawī (d. 1325) wrote:

> When Khusrau opens the Book of Love for prognostication,
> From the first page of grief my story appeared.[41]

Frequently, the heart is compared to a Qur'ān copy, and the custom to write the Holy Book in thirty parts, *juz'*, made many a poet think that his heart is also a collection of thirty parts. Kalīm, however, expresses his concern differently:

> I tore my heart to pieces page by page,
> For from this book one has rarely seen the prognosis of well-being.[42]

The comparison of the heart with the Qur'ān leads sometimes to strange exaggerations. Thus, Mīr Dard of Delhi (d. 1786), never exactly modest in his mystical claims, compares himself in a subtle way to the Prophet, his ancestor, by remarking:

> I am unlettered, but I have a heart
> thanks to whose mystical grace, *faiz*, every letter of mine is a book in the world.[43]

That is, wisdom is poured onto his heart, which thus produces wonderful, inspired books (he indeed claimed that all his Persian and Urdu works were written under inspiration).

Two centuries before him, 'Urfī (d. 1591), noted for his grand ambitions, had claimed:

> Every book for which I am the last chapter—
> Its first page is the well-preserved Tablet.[44]

This, again, sounds rather like a claim if not to prophethood, at least to the status of the Perfect Man.

However, not every poet used the imagery of the book in this way. More common, and probably easier to appreciate, are verses in which the garden is seen as a book, just as books were compared, by earlier writers, to a garden. Everyone who has studied the elements of Persian is aware of Sa'dī's line in his *Dīwān*:

> Every leaf on the green trees is in the eyes of those who understand
> a page from the hook of the Creator's wisdom.[45]

Jāmī sees the "children of spring" practice the letter *alif* in the garden,[46] and Kalim takes up this idea when he says:

Every spring is a child in the school "Garden"
Every bud that ovens becomes his book.[47]

The poets in the Islamic world, as elsewhere, loved especially the rose and saw it as a wondrous book with a hundred petals, that is, pages. Most of the later writers would agree with the Mughal poet Umīd:

Umīd, speak like the rose of your heart that is in a hundred pieces;
talk about one page, for this book is all blood.[48]

The combination of the red centifolia with bloodstained pages that resemble the bleeding heart of the lover is quite common in later Persian poetry and is particularly well expressed in Fighānī's lines:

Who washed the booklet of the rose with the spring cloud's weeping?
For every petal is a booklet filled with the blood of the suffering ones![49]

If I understand his train of thought correctly, he means that it was not right that the rain was washing the roses, as these are signs of the martyrs, those who died in unfulfilled longing—and according to Islamic law, martyrs' bodies are not washed before burial.

In earlier centuries, however, the cheerful, or at least delightful, aspect of the "book Rose" is more prominent:

The rose has made correct its page with dew—
the stamp on this page is all pearls![50]

Thus says Amīr Khusrau, and he continues this line with the remark that the line, *khaṭṭ*, of greenery is even prettier than this page. Whether he intends the vernal green in the meadow or the fresh down on his friend's rose-cheek remains an open question.

But Fighānī also looks at the *safīnah*, the anthology, of the heart and wishes that every page of the booklet might be in the hand of some charming person:

I want that the *safīnah* of the heart be opened like the rose, page by page (or, petal by petal),
and that every page be in the hand of some angelic beauty![51]

Is not the "rose of the cheek" a lovely book that contains innumerable love songs? Ḥāfiẓ, as so often, coined the classical formulation of this thought:

Not I alone sing *ghazals* for the rose of the cheek,
for you have thousands of nightingales on all sides[52]

a verse which inter alia contains a fine pun on *hazārān*, "thousands" and "nightingales".

The morning breeze opens the "notebook of the rose" to sing of the curls of the beloved.[53] Thus thinks Amīr Khusrau, and even a nearly contemporary poet like Iqbāl (d. 1938) sees the Creator writing His message on the petals of the tulip.[54]

Persian poets sometimes invented strange metaphors in their spring songs. One wonders what lead Fānī Kashmīrī to compose the verse:

> The rose wrote with writing, *khaṭṭ*, of greenery in the book of spring:
> The cloud of the wine bottle is better than the sun of spring.[55]

Does he mean to say that rain would be more welcome than sun at this point in time, or else does he claim to prefer wine indeed to the radiant sunshine of a Kashmiri spring day. . .?

Yet, one is not surprised when the nightingales are heard reciting the *Manṭiq al-ṭayr* from the book of the roses,[56] for rose petals can play various roles in the imagery of the book. They may just be a book filled with mysterious tales, as in the previous example, or else a book that contains the story of grief:

> Every rose petal is a tongue to explain the commentary of grief—
> Not in vain does the nightingale lament when it sees the rose.[57]

Thus says one of the greatest Turkish poets, Fuẓūlī (d. 1556). One of his predecessors, Jāmī, who influenced him considerably, remarks, however:

> I struck together the booklet of the rose like the wind,
> because in these pages there is no letter about your beauty![58]

How could one leave intact a book which does not speak of the rose-like cheek of the beloved? Fānī even wants to blacken rose petals with the color of the tulip;[59] he alludes to the black scar on the heart of the tulip which is compared to the black scar in the suffering lover's heart, from which one can easily produce a collection of poetry.

To this century, poets have invented comparisons between the book and the garden; thus, the Egyptian poet Sāmī al-Bārūdī (d. 1904) wrote, at the beginning of this century:

> The hand of wind writes letters on the pond that could be read and sung by birds.[60]

Perhaps the finest verses that compare gardens and books are not those in which birds recite from the booklet Rose, but rather the colorful descriptions of the autumnal garden. Jāmī sees it as a notebook colored by red and yellow leaves—a notebook from which the insightful spectator understands that the "white book", that is, the snow-covered ground, will soon appear.[61] Fuẓūlī similarly takes up the radiant colors of autumn, but uses the image ever more ingeniously than Jāmī:

> The scribe of Destiny made from the autumnal leaves a golden sprinkling for the pages of the garden;
> Cutting off the stitching, *shirāzah*, of running water [which held in shape the book], autumn has confused the pages of the manuscript of the garden.[62]

Similarities with books could be discovered in all of nature: An early poet of Baghdad did not see the garden or flowers as a book, but discovered a book with lines in the glittering skin of a snake.[63]

One often finds a concretion of abstracts in Persian poetry, and almost "mythical" transformation of material and spiritual objects. An early Persian poet, Akhsikatī, speaks of the "book of poverty",[64] and Maulānā Rūmī mentioned "the library of my needs", which the beloved is supposed[65] to study. When Sanā'ī claims:

> As much as I read the booklet of the lovers,
> Yet, in love of you I am still a beginner who learns the alphabet,[66]

he alludes to the fact that love, in its true essence, can never be understood by studying the books that speak about it, and that everyone has to start again with a new experience, with new suffering. Naẓīrī (d. 1612), the leading poet of Mughal India, took up the same idea:

> Ever so many books and Qur'ān copies are the register for the chapter Love—
> When you find the real tale, you don't read any page any more![67]

Jāmī sees it somewhat differently: Although intellectually he wanted to give up loving, yet, the friend's *khaṭṭ* (down, script) seduced him again:

> I washed off the book of Love with the management of reason,
> But again, your *khaṭṭ* brought the lesson of the alphabet, *abjad*, into my head.[68]

The manuscript of Love is usually black—one can combine it with the term *muswaddah*, "black copy" (i.e., rough draft). This is so, on the one hand, because lovers suffer from melancholia, "black liver," and from *bakht-i siyāh*, "black fortune," that is, misfortune, but also because this misfortune is caused by the black tresses and black down of the beloved. Bēdil (d. 1721), in good Sufi manner, gratefully acknowledges that this black manuscript became radiant when the lesson of beauty was written on it, so that by looking at the friend's beauty the reader became aware of himself,[69] for the lover is nothing but a mirror for the beloved's beauty. And one should not forget that even though the book of Love is black, it need not be afraid of God:

> for this sin [that is love] was not written in the account-book, *jarīdah*, of the [black] tress.[70]

That, at least, is what Fānī claims.

Poets might boast of their intimate relation with the primordial book or with the Book of Love. Thus, an Indo-Persian poet whose name is barely found in any history of Persian literature claims:

> The title of the books of mystery is our fate [*sarnivisht*], "what is written on the forehead"
> The exordium of the book of Love is our disposition.[71]

But many of them were aware that one should never trust the book of Love. Is it not strange that:

> His (the friend's) mole is in the eyes of the rival and the scar of longing is in my heart—
> In the book of love-game the dots have fallen on the wrong places!

Is it right that the rival can study the friend's beauty spot from a close distance while the poor lover only suffers from the black scars which unfulfilled longing has stamped into his heart? There must be some *taṣḥīf*, a wrong placement of the diacritical marks, in this strange book![72]

At a rather late stage of Indo-Persian poetry, combinations of the reed pen, which is used for writing, and the reed mat, *buryā*, on which the derwish, the true lover, is supposed to sleep, can be found. The reed, in its different aspects as pen, as flute, and as sugarcane, had been praised and described in earlier poetry, but the "Indian style" of Persian poetry abounds in allusions to the reed mat. Thus, Bēdil, the most difficult of the poets who wrote in the "Indian style," excels here, as elsewhere, in difficult cross references:

> You break a hundred reed pens to reach the practice of good behavior, *adab*:
> There are lines in the book of the school of the reed mat![73]

For if one sleeps on the reed mat (which was even compared by the poets to the ruler, *masṭarah*, that is needed for good writing),[74] the lines of the hard mat leave their marks on the body and thus "educate" it in proper modest behavior.

Many poets knew that:

> The book of generosity and kindness is a sign, *āyah*, of Mercy,
> But the pages of this book do not come together.[75]

For it is hard to find more than a few scattered pages of such books as much as everyone looks out for them.

A book, however, should be stitched carefully in order to keep the pages in the right sequence, and the *shirāzah*, "stitching," occurs frequently in later Mughal verse—so much so that ʿAbdul Jalīl Bilgrāmī *(d. 1743) sees the "wave of the khaṭṭ*" appear as the "*shirāzah* off the book of Beauty."[76]

At about the same time, Bēdil saw the vein of the rose petal as the thread of binding for the collection, *majmūʿah* of life and love, a collection in which one finds the blackness of, or the passion for, *sawdā*, the friend's *khaṭṭ*.[77]

Naẓīrī appears more matter-of-fact when he describes his state:

> Your love is the stitching of my parts;
> Longing for you is the register, *fihrist*, of my whole being.[78]

A century earlier, Fuẓūlī, in the Turkish area, had used the idea of "stitching together" in a somewhat more elegant way:

> The true lovers stitch together with the thread of the soul
> Every book in which the tale, ḥadīth, of your ruby lips is written![79]

In the nineteenth century, Ghālib (d. 1869) (who even speaks, in his Urdu verse, of "looking" as the *shirāzah* of the eyelashes)[80] invented a fine image:

> The story of longing does not fit into binding, alas!
> Let this manuscript remain in parts![81]

Iqbāl, on the other hand, expressed his philosophy of development and longing in a related image:

> Wish is the stitching for the book of actions—[82]

It is only man's burning wish and striving that makes true, useful action possible.

He is thus quite different from his predecessors in whose verses a melancholy mood overshadows everything, including, and perhaps especially, images connected with the book:

> The sign of cheerful life is not to be found in the pages of this time, *dahr*—
> Someone has made a wrong selection from this book![83]

Poets did not believe much in hope and expectation, and knew from experience that:

> It is not good when a goal is attained;
> When the page is complete it is turned over.[84]

Probably the most outspoken criticism of the Book of Life comes from Sarmad, the Judeo-Persian convert to mystical Islam, who paid with his life for his daring and often seemingly blasphemous utterances after his protector, the Mughal heir apparent Dārā Shikōh, had been executed in 1659. The content of his famous quatrain turned out to be true:

> To trust the promises of humans in the world is wrong.
> "Yes": wrong. "Sure": wrong. "Tonight": wrong. "Tomorrow": wrong.
> Don't ask how the manuscript of the *dīwān* of my life looks;
> The script wrong, the meaning wrong, the composition wrong, the orthography wrong!

No, there was no reason in hoping against hope:

> Behold my magnanimity: a hundred leaves from the book of Hope have
> I torn into a hundred pieces and washed them off with tears of blood![86]

This little-known poet from the days of Emperor Akbar still sees the possibility of casting away the pages of hope; Ghālib, in nineteenth-century Delhi, is even less positive:

> Future and past are wish and longing,
> It was a "Would it were!" which I wrote in a hundred places.
> Not in a single manuscript was the meaning of the word "hope"
> [as much as] I had written the register of the chapters of wishes.[87]

What is existence but a strange, often incomprehensible book? What is left to mankind but *tajrīd*, complete isolation from all created beings, abstaining from wishes and hopes? Perhaps the most impressive description of a wise person's attitude comes from Khāqānī, whose verse seems unsurpassable in depth and expressiveness:

> I wrote the alphabet of isolation, *tajrīd*, and then, I painted it with the
> red and yellow of the [red] tears and [pale] face as though it were
> a *nashrah* [an amulet for children painted in several color].
> When I had learned by heart this alphabet, whose beginning is from nothingness,
> I forgot the riddle whose title is "Existence"[88]

There seems little doubt that this line has inspired one of the famous verses by Mirzā Ghālib who wrote, in his Persian *Dīwān*:

> Death is a letter whose title is "Life."[89]

Poets in former centuries often spoke of God the Creator as the master calligrapher, for they knew:

> Creation was not prepared without a creator;
> To decorate pages is impossible without the scribe's writing.[90]

Thus thought Anvarī in the twelfth century. The same concept of the Divine Scribe, so frequently used in a positive way, as in Maulānā Rūmī's poetry,[91] is transformed in Ghālib's introductory lines to his *Urdū dīwān* into a rebellious outcry of the letters against the Divine Master who put them "in a paper shirt," that is, who wrote them the way He wanted, without apparently caring for the letters' feelings.[92] What, then, do we know about the meaning of the world?

Kalīm admits his ignorance about creation and world in his oft-quoted verse:

> We do not know anything of the beginning and the end of this world—
> The first and last page of this old book have fallen off.[93]

The mystics had always pretended to be averse to bookishness, and many of them pretended, also, to follow the example of the "unlettered Prophet," or else to know only one letter of the alphabet, that is, *alif.* But we cannot deny that they probably wrote more books than those whom they criticized for their literary and scholarly activities, so that the output of mystical writings in Arabic, Persian, Turkish, Urdu, as well as the regional languages of Indo-Pakistan, Southeast Asia, and Africa, seems to have no limits. Yet a book was only a medium which should be studied under the supervision of a master who would know what to teach the disciple and how to explain the difficulties, the inner meaning, according to time-honored and often experiential methods. That is why one finds numerous remarks, especially among Sufis, against the use of books. But even Muḥammad Iqbāl, the poet-philosopher of the Indian Muslims and spiritual father of Pakistan, criticized the reliance on books, be they philological or scholastic. Is not the Muslim jurisconsult of modern times who knows only books and does not feel true religious experience like Qārūn? Under the weight of the dead load of books on Arabic grammar he sinks into the earth, as did Qārūn under the burden of his useless treasures, instead of breathing the air of divine Love.[94]

In another metaphor, Iqbāl juxtaposes the bookworm, which leads a miserable life in the pages of manuscripts of Fārābī and Avicenna, with the moth that casts itself lovingly and longingly into the candle to burn there in ecstasy.[95] He also coined the fine expression:

> Love is *umm al-kitāb*, "Mother of the Book," scholarship is the "Son of the book."[96]

Love is the primordial basis for revelation, while scholarship is dependent upon written, that is, second-hand, knowledge.

Long before him, Jāmī had admonished the reader of his *Lawā'iḥ*:

> Strive to lift the veils, not to collect books,
> For by collecting books the veils are not lifted.
> Where would be the joy of love in traversing books?
> Roll up all of them, return to God, and repent![97]

Rūmī had combined the book and the garden, expressing his pity for those who look only at books and, as it were, turn themselves into a library:

> If you are a library, you are not someone who seeks the garden of the soul.[98]

For, as he sings in the *Mathnawī*:

> For the lovers, the friend's beauty is the teacher,
> his face is the notebook and lesson and instruction for them.[90]

For it is the page of the heart that matters:

> From the undecorated page of the heart I found
> the reality which you seek in books.[100]

The heart, however, is perfected when it has been polished as a mirror to reflect the beloved's beauty, which confuses everyone. Therefore, a minor Mughal poet sings:

> I keep the sheet of the mirror under the arm instead of a book;
> I am the child that reads the alphabet in the schoolhouse of confusion.[101]

What would be a book when one wants the radiant reflection of beauty? Gēsū Darāz, whose description of the book as beloved we quoted in the beginning, seems to have changed his opinion and, refuting his own previous statement, writes in another quatrain:

> If you have a book as your beloved,
> Then you have something that has a black heart!
> God forbid that a book be your beloved—
> What kind of friendship with Abyssinians and Barbarians![102]

Maulānā Rūmī admonished himself in hundreds of *ghazals* to be silent, and Mīr Dard, more than 500 years later, emphasizes the importance of silence, so that the true Speaker and Author, God, can speak:

> O you who has wasted this life in debate:
> One point of silence is better than a hundred kinds of books![103]

Could any book describe properly what the lover feels?

> This notebook has reached its end, but the story still goes on:
> One cannot tell the situation of a longing heart even in a hundred notebooks![104]

Thus said Saʿdī, and, confronted with the dilemma of wanting to write books and yet knowing that all of them are but a veil, what can one do except follow Sanā'ī's remark:

> First I wrote books with effort great—
> At last I broke the pen, confused![105]

NOTES

1. *Fīhi mā fīhi*, trans. Arthur John Arberry, Discourses of Rumi (London, 1961).

2. "Comprendre l'Islam," in *La Voie des Lettres*, ed. Jean Canteins (Paris, 1981), p. 76, note 21.

For the whole problem of calligraphy's influence on the art of the book, literature in general, and Sufism, see Annemarie Schimmel, *Callugraphy and Islamic Culture* (New York, 1984; paperback, 1989).

3. *Armaghān-i Pāk*, ed. Shaykh Muḥammad Ikrām (Karachi, 1953), p. 259.

4. ʿAbdul Bāqī Nihāwandī, *Ma'āthir-i Raḥīmī*, 3 vols., ed. M. Hidayat Hosain (Calcutta, 1916–1931), is devoted to the Khānkhānān's political and cultural activities. For the deplorable decay of such libraries, however, see Aloys Sprenger, *A Catalogue of the Arabic, Persian, and Hindu'stany manuscripts of the Libraries of the King of Oudh, compiled by Order of the Government of India* (Calcutta, 1854, repr. Osnabüch, 1979) 1: x: "The books are kept in about forty dilapidated boxes—camel trunks, which are at the same time tenanted by prolific families of rats, and any admirer of Oriental lore who wants to visit this collection will do well to poke with a stick into the boxes before he puts his hand into them, unless he be a zoologist as well as an orientalist."

5. ʿAbdurraḥmān Jāmī, *Dīwān-i kāmil*, ed. Hāshim Riẓā (Tehran, 1341 H solar/1962), *rubāʿī* no. 49.

6. J. Christoph Bürgel, "Von Freud und Leid mit Büchern. Gereimtes und Anekdotisches aus dem arabischen Mittlealter," in *Einheit in der Vielfalt*, Festschrift Peter Lang (Bern/Frankfurt/Paris, 1988).

7. Annemarie Schimmel, *Die orientalische Katze*, 2nd ed. (Munich, 1989), pp. 87–92. The book lover was Abū Jaʿfar al-Awsī.

8. Laṭīfī, in Elias J.W. Gibb, *History of Ottoman Poetry*, 6 vols. (London, 1900–1909; repr. London, 1958–63) 6:165.

9. Ikrām, *Armaghān-i Pāk*, p. 161.

10. Afḍaladdīn Ibrāhīm Khāqānī, *Dīwān*, ed. Ẓiā'addīn Sajjādī (Tehran, n.d.), p. 326.

11. Jalāladdīn Rūmī, *Mathnawī maʿnawī*, 7 vols., ed. and trans. Reynold Alleyne Nicholson (London, 1925–40), 4: line 5722ff. The story is found in Abū Ḥāmid al-Ghazzālī, *Iḥyā' ʿulūm al-dīn, v. 4, bāb al-tawakkul*, "The Chapter of Trust in God", which is Rūmī's source.

12. Jāmī, *Dīwān-i kāmil, rubāʿī* no. 48.

13. Stuart Cary Welch et al., *The Emperors' Album* (New York, 1987), pp. 42–43.

14. Annemarie Schimmel, "Islamic Literatures in India," in *History of Indian Literature*, vol. VII, ed. Jan Gonda (Wiesbaden, 1973), p. 46.

15. Ikrām, *Armaghān-i Pāk*, p. 142.

16. Garcin de Tassy, *Les Oeuvres de Wali: publiés en Hindoustani* (Paris, 1834; traduction et notes, Paris 1838).

17. Ḥāfiẓ, *Dīwān*, eds. Nadhīr Aḥmad and Jalāl Nā'inī (Tehran, 1971), p. 75.

18. Jāmī, *Dīwān-i kāmil, p. 470, ghazal* no. 778.

19. Jāmī, *Dīwān-i kāmil*, p. 185, *ghazal* no. 137.

20. Edward Granville Browne, *A Literary History of Persia*, 4 vols. (Cambridge, 1921), 2:232.

21. Muḥammad Nāṣir 'Andalīb, *Nāda-i 'andalīb*, 2 vols. (Bhopal, 1309/1890–91), 1:646.

22. Muḥsin Fānī Kashmīrī, *Dīwān*, ed. G.L. Tikki (Tehran, 1964), p. 82.

23. Fānī, *Dīwān*, p. 10.

24. Bābā Fighānī, *Dīwān*, ed. A.S. Khwānsarī, 2nd ed. (Tehran, 1340 H solar/1961), *ghazal* no. 358.

25. Professor Vincent M. Monteil, Paris, in an oral communication, remarked that in Omar Khayyam's famous quatrain about the "book under a tree, and wine," the correct reading is not *kitāb*, "book," but with the change of one dot, *kabāb*, "roast meat," which makes much more sense both in the context and in the usage of the term *kitab*.

26. Annemarie Schimmel, *And Muhammad is His Messenger* (Chapel Hill, 1985), Index: s.v. *ummī*, especially pp. 71–74.

27. Annemarie Schimmel, *Calligraphy and Islamic Culture*, p. 79. relying on Sulaimān, Sa'daddīn Mustaqīmzādah, *Tuḥfat al-khaṭṭaṭīn*, ed. Ibnul Emin Mahmud (Istanbul, 1928), p. 7 (among the forty *ḥadīth* on writing).

28. Majdaddīn Majdūd Sanā'ī, *Ḥadīqat al-ḥaqīqah*, ed. Mudarris Riẓawī (Tehran, 1329 H solar/1950), p. 457.

29. Ikrām, *Armaghān-i Pāk*, p. 193.

30. Fānī, *Dīwān*, p. 144.

31. Muḥammad Aṣlaḥ, *Tadhkirat-i shu'arā-yi Kashmīr*, 5 vols., ed. Sayyid Hussāmuddīn Rāshdī (Karachi, 1967–68) 4: 1736. *A* is the basic text, I-IV the additional notes supplied by the editor.

32. Schimmel, *Calligraphy and Islamic Culture*, Index: s.v. *khaṭṭ*, especially pp. 128–34.

33. Aṣlaḥ, *Tadhkirat A*, p. 107.

34. Muṣliḥaddīn Sa'dī, *Kulliyāt*, ed. Furūghī (Tehran, 1342 H solar/1963), *ghazal* no. 517, p. 498, line 8.

35. Aṣlaḥ, *Tadhkirat A*, p. 363.

36. Fānī, *Dīwān*, p. 135.

37. Aṣlaḥ, *Tadhkirat A*, p. 275.

38. Ḥāfiẓ, *Dīwān, p. 363 (mīm* no. 9).

39. Schimmel, *Calligraphy and Islamic Culture*, pp. 106–11.

40. Ismā'īl Bakhshī, quoted in Mīr "Alīsīr Qāni', *Maqālāt al-shu'arā'*, ed. Sayyid Ḥussāmuddīn Rāshdī (Karachi, 1956), p. 44.

41. Amīr Khusrau, *Dīwān-i kāmil*, ed. Maḥmūd Darwīsh (Tehran, 1343 H solar/1965).

42. Abū Ṭālib Kalīm, *Dīwān*, ed. Partaw Baiḍā'ī (Tehran, 1336 H solar/ 1957), *ghazal* no. 214.

43. Khwājah Mīr Dard, *Dīwān-i fārsī* (Delhi, 1310/1891–92), p. 65. About Dard's attitude to writing and books, see Annemarie Schimmel, *Pain and Grace* (Leiden, 1976), pt. 1.

44. Muḥammad 'Urfī Shīrāzī, *Kulliyāt*, ed. Ghulām Ḥusain Jawāhirī (Tehran, 1336 H solar/1957), *ghazal* on p. 283, line 5.

45. Sa'dī, *Kulliyāt I*, *ghazal* no. 296, p. 282, line 4.

46. Jāmī, *Dīwān-i kāmil, rubā'ī* no. 90.

47. Kalīm, *Dīwān*, *ghazal* no. 539. Cf. also Khāqānī, *Dīwān*, p. 42, "birds in the garden learn the alphabet like little children."

48. Aṣlaḥ, *Tadhkirat A*, p. 569.

49. Fīghānī, *Dīwān, ghazal* no. 151.

50. Amīr Khusrau, *Dīwān-i kāmil*, no. 336.

51. Fīghānī, *Dīwān, ghazal* no. 363.

52. Ḥāfiẓ, *Dīwān*, p. 119, *ghazal* no. 59. This verse, which is usually quoted as one of Ḥāfiẓ's finest puns, appears only in a footnote.

53. Amīr Khusrau, *Dīwān-i kāmil*, no. 476.

54. Muḥammad Iqbāl, *Zabūr-i ʿajam* (Lahore, 1927), pt. 2, no. 29.

55. Fānī, *Dīwān*, p. 109.

56. Gibb, *History of Ottoman Poetry*, 6:80.

57. Fuẓūli, *Diwān*, ed. Abdulbaki Gölpinarli (Istanbul, 1948), no. 34.

58. Jāmi, *Diwān-i kāmil*, p. 260, *ghazal* no. 331.

59. Fāni, *Diwān*, p. 140.

60. Carl Brockelmann, *Geschichte der arabischen Literatur* (Leiden, 1938), suppl. 3: 12.

61. Jāmi, *Diwān-i kāmil*, p. 401, *ghazal* no. 598.

62. Fuẓūli, *Diwān*, no. 132.

63. Ibn Abi ʿAwn, *Kitāb al-tashbihāt*, ed. M. Muʿid Khan (London/Leiden, 1960), p. 58.

64. Daulatshāh, *Tadhkirat al-shuʿarā'*, ed. Edward Granville Browne (Leiden, 1900), p. 136.

65. Jalāladdin Rūmi, *Diwān-i kābir yā Kulliyāt-i Shams*, 10 vols., ed. Badiʿuzzamān Furūzānfar (Tehran, 1957), *ghazal* no. 1425.

66. Sanā'i,*Diwān*, ed. Mudarris Raẓawi (Tehran, n.d.), p. 899.

67. Naẓiri Nishāpūri, *Diwān*, ed. Maẓāhir Muṣaffā (Tehran, 1340 H solar/1961), *ghazal* no. 520.

68. Jāmi, *Diwān-i kāmil*, p. 884.

69. Bēdil, *Diwān* (Bombay, 1302/1885), p. 207.

70. Fāni, *Diwān*, p. 100.

71. Aṣlaḥ, *Tadhkirat I*, p. 118, line 7 (Ilāhi).

72. About *taṣḥif*, see Ḥamzah al-Isfāhāni, *al-Tanbih ʻalá ḥudūth al-taṣḥif*, ed. al-Shaykh Muḥammad Ḥasan Āl Yāsin (Baghdad, 1967). See A. Schimmel, *Calligraphy and Islamic Culture*, ch. 4, notes 4–6.

73. Bēdil, *Kulliyāt*, 4 vols. (Kabul, 1962–65), 1:5.

74. Kalim, *Diwān*, *ghazal* no. 316.

75. Fāni, *Diwān*, p. 124.

76. Qāniʻ, *Maqālāt al-shuʻarā'*,. p. 412.

77. Bēdil, *Kulliyāt*, 1:32.

78. Naẓiri, *Diwān*, *ghazal* no. 483.

79. Fuzūli, *Diwān*, no. 71.

80. Mirzā Asadullāh Ghālib, *Urdū diwān*, ed. Ḥāmid Aḥmad Khān (Lahore, 1969), p. 155.

81. Ghālib, *Kulliyāt-i fārsi*, 17 vols. (Lahore: University of the Punjab, n.d.), 5: *qasidah* 36.

82. Iqbāl, *Asrār-i khudi* (Lahore, 1915), line 285.

83. Aṣlaḥ, *Tadhkirat A*, p. 593, line 27.

84. Qudsi, in Aṣlaḥ, *Tadhkirat III*, p. 1249.

85. Ikrām, *Armaghān-i Pāk*, p. 239.

86. Jaʻfar Beg Asaf Khān Qazwini, in Badaoni, *Muntakhab al-tawārikh*, 3 vols., eds. William Nassau Lees and Ahmad Ali, trans. George S.A. Ranking, W.H. Lowe, and Wolseley Haig, (Calcutta, 1865–89; repr. Patna: Academia Asiatica), 3: text 217, trans. p. 301.

87. Ghālib, *Kulliyāt-i fārsi*, 1: no. 284.

88. Khāqāni, *Diwān*, p. 209.

89. Ghālib, *Kulliyāt-i fārsi*, 1: no. 284.

90. Anvari, *Diwān*, ed. Sa'id Nafisi (Tehran, 1958), qaṣidah fi al-tawḥid, p. 175, line 10.

91. For examples, see Annemarie Schimmel, *The Triumphal Sun* (London/The Hague, 1978), chapter on "Divine Calligraphy."

92. Ghālib, *Urdū diwān*, no. 1. For the interpretation, see Annemarie Schimmel, *A Dance of Sparks: Studies in Ghalib's Imagery* (New Delhi, 1979), chapter on "Calligraphy and Poetry."

93. Ikrām, *Armaghān-i Pāk*, p. 227.

94. Iqbāl, *Bāl-i Jibril* (Lahore, 1936), p. 50.

95. Iqbāl, *Payām-i mashriq* (Lahore, 1923), p. 119.

96. Iqbāl, *Ẓarb-i Kalim* (Lahore, 1937), p. 14.

97. Jāmi, *Lawā'iḥ*, no. 40. Bēdil, too, combines book collecting with *afsurda dili*, "having a frozen, dried-up heart," *Kulliyāt*, 1:226.

98. Jalāladdin Rūmi, *Diwān-i kābir, ghazal* no. 2481.

99. Jalāladdin Rūmi, *Mathnawi*, 3: line 3847.

100. Fāni, *Diwān*, p.42.

101. Aṣlaḥ, *Tadhkirat A*, p. 320 (*Qalandar*).

102. Gēsū Darāz, *Anis al-'ushshāq* (Hyderabad/Deccan, 1940), p. 188.

103. Dard, *Diwān-i fārsi, rubā'i* no. 82.

104. Sa'di, *Kulliyāt*, 23: no. 586.

105. Sanā'i, *Diwān*, p. 801.

6

Biographical Dictionaries: Inner Structure and Cultural Significance

Wadād al-Qāḍī

Biographical dictionaries seem to be, for the researchers in the Islamic Arabic library, both a blessing and a curse. When a researcher seeks to identify a relatively unknown person whose identification is crucial for his/her research, finding this person's biography in a biographical dictionary produces unparalleled relief, joy, and a sense of salvation. When he/she does not, however, the frustration is great, and the chances of coming out with solid results are postponed—perhaps indefinitely. And, in fact, it is quite possible that a researcher would not find what he/she is looking for, not only because the Arabic biographical dictionaries, or what has survived of them, do not, and perhaps could not, include the biographies of every single person mentioned in the history of Islamic peoples across the centuries, but also because the promise that those dictionaries have, and the actual evidence of their tremendous usefulness, raise the hopes and aspirations of the researcher, creating thereby an image which does not necessarily stand up to the reality. If X were to identify a poet named Muḥammad, my expectation would be that, even if I failed to find his biography in all the available dictionaries on poets, I would eventually find him in Jamāl al-Dīn al-Qifṭī's (d. 646/1248)[1] dictionary, *al-Muḥammadūn min al-shuʿarāʾ wa ashʿaruhum*, which has entries for the Arab poets called "Muḥammad." I may not, however, find him there either, the fact being that the book has not survived in its entirety. And there is, after all, another obstacle, namely the sheer number of these biographical dictionaries: they seem to be endless—"in their hundreds or thousands," as Stephen Humphreys aptly put it[2]—and one is always afraid that one may have forgotten to consult a relevant dictionary, or that a new dictionary has been published without one being aware of it.

Whereas all this is true for anyone who has had to use Arabic biographical dictionaries extensively what is certainly as true is that having to handle these, dictionaries is an experience that puts one in the very midst of one of the major areas of medieval Islamic book production. After all, biographical composition is a form of *historical* composition: this is a fact that had been recognized by Muslim scholars of old,[3] and its echoes continue to be heard in modern scholarship today.[4] It is also a fact that is true of other cultures with well-developed historical traditions,[5] although in the Islamic one in particular, the biography, especially in the form of biographical dictionaries, has had an unparalleled level of prominence[6] for a variety of specific, historical reasons.[7]

Given the importance of this genre of writing, it is not surprising that there has been a sizeable number of studies on it. Some of these studies are brief, or detailed, surveys of the literature;[8] others are more analytical.[9] The latter discuss issues such as the motives for writing biographical dictionaries,[10] their origin,[11] provenance,[12] sources,[13] or organization,[14] the criteria for inclusion used by compilers,[15] typical contents of biographies there,[16] and so forth. Few of the studies venture to dwell at length on the question of the development of the genre,[17] and even fewer try to discern a relationship between this development and stations of change in Islamic society and civilization across time.[18] Though admitted,[19] this aspect of studying biographical dictionaries remains almost absent; generally, one gets perceptive remarks about the genre,[20] but the remarks are not linked to social and cultural development.

It is this last idea that the present paper wishes to investigate. The investigation is based on my belief that biographical dictionaries are indeed a mirror in which are reflected some important aspects of the intellectual and cultural development of the Islamic community, at least in the first nine centuries of Islamic civilization. What this study will attempt to do is to highlight these aspects by concentrating mainly, but not exclusively, on the inner structure and organization of biographical dictionaries, produced during these early centuries of Islam.

But let me, before going into the heart of the topic, define what I mean precisely by "biographical dictionaries." This is necessary not only because there is no equivalent in Arabic for the term "biographical dictionaries" (although the expressions "*kutub al-ṭabaqāt*"[21] [books on "classes"] or "*kutub al-tarājim*" [books on biographies] are frequently used), but also, and more importantly, because there are many genres of writing that come close to being identified as biographical dictionaries when they are, strictly speaking, not: one is to be reminded of how closely biographical dictionaries have been associated with history for example.[22] Thus, a biographical dictionary, as I would define it, is a prose work whose primary structure is that of a series of biographies, regardless of the order in which these biographies succeed each other.

According to this definition, the works that fall into the category of biographical dictionaries in the Arabic Islamic library can be one of two kinds. The first is what I would call "general biographical dictionaries." These works include: biographies of individuals from all walks of life, professions, epochs, places, ranks, beliefs, and so forth. Two good examples of this kind are Ṣalāḥ al-Dīn al-Ṣafadī's (d. 764/1362) voluminous *al-Wāfī bi-al-wafayāt* and Ibn al-ʿImad al-Ḥanbalī's (d. 1089/1678) large *Shadharāt al-dhahab*. The second type is what I would term "restricted biographical dictionaries," dictionaries which contain biographies of individuals who share one common, yet specific, trait. Most frequently these individuals belong to the same discipline of scholarship: Jalal al-Din al-Suyuṭi's (d. 911/1505) *Ṭabaqāt al-mufassirīn* records only the biographies of the interpreters of the Qur'an; Jamāl al-Dīn al-Mizzī's (d. 742/1341) *Tahdhīb al-kamāl* those of the transmitters of hadith; Abū Isḥāq al-Shirāzī's (d. 476/1083) *Ṭabaqāt al-fuqahā'* those of the jurists; ʿIzz al-Dīn Ibn al-Athīr's (d. 630/1232) *Usd al-ghābah* those of the companions of the Prophet; Ibn Qutaybah's (d. 276/989) *al-Shiʿr wa-al-shuʿarā'* those of the poets; al-Qifṭī's *Inbāh al-rūwāt* those of the grammarians and philologists; pseudo-Abū Sulaymān al-Manṭiqī al-Sijistānī's (d. ca. 380/990) *(Muntakhab) Ṣiwān al-ḥikmah* those of philosophers, both Greek and Muslim; and Yaqūt al-Ḥamawī's (d. 626/1228) *Muʿjam al-udabā'* (known as *Irshād al-arib ilā maʿrifat al-adīb*) those of the compilers among the litterateurs, for example. Often, too, these "restricted dictionaries" record the biographies of individuals who share a certain theological or religious orientation, like Ibn al-Murtaḍá's (d. 840/1436) *Ṭabaqāt al-muʿtazilah*, for the Muʿtazili theologians of the Muslim community until the time of the author, and Abu Nuʿaym al-Iṣfahānī's (d.430/1038) *Ḥilyat al-awliyā'*, for the Muslim ascetics and the Sufis until his day. Others include entries on those individuals who have lived in or passed by a particular city or district, such as al-Khaṭīb al-Baghdādī's (d. 463/1070) *Ta'rīkh Baghdād*, which records the biographies of figures connected with the city of Baghdad, or Ḥamzah ibn Yūsuf al-Sahmī's (d.427/1035) *Ta'rīkh Jurjān*, which has entries only for the scholars connected with the town of Jurjān. In still other works, the individuals entered all belong to a particular profession, as one finds in Muḥammad ibn Khalaf Wākī's (d.306/918) *Akhbār al-quḍāt*, for the judges, and Ibn Abi Uṣaybiʿah's (d. 668/1270) *ʿUyūn al-anbā' fi ṭabaqāt al-aṭibbā'*, for the physicians and related medical professionals. Or, in other instances, those covered may be individuals who share a peculiar characteristic, no matter how significant or insignificant it is for their work, such as Abū Ḥātim al-Sijistānī'a (d. 248/862) *al-Muʿammarūn wa-al-waṣayā*, which has entries for prominent figures known for longevity, Ṣalāh al-Dīn al-Ṣafadī's *Nakt al-himyān fi nukat al-ʿumyān*, whose entries deal with blind men, and al-Jāḥiẓ's (d. 255/868) larger *al-Burṣān wa-al-ʿurjān wa-al-ʿumyān wa-al-ḥūlān*, which handles the biographies of litterateurs who were lepers, lame, blind, and squint-eyed.

What this definition would exclude are works whose primary structure is not that of a series of biographies, in spite of the fact that they may contain a large number of biographies, and, in fact the biographies included in them may be an essential component of the books, and may be extremely useful for the researchers. Books on genealogies, *ansāb*, for example, often look as if they were biographical dictionaries, but they really are not, since the primary criterion in them is the tribe, clan, and so forth. Accordingly, a work very rich in biographies like al-Baladhuri's (279/892) *Ansāb al-ashrāf* is not to be considered among the biographical dictionaries, for it is, essentially, an indirect history of the early Muslim community as it is envisioned through the achievements of its prominent Arab men. Similarly, several annalistic histories, such as those of al-Ṭabarī (d. 310/922) and Ibn Taghribirdī (d. 874/1470), which often include biographies of individuals at the end of the historical reportings of many years, are by no means biographical dictionaries, just as geographical dictionaries containing many biographies, such as Yaqut al-Ḥamawi's *Muʿjam al-buldān*, are not either, because the city, district, or locale is their primary structural criterion. On a more subtle level, a great deal of biographical information, in biographical form, is available in some lexicons, like al-Murtaḍā al-Zabidī's (d. 1205/1790) *Tāj al-ʿarūs* (most frequently under *al-mustadrak* at the end of the entries), or in works which specialize in documenting the correct spelling and pronunciation of proper names, such as Ibn Makūlā's (d. 475/1082) *al-Ikmāl* or Ibn Ḥajar al-ʿAsqalāni's (d. 852/1448) *Tabṣīr al-muntabih*; but, there again, the essential format is not that of biographical dictionaries, properly speaking. Several other kinds of quasi-biographical books also cannot be considered biographical dictionaries since biographies are not the determining factor in their construction. Examples of these include travel books, especially late medieval Maghribi ones, like Ibn Rushayd al-Sabtī's (d. 721/1321) *Riḥlat ibn Rushayd*; bibliographical books, like the famous *al-Fihrist* of Ibn al-Nadīm (d. 380/990 or 412/1021); *mashyakhat* or *baramij* books, that is, books which record the life and times of the authors' teachers,[23] such as the *Mashyakhah* of Ibn al-Jawzi (d. 597/1200) or the *Barnāmaj* of al-Wadi'ashī (d. 749/1338); large compendia which are encyclopaedic in their scope, such as Ibn Faḍl Allāh al-ʿUmarī's (d. 749/1348) *Masalik al-abṣar*, even if their scope were somehow restricted (such as al-Maqqarī's [d. 1041/1631] *Nafḥ al-ṭīb*, which is concerned only with the news of Andalusia); major commentaries on famous, important or widely-read early texts, like Ibn Abī al-Ḥadīd's *Nahj al-balāghah*, which is a commentary on the sayings, orations, and letters of ʿAlī ibn Abī Ṭālib; or even books which are concerned with recording the available information on "the firsts," *awā'il*, that is, the first persons to perform certain things, such as Abū Hilāl al-ʿAskarī's (d. 395/1004) *Kitāb al-awā'il*.

With this clarification out of the way, we can now begin to look at the manner in which the biographical dictionaries reflected some traits of the intellectual and cultural development of the Muslim community in the first nine centuries of Islamic civilization.

1. One of the most striking features of the Arabic biographical dictionaries is that they do not make their appearance until the beginning of the third/ninth century, the two earliest extant dictionaries[24] being Ibn Sa'd's (d. ca. 230/845) *Kitāb al-ṭabaqāt al-kabīr* and Ibn Sallām al-Jumāḥi's (d. ca. 231/846) *Tabaqat fuḥūl al-shu'arā'*. This by itself is a significant fact, for it indicates that the genre of biographical dictionaries evolved in Islamic civilization at the time when that civilization was beginning to develop a clear self-image, and when it was reaching towards formalizing its stances. It is therefore a genre which is by no means "preliminary" or "simple"; it is one which belongs to the age of the maturing of the civilization in which it arose. This is further confirmed by the fact that this genre was preceded by a presumably simpler genre of writing, namely that of the single biography, or monograph.[25] Unfortunately, none of these monographs, with the exclusion of the Prophet Muhammad's *Sīrah*, have survived. However, Ibn al-Nadīm's *Fihrist* provides us with ample examples of them, such as Abū Mikhnaf's (d. 157/774) *Kitāb al-Mukhtār ibn Abī 'Ubayd* and *Kitāb Zayd ibn 'Alī*,[26] Ibn al-Kalbī's (d. 206/821) *Akhbār al-'Abbās ibn 'Abd al-Muṭṭalib* and *Kitāb Musaylimah al-kadhdhāb wa-Sijāh*,[27] and al-Haytham ibn 'Adī's (d. 207/822) *Kitāb akhbār Ziyād ibn Abīhi* and *Akhbār al-Ḥasan ibn 'Alī wa-wafatihi*.[28] These and similar works must have been among the basic sources for the early biographical dictionaries. What the biographical dictionaries essentially did was to compile them and to create from them, in addition to other historical and literary sources, complex and elaborate structures.

But perhaps the best evidence we have of the complexity and maturity of the genre of biographical dictionaries in its earliest stages is the structure of the dictionaries themselves. For an examination of the structures of the two works mentioned above (Ibn Sa'd's and Ibn Sallām's) reveals that their authors were struggling hard to simplify complex material, and, where possible, to create clear and comprehensible presentations of their materials, go beyond the unitary vision of things dictated by the earlier, single-format works, and present comprehensive and global visions of the two disciplines they were addressing in their works.

Of the two earliest dictionaries, Ibn Sa'd's *Ṭabaqāt* is the more complex and much longer one,[29] for in it the author uses so many criteria in organizing his material that one senses that he is working against serious odds to achieve clarity side by side with comprehensiveness. The work is without an introduction; it begins with a lengthy *Sīrah*, biography, of the Prophet, together with an account of the *maghāzi*, the early campaigns. Immediately following the Prophet's biography, there is what amounts to a statement of purpose: "Naming those whom we have counted from the companions of the Messenger of God, from the *Muhajirūn* and the *Anṣār*, and those who lived after them from their offspring (*abnā'ihim*) and their followers, of the people of knowledge (*fiqh*), learning (*ʿilm*), and transmission of *ḥadīth*, and what has come down to us about their names, genealogies, agnomens (*kunā*), and reports (*ṣifātihim*), class by class (*ṭabaqatan ṭabaqah*)."[30] This sentence gives us a clear idea of the comprehensiveness that the author is aiming for; it does not, however, tell us how he is going to arrange the massive amount of material he has: the biographies of the religious scholars who lived in the first two centuries of Islam. In the next main part of the book, however, the reader begins to have a sense of the arrangement. This second part covers the biographies of the Prophet's Companions, and its organization indicates that the author has decided to choose the criterion of "*sābiqah*" (precedence of priority in accepting Islam) in arranging his entries. Thus, the biographies of first converts to Islam—those who fought in the first major battle which the Prophet fought (the battle of Badr, in the year 2 A.H.)—are entered first. But within this section, another criterion is introduced, namely that of the precedence of the *Muhājirūn* (mainly the earliest Meccan converts from the tribe of Quraysh) over the *Anṣār* (mainly the later converts from the city of Medina): a tribal/place criterion. In the next section, this criterion is dropped, and the *sābiqah* criterion is resumed, so that the biographies of both the *Muhājirūn* and the *Anṣār* who fought at the battle of Uḥud (in the year 3 A.H.) and the following battles are mentioned, albeit only if they had been among the emigrants to Abyssinia—still an additional criterion. The last section retains the *sābiqah* criterion, with a slight twist to it: it includes the biographies of the Muslims who accepted Islam prior to the conquest of Mecca (in the year 8 A.H.). This section concludes the first part on the Companions of the Prophet.

In the following part, which covers most of the remainder of the book, the author abandons the *sābiqah* criterion completely and assumes two concurrent criteria: place and time. Accordingly, the biographies of the Followers of Medina—the Prophet's adopted city—are, first, followed by the biographies of the Followers of Mecca, then those of Ṭā'if, Yemen, Yamāmah, Bahrain, Kufah, Basrah, Wāsiṭ, Madā'in, Baghdad, Khurasān, Syria, the Jazirah, Egypt, then Ayla.[31] Within each of the sections on each center of learning, the biographies are arranged in classes, *ṭabaqāt*, usually carrying an ordinal number, that is, the first *ṭabaqah*, second, third, et cetera. This structure shows not only the place criterion most clearly and the time one a little less,[32] but also the factor of transmission of ḥadīth or religious learning in general, where there are instances when an older person may narrate from a younger one or from a peer. This factor comes into play in particular in the sections on Kufah and Basrah, where there are many sub-sections within a class depending on which scholars the members of this class narrated ḥadīth from. Thus, in the section on Kufah, and within the first class, there are ten sub-sections, each of which includes the biographies of those who narrated ḥadīth from ʿUmar alone,[33] from ʿUmar and ʿ'Alī,[34] from ʿAlī alone,[35] from ʿAlī and Ibn Masʿūd,[36] from Ibn

Mas'ūd alone,[37] and so forth. The presence of this factor in the two sections of this third part is so strong that it amounts to being an independent, additional criterion, thus adding all the more to the complexity of the book's structure. The book ends with a special part on women, with no subdivision.[38] There the criterion of *sābiqah*/time/piety/fame come into play all at once.

The conclusion one can draw from this analysis is that Ibn Sa'd, in the earliest surviving biographical dictionary, achieved comprehensiveness and attempted to achieve clarity regardless of complexity. In spite of all the intertwined criteria, clarity was not far from being reached: we have a large eight-volume work,[39] with over 4,250 entries, recording the biographies of the Companions of the Prophet, then of the Followers of the Companions, then their Followers, then of the Muslim women who played a role in early Islamic society and Islamic learning. It must be noted, however, that the complexity of the work was bound to be overwhelming for any author attempting this genre at such an early point in Islamic culture. The result was that many prominent Muslims came to have more than one biography in the book, simply because they fulfilled several of the criteria the author was struggling to organize and put under control. Also, some information is repeated in several places in the book (though sometimes in different versions), thus pointing to the hardships endured in compiling this pioneering biographical dictionary.

In Ibn Sallām's *Ṭabaqāt*,[40] no such overlapping takes place and no poet has more than one entry. The book is better controlled, with a relatively lengthy introduction on literary criticism and the author's method. Ibn Sallām explains that he is going to divide the Arab poets into two main groups: the pre-Islamic poets and the Islamic poets. Within each group, he is going to have ten classes, and in each class there will be biographies of four poets who are similar to each other in poetical achievement. The book, then, takes into consideration two main criteria: time, then artistic achievement/fame. In general, the book has a much clearer structure; it is also much shorter and its material is more limited. And yet, signs of pioneering efforts persist. The time factor is not always an absolute one: the biographies of the "*mukhadramūn*," that is, poets who lived partially after its advent, are sometimes put among those of the pre-Islamic poets and sometimes among those of the Islamic ones. The number of classes selected and the strict number of four within each class is so arbitrary that it defies explanation, inasmuch as it is sometimes very difficult to figure out why certain poets were lumped together in one class. But, we have to remember, all this is the result of the struggle of an ambitious author treading on strange, virgin soil: he tries his best, and achieves as much as he can.

This analysis of the inner structure of the two earliest of our biographical dictionaries, written at the beginning of the third/ninth century, point out that in addition to the attempt at complexity and comprehensiveness at that moment in time in Islamic civilization, the civilization had already begun to mature and define itself more clearly.

Ibn Sallām's dictionary is but a culmination of that civilization's enduring tendency to compare and contrast poets in terms of output and artistic achievement—eventually with fame. It is a record of the "*fuḥūl*" among the poets, the best of them, that is, those who set the linguistic and artistic standards for other poets for a long time. On the other hand, Ibn Sa'd's dictionary is, above all, a presentation of the self-image of Islamic civilization at that time, which considered participation in Islamic learning a criterion for prominence in it. And the details of that structure reveal without doubt the importance of the idea of the *sābiqah* which was developing then: the earlier one adhered to Islam, the higher his position in learning would be. Thus the Companions come before the Followers. Interestingly enough, the criterion of tribe or tribal grouping had great significance, too. In the Companions' part, the biographies of the *Muhājirūn* come before those of the *Anṣār*: the Quraysh comes first. The Quraysh is the tribe of the Prophet, and Ibn Sa'd is telling us that the Prophet has a special position. This is why Ibn Sa'd's work begins with Muḥammad's *Sīrah*, and two volumes, or almost a quarter of the work, are accorded to it. But the Quraysh is also the stock of the caliphs, the supreme rulers of the Islamic community, now already in power for two centuries. The Quraysh are also the paramount notables, *ashrāf*, among the Arab Muslims. Thus, even after centuries of urbanization and of Islamization of non-Arabs, the supreme Arab tribe, that of the Prophet and the caliphs, is still accorded a distance treatment (cf. Baladhurī's *Ansāb al-ashrāf*). On the other hand, we have to remember that the *Muhājirūn* mean also Meccans versus Medinans. The precedence of the first vis-à-vis the second, however, is adhered to by the author only in the Companions' part; in the Followers' part, the order is reversed: Medina comes first and is then followed by Mecca. But this is understandable. Islamic civilization then saw Medina as THE center of learning since the main Companions lived in it after the death of the Prophet, and it was in Medina that the Followers took their religious knowledge from the Companions. Medina was also the capital of the first caliphs, the center of the emerging Islamic state, the heir to which was the contemporary Islamic state. After Ibn Sa'd is through with Medina and Mecca, he opts for treating other centers of learning in Arabia, and then he moves to Iraq. In the section on Iraq, he begins with Kufah rather than Basrah, a fact which is significant. Kufah, again, was a kind of capital for a part of rule of the last "Rāshidi" caliph, 'Alī; also, more Followers who had transmitted ḥadīth and religious learning from the Companions lived there. These two facts, at least, give it precedence over Basrah, in the view of the formative scholars of the early third/ninth century. But Kufah also, much more than Basrah, was the center of the largest number of religious controversies; hence the introduction by the author of the criterion of "the narrator": who your authority is in learning affects the stance you take on various issues, be they legal, political, or theological. The overall image of the Islamic community, as advanced by Ibn Saʿd, is represented by its religious scholars, after the part on the Companions; the mere division of the book into locales, places, or centers of learning indicates how the early Muslims saw their tradition, as one that grew in separate milieus (hence the contemporaneous *riḥlah fī ṭalab al-ʿilm*). Finally, Ibn Saʿd's handling of women in a separate part is indicative of the view Islamic civilization then took of women's role, as one which is distinct from the role of men in religious learning: the criteria that apply to the latter need not apply to the first.

2. Looking again at the two earliest biographical dictionaries, one cannot but be struck by the fact that the genre of biographical dictionaries deals with the fields of poetry and religious learning, with an underlying, hidden stratum of history. This is significant, for it indicates that at the time when Islamic civilization had begun to define itself, at the beginning of the third/ninth century, poetry and religious learning came to the forefront as fundamental, defining criteria. Hardly anything need be said about religious learning: without adherence to Islamic learning, its roots as well as its perpetuation, there is no such thing as Islamic civilization, and this is precisely the message of our earliest biographical author, Ibn Saʿd. As for poetry, and *Arabic* poetry in particular, it is the most firmly rooted *pre*-Islamic genre which continued in great force after Islam, in spite of early Islamic reservations about its sources and function. This is not the right place to go into the reasons for this continuation; what is relevant to our discussion here is that the major figures in this genre get their biographies recorded at the same time as the religious scholars do, right at the outset of the self-definition of Islamic civilization. Does one sense a dichotomy here? Only in appearance, perhaps, but not in reality. After all, our first comprehensive biographer of the poets chose the *fuḥūl* from those poets. The meaning of the word "*fuḥūl*" is ambiguous, but it must include at least two things: the artistic and the linguistic abilities of the poets concerned. The artistic component keeps us in the realm of poetry proper, but the linguistic component takes us a little out of it, into an area which brings us back to the religious sphere: Arabic is, after all, the language of the Qur'an. This way, poetry becomes a supporting factor for the definition of a civilization which conceived of itself as primarily religious.

The role of history alongside the two fields of religious learning and poetry at the outset of the genre of biographical dictionaries is quite obvious. In order to be comprehensive requires in the first place that one think in historical terms. Actually, the criterion of time, or a certain chronological setup, is present in both works we have been discussing.[41]

3. The two books under study can be the starting point for examining yet another way in which the biographical dictionaries of the Arabic Islamic library reflected important traits of the intellectual development of the Muslim community. This way revolves around the question of specialization.

One of the most striking things about biographical dictionaries is that they were, right from the start of the genre, and for at least the four following centuries, solely of the "restricted" rather than the "general" kind:[42] most of them dealt with specific fields mostly, although some of them were restricted by criteria other than field. This field-related restriction makes them, in a way, "specialized" books: one does not look up biographies of other than poets in Ibn Sallam's *Ṭabaqāt*, nor for biographies of other than religious authorities in Ibn Saʿd's *Ṭabaqāt*. This phenomenon needs explanation, for an observer of any given civilization might expect the reverse: that within a certain genre there should be a tendency towards recording the general first, then the particular. We must not forget two things, however. The first is that the genre of biographical dictionaries belongs to the age of maturity of early Islamic civilization, not of infancy; and the second is that this civilization perceived itself primarily as a religious one, with a necessary linguistic component and a linguistic/poetic one. Specialization was unavoidable; indeed, it is a marker of the civilization at hand. A comparison of the genre of early biographical dictionaries with the related genre of history in its early stages, for example, shows that the tendency towards specialization rather than generality is common between them; it is even stronger in the early historical works than it is in the early biographical dictionaries, as the chapter on the historians in Ibn al-Nadīm's *Fihrist* shows.

But there is something else to note with regard to "specialization" in the development of the genre of biographical dictionaries, namely that with the passage of time, the tendency towards specialization actually increases. Whereas *all* the religious scholars are biographical subjects in Ibn Saʿd's dictionary, a few decades later, Bukhari (d. 256/869) includes in his *al-Ta'rīkh al-kabīr* only the biographies of the ḥadīth transmitters; and, two centuries later, Abū Isḥāq al-Shirāzī includes in his *Ṭabaqāt al-fuqahā'* only the biographies of the jurists. The circle becomes even narrower, and more specialized, later on. Instead of al-Shirāzī's jurists of all schools, we begin to observe, after him, dictionaries concerned only with jurists from the Maliki (e.g. al-Qāḍī ʿIyād's [d. 544/11491 *Tartīb al-madārik*), Ḥanafi (e.g. Ibn Abī al-Wafā''s [d. 775/1373] *al-Jawāhir al-muḍiyah*), Ḥanbali (e.g. Ibn Abū Yaʿla al-Farrā's [d. 526/1131] *Ṭabaqāt al-hanābilah*) or Shāfiʿi (e.g. Tāj al-Dīn al-Subki's [d. 771/1369] *Ṭabaqāt al-shafiʿiyah al-kubrā*) rites. And instead of Bukhārī's ḥadīth transmitters, we get special books on reliable transmitters (e.g. al-Mizzī's *Tahdhīb al-kamāl*), or fairly reliable transmitters (e.g., Shams al-Dīn al-Dhahabī's [d. 748/1374] *Mizān al-iʿtidāl*), or weak transmitters (e.g., Ibn Ḥajar's *Lisān al-mizān*). What this tells us is that although the genre of biographical dictionaries began as a specialized genre, its specialization was limited to what the civilization perceived as *broadly* indicative of itself; it was an "inclusive" rather than an "exclusive" kind of specialization. As for later "sub-specialization" within the genre, it was bound to happen, as the civilization became more and more advanced and sophisticated. Paradoxically, the writing of general rather than restricted biographical dictionaries began quite late in Islamic civilization, six and a half centuries after the advent of Islam, with Ibn Khallikān's (681/1282) *Wafayāt al-aʿyān*. But, again, this is quite natural. A great deal of time was needed before one could see the general picture and record biographies of distinguished men in all fields, places, eras, and walks of life.

4. Another feature of biographical dictionaries that appeared rather late in the history of the development of the genre is that of the "continuation," *dhayl*. By "continuation" I mean that a compiler would take the biographical dictionary of a predecessor, possibly, but not necessarily together with the predecessor's criteria, and, write his own biographical dictionary, including the biographies of the people who lived in the period between the predecessor's time and his own. Interestingly enough, this phenomenon appeared for the first time not in the Islamic East but in the Islamic West, in Andalusia and the Maghrib. The first person to attempt it was Ibn Bashkūwāl (d. 578/1183);[43] the very title of his book, *Kitāb al-ṣilah* [= the book of addendum], clearly conveys a sense of "continuation," and the book is indeed a continuation of Ibn al-Faraḍi's (404/1013) *Ṭabaqāt al-fuqahā' wa-al-rūwat lil-ʿilm bi-al-Andalus*, on Andalusian religious scholars. Ibn Bashkūwāl's book itself was picked up for continuation in the following century, when Ibn al-Abbār (d. 658/1259), again with an indicative, explicit title, wrote his longer *Kitāb al-takmilah* [= the book of supplement] *li-kitāb al-ṣilah*. A few decades later, Ibn ʿAbd al-Malik al-Marrākishī (d. 703/1303) did the same thing with Ibn al-Abbār's book in his large compendium, *al-Dhayl wa-al-takmilah wa-al-mawṣūl baʿd al-ṣilah*. As the title indicates, this book was meant by the author to be not simply a continuation but also a comprehensive record of the Andalusian and Maghribi scholars until his time, hence the duplication in it of some of the previously recorded biographies.

The phenomenon of continuing the work of a previous compiler in biographical dictionaries is, in my opinion, indicative of the confidence that this genre gained over time, and hence its emergence rather late, a number of centuries after the genre had made its first appearance. The fact that it surfaced for the first time in Andalusia and the Islamic West has its cultural significance. At the time when Ibn Bashkūwāl wrote his *Kitāb al-ṣilah*, there was a great deal of intellectual restlessness in Andalusia, expressed in the form of a rebellion against servility to the Islamic East, against considering Andalusia a mere subservient follower of the cultural traditions of the East, or an echoer of every line of intellectual or artistic production taking place there. The most outspoken intellectuals to express this rebellion are three of Andalusia's greatest thinkers and historians: Ibn Ḥazm (d. 456/1064), Ibn Ḥayyān (d. 469/1076), and Ibn Bassām (d. 542/1147).[44] In fact, Ibn Ḥazm wrote a whole treatise on the merits of the Andalusians (*Risālah fī faḍl ahl al-Andalus*),[45] whose main message was that the Andalusians made their own undoubted original contribution to Islamic civilization and culture, and his treatise was soon complemented by other Andalusian intellectuals.[46] Ibn Bassām, in the introduction to his huge biographical compendium, *al-Dhakhīrah fī maḥāsin ahl al-Jazīrah*, quoted Andalusia's great historian, Ibn Ḥayyān, in his rebellion against servility to the traditions of the East, and after that he went on to record the biographies of his Andalusian contemporaries from the litterateurs in the rest of his book. It appears to me that by using the "continuation" format to record the biographies of the religious scholars up to their respective times, what Ibn Bashkūwāl, Ibn al-Abbār, and Ibn 'Abd al-Malik were doing was to precisely highlight the Islamic West's continued tradition of original scholarship—and on its own; hence the close relationship between the appearance of this phenomenon in the genre of biographical dictionaries and in the Islamic West.

The genre, having taken this direction, could not remain restricted to the West, but was bound to come to the East. Only a few decades after Ibn Bashkūwāl wrote his first continuation, Ibn al-Dabithī (d. 637/1239), in the East, wrote a continuation to al-Khatīb al-Baghdādi's (d. 463/1070) *Tā'rīkh Baghdād*, entitled *Dhayl tā'rīkh madinat al-salām Baghdād*. In this work, Ibn al-Dabithī brought up to date the biographies of long- and short-term residents of Baghdad who contributed to Islamic civilization. Shortly thereafter, another, longer continuation to the same book appeared, Ibn al-Najjār's (d. 643/1245) *Dhayl tā'rīkh Baghdād*. A similar process was undertaken a century later by Ibn Shākir al-Kutubi (d. 763/1361), who, in his *Fawāt al-wafayāt*, recorded and brought up to date the biographies which were left out by Ibn Khallikān (in his *Wafayāt al-a'yān*), and brought them up to date. At the same time, al-Kutubi's contemporary, al-Ṣafadī (d. 763/1361), wrote a comprehensive biographical dictionary, his voluminous *al-Wāfī bi-al-wafayāt*, duplicating most of the biographies present in Ibn Khallikān's and Ibn Shākir al-Kutubi's dictionaries, thereby doing the same thing Ibn 'Abd al-Malik al-Marrākishi did with the works of Ibn Bashkūwāl and Ibn al-Abbār in the Islamic West.

5. Going back to the inner structure of the biographical dictionaries, one notes that, with the passage of time, these structures become smoother and easier for the user to handle. It was noted above how the signs of complexity, and even abstruseness, marred the structures of the earliest dictionaries (Ibn Sa'd's and Ibn Sallām's), making it frequently impossible to predict where a particular biography is to be found, and making it very difficult to use these books without the help of indexes—unless one reads the books in their entirety, of course. This changed rather quickly, progressing step by step. A few decades after these two works appeared, Bukhārī (d. 256/870) produced his *al-Ta'rīkh al-kabīr*, including in it brief biographies of the transmitters of ḥadīth. At almost the same time, Ibn Ḥibbān al-Busti (d. 254/868) wrote his *Kitāb al-majrūḥīn*.

The structure of these latter two dictionaries clearly represent attempts at smoothness; their order is, in principle, based on the letters of the alphabet in their oriental sequence. But the smoothness does not go very far: only the first letter of the first name of a given ḥadīth-transmitter is taken into consideration. Thus people with names like "Ibrahīm," "Aḥmad," "Isḥāq," and "Adam" come first simply because the first letter of their names is an *alif*. Within this letter, as in all other letters, however, there is no particular order whatsoever: the second letter of the name is not taken into consideration, nor the following letters in the first names. The reader thus knows approximately where the biographies of certain persons are going to be, but only within the large range of the first letter of their first names. A mechanism for smoothness, is, however, added by Bukhārī (and Ibn Ḥibbān) to make things a little easier for the user: all the biographies of persons with the same first name are grouped together. Thus, for example, all the "Ibrahims" are grouped together, and all the "Muḥammads" are grouped together. This structure proved to be quite influential in the early history of the genre of biographical dictionaries, especially in the field of ḥadīth-transmission, maybe due to the great stature of Bukhārī and Ibn Ḥibbān. Almost a century after these two scholars, al-ʿUqayli (d. 322/934) used their structure in compiling his *Kitāb al-duʿafā' al-kabīr*, and Ibn Abī Ḥātim al-Rāzi (d. 327/938) used it in putting into final form what were mainly his father's notes, his voluminous *Kitāb al-jarḥ wa-al-taʿdīl*.

It was not until the seventh/thirteenth century that complete smoothness was reached in the inner structures of biographical dictionaries, and that came with the appearance of Yaqūt al-Ḥamawī's *Muʿjam al-udabā'* (or *Irshād al-arīb*). From the time that book appeared onwards, the arrangement of biographies in biographical dictionaries became more and more frequently alphabetical, with all the letters of the first name, as well as those of the father's name, and sometimes even the grandfather's name, being taken into consideration. This phenomenon came rather late in the genre of biographical dictionaries in Islamic civilization, but here again, the amount of time needed for the establishment of and confidence in a tradition has to be taken into account. It is to be noted that although the smoother style came to be dominant in the majority of the biographical dictionaries produced, traces of the older, Bukhari/Ibn Ḥibbān style did not disappear. Thus it is that some of our most influential later books carry those traits, namely al-Khaṭīb al-Baghdādi's (d. 464/1071) *Ta'rīkh Baghdād*, and, to a lesser extent, Ibn Khallikān's *Wafayāt al-aʿyān*.

6. In al-Khaṭīb al-Baghdādi's book, there appears another characteristic of some, but not many, of the later biographical dictionaries in regard to the degree of strictness to which their authors adhered to alphabetical arrangement. Like Bukhārī, al-Khaṭīb adhered only to partial, rather than to full, alphabetization. He followed Bukhārī in another very interesting phenomenon, namely

that he set aside the biographies of those persons called "Muḥammad" and began his book with them, and only after that did he go to the normal sequence of the letters of the alphabet, beginning with the letter *alif*. Why Bukhārī and al-Khaṭīb chose that particular break from the order that they otherwise adhered to in their respective books is not difficult to explain. "Muḥammad" is the name of the Prophet, and it is in deference to him that anybody called by his name is given precedence over people called by other names. In other words, this is an act of piety. Mixing piety with scholarship in a civilization that perceives itself primarily as religious is not strange at all; indeed, one may expect more such expressions of piety. One does find these, in fact. In later works, one meets some biographical dictionaries which not only begin with the "Muḥammads," but also give precedence to the "ʿAbd Allāhs" within the compound names starting with the letter *ʿayn* (ʿAbd al-Raḥmān, ʿAbd al-Malik, ʿAbd al-Waḥīd, etc.)—a thing that breaks their alphabetical structures much more than does beginning them with the "Muḥammads." A good example of this is al-Ṣafadī's *al-Wāfī bi-al-wafayāt*, which begins with the "Muḥammads" and puts the "ʿAbd Allāhs" before the other compound names within the letter *ʿayn*. Ibn Ḥajar's *Tahdhīb al-tahdhīb* does not begin with the "Muạmmads," but its author follows al-Ṣafadī in giving priority to the "ʿAbd Allāhs" within the letter *ʿayn*. All this is done, again undoubtedly, as an expression of piety: Allāh's name should precede any other names (although al-Raḥmān, al-Malik, al-Waḥīd, etc., too, are names of God, but they are descriptive in nature). As acts of piety, such interference with the normal order of the biographical materials was bound to increase rather than decrease with the passage of time: in religious civilizations, the farther away one is from the source, the more one is desirous of expressing piety.

7. Returning to the issue of smoothness, one notes that with the development of the genre of biographical dictionaries and its increasing tendency to make its materials more easily accessible to the readers, methods of organization other than alphabetization were used. The most notable method used is that of arranging biographies within fixed time spans or periods, though arbitrary they may often be. The seeds of this system, it appears to me, were sown by Bukhārī's *al-Ta'rīkh al-ṣaghīr*, a relatively short biographical dictionary whose biographies are arranged, in principle, according to time spans. These time spans, however, are not always the same: the first time period is defined by the lifetime of the first prominent men of Islam, the Prophet and the first four caliphs, that is, until the year 40 A.H. After that, decades are used: "[the biographies of those who died between [the years] 40 [A.H.] and 50 [A.H.]," and so on. Decade-long spans are adhered to in much of the book, but sometimes they change to spans of five years (e.g., the years 211 to 215, 216 to 220), and, towards the end of the book, beginning with the year 250, they change to one-year time spans.

But this was only the beginning, and beginnings are normally rather crude. With time, this system was refined and it became a prime server of the principle of smoothness and ease. Most frequently, time spans of either decades or centuries were used. A good example of the first is the biographical part of al-Dhahabi's comprehensive *Ta'rīkh al-Islām*. An example of the latter is Tāj al-Dīn al-Subki's *Ṭabaqāt al-shafi'īyah al-kubrá*, a dictionary of the scholars who followed the Shafi'i rite in law. This book is structured according to centuries, but not for convenience, rather because al-Subki believed that a paramount position should be given to the tradition of the Prophet which says that there will be a reformer (*mujaddid*) of Islam at the beginning of every century. According to al-Subki, the reformer at the top of the second century [A.H.] was al-Shāfi'ī himself, the founder of the Shāfi'ī school (d. 204/819). Every following century until al-Subki's time is shown to have had one great scholar, the reformer, and he is, of course, from the Shāfi'ī school; in al-Subki's book, this reformer normally gets a very long biography within that particular century. By choosing this particular structure for his biographical dictionary, then, al-Subki rendered a clear service to his school, in addition to serving the principle of ease and smoothness.

8. Centuries and decades refer to time, But other biographical dictionaries made place the basis of their structures, with or without considerations of time. Those works that took place as their sole criterion are the biographical dictionaries of cities, and those that took both time and place as their joint criteria are some of the biographical dictionaries of litterateurs.

The biographical dictionaries of cities are numerous in the Arabic Islamic library. We have dictionaries of the outstanding men of Damascus, Baghdad, Cairo, Aleppo, Jurjān, Herat, Naysābūr, Isfahan, Granada, Bijayah, and others; even a small town like Dārayyā, in the vicinity of Damascus, found a historian who recorded the biographies of its illustrious men in 'Abd al-Jabbār al-Khawlānī (d. after 365/975), in his *Ta'rīkh Dārayyā*. Two things must be noted about this category of biographical dictionaries. The first is that they begin to appear clearly only by the fourth/tenth century.[47] The second is that the first products in this category, al-Narshakhī's (d. after 322/943) *Ta'rīkh Bukhārā*, and Abū al-'Arab Tamīm's (d. 333/954) *Ṭabaqāt 'ulama' Afrīqīyā wa-Tūnis*, were not centered around any of the larger centers of learning in the heart of the caliphal lands (Damascus, Baghdad, Cordoba, Cairo), but around farther and less central Islamic cities. These two things, when they are put together, are quite telling: the branch of "histories of cities" within the genre of biographical dictionaries is not an early one; it starts with the beginning of the weakening of the central caliphate and the emergence of other centers of political power in the Islamic empire. Narshakhī's book on the history of Bukhārá is a case in point. Although its Arabic original has been lost (only a Persian abridgement has survived[48]), what is certainly known about it is that it was presented in 322/943 to the Samanid *amīr* Naṣr ibn Nūh. As is well known, the Samanids, with their capital at Bukhārā, had been one of the earliest assertive dynasties who in reality, though not in appearance, were practically independent of the central government in Baghdad. As I see it it was only natural that their assertiveness and practical independence should express itself in a separate history of the city of Bukhārā. One finds a similar case in the later work of ʿAbd al-Ghāfir ibn Ismāʿil al-Fārisī's (529/1134), *Kitāb al-siyāq li-ta'rīkh Naysābūr.* This biographical history of the city of Nishapur did not get written until Nishapur had become a regional capital under the Seljuks. Abū al-ʿArab Tamim's book on the scholars of Qayrawān and Tunis also has something to do with assertiveness, albeit in a different way. Abū al-ʿArab wrote his book in a distant province that had already been virtually independent from the central government in Baghdad for over a century, under the Aghlabids. But in the meantime, another power had come to take control in Tunis (in 909): the Ismāʿīlī Shiʿites—the Fatimids. As a staunch Sunni, Maliki scholar, Abū al-ʿArab not only refused to admit the new political realities, he actually fought against them. And one way in which he showed his combative, assertive attitude was by writing a book on the scholars of his proud province in its good, pre-Shiʿite days. Thus, only Sunni, mainly Maliki, scholars are included in his book, and no Ismāʿili Shiʿite ones are mentioned.

Once the "histories of cities" had become a fixed genre, other books on other cities followed. But Baghdad did not get its share until one century and a half after Bukhārā, with al-Khaṭīb al-Baghdādi's *Ta'rīkh Baghdād*, and Damascus had to wait over a century after that to get its own history with Ibn ʿAsākir's (d. 571/1175) *Ta'rīkh madinat Dimashq.*

Finally, whereas most of the biographical dictionaries of cities include the biographies of persons of all disciplines who lived in those cities, there were some works whose biographies were restricted to people of specific disciplines or professions, within specific cities. A good example of this comes, once again, from Andalusian namely al-Khūshāni's (d. 366/976) book on the judges of Cordoba, *Quḍāt Qurṭubah*. Though relatively early, this restriction to the genre never took root in Islamic writing, for understandable reasons, and the books that were produced along its lines remained very few.

9. The regional histories of literature were also late to appear, for reasons similar to those which led to the relatively late appearance of the genre of histories of cities, and none of them appears before the breakup of the central government in Baghdad and the emergence of mini-states, which were often ruled dynastically. The rulers of these states took it upon themselves to play the role of the patrons of art, in imitation of the former, reigning dynasty of the Abbasids and their magnanimous great viziers. Abū Manṣūr al-Thaʿālibī (d. 429/1037) was the first author to attempt such a regional history of literature. In his famous *Yatīmat al-dahr*, he recorded the biographies of only contem-

poraneous and near-contemporaneous literary figures, those of the fourth/tenth and early fifth/eleventh centuries. To this general criterion of time, the more specific criterion of place is added, and is made to act as the basic structural element on the book. As the author says in his introduction, the *Yatīmah* is divided into four "geographical" parts (with a strong "dynastic" slant to most of them):

a. the litterateurs of the Ḥamdanids and the poets of their court (i.e., Aleppo, the Jazīrah, and northern Syria) among others of the litterateurs of Syria, Mosul, and the Maghrib;

b. the litterateurs of Iraq and those connected with the Buyids;

c. the litterateurs of the provinces of al-Jabal, Fars, Jurjān, Ṭabāristān, and the city of Isfahan;

d. the litterateurs of the provinces of Khurasān, especially Nishapur, and Transoxiana. and those connected with the Samanids and the Ghaznavids.[49]

In each of the parts of this main structure, there are sections, or subdivisions, constructed along geographical lines; the biographies of the individual litterateurs fall into the various sections in accordance with the city or region with which they are most closely affiliated. Thus, we have a chapter on the poets of Jurjān, another on the poets of Baghdad, and so forth; even a relatively small town like Bust gets a separate section.

It is not surprising that a number of biographical dictionaries dealing with regional literary history appeared in Andalusia. Here this phenomenon expresses the same vein of self-assertion and rebellion against the accusation of servility to the East that we have met in the "continuation" sub-genre of biographical dictionaries. Ibn Bassām made this very clear in his introduction to *al-Dhakhīrah*, as mentioned above.[50] His book is actually a clear example of a regional literary biographical dictionary which takes the criterion of place, within Andalusia, as a major structural criterion.[51] One gets the biographies of the Central Andalusians, including the Cordobans, first, then the Andalusians of the West, including the Sevilleans, then those of the East, including the Valencians, and finally the biographies of the non-Andalusians who flourished in Andalusia.[52] A century later, another literary history of Andalusia was written, *al-Mughrib fī ḥulá al-Maghrib*, by Ibn Saʿīd al-Andalusī (d. 685/1286). This book also followed the regional divisions, beginning with Western Andalusia, followed by Central Andalusia and ending with Eastern Andalusia.[53]

10. The dictionaries which record the biographies of the Twelver Shiʿites and those of the Sufis require special attention, since their inner structures and the way these structures changed over time are culturally significant.

The first thing one notes about Twelver Shiʿite biographical dictionaries is that none of them appears before the beginning of the fourth/tenth century. This is as understandable as it is significant. The twelfth imam went into occultation in the second half of the third/ninth century, and some time was needed after that to figure out who was going to continue to believe in him, thereby finishing the cycle of adherence to the basic Imami cause. The fourth/tenth century was also the period when Imami theology and law began to crystallize and be articulated in the works of such scholars as al-Kūlīnī (d. 329/941) and al-Shaykh al-Mufīd (d. 412/1022). That compiling biographical dictionaries came about at the same time or slightly thereafter is, thus, entirely understandable.

The first Twelver biographical dictionary we have is that of al-Kishshī (d. ca. 360/970), entitled *Ikhtiyār maʿrifat al-rijāl* or *Rijāl al-Kishshī*. The structure that the author chose for his book is very difficult to ascertain. At first sight the structure seems to be chronological, but then this principle falters here and there; at times one thinks that the order of the biographies follows a vague alphabetical arrangement, but then this principle also falters. Two things make the structure of the book even more obscure. These are the sparsity of dates in the biographies, and the fact that it is so filled with ḥadīth material that one almost loses sight of its essential biographical set-up. All these considerations are culturally significant. Above all, they indicate that, for the Twelver Shiʿites, the vision of what constituted a member of their community had not been sufficiently clarified yet, and that writing a biographical dictionary meant, at that time, embarking on a new genre unattempted before. In this particular respect, the multiplicity of criteria in the inner structure of al-Kishshi's book can perhaps be compared to that of Ibn Saʿd's *Ṭabaqāt*; after all, both were pioneering dictionaries in their respective spheres.

After al-Kishshī, the Twelver Shiʿite biographical dictionaries become clearer in inner structure. One sees this in the two dictionaries which succeeded Kishshī's work immediately, namely al-Najāshī's (d. 450/1058) *Rijāl al-Najāshī* and al-Ṭūsi's (d. 460/1067) *Rijāl al-Ṭūsi*. Since these two authors were contemporaries, it is difficult to ascertain which of their books appeared first. However, judging by the structures of these books, it seems to me that Ṭūsi's *Rijāl* was compiled before al-Najāshī's. The reason is that whereas al-Najāshī arranged his biographies essentially alphabetically (according to the earlier Bukhari model), indicating a simplification and refinement of the genre within Twelver Shiʿism, al-Ṭūsī arranged them according to the rather more complex principle of "discipleship" to the various imams, beginning with the disciples of ʿAli and ending with the disciples of the twelfth imam. Al-Ṭūsī's arrangement, in principle, should have made his biographies roughly chronological in order. But this actually does not happen, especially since one person could have been the disciple of more than one imam, whence his biography would be repeated twice, three times, or even more. To this already complex set-up another factor is added, namely the manner in which the biographies are to be arranged within the discipleship of the individual imam. Al-Ṭūsī chose the rough alphabetical principle (all the people with the same first name are grouped together), thereby easing the flow of his biographies to some extent. The sum total of the situation is that al-Ṭūsī's book reveals certain, if few, traits of struggle with the genre; whence my assumption that it was written before al-Najāshī's only relatively smoothly structured book.

11. The biographical dictionaries of the Sufis are interesting in what they reveal. Like many other sub-genres of biographical dictionaries, they do not begin to appear until quite late, at the beginning of the fifth/eleventh century. As in the case of the Twelver Shiʿite biographical dictionaries, this is as understandable as it is significant. Sufism is a phenomenon that does not belong to the founding decades of Islam, but to a later period, after asceticism had taken root in society and had undergone a deep metamorphosis in the direction of spirituality and social and intellectual complexity. The first book we have of this genre, al-Sulamī's (d. 412/1021) *Ṭabaqāt al-ṣūfīyah*, does not reveal a particular sensitivity to this issue of late date, although one does find in it a certain desire for "historicizing" Sufism. The biographies in the book are arranged chronologically, beginning with the earliest Sufi (al-Fuḍayl ibn ʿIyād) and ending with contemporary Sufis (the last one is Abū ʿAbd Allāh al-Dīnawari), but no attempt is made to consider patricians like ʿAli or al-Ḥasan al-Baṣrī as forerunners of Sufis or as Sufis proper. And the same principles are noted in some of the later dictionaries, such as al-Qushayrī's (d. 465/1072) *al-Risālah al-qushayrīyah*. When, however, one reaches the work of Abū Nuʿaym al-Iṣfahāni (d. 430/1038), his *Ḥilyat al-awliyā'*, the situation changes completely. There, almost all the great figures of Islam who have been known for their outstanding piety, asceticism or great learning are considered "*awliyā*" just like the Sufis. Thus, the biography of the Companion ʿUmar ibn al-Khaṭṭāb stands side by side in the book with that of the Follower al-Ḥasan al-Baṣrī, the jurist al-Shāfiʿi, and the Sufi al-Junayd. The underlying assumption of the author is further strengthened by lengthy citations from the words/works of all those people, giving credibility to the criterion used. Over a century after Abū Nuʿaym, Ibn al-Jawzī (d. 597/1200) had the opportunity to write a biographical dictionary of the Sufis, his *Ṣifat al-ṣafwah*, in whose introduction he criticized Abū Nuʿaym for placing so many non-Sufis among his "*awliyā'*." He, however, not only followed the wide criterion of Abū Nuʿaym, he widened it even further by including in his book a long biography of the Prophet, and a large number of biographies of people without names (for examples *ʿĀbidah min jabal Lubnān*). This way, Sufism, through the later expressions of the genre of biographical dictionaries, was given greater validity, legitimacy, and even roots, in the very foundation of Islam.

CONCLUSIONS

I have tried to examine biographical dictionaries as a cultural and intellectual phenomenon in classical Islamic civilization, rather than as merely a large number of compilations within the Arabic Islamic library. This point of departure permitted me, first, to consider all the biographical dictionaries as variant expressions of one single genre, and, second, to relate the appearance (or lack thereof) of one sub-genre or another of biographical dictionaries to the progressive intellectual and cultural development of the Islamic community in the first nine centuries of Islam. There were several consequences for taking this approach, among them that this paper could not lay any claims to exhaustiveness whatsoever; a single example sufficiently representative of one facet or another of the genre under discussion would be enough. Furthermore, the discussion, in the latter part of the paper, of the biographical dictionaries in some specific areas (Twelver Shiʿism, Sufism) is also not exhaustive; one may wish to experiment with other specific types of biographical dictionaries (those on the philosophers and physicians, for example). But even there the results reached should not be significantly different from what the sample study here offers. On a constructive level, the approach has permitted me to draw some conclusions. The first of these is that the genre of biographical dictionaries emerged only at the time when Islamic civilization was starting to have a definite identity, one which was primarily religious, with a linguistic (Arabic-Qur'anic) and poetic touch to it. In the latter capacity, it portrayed its incorporation of the pre-Islamic Arabic tradition; in the former, although it perceived itself as an heir to the religious heritage of the Near East, it had a definite, specific, individual color to it: an *Islamic* one, with a new beginning to the tradition. It is because of this that the first biographical dictionary we have, Ibn Saʿd's *Ṭabaqāt*, begins with the *Sirah* of the Prophet, and the *Sirah* assumes almost a quarter of the size of his multivolume book. But if the Prophet represents the main symbol of the new identity, others also are made to contribute to this identity and to pose as models for the new community through innumerable details of their lives, careers, behaviors, and attitudes. Moreover, those symbols are judged first and foremost in accordance with their temporal proximity to the new phase of human history; hence the introduction of the criterion of "*sābiqah*" in the first, fundamental part of the book. The second part, based essentially on the criterion of place or locale, is also connected with the nature of the development of the new community. Its habitat now covers (after the conquests) a large area from Egypt in the west to Khurāsān in the east. These new, pride-evoking physical realities bring with them, as the structure of Ibn Saʿd's biographical dictionary would indicate to us, other new realities which may not be as positive as the first, namely that they cause the Muslim authorities to live far apart from each other and to develop variant visions of the new religion; hence the primacy of the "narrator-source" criterion (within the geographical one) in the part on the Followers and their followers in the book. Even if perceived as regrettable, the fact is admitted. And admission means confidence: the variations can be recorded only because the finalization of the identity is already in place, on its way to being complete. Let us remember that Ibn Saʿd wrote his book just at the time when the *miḥnah* was underway, and when the opposition to its course, though small, was not unpromising. A new era was coming, and Ibn Saʿd's biographical dictionary conveys a sense of the approach of the new identity of the majority of the Muslim community, along with the seeds of a final vision of Islam.

The genre of biographical dictionaries, once begun, continued and developed. This development took a clear line of greater specialization, reflecting the further identification of Muslim groups within the community. At the time when Ibn Saʿd was writing, specialization was as yet unclear among the religious authorities. By the next generation, that of Aḥmad ibn Ḥanbal al-Bukhārī, the ḥadīth transmitters had already emerged as a specialized (and victorious) group, after decades of unconscious building of the image (and reality) of that specialty; hence the beginning of a series of biographical dictionaries right from that generation onwards. The jurists came to emerge as a specialized group shortly thereafter. Biographical dictionaries about them, however, did not emerge until much later, in the fifth/eleventh century, and that was due to developments within the ranks of the jurists themselves. Right from the beginning, the jurists posed as representatives of different local traditions (the Ḥijāz, Iraq, Syria, Egypt), thereby ending up with "founding" followers, of "schools," as they are called, each having varying positions in legal details and outlook. It was not until these schools were fully established (with some dying out), at the end of the fourth/tenth century, that the image of the jurists was clear enough to warrant biographical dictionaries which recorded their numbers, views, and achievements; hence the appearance of Abū Isḥāq al-Shīrāzī's *Ṭabaqāt al-fuqahā'* in the fifth/eleventh century. With the development of serious animosities between the schools, however, especially in Baghdad and the East in the fourth/tenth and fifth/eleventh centuries, more specialized biographical dictionaries of the jurists of each school began to be compiled. Something similar happened in the field of ḥadīth, albeit for different reasons, essentially that of authentication—a matter considered of great importance right from the appearance of the first biographical dictionary of the genre, Bukhārī's *al-Ta'rīkh al-kabīr*.

As in the case of the people of ḥadīth and law, other groups came to have biographical dictionaries of their own people, but only after their groups could be identified clearly. Since the identity of the Twelver Shiʿites did not become final until the disappearance of the twelfth imam in second half of the third/ninth century, no Twelver biographical dictionary could appear before the following century. Similarly, the tardiness in the emergence of Sufism until the beginning of the third/ninth century caused the delay in the appearance of the first Sufi biographical dictionary until the next century.

The appearance of biographical dictionaries dealing with people associated with particular cities is related to the emergence of some cities as regional capitals for semi-independent dynasties, the result of a dwindling of the power of the central caliphate; hence its first systematic expressions did not come out before the fourth/tenth century, in connection with cities in the peripheries, not in the center. Bukhārā, the capital of the Samanids, was probably the first to come out. It is to be noted, however, that there are some biographical dictionaries in this sub-genre whose explanation cannot stem from this particular political development, ʿAbd al-Jabbār al-Khawlānī's *Ta'rīkh Dārayyā* being a stark example. In a case such as this, one has to think of the author's individual motives. In the case of ʿAbd al-Jabbār al-Khawlānī, pride in his town and stock was the reason behind his compiling his book. In the cases of the two huge compendia, al-Khaṭib al-Baghdādī's *Ta'rīkh Baghdād* and Ibn ʿAsākir's *Ta'rīkh madinat Dimashq*, the motive was not only pride but also, perhaps, a combination of hope and the fear of change; the winds of change were blowing strongly in Baghdad in the latter half of the fifth/eleventh century, and in Damascus in the latter half of the following century.

Of all the regions addressed by biographical dictionaries in the Arabic Islamic library, Andalusia (and, by extension, the Maghrib) deserves special attention. Its output of biographical dictionaries is connected to a great extent with the intellectual and cultural crisis that its scholars underwent at the beginning of the fifth/eleventh century, following several years of devastating civil strife at the close of the previous century, the notorious "*al-fitnah al-barbarīyah*," and the subsequent loss of political unity in the peninsula. This crisis, as expressed by two of the most towering intellectuals of Andalusia, Ibn Ḥayyān and Ibn Ḥazm, both of whom had witnessed the civil war, centered around the widespread vision that the Andalusians adored any model of thought or literature that came from the East, and that, subsequently, Andalusian literature and thought were a mere imitation of their counterparts in the East; they thus lacked originality and a local identity. It is in this atmosphere that the Andalusian biographical dictionaries grew larger and larger in number. Building on the pre–civil war, though young, tradition of biographical dictionaries (al-Khūshānī's *Quḍāt Qurṭubah* and Ibn al-Faraḍi's *Ṭabaqāt al-ʿulamā' wa-al-rūwāt lil-ʿilm bi-al-Andalus*), the post–civil war authors concentrated heavily on their peninsula, and produced many biographical dictionaries and continuations thereof. It is within this vision that we have to see the biographical dictionaries of Ibn Bassām, Ibn Bashkūwāl, Ibn al-Abbār, Ibn ʿAbd al-Malik al-Marrākishī, Ibn Saʿīd al-Andalusi, and even the later works of Ibn al-Khaṭīb and al-Maqqarī. The large accumulation of literary output was probably at the basis of the appearance of regional literary histories such as al-Thaʿālibī's *Yatīmat al-dahr* and later al-ʿImād al-Katib's *al-Kharīdah*. As expected, Andalusia had its share in this sub-genre.

Although Arabic Islamic biographical dictionaries emerged at the time of the maturity of Islamic civilization, in their first expressions they reveal a relative degree of difficulty in the presentation of their materials. This is due to their attempt at comprehensiveness—a thing quite new in compilation at the beginning of the third/ninth century. What was common before that was the format of the single biography, and they were attempting to put scores of biographies together, making them, at the same time, portray their respective visions of the contemporary stage of the intellectual and cultural development of the Islamic community then. This relative crudeness in inner structure, however, was soon made more refined, and, with the passage of time, achieved complete smoothness when full alphabetization became more or less the standard in compiling biographical dictionaries. It has to be noted, however, that this process took a very long time, and that the cruder forms continued to co-exist with the smoother forms. In the area of ḥadīth in particular, the older forms survived for some time, due to the nature of the discipline (the importance of locating the transmitters in time for the authenticity question), and Dhahabi's huge *Sīyar a'lām al-nubalā'* of the eighth/fourteenth century is an instructive example in this respect. And even when full smoothness was achieved, its form was sometimes interrupted by the piety element (beginning biographical dictionaries with "Muhammads," among other things), making the inner structures of some biographical dictionaries occasionally less than straightforward.

Perhaps what still needs explanation is the whole phenomenon of biographical dictionaries, for it seems that there are few cultures which have been as prolific in producing biographical dictionaries in premodern times as the Arabic branch of Islamic culture.[54] But this is a huge topic that requires separate examination.

NOTES

1. The death date of an author will be mentioned only at the first occurrence of that author's name, unless it proves particularly useful in a certain context to repeat that information.

2. R. S. Humphreys, *Islamic History: A Framework for Inquiry* (revised edition, Princeton, 1991), p. 188.

3. The close association between "*ṭabaqāt*" and "*ta'rīkh*" is very old indeed and dates back to the early stages of the development of the genre in Islam. For one thing, the titles of a sizeable number of biographical dictionaries begin with the word "*ta'rīkh*," history [of], such as Bukhārī's *al-Ta'rīkh al-kabīr* and Ibn 'Asākir's *Ta'rīkh madinat Dimashq* (on which see below). For another, several of the foremost compilers of biographical dictionaries have identified their respective works as works of history. Ibn Khallikan, for example, says in his introduction to his celebrated *Wafayāt al-a'yān*, ed. Iḥsān 'Abbās, 8 vols.

(Beirut, 1971–75), 1:19 (on which see below): "This is a concise work in the science of history [*hadha mukhtaṣarun fi al-ta'rīkh*]"; there is also (perhaps consequently) a discussion as to whether or not Ibn Khallikān's *Wafayāt* is actually his very same *al-Ta'rīkh al-kabīr* (see Iḥsān 'Abbās' study of the *Wafayāt* in *ibid.*, 8:69–71 (of the pagination in Arabic numerals). More significantly, the late medieval Muslim historiographers place the various kinds of biographical dictionaries among the branches of historical writing. The most notable among these are Shams al-Dīn al-Dhahabi (d. 748/1347), whose exposé is preserved in al-Sakhāwī's *al-I'lān bi-al-tawbīkh li-man dhamma al-ta'rīkh* (Cairo, 1349 [A.H.]), pp. 84–108, tr. in F. Rosenthal, *A History of Muslim Historiography* (Leiden, 1952), pp. 316–58; al-Sakhāwī (d. 902/1496), in his *al-I'lan*, ibid., pp. 104–69, tr. Rosenthal, pp. 358–450; Tāshköprüzādah (d. 968/1560), in his *Miftāḥ al-sa'ādah* (second edition, Haydarabad, 1977), 1:231–48, 263–66 (under the rubric *'ilm al-tawārīkh*), tr. Rosenthal, pp. 452–56; and Ḥājjī Khalīfah (d. 1067/1657), in his *Kashf al-ẓunūn 'an asāmī al-kutub wa-al-funūn* (Offset copy of the Istanbul edition, Baghdad, n.d.) 1:271–333 (under the rubric "*'ilm al-ta'rīkh*"), but also 2:1095–1107 (under the rubric "*'ilm al-ṭabaqāt*").

4. Several works on Islamic history and historiography discuss biographical dictionaries. See, in chronological order, H.A.R. Gibb, "Ta'rīkh," in *Encyclopedia of Islam* (first edition), Supplement, pp. 233–45; I. Lichtenstadter, "Arabic and Islamic Historiography," *Muslim World* 35 (1945), pp. 126–32; F. Rosenthal, op. cit., pp. 88–94 and passim.; and R.S. Humphreys, *Islamic History*, op. cit., pp. 188–207 and passim. Sir Hamilton Gibb, in his article "Islamic Biographical Literature" (in *Historians of the Middle East*, ed. B. Lewis and P.M. Holt [London, 1962], p. 54), says that "the composition of biographical dictionaries in Arabic developed simultaneously and in close association with historical composition." Rosenthal (p. 89) goes even further and states that "In many Muslim minds, history thus became synonymous with biography." Much of T. Khalidi's discussion in his article "Islamic Biographical Dictionaries: A Preliminary Assessment," *Muslim World* 63 (1973), pp. 53–65, is based on the relationship between history and biographical dictionary.

5. Rosenthal, op. cit., pp. 88–89, where the biographical component of Greek and Roman historical literature is mentioned.

6. According to Rosenthal (ibid., p. 89), "That biography shared in Muslim historiography from the beginning and that it eventually achieved a dominating position in it is obvious."

7. Ibid., pp. 89–90. Rosenthal mentions among those reasons the interest in the Prophet Muhammad's biography, the dogmatic struggle in Islam, the desire

of the, historians to be useful and employable, and the Muslims' "firm conviction that all politics was the work of individuals and understandable in the light of their personal qualities and experiences. . . .Under the influence of theology, even the history of the various branches of learning was conceived as a collection of biographies of the outstanding scholars" (p. 89). This last point was mentioned also by Gibb in "Islamic Biographical Literature," p. 54.

8. For the brief surveys, see Heffening, "Tabakat," in *Encyclopaedia of Islam* (first edition), Suppl.: 214–15; M. Abiad, "Origine et développement des dictionnaires biographiques arabes," *Bulletin d'Études Orientales* 31 (1979 [1980]), pp. 7–15. For detailed surveys, see I. Hafsi, "Recherches sur le genre tabaqat," *Arabica* 23 (1976), pp. 227–65 and 24 (1977), pp. 1–41, 150–86, which deals with the biographical dictionaries reported in the sources, regardless of whether they have survived or not; P. Auchterlonie, *Arabic Biographical Dictionaries: A Summary Guide and Bibliography* (Durham, 1987), which, contrary to Hafsi's work, lists only the published works, and "only the best-known, fullest and most useful biographical dictionaries" (p. 1). All of the medieval Muslim historiographers mentioned in n. 3 above include in their respective exposés surveys of the biographical dictionaries known to them. See also O. Loth, "Ursprung und Bedeutung der Tabakat vornehmlich der des Ibn Saʿd," *Zeitschrift der Deutschen Morgenlandischen Gesellschaft* 23 (1869), pp. 593–614; G. Levi Della Vida, "Sira," in *Encyclopaedia of Islam* (first edition), 4:439–43; N. Abbott, *Studies in Arabic Literary Papyri, I: Historical Texts* (Chicago, 1957), pp. 5–31, esp. 7–8; W. al-Qāḍī, "Biography," in *Companion to Arabic Literature*, ed. J. Meisami (London: Routledge, forthcoming).

9. In particular, the works of Gibb and Khalidi mentioned above, but mainly those of Rosenthal and Humphreys. Hafsi's long article has many analytical insights, but its structure does not permit these insights to stand out clearly.

10. Khalidi, for example, says (p. 55): "The final purpose, for all these writers, is moral edification and/or the acquisition of a skill which would enable the Muslim to understand and practice his religion to better advantage." Gibb's concept (p. 54) is more complex: "the conception that underlies the older biographical dictionaries is that the history of the Islamic community is essentially the contribution of individual men and women to the building up and transmission of its specific culture; that it is these persons (rather than the political governors) who represent or reflect the active forces in Muslim society in their respective spheres; and that their individual contributions are worthy of being recorded for future generations."

11. There is agreement among scholars that biographical dictionaries are an indigenous, not "imported," Arabic Islamic genre; see Gibb, op. cit., p. 54; Khalidi, op. cit., p. 53; Abiad, op. cit., p. 9.

12. Modern scholars have suggested a number of "disciplines" as "predecessors" for the biographical dictionaries, notably history, ḥadīth/ḥadīth criticism, or both; see, Loth, op. cit., pp. 593–601; Heffening, op. cit., p. 215; Gibb, opo. cit., p. 54; Khalidi, op. cit., pp. 53, 59–60; Hafsi, op. cit., p. 227.

13. This overlaps with the previous category somewhat. In addition to history and ḥadīth/ḥadīth criticism, the genres of *ayyām* (pre-Islamic battles of the Arabs), genealogy, *ma'āthir-mathālib* (virtues and vices) literature, and biography are suggested; see Loth, op. cit., pp. 598–99; Della Vida, op. cit., p. 440; Lichtenstadter, op. cit., p. 129; Rosenthal, op. cit., p. 88; Gibb, op. cit., pp. 54–58; but mainly Abiad, op. cit., pp. 9–12.

14. Organization is particularly discussed by Abiad and Hafsi.

15. These are very difficult to enumerate, since they vary tremendously from author to author; nevertheless, see Gibb, op. cit., p. 55; Khalidi, op. cit., pp. 60–62.

16. Such as name, descent, field, craft, teachers, students, date of death, character, virtues, resumé of career, revealing anecdotes, compilations, and so on; see Gibb op. cit., pp. 56–57; Rosenthal, op. cit., pp. 90–91; Khalidi, op. cit., pp. 62–64; but above all, Humphreys, op. cit., pp. 190–93.

17. Such as Rosenthal and Humphreys. Khalidi is interested in the later medieval period (fifth/eleventh through the twelfth/eighteenth century). Hafsi makes many comments about the development of the genre, but the structure(s) he chose for his article make those comments diffused here and there, and hence less clear than they could be. In spite of the promise in its title, Abiad's article does not have much to say on the question of development.

18. One remark in which the relationship is made is in Humphreys' discussion of the change in the criteria of inclusion in biographical dictionaries between the early dictionaries and those compiled in the fourth/tenth century. He says (op. cit., p. 189) "The earlier dictionaries attempted to provide comprehensive coverage for those broad classes (ḥadīth specialists or poets, usually) which they included in their purview. But in the 4th/10th century we see a growing tendency to include only subgroups, defined by place of residence, legal or theological sect, etc. Such changes in the criteria for inclusion have important cultural implications, obviously; thus there seems to be a feeling that one's Islam is not defined by his fidelity to Scripture (Qur'an and ḥadīth), but by the way in which he interprets it, or that a locality can properly be a Muslim's primary (though not ultimate) focus of cultural identity."

19. Gibb (op. cit., p. 54) suggests, for example, that the study of biographical dictionaries entails finding "the evidence it supplies or indicates as to changing or enduring social and intellectual attitudes or trends."

20. Several scholars note, for example, that the early dictionaries were concerned mainly with religious scholars and then broadened their scope (see n. 18 above). Other scholars make additional remarks here and there. Gibb (op. cit., p. 58), for example, notes how the dictionaries "supply almost the sole materials for the social activities and status of women in Muslim communities" and that the "agricultural and industrial arts are thinly represented. . .although trade and economic activities are by no means neglected in the Mamluk and later dictionaries." Similarly, Humphreys notes (op. cit., p. 189) that it is "striking and instructive" that "the productive classes of society—the farmers, merchants, and artisans—never made it into the dictionaries as such, though a few persons of such background do appear under a more respectable rubric."

21. Some scholars, notably Hafsi (op. cit., pp. 229–34), and before him Heffening (op. cit., pp. 214–15), discussed the various meanings of the word "*ṭabaqāt*." The numerous identifications offered by Hafsi, in particular, are quite revealing, as they demonstrate the rather complex meaning(s) of the term when it is used in different contexts over the ages. He says (p. 229): "Le terme *tabaqa*, au singulier, designe le rang attribué a un groupe de personnages ayant joué un role dans l'histoire a un titre ou a un autre, classe en fonction de critères determinés d'ordre religieux, culturel, scientifique, artistique, etc."; and on p. 230, he adds: "*tabaqa* signifie, suivant les epoques: classe, valeur, generation, merite, degré et groupe." Still on p. 233, he says: "*tabaqa* évoque egalement l'idée de gradation." As for Heffening, his identification is shorter and more direct: "The word means when used of place: similar, lying above one another, and with regard to time: similar, following one another. . .and especially:. . .generation, stratum or category. . .in hadith: the men included in one *tabaqa* are those who have heard traditions from those in the preceding one and have transmitted to the members of the following category."

22. See above, n. 4.

23. The words "*mashyakhah*" and "*barnāmij*" are identical in signification, but the first term is used in the Muslim East, the second in the Muslim West. In Andalusia and the Maghrib, the term "*fahrasah*" is also used (as in *Fahrasat ibn Khayr*).

24. There are other, earlier dictionaries which have been lost and whose structure is, hence, impossible to determine. They include: *Ṭabqaāt ahl*

al-ʿilm wa-al-jahl (classes of the learned and the ignorant), by Wāṣil ibn "Atā' (d. 131/748); *Ṭabaqāt al-shuʿarā'* (classes of poets), by al-Yazīdī (d. 200/815); *Ṭabaqāt al-fuqahā' wa-al-muḥaddithīn* (classes of jurists and ḥadīth transmitters/traditionists) and *Ṭabaqāt man rawa ʿan al-Nabi* (classes of transmitters from the Prophet), by al-Haytham ibn ʿAdī (d. 207/822); *Ṭabaqāt al-fursān* (classes of cavaliers), by Abū ʿUbaydah (d. 208/823); see Heffening, op. cit., p. 215 (copied in Abiad, p. 14). See also Hafsi, op. cit., p. 245. It is, however, to be kept in mind that Ibn Saʿd's book may be very closely related to the work of his teacher al-Wāqidī (d. 207/822), who was of the same generations al-Yazīdī, al-Haytham ibn ʿAdī and Abū ʿUbaydah.

25. Cf. nn. 12 and 13 above.

26. *al-Fihrist* (ed. Riḍā Tajaddud, Tehran, 1971), pp. 105, 106.

27. Ibid., pp. 108, 110.

28. Ibid., p. 112.

29. See on this book and its structure, the old study of Loth mentioned in n. 8 above, especially pp. 603–5; Gibb, op. cit., pp. 54–55 (where there is a very brief survey of structure); and Hafsi, op. cit., pp. 229–30, 235, and 242–44, where the structure and criteria for organization are discussed without an attempt at comprehensiveness.

30. Ibn Saʿd, *Kitāb al-ṭabaqāt al-kabīr* (ed. E. Sachau, Leiden, 1905–40), 3:1.

31. For the significance of this order of the cities, see above the end of section 1.

32. Since the term "*ṭabaqah*" need not indicate, strictly speaking, solely the time factor (although Ibn Saʿd does mention "age" at some points); cf. the meanings of "*ṭabaqah*" in n. 21 above.

33. See Ibn Saʿd, 6:90ff.

34. Ibid., p. 84ff.

35. Ibid., p. 151ff.

36. Ibid., p. 115ff.

37. Ibid., p. 126ff.

38. That a whole volume is devoted to women is indeed noteworthy; see also Gibb's remark in n. 20 above.

39. The last, ninth, volume of the printed edition contains only the editor's notes.

40. On the structure of this dictionary, see Hafsi, op. cit., pp. 230, 239, 245–46. In the introduction to the best edition of the book (ed. Muḥammad Maḥmud Shākir, second edition, Cairo, 1974), the editor provides an excellent study of the work, including its structure.

41. See above, n. 3.

42. Cf. Humphreys' remark in n. 18 above.

43. Jim Lindsay, of Westmont College, attracted my attention to a possible earlier "*dhayl*," namely *Dhayl ta'rīkh mawālīd al-'ulamā' wa-wafayātihim* by 'Abd al-'Aziz ibn Aḥmad al-Kattānī (d. 466/1074), which could be a continuation of Muḥammad ibn 'Abd Allāh al-Rabā'i's (d. 379/989) *Ta'rīkh mawālid al-'ulamā' wa-wafayātihim*. Both books have been recently published in Riyad in 1989 and 1990 respectively. Like Lindsay, however, I have not been able to see those books, nor am I able to identify their authors.

44. On this phenomenon in Andalusia, see Ibn Bassām's sharp statement in the introduction to his *al-Dhakhīrah* (ed. Iḥsān 'Abbās, Beirut, 1979), 1:11–16.

45. Preserved in al-Maqqari, *Nafḥ al-ṭīb* (ed. Iḥsān 'Abbās, Beirut, 1968), 3:156–79.

46. Ibn Sa'īd also wrote an addendum to this epistle; see ibid., pp. 179–86, as did al-Shāqundi; see ibid., pp. 186–222.

47. A few books appeared slightly earlier, but they are not typically biographical dictionaries. Ibn Abi Ṭāhir Ṭayfūr's (d. 280/893) *Kitāb Baghdād*, which has partially survived (Baghdad, 1968), is a literary chronicle, not a biographical dictionary. Bahshal's (d. 292/905) *Ta'rīkh Wāṣiṭ*, which has survived (ed. Kurkīs 'Awwād, Baghdad, 1967), is similar to most other dictionaries of cities in that it begins with an exposé of the town of Wāsiṭ; however, the entries in it can hardly be called biographies at all: their titles carry persons' names, but the material under each rubric contains nothing other

than the ḥadīths which those persons have transmitted. In that sense, the book is closer in genre to Bukhārī's *al-Ta'rīkh al-kabīr* and similar works. See Rosenthal, op. cit., pp. 83, 144–45.

48. Published in Tehran, 1351 [A.H.]. The book has been translated into English as *The History of Bukhara* by Richard N. Frye (Cambridge, MA 1954).

49. See *Yatimat al-dahr* (reproduction of the Damascus edition, Beirut, 1979), 1:8–9.

50. See above, n. 45.

51. In addition to the criterion of time, whence only contemporaries receive biographies.

52. *al-Dhakhīrah*, 1:22–32.

53. Ibn Sa'īd al-Andalusi, *al-Mughrib fi ḥulā al-Maghrib* (ed. Shawqī Ḍayf, Cairo, 1953), 1:33.

54. See above, n. 6.

7

The Book in the Grammatical Tradition: Development in Content and Methods

Ramzi Baalbaki

Through sheer coincidence, the word *Kitāb* has acquired special significance in the field of Arabic grammar. The sudden and premature death of Sībawayhi meant that his huge but unfinished and unnamed grammatical treatise had to be given a name by his contemporaries. What better a name than "*al-Kitāb*" could they come up with to reflect the grandeur and exhaustiveness of Sībawayhi's (d. ca. 180/796) work? The term "*al-Kitāb*," which is an example of an *'alam bi-al-ghalabah*,[1] can thus refer either to the Qur'an or to Sībawayhi's treatise, which came to be known as *Qur'ān al-naḥw*.[2]

The *Kitāb* of Sībawayhi is striking in another aspect related to the concept of "book" in Arabic grammatical tradition. It is the first grammatical work written, and, at the same time, the most comprehensive and imposing among a host of grammatical works that have survived. *al-Kitāb*, of course, did not emerge from a vacuum, but it is overwhelming in its material, technical terms, and analytic methods, given the relative scarcity of grammatical activity in the pre-Sībawayhi period. What is more striking than the unexpected appearance of this major work in grammar is that, unfortunately the later authors added to it hardly anything of real value or importance as far as material and terms are concerned, but tried to depart from some of the analytic methods of Sībawayhi and from the delicate balance he established between *qiyās* and *samā'*. This departure is largely to blame for the post-Sībawayhi grammarians' inclination to prescriptiveness, and their subjugation of attested usage to a rigid set of rules and to far-fetched explanations which have tarnished the image of *naḥw* and disgraced the *naḥwiyūn*, causing them to be viewed not only as poor interpreters,[3] but also as insensitive to the intricacies of Arabic usage. This very insensitivity was at the heart of the emergence of *balāghah* as a discipline distinct from *naḥw*, and the main reason for the lack of originality in the post-Sībawayhi period, characterized by concern for the permissibility of usage—according to the grammarians' criteria. Rather than be concerned with meaning and the disclosure of the impact of the context and the speaker's intention in using the *'awāmil* (operants, regents), the grammarians' regimen converged on exhausting the different kinds of *'awāmil* and so-called *'ilal* (reasons).

It is obvious that Sībawayhi's *Kitāb* is the focal point in the history of Arabic grammatical writing. Consequently, any study of the "book" in this grammatical tradition is bound to have the *Kitāb* as its point of departure. The present author proposes, in order to trace the development of the grammatical book, to examine three stages in the history of Arabic grammar, based on Sībawayhi as the focal point in this history, and according to the following scheme:

1. The pre-Sībawayhi stage, that is, the early grammatical activity leading to and preceding the phase of *ta'līf*, and the reports about grammatical writings in this period;
2. Sībawayhi's *Kitāb*, that is, its content, and the set of grammatical notions and methods it portrays; and
3. The post-Sībawayhi stage, that is, the departure from Sībawayhi's methods of grammatical analysis as exemplified in the work of the main figure after Sībawayhi, namely, Mubarrad.

Although this scheme might appear to have been oversimplified so as to suit the purpose of a general survey, it is basically an accurate representation of the development of grammatical activity. It is lamentable that after Sībawayhi one cannot discern any serious attempt at originality. Thus, the satisfaction with only one post-Sībawayhi stage is a reflection of the irreversible tendency of the grammarians of the third century onward toward complication, standardization and prescriptiveness, rather than a deliberate effort on our part to magnify the schism between Sībawayhi and the later grammarians, at least with regard to grammatical analysis.

The first reference to a "book" in the grammatical tradition is encountered in the biography of the allegedly first grammarian, Abū al-Aswad al-Du'alī (d. 69/688).[4] It is, however, highly improbable that Abū al-Aswad, or anyone trying to write preliminary notes on grammar, could have written a book on grammar, as the account quoted by al-Suyūṭī claims, unless by "book" no more than a few pages are meant (hence the reference to it as *al-Mukhtaṣar*[5]). It is also highly improbable that this "book" could have covered *naḥw* as such—as other accounts, again quoted by al-Suyūṭī, indicate—at this early stage. We are thus left with the limited subjects mentioned in the different accounts.[6] These are the following:

1. The parts of speech (*kalām*): the noun (*ism*), which indicates a denominative (*mā anba'a 'an al-musammā*), the verb (*fi'l*), which is a movement (*ḥarakah*, i.e., in time), and the particle (*ḥarf*), which has a meaning not signified by the first two parts. The nouns are further divided into explicit nouns, pronouns, and what is neither of those.

2. The particles governing the accusative: *inna, anna, laysa* (!), *la'alla, ka'anna*, and *lākinna*. A few other "operants" are mentioned in other accounts, namely, those which govern *raf'* (nominative and/or indicative), *naṣb* (accusative and/or subjunctive), *khafḍ* (genitive) and *jazm* (jussive).

3. Three disparate topics: subject and object, admirative constructions, and the construct state.

These subjects, apart from the first, might well have been those that captured the attention of the grammarians of the first and early second centuries, especially since they are the very subjects liable to solecism (*laḥn*), which is a major factor in the initiation of Arabic grammatical thinking.[7] The division of *kalām* into parts could hardly have taken place at this stage, as it was of no great importance to the pedagogical aims of the grammarians then. Moreover, the resemblance between the division into parts of speech and their functions, in the accounts of Abū al-Aswad writing down 'Alī's views, on the one hand, and Sībawayhi's treatment of the subject, on the other, can be understood as part of the attempt to credit 'Alī with laying the foundations of grammar, especially since parts of speech are given precedence in the *Kitāb*, and are discussed in its very first lines.[8]

It seems absolutely clear that the concept of *qiyās* did not cross the minds of grammarians at this stage. Not only is there no mention of it in the accounts, but also the timid and confused attempt at classifying particles (manifested in the inclusion of *laysa* with five other particles followed by nouns in the accusative) does not seem to correspond at all to the concept of *qiyās* as used by later grammarians. Neither does it indicate that *'āmil* and *'amal* were of interest in themselves at this stage, as the arrangement according to regimen seems to be initiated only for didactic purposes. One can therefore safely dismiss Ibn Sallām's statement that Abū al-Aswad was the one who laid the foundation of Arabic (grammar) (*awwal man assasa al-'Arabiyah*), and was also the first one to have devised grammatical *qiyās*.[9]

Unlike the largely unrealistic and unfounded reports on the grammatical activity—especially in writing—of Abū al-Aswad and his contemporaries, we possess reliable material on the pre-Sībawayhi grammarians of the second century, mainly from Sībawayhi himself. The importance of the grammatical stage following the primitive beginnings of grammatical activity, and preceding that of Sībawayhi, lies in the use of *qiyās* as a method of grammatical analysis, an analytical technique which later became the backbone of Arabic grammar.

The main figures of this intermediate stage are:

1. 'Abd Allāh ibn Abī Isḥāq (d. 117/735): He is mentioned seven times by Sībawayhi,[10] and these mentions hardly substantiate the view that he represents a trend highly dependent on *qiyās*,[11] or that he is the first grammarian who can be identified as "Basran."[12]

2. ʿĪsā ibn ʿUmar (d. 149/766): From the twenty references to him in the *Kitāb*, a number of which simply quote him as a transmitter of certain specific usages, ʿĪsā cannot be considered as a representative of the *qiyāsī* trend[13] in the same sense the term came to acquire with Sībawayhi and the later grammarians. In other words, the sophistication characteristic of later *qiyās* cannot apply to him, although one can detect in some of his ideas[14] a tendency to compare two sentences or phrases and infer that one was given the same treatment as the other on the grounds of their similarity.

3. Abū ʿAmr ibn al-ʿAlā' (d. 154/770): In his *Ṭabaqāt*,[15] Zubaydī lists him both under the *naḥwiyūn* and the *lughawiyūn*. However, evidence from the *Kitāb*, in which he is quoted fifty-seven times, shows that while the term *lughawī*, lexicographer, is easily applicable to him, the term *naḥwī*, grammarian, is hardly so. He is quoted mainly in relation to Qur'anic readings,[16] transmission of poetry,[17] and usages by Arabs,[18] in addition to some of his explanations and reasoning in matters related to *lughah*, rather than *naḥw*.[19]

4. Abū al-Khaṭṭāb al-Akhfash al-Kabīr (d. 177/793): Although Zubaydī[20] lists him under the *naḥwiyūn*, and not the *lughawiyūn*, the evidence furnished by Sībawayhi's *Kitāb* strongly suggests that the opposite is more likely true. There are fifty-eight mentions of him in the *Kitab*, all, without exception, on matters concerning *lughah*, not *naḥw*.[21] Eight of these are on lines of poetry,[22] the rest being on prose material Abū al-Khaṭṭāb heard from Arabs whose Arabic was usually described by Sībawayhi as being reliable or trustworthy (*mawthūq bi-ʿArabiyatihim*).

5. Yūnus ibn Ḥabīb (d. 182/798): There are 217 mentions of him in the *Kitāb*.[23] In many instances he is quoted as a transmitter of certain usages: two concerning Qur'anic verses,[24] twenty concerning lines of poetry,[25] eighteen concerning usages reported by Abū ʿAmr, or views held by him,[26] and many other cases concerning prose.[27] Apart from al-Khalīl (see below), Yūnus is the earliest grammarian in whose work a definite system can be discerned, sufficiently supported by textual evidence. Elaboration on this system is beyond the scope of this paper, but it should suffice us to point out briefly the main features of his methods of grammatical analysis:

a. He made extensive use of *taqdīr* as an analytical tool. This involved the suppletive insertion of parts of the sentence, mainly the operants which he assumed to be elided.[28]

b. He often formulated grammatical "rules" of universal validity[29]—an extremely important step in the history of grammatical analysis which so far had been mainly concerned with particulars, rather than "rules" which embraced these particulars.

c. He often relied on anomalous examples in drawing conclusions or formulating "rule."[30] His approach was thus highly reliant on *samāʿ*,

with an obvious unwillingness to dismiss usages only scarcely used or documented.

6. al-Khalīl ibn Aḥmad (d. 175/791): Unlike those of the five grammarians above, the role of al-Khalīl in the *Kitāb* is integral to the whole work. There are 608 mentions of him in the *Kitāb*, many of which cover whole chapters.[31] Indeed, al-Rāzī asserts that Sībawayhi's *Kitāb* contains data (*'ulūm*) gathered from al-Khalīl.[32] It would therefore be completely unrealistic to claim that it is possible to examine the linguistic analysis of either al-Khalīl or Sībawayhi in isolation. Any conclusion here referring to Sībawayhi's methods refers, by definition, to him as well as to his master.

Apart from individual grammarians, Sībawayhi refers seventeen times to a group which he calls *naḥwiyūn*.[33] The sense of the designation is not very clear,[34] but it should be noted that six out of these seventeen mentions are in relation to hypothetical examples they constructed, as opposed to what Arabs actually said.

The grammatical activity surveyed above, apart from furnishing the background of Sībawayhi's book, and indeed, of the grammar book for centuries to come, reveals that despite the preoccupation of Sībawayhi's predecessors with some basic grammatical phenomena, no grammar book seems to have preceded the *Kitāb*. It is unimaginable that Sībawayhi, who frequently quotes his predecessors and gives them due credit, should have intentionally ignored reference to a grammar book before his. As for the reports that 'Īsā ibn 'Umar wrote two grammar books, *Jāmi'* and *Ikmāl*,[35] we have no single reference to or quotation from either book in Sībawayhi's *Kitāb*, or indeed in any later grammatical work, and thus very much doubt the existence of either title.

We are left with no more than a single grammar book which might be claimed to have been written before the *Kitāb* or in the same period; namely, *Muqaddimah fī al-naḥw*, by Khalaf al-Aḥmar (d. 180/796). There is, however, compelling evidence that this book could not have been written in the second century, let alone that Khalaf al-Aḥmar is its author:

1. The book is not attributed to Khalaf in the sources, which do not even accept him as a proper *naḥwī*, since his contribution was mainly in poetry and, to a lesser extent, lexicography.[36] Asmā'ī, himself not accepted as a *naḥwī* was nevertheless said to have been a better *naḥwī* than Khalaf.[37]

2. The purpose of the book, as explained by the author, is to enable its reader to "improve his language in any book he might write, in poetry he might recite, or in an oration or treatise he might compose."[38] This is not in tune with the trend in the second part of the second century. In spite of the fact that the beginning of Arabic grammatical activity was related to a didactic purpose, its development thereafter was largely on different lines, and the didactic element does not distinctly re-emerge until late in the third century.

3. The author speaks of grammatical principles (*uṣūl*), particles (*adawāt*), and operants (*'awāmil*),[39] and arranges many parts of his book according to the government of these operants, listing those governing the nominative, accusative, genitive, and so on, under separate headings. This arrangement, and more particularly the *uṣūl*, betrays the fact that the author was writing later than the second century, for this term was not yet used in the sense of grammatical principles or fundamentals of grammar, nor was such an arrangement of headings—characteristic of the fourth century onward—likely to have been used.

4. The author mentions the Basrans and the Kufans in two places, both concerning terminology, saying that the Kufans use the term *istitā'* for the Basran *qaṭ'* or *ijrā'*[40] (instigation), and *ījāb* for *taḥqīq*[41] (void, exception, lacking the general term). But how could such a reference be made at a time when the two "schools" could not yet have been formed?!

The formative elements of Sībawayhi's *Kitāb* can thus be reduced to the general grammatical activity preceding him, and especially that of the grammarians he quotes. Having discarded the *Muqaddimah* attributed to Khalaf as a work of the third or even fourth century, we can confidently conclude that Sībawayhi's *Kitāb* is the first book of Arabic grammar. It is interesting to note that this first attempt, which laid the solid foundations of terms and methods alike, has never been surpassed by later authors, nor has its author's approach to linguistic analysis been seriously challenged, with the single exception of Ibn Maḍā''s refutation of the grammarians in his *al-Radd 'alá al-nuḥāt*.

Having studied the stage leading to the appearance of the first grammatical treatise, the developments that took place in the nature and methods of grammar books can best be traced by comparing Sībawayhi's work, on the one hand, with the work of the later grammarians, on the other. We have already suggested that post-Sībawayhi grammarians may be identified as a single group to stress the fact that, from the third century onward, there was an irreversible trend away from some of the essential components of Sībawayhi's method, resulting in a major change in the concept of what constitutes a grammar book, and for what purpose it is written. Although a detailed study is warranted to trace this development in its various aspects and appreciate the range of differences among grammarians within the general trend, we shall limit this part of the paper to the main features as portrayed in a comparison between Sībawayhi's *Kitāb* and the first major grammar book to be written after it, namely, *al-Muqtaḍab*, by Mubarrad (d. 285/898).

It should be stressed here that Sībawayhi set the main features which characterize the grammar book in general. The difference that one detects between him and the later authors is in aspects of the methods of grammatical analysis; most other features were largely preserved, and the broader ones among them—which should not be lost in the mass of details one encounters in the process of comparison—are the following:

1. The separation between *lughah* and *naḥw*: The realm of *naḥw*, as presented by Sībawayhi, remained distinct from that of *lughah*, which has an altogether different history of development.

2. The inclusion of *ṣarf*: Although there was an early realization that the themes of *ṣarf* form a distinct entity and may be the exclusive subject of a whole treatise—as they were indeed as early as Māzinī's (d. 247/861) *Taṣrīf*—most of the later authors followed Sībawayhi's example in treating the themes of *ṣarf* in one treatise, side by side with the linguistic subjects which deal with the *jumlah* rather than the *kalimah*. Mubarrad's (d. 285/898) *Muqtaḍab*, Ibn al-Sarrāj's (d. 316/928) *Mūjaz* and *Uṣūl*, and Zubaydī's (d. 379/989) *Wāḍiḥ* are but a few examples of the continuity of Sībawayhi's method.[42] The phonetic part of *ṣarf*, which Sībawayhi considers late in his second volume, also continued to be included in most later books.

3. The *shawāhid*: Not only did the bulk of Sībawayhi's *shawāhid* form the main body of material for the later authors, but they had few additions to make, as they absolutely refused to extend the period of accepted *shawāhid* beyond the second century. It is interesting to note that it was only on the linguistic merit of ḥadīth that there was a departure from this approach, and then a minor and short-lived one, propagated by proponents of one line of thought—harshly criticized by proponents of another—quite late in the history of grammar.[43]

4. The arrangement of material: Despite minor variations, the arrangement Sībawayhi adopts in the *Kitāb* is generally observed by the later grammarians.

5. The tools of grammatical analysis: Whatever the later grammarians might have introduced to the study of grammar or however they might have drifted away from the delicate balance which Sībawayhi established in his analysis—as between *samā'* and *qiyās*, for example—there remains the fact that the "tools" of grammatical analysis used by Sībawayhi—in our view, largely under the influence of al-Khalīl—were completely adopted by the later grammarians. Concepts such as *taqdīr, ḥadhf, 'illah, 'āmil, ma'mūl, aṣl*, and so forth, are featured in the later sources with practically the same range of application as in the *Kitāb*. Furthermore, Sībawayhi's host of terms—again, largely from al-Khalīl[44]—carried through to the later grammarians with only a few additions.[45] It is remarkable that even the Kufan terms, despite some of their idiosyncrasies, are largely similar to the terms used and elaborated on by Sībawayhi.

The major areas of difference between Sībawayhi and the later grammarians—represented here by Mubarrad—that reveal the changes that occurred in grammatical writing are the following:

1. On *qiyās* and *samāʿ*: Both authors use these terms in a largely similar sense, but Mubarrad gives more prominence to the first at the expense of the second. For him, *qiyās* is not only a method of grammatical analysis, but also a purely intellectual process which could be the arbiter in grammatical questions. His use of terms like *minhāj al-qiyās*[46] and *ḥaqīqat al-qiyās*[47]—which do not occur in the *Kitāb*—points to a more closely defined view of *qiyās*, whereby it is not only used as a grammatical tool, but also referred to as one.

More importantly, Mubarrad seems to have changed the delicate balance Sībawayhi established between *qiyās* and *samāʿ*. In his system, Sībawayhi puts limitations on *qiyās*, and respects *samāʿ*, so that, apart from four examples,[48] he does not dismiss attested forms as wrong. Mubarrad, on the other hand, frequently considered attested forms as unacceptable or wrong and resorts to dismissing the *riwāyah* to prove his point.[49] The matter takes more serious dimensions when Mubarrad's preference of *qiyās* over *samāʿ* prompts him to apply the former, resulting in forms that are contrary to those attested to by the Arabs through the latter. In his refutation of Mubarrad, Ibn Wallād points out that he and the grammarians are not allowed to apply a *qiyās* which would, even if it were sound, result in something that does not exist in their language, and endorses Sībawayhi's view that the application of *qiyās* for generating forms is only acceptable if these forms conform to the speech of the Arabs.[50] Unfortunately, Ibn Wallād's support of Sībawayhi is outweighed by the growing acceptance by the later grammarians of the approach which gives *qiyas* preeminence over *samāʿ*—an approach which brought about a major change in the nature of a grammar book, the *Kitāb*, leading to a futile exercise in the application of criteria externally imposed by the grammarian on linguistic data.

2. On *ʿamal* (regimen) and *taʿlīl* (causation): The idea that any grammatical phenomenon in an utterance must have a cause to explain it, and that this cause can often be represented by the relation of the element that governs to the element governed by it, has dominated the thinking of almost all Arabic grammarians, mainly through the influence of al-Khalīl and Sībawayhi. Furthermore, most of the reasons Sībawayhi cites for particular phenomena are adopted by the later grammarians, including Mubarrad.[51] However, a study of Mubarrad's employment of the two concepts of regimen and causation reveals basic differences between his approach and that of Sībawayhi, especially as evidenced by the terminology expressing the concept of "operant." In the *Kitāb*, there are fifty occurrences of the terms *ʿāmil, ʿāmilah,* and *ʿawāmil*. However, the majority do not express the concept of "operant."[52] In an expression like *wa-kāna al-ʿāmil fīhī mā qablahu min al-kalām* (the operant in it was the preceding sentence),[53] the word *ʿāmil* cannot be said to stand for the concept of "operant," as it lacks the degree of abstraction needed for such a concept. In a few other instances,[54] however, the concept is more clearly expressed. Mubarrad, on the other hand, not only expresses this concept with precision,[55] but also speaks

of the different sorts of *'awāmil*, and uses expressions like *'awāmil al-af'āl*,[56] *'awāmil al-asmā'*,[57] *taṣarruf al-'āmil*,[58] and *al-'aṭf 'alá 'āmilayni*.[59] Another expression Mubarrad uses is *bāb al-'awāmil*,[60] which shows that the concept of "operant" has become a "class" in itself. Indeed, he applies language drawn from logic in his discussion of *'awāmil*, as in the following passage: *fa-idhā ja'alta lahā 'awāmil ta'mal fīha lāzimaka an taj'al li-'awāmilihā 'awāmil wa-kadhālika li-'awāmil 'awāmilihā ilā mā lā nihāyah* (if you assign to it operants to act on it, you would need to assign operants to its operants, likewise to the operants of its operants, indefinitely).[61] This approach to *'awāmil* continued to be used by the later grammarians and culminated in works devoted totally to *'awāmil*, complete with complex internal division[62]—another noteworthy development in the grammar book.

As for *ta'līl*, Mubarrad, like Sībawayhi, assigns causes to explain grammatical phenomena, but his use of this tool is far more sophisticated than Sībawayhi's. First, he uses the term *'illah* to refer to several phenomena, such as *labs*,[63] *ḥadhf*,[64] *ikhtilāf*,[65] and *jawāz*.[66] Moreover, he uses the term *'ilal* to refer, collectively, to the issues or particulars of a certain *bāb*.[67] This shows how the uninterrupted application of *'illah* resulted in a shift of meaning, whereby a grammatical *bāb* can be said to be made up of a number of *'ilal*.

The major features of the difference between Sībawayhi's use of *ta'līl* and that of the later grammarians, represented here by Mubarrad, can be further demonstrated through the following observations:

a. Many of the phenomena for which Mubarrad assigns an *'illah* are not given causes by Sībawayhi. Examples include the *'illah* for the suffix of the third-person masculine plural being *sākin* (as in *ḍarabū*), while that of the third-person feminine plural is not (as in *ḍarabna*),[68] for many peculiarities of numerals and the *tamyīz* following them,[69] and for the vocative which is *mufrad* and ending in *ḍammah*.[70]

b. Many of the phenomena to which Sībawayhi assigns one *'illah* are explained by Mubarrad by two or more *'ilal*.[71] Expressions like *wa-sanadhkuru dhālika bi-istiqṣā' al-'illah fīhi*[72] show Mubarrad's tendency to exhaust all the possible reasons for a particular phenomenon.

c. Many of the causes Mubarrad mentions are more complex and sophisticated than those given by Sībawayhi. For instance, whereas Sībawayhi mentions *takhfīf* as the cause for the *kasrah* after the *kāf* in *aḥlāmikim*, used by Bakr ibn Wā'il (*akhaff min an yuḍamm*),[73] Mubarrad dismisses the usage as unacceptable to *ahl al-naẓar*.[74] And whereas Sībawayhi asserts that the elision of the *nūn* of the dual and plural when the geminate energetic *nūn* is suffixed to a verb in the dual or plural is to avoid disambiguity between the singular and the dual or plural,[75] Mubarrad resorts to *qiyās*,[76] the complexity of which becomes the target of Ibn Wallād's criticism.[77]

Just as the approach to *'awāmil* (in 1 above) gave rise to a new genre of grammatical books, namely, books on *'awāmil*, the approach to causation is the main reason for another genre of grammatical books, this time works on *asrār* (i.e., *'ilal*), as exemplified in Ibn al-Anbārī's *Asrār al-'Arabiyah* and *al-Ighrāb fī jadal al-i'rāb*, where causation is pursued as a mental exercise in logic more than as a tool of grammatical interpretation.

3. Regarding subdivisions, Mubarrad and the later grammarians, in general, tend to divide and subdivide grammatical phenomena to treat them more precisely, but often, too, to demonstrate their ability to expand on the subject at hand and present all its particulars under one heading. For example, in dealing with the types of definite nouns, Mubarrad divides them according to the degree of their "definiteness,"[78] whereas Sībawayhi makes no such distinction.[79] Similarly, Mubarrad lists four types of *badal*,[80] whereas Sībawayhi mentions them in different places,[81] without any attempt to show that they are different types of one concept.

4. As for "logical" considerations, several of these have already been mentioned, and this subject deserves detailed study. One can point out here, however, just a few manifestations of Mubarrad's "logical" approach to grammar as an example of a drastic change in the nature of the grammar book. These include "*fanqala*"[82] (hypothetical questions and answers), "*iḥālah*"[83] (*reductio ad absurdum*), and "*tasalsul*"[84] (successivity). Furthermore, some of the terms and expressions specific to logic and philosophy clearly feature in passages like the one in which he arranges the degrees of definiteness,[85] where he says: "*fa-al-shay' a'amm mā takallamta bihi, wa-al-jism akhaṣṣ minhu, wa-al-ḥayawān akhaṣṣ min al-jism. . . bi-annaka taqūl kull rajul insān wa-la taqūl kull insān rajul*" (the *thing* is the most general connotation of a term, and the *body* is more specific, and *animal* is more specific than *body*. . . so you say every male is a human being but not every human being is a male).

Sībawayhi's originality was not to be matched by any of the later grammarians. It was only when the new approach of the *balāghiyūn* emerged—mainly out of the preoccupation of the *naḥwiyūn* with imposing their own norms on attested usage, and their inability to provide a theory of meaning compatible with their theory on *qiyās*, *'amal*, and so on—that originality made another appearance. This came with Jurjani's theory, mainly in his *Dalā'il al-i'jāz*, where he asserts that *naḥw* should be the study of meaning, but that the *naḥwiyūn* failed to approach their subject from that angle.[86] But this attempt was again short-lived, and *balāghah* itself was later plagued with rigidity and the lack of continued revision of theory, Once again, later authors seem to have corrupted the basically sound systems of their forerunners, and thwarted the efforts they made in their first and major books in each of the two subjects.

NOTES

1. Ibn ʿAqīl's *Sharḥ ʿalá alfiyat Ibn Mālik*, 4 vols., ed. M.M. ʿAbd al-Ḥamīd (Cairo, 1967), 2:185–86.

2. Abū al-Ṭayyib al-Lughawī, *Marātib al-naḥwiyīn*, ed. M.A. Ibrāhīm (Cairo, 1974), p. 106.

3. Cp. the saying: *aḍʿaf min ḥujjat naḥwī*, in Ibn Khallikān's *Wafayāt al-aʿyān wa-anbāʾ abnāʾ al-zamān*, 8 vols., ed. I. ʿAbbās (Beirut, 1968–72), 1:119. Examples of some of their poor interpretations are discussed by Ibn Maḍāʾ al-Qurṭubī in his *al-Radd ʿalā al-nuḥāt*, ed. Sh. Ḍayf (Cairo, 1947). See also F. Tarazī, *Fī uṣūl al-lughah wa-al-naḥw* (Beirut, 1969), pp. 132–33.

4. al-Suyūṭī, *Sabab waḍʿ ʿilm al-ʿarabiyah*, in *al-Tuḥfah al-bahīyah wa-al-ṭurfah al-shahiyah* (Constantinople, 1885), p. 49ff. For the different accounts on the "first Arab grammarian," see R. Talmon, "Who Was the First Arab Grammarian? A New Approach to an Old Problem," *Zeitschrift für arabische Linguistik* 15 (1985), pp. 128–46.

5. Ibn al-Anbārī, *Nuzhat al-alibbāʾ fī ṭabaqāt al-udabāʾ*, ed. I. Sāmarrāʾī (Baghdad, 1970), p. 20. Ibn al-Nadīm reports that he once saw four Chinese papers containing material from Abū al-Aswad's grammatical treatise in the handwriting of Yaḥyā ibn Yaʿmar; see *al-Fihrist*, ed. R. Tajaddud (Tehran, 1971), p. 46. It is very doubtful, however, whether Chinese paper was known to the Arabs by the time of Yaḥyā (d. 129/746), and if Ibn al-Nadīm indeed saw such a manuscript, it was, most probably, forged.

6. In addition to al-Suyūṭī and Ibn al-Anbārī, see Ibn Sallām, *Ṭabaqāt al-shuʿarāʾ*, ed J. Hell (Leiden, 1916), p. 5; and Zubaydī, *Ṭabaqāt al-naḥwiyīn wa-al-lughawiyīn*, ed. M.A. Ibrāhīm (Cairo, 1973), pp. 11–12.

7. This is continuously stressed by the sources, and errors like "*mā ashaddu al-ḥarri*," for "*mā ashadda al-ḥarra*," and "*inna Allāha barīʾun min al-mushrikīna wa-rasūlihi*" for "*rasūlahu*" are invariably cited.

8. Sībawayhi, *Kitāb*, 2 vols. (Būlāq, 1316–17/1898–99, repr. Baghdad, 1965), 1:2.

9. *Ṭabaqāt al-shuʿarāʾ*, p. 5; cp. Zubaydī's *Ṭabaqāt*, p. 21. Equally untrustworthy is the reference to Naṣr ibn ʿĀsim as having opened *qiyās* wide (*fataqa al-qiyās*). This is incompatible with Naṣr's grammatical activity, which is usually mentioned along with that of Abū al-Aswad, and said to be similar

to it. See al-Qifṭī, *Inbāh al-ruwāh ʿalá anbāh al-nuḥāh*, 4 vols., ed. M.A. Ibrāhīm (Cairo, 1950–73), 3:343.

10. For this and other statistics about grammarians mentioned in the *Kitāb*, see W. Reuschel's *al-Ḫalīl ibn Aḥmad, der Lehrer Sībawaihs, als Grammatiker* (Berlin, 1959), pp. 67–75; and the additions and corrections made by G. Troupeau in "À propos des grammairiens cités par Sībawayhi dans le Kitāb," *Arabica* 8 (1961), pp. 309–12. See also G. Troupeau's *Lexique-Index du "Kitāb" de Sībawayhi* (Paris, 1976), pp. 227–31; and ʿA.M. Hārū's indexes to his edition of the *Kitāb* (Cairo, 1977), pp. 181–961.

11. As suggested, for example, by A.M. Anṣārī in "al-Tayyār al-qiyāsī fī al-madrasah al-Baṣriyah," *Bulletin of the Faculty of Arts, Cairo University* 24 (1962), p. 20.

12. Sh. Ḍayf speaks of him as "ustādh *al-madrasah al-Baṣrivah*"; see *al-Madāris al-naḥwiyah* (Cairo, 1968), p. 22; while M.S. Belguedj says: "on avait en effèt quelques raisons de le présenter parfois comme le premier grammarien 'basrite' "; see "La démarche des premiers grammairiens arabes dans le domaine de la syntaxe," *Arabica* 20 (1973), pp. 168–85.

13. This is contrary to Ḍayf's interpretation of ʿĪsá's views, in *al-Madāris al-naḥwiyah*, p. 25.

14. See, for example, *Kitāb*, 1:272, where he allows the accusative in *hādhā awwalu fārisin muqbilan* by comparing it with the accusative in *hādhā rajulun munṭaliqan*, that is, treating it as a circumstantial accusative, not as an adjective. See also *Kitāb*, 1:313, where he reads *yā maṭaran*, likening it to *yā rajulan*, and explains the accusative through the nunation (i.e., the sign of indefiniteness) common to both.

15. *Ṭabaqāt al-naḥwiyīn*, pp. 35, 159.

16. *Kitāb*, 1: 238, 316; 2: 167, 289, 297, 358, 417. Note that Abū ʿAmr was one of the seven authorized readers.

17. Ibid., 1: 253, 437, 446.

18. Ibid., 1: 293, 320, 396; 2: 81, 167.

19. Ibid., 1: 208, 265; 2: 15, 28, 63, 149, 208, 237.

20. *Ṭabaqāt al-naḥwiyin*, p. 40.

21. In Zajjājī's *Majālis al-'ulamā'*, ed. 'A.M. Hārūn (Kuwait, 2nd ed., 1983), p. 124, Abū al-Khaṭṭāb has only one *majlis* (no. 75), again on *lughah*.

22. *Kitāb*, 1: 40, 103, 153, 271, 369, 462; 2: 12, 17. For the rest of the quotations, see Troupeau's *Lexique-Index*, pp. 227–28.

23. In addition to Reuschel and Troupeau, see A.M. Ansari, *Yūnus al-Baṣrī: ḥayātuhu wa-āthāruhu wa-madhāhibuhu* (Cairo, 1973), pp. 320–21.

24. *Kitāb*, 1: 173, 236.

25. Ibid., 1: 25, 77, 131, 140, 161, 182, 201, 207, 241, 253, 289, 333, 359, 422, 423,468, 486; 2: 54, 160, 174.

26. Ibid., 1: 1, 194, 201, 208, 265, 273, 293, 360, 397, 453; 2: 23, 48, 53, 63, 74, 81 1.12, 81 1.15, 125, 183.

27. See, for example, *Kitāb*, 1: 115, 174, 203, 207, 213, 231, 248, 249, 258,275, 284, 311, 316, 317, 322, 345, 361, 363, 372, 379, 382, 402, 404, 470; 2: 26, 31, 35, 54, 70, 73, 88, 110, 113, 122, 125, 127, 142, 148, 153, 190, 191, 192, 201, 203, 226, 249, 273, 278, 288, 388.

28. Some of the clearest examples of this can be found in *Kitāb*, 1: 147, 173, 252, 256, 328, 398, 412.

29. Examples of this are his assertion that any noun made of two conjoined nouns is a diptote (2:50), and that the diminutive (*taḥqīr*) invariably reveals the origin of the word's radicals (2:85). See also 2:283, concerning *ishmām*.

30. One example is his claim, based on the form *manūn*, the plural of the interrogative particle *man*, and on the sentence *ḍaraba mannun mannan* which he heard from an Arab, that *manah* can be considered to be declinable as is *ayyah*, and it is therefore permissible to use the forms *manatun, manatan,* and *manatin*. See *Kitāb*, 1:402; cf. Suyūṭī, *Ham' al-hawāmi' sharḥ jam' al-jawāmi'* (Cairo, 1909), 2:153. Similarly, he allows *iyyāka Zaydan* on the basis of a poetic *shāhid* (1:140; cf. Zubaydī's *Ṭabaqāt*, p. 53).

31. Reuschel, *al-Khalīl*, p. 18.

32. al-Suyūṭī, *al-Iqtirāḥ fī 'ilm uṣūl al-naḥw*, ed. A.M. Qāsim (Cairo, 1976), pp. 205–6.

33. *Kitāb*, 1: 167, 194, 216, 223, 227, 242, 257, 383, 393, 395, 415, 433, 437; 2: 18, 107, 157, 315. Cf. Troupeau, *Lexique, NHW*, where three other mentions are cited, but only in the context of the seventeen occasions.

34. For an examination of this term, see M.G. Carter, "Les origines de la grammaire arabe," *Revue des Études Islamiques* 40 (1972), pp. 69–97.

35. Fayrūzābādī, *al-Bulghah fī tārīkh a'immat al-lughah*, ed. M. Miṣrī (Damascus, 1972), pp. 180–81; and al-Suyūṭī *Bughyat al-wu'āt fī ṭabaqāt al-lughawiyīn wa-al-nuḥāt*, ed. M.A. Ibrāhīm (Cairo, 1964–65), pp. 237–38.

36. Note that Zubaydī lists him under the *lughawiyūn* in his *Ṭabaqāt*, p. 161.

37. Ibid., p. 163; cf. *Nuzhat al-alibbā'*, pp. 90–91.

38. Khalaf al-Aḥmar, *Muqaddimah fī al-naḥw*, ed. 'I. Tanūkhī (Damascus, 1961), p.34.

39. Ibid., p.34.

40. Ibid., p. 53.

41. Ibid., p. 80.

42. R. Baalbaki, "The relation between naḥw and balāġa: a comparative study of the methods of Sībawayhi and Ǧurǧāni," *Zeitschrift für arabische Linguistik* 11 (1983), p. 7.

43. For grammarians who included ḥadīth as a main source of linguistic data, and those who argued the case for its inclusion, see Baghdādī's *Khizānat al-adab wa-lubb lubāb lisān al-'arab* (Bulaq, 1299) 1:3ff.; and Kh. Ḥadīthī, *Mawqif al-nuḥāt min al-iḥtijāj bi-al-ḥadīth al-sharīf* (Baghdad, 1981) ch. 3: 191–365.

44. See the section on *muṣṭalaḥāt* in G.N. 'Abābinā's *Makānat al-Khalīl ibn Aḥmad fī al-naḥw al-'arabī* (Amman, 1984), pp. 157–76.

45. For example, the addition of *ism al-āla* (in *Kitāb*, 2:249, "*hādhā bāb mā 'alá ta bihi*"), and *ism al-marrah* (in *Kitāb*, 2:246, "*hādhā bāb naẓā'ir ḍarabtuhu ḍarbatan wa-ramaytuhu ramyatan*"). For other examples, see Ḍayf's *al-Madāris al-naḥwiyah*, pp. 61–62.

46. Muḥammad ibn Yazīd al-Mubarrad, *Kitāb al-Muqtaḍab*, 4 vols., ed. M.A. 'Uḍaymah (Cairo, 1965–66), 3:147; hereafter *Muqtaḍab.*

47. Ibid., 1:177.

48. These are the passages in which Sībawayhi describes observed linguistic data as unacceptable; see *Kitāb*, 1: 290; 2: 127, 278, 367.

49. See, for example, *Muqtaḍab*, 2: 22, 116–17, 132–33 (cf. *Kitāb*, 1:408); 3:285; and *Kāmil*, ed. W. Wright (Leipzig, 1864–92), p. 22. For evidence of Mubarrad's rejection of *riwāyah* from other sources, see Ibn al-Sarrāj's *Kitāb al-uṣūl fī al-naḥw*, 3 vols., ed. 'A Fatalī (Baghdad, 1973), 1:123; and Ibn Jinnī's *al-Khaṣā'iṣ*, 3 vols., ed. M.A. Najjār (Cairo, 1952–56), 1:75. As for usages which Mubarrad dismisses but that Sībawayhi accepts, or only describes as weak but not to be dismissed, cf. five examples from *Kitāb*, 1: 235, 435; 2: 121, 144, 294, with their corresponding passages in *Muqtaḍab*, 2: 146, 72–73, 249, 336; 1: 269–70.

50. *Intiṣār Sībawayhi 'alá al-Mubarrad*, in *Muqtaḍab*, 3:313, margin.

51. Examples of this are the agreement that the implicit verb is the operant which brings about the accusative in certain vocative constructions (*Kitāb*, 1:303; *Muqtaḍab*, 4:202), and that *ibtidā'* is the operant causing the nominative in the *mubtada'* (*Kitāb*, 1:278; *Muqtaḍab*, 2:49). But for disagreement, see their discussions of the *mustathná (Kitāb*, 1:369; *Muqtaḍab*, 4:390), and of the apodosis (*Kitāb*, 1:449; *Muqtaḍab*, 2:82).

52. As in *Kitāb*, 1: 27, 37, 64, 74, 79, 92, 104, 108, 121, 134, 179, 202, 228, 243, 248, 277, 345, 360, 362, 440, 456, 457, 465.

53. Ibid., 1:369.

54. For example, 1: 3, 48, 231, 245, 347; 2: 61. See also F. Praetorius, "Die grammatische Rektion bei den Arabern," *Zeitschrift der deutschen morgenländischen Gesellschaft* 63 (1909), p. 499, where specialized terms connected with *'awāmil*, not found in the *Kitāb, are pointed out.*

55. As in Muqtaḍab, 2:5; 4:302, for example.

56. Ibid., 2:10, 75.

57. Ibid., 2:6, 7, 38, 345.

58. Ibid., 4: 156, 300.

59. *Kāmil*, pp. 163, 448.

60. *Muqtaḍab*, 4:317.

61. Ibid., 4:80.

62. As in Jurjānī's *al-ʿAwāmil al-mi'ah al-naḥwiyah fī uṣūl ʿilm al-ʿarabiyah*, ed. al-Badrāwī Zahrān (Cairo, 2nd ed., 1988).

63. *Muqtaḍab*, 3:142.

64. Ibid., 2:269; 3:166.

65. Ibid., 2:153.

66. Ibid., 3: 101, 217.

67. Cf. the expression, "*bāb anna wa-inna bi-jamīʿ ʿilalihi*" (*Kāmil*, p. 49), with "*wa-hādhā yushrah ʿalā hiyālihi bi-jamīʿ ʿilalihi*" (*Muqtaḍab*, 2:31–32).

68. Ibid., 1:271.

69. Ibid., 2:163–69, esp. p. 166 1.12, and p. 167 1.1.

70. Ibid., 4:204.

71. Cf., for example, *Kitāb*, 2:153, with *Muqtaḍab*, 3:19, for the *fatḥah* in the imperfect followed by the energetic *nūn*, and *Kitāb*, 2:36–38, with *Muqtaḍab*, 3:374 (cf. *Kāmil*, p.268, and Ibn al-Sarrāj's *Uṣūl*, 1:424; 2:90), for the final *kasrah* of feminine forms of the pattern *faʿālī*.

72. Ibid., 2:136.

73. *Kitāb*, 2:294.

74. *Muqtaḍab*, 1:270.

75. *Kitāb*, 2:154.

76. *Muqtaḍab*, 3:22.

77. *Intiṣār*, in *Muqtaḍab*, 3:21, margin.

78. *Muqtaḍab*, 4:281.

79. *Kitāb*, 2:260ff.

80. *Muqtaḍab*, 4:297; cf. *Kāmil*, pp. 438–39.

81. *Kitāb*, 1: 75ff., 218ff., 224ff., 393ff.

82. For example, *Muqtaḍab*, 2:3–4,; 4:173–76.

83. Ibid, 1:36; 4:8. See also his use of *iḥālah* as reported in *majlis* 55 of Zajjājī's *Majālis*, p. 96; and in Ibn Jinnī's *Khasā'is*, 1:89.

84. *Muqtaḍab*, 3:374; 4:80.

85. Ibid., 4:280. Cf. Abū al-Baqā', *al-Kulliyāt* (Cairo, n.d.), p. 358.

86. For the relation between *naḥw and balāghah*, the emergence of the latter as a reaction to the former, and a detailed comparison between the two key figures of the two fields, namely Sībawayhi and Jurjānī, see my article mentioned in note 42 above.

8

Women's Roles in the Art of Arabic Calligraphy

Ṣalāḥ al-Dīn al-Munajjid

Those scholars who study the role of women in Islam will notice that throughout the different periods of history, women were actively engaged in every field of endeavor, be it politics, government, or learning. Women were not confined, as some have assumed, to mothering and household occupations.

Women achieved a distinguished position in society by becoming skilled in Arabic composition, and by excelling in penmanship and calligraphy. Quite often, women managed the affairs of palaces, acquired knowledge and became important scholars, and copied books of all genres, including literature, poetry, and Traditions (ḥadīth). They copied books in a most beautiful way, and competently checked the copies against the originals for correctness. They copied Korans (*maṣāḥif*) and excelled in the manner of presenting them. People in government often relied on women to write the texts of political treaties because of their superior writing abilities.

ISLAM ENCOURAGES LEARNING AND WRITING

At the advent of Islam, only seventeen men and three women of the clan of Quraysh knew how to write. When the Prophet came, he called upon his followers to become learned, to learn how to read and write. The Holy Koran is explicit in this regard. God swore by the pen. He said, "*Nūn*, by the pen and what they write,"[1] and God commanded His Messenger to read. He said, "Recite (or read, *iqra'*) in the name of thy Lord who created, created man from a blood-clot. Recite, and thy Lord is the Most Bountiful, who taught by the pen, taught man what he did not know."[2] God also ordained the cultivation of learning. He said, "Seek ye knowledge even in China." China, in this context, refers to a remote point, extremely distant from Mecca and Medina (in the absence of modern means of travel and communication), and very hard to reach. He ordained teaching. He said, "He who is learned among you should teach the others." God instructed the Messenger to seek knowledge, despite its being a difficult undertaking.

One of the earliest verses of the Koran, revealed just after the emigration of the Prophet to Medina, had to do with debt. God ordained the writing, or recording (*kitābah*), of debts. He said, "O, ye who believe, when you contract a debt one upon another for a stated term, write it down and let a scribe write it between you in equity."[3] Henceforth, writing came into fiscal legislation for the recording of contracts and for the protection of peoples' rights.

The Messenger ordained writing in another area, namely writing a will before death. He encouraged every person to write a will before his death, and to divide his personal property among his heirs or donate it to the poor.

Great interest was shown in studying script and writing, in particular writing down the revelation of the Koran. The Messenger was illiterate, in that he did not know how to read or write. God said, "Not before this didst thou recite any Book, or inscribe it with thy right hand."[4] The Prophet appointed several from among those Companions of his who knew how to write to be his writing secretaries. These included Abū Bakr, ʿUmar ibn al-Khaṭṭāb, ʿUthmān ibn ʿAffān, ʿAlī ibn Abī Ṭālib, Zayd ibn Thābit, Ubbay ibn Kaʿb, Muʿāwīyah ibn Abī Ṣufyān, and Zayd ibn Arqum. He assigned each one of them a specific task. To Zayd ibn Thābit he assigned the writing down of the revelation, for example. The Messenger, furthermore, set up a special desk (*ṣuffah*) in the mosque for the purpose of teaching, and he appointed a special staff of teachers to teach writing. Among the teachers were ʿAbd Allah ibn Saʿid ibn al-ʿAṣṣ and ʿUbādah ibn al-Samiṭ. He also sent Muʿādh ibn Jabal to Yemen and Hadramaut as a teacher.

The Prophet's interest in teaching was not limited to the education of men; he directed that women, too, should receive proper education. He asked a woman called al-Shafāʾ bint ʿAbd Allah al-ʿAdawīyah, who was conversant in the art of writing, to teach his daughter Hafṣah that art.

The Companions of the Prophet later called on people to learn how to write. ʿAli ibn Abī Ṭālib said, "Teach your children writing and marksmanship." He also said, "Beautiful writing makes the truth clearer," and "Take up beautiful writing, it is the key to livelihood." ʿAbd Allah ibn al-ʿAbbās said, "Calligraphy is the tongue of the hand."

One more thing should be pointed out, as it clearly indicates the Prophet's concern for promoting learning. When the battle of Badr ended with the victory over the clan of Quraysh, the number of prisoners was high. Most of them did not have the necessary funds for a ransom. The Messenger consented that each prisoner ransom himself by teaching ten Muslims who were versed in the tenets of Islam to read.

The above considerations, together with enthusiasm for learning, directed the Muslims toward the high road of knowledge and the pursuit of writing capability. These same considerations led also to the diffusion of the Arabic script and to the writing of works that numbered in the millions, including works on religion as well as in the humanities. Muslim scholars who got involved in authoring did so prolifically. The works of some individual scholars reached four hundred in number. Mention can be made here of al-Kindī the philosopher, al-Jāḥiẓ the writer, al-Madā'inī the historian, Ibn ʿArabī the mystic, and al-Suyūṭī the theologian.

THE ARABS' EXCELLENCE IN CALLIGRAPHY

In Mecca, the Arabs wrote in a script called the Meccan, an offshoot of the Nabatean script. After the *hijrah*, the emigration of the Prophet to Medina in 622 C.E., a script called the Medinian evolved. It differed little from the Meccan. The Kufi script appeared after the establishment of the city of Kufah in 638 C.E. It marked the beginning of a new era in the history of scripts in that this last and newest script manifested tendencies for improvement and variation.

The Kufi script spread along with Islam in all the conquered countries. Each country, however, stamped it with its own particular character, so we began to see the Damascene, or Syrian; the Baghdadi; the Iraqi, or *Muḥaqqaq*; the Egyptian; the Qayrawānī; and the Andalusian scripts. Some scripts came to be known after the name of a ruling dynasty, such as the Fatimid, Ayyubi, and Mamluk Kufi scripts. The Kufi script, in all its variations, remained the script of the *maṣāḥif*, Korans, until the fourth/tenth century. It was then that Ibn Muqlah and Ibn al-Bawwāb appeared, and the writing of the *maṣāḥif* in the Naskhi (cursive) script began. The sixth/twelfth century witnesses the complete disappearance of Kufi as the script of Korans; however, it remained used for the decoration of mosques and inscriptions on tombstones. New and more developed styles of script appeared with the passage of time, such as the new Naskh, Ruqāʿ, Thulūth, Dīwānī, and Taʿlīq. Both the Persians and the Turks later excelled in producing other beautiful styles of script.

Using this wealth of scripts, the Muslims produced millions of works and millions of *maṣāḥif*. None of the other ancient civilizations produced as great a number of works as did the Islamic and Arab civilizations, and that includes the Greek, the Syriac, and the Roman.

THE PLACE OF CALLIGRAPHY IN ISLAM

Calligraphy occupied a high position in Islam and played an important role in society for the following reasons:

1. Islam encouraged reading and writing from the very beginning.
2. Calligraphy became an official and religious tool.
3. Arabic script was beautiful and amenable to development.
4. Calligraphers were accoladed and supported by Muslim states.
5. Muslim calligraphers were possessed of genius.

Calligraphy invaded all areas of culture and society. Korans, as well as scientific, religious, and literary works, were penned in beautiful styles of calligraphy. Mosques, tribunes (*minbars*), palaces, baths, rugs, pillows, seats, swords, helmets, and even scientific instruments, such as astrolabes and globes, were all embellished with calligraphy and calligraphic designs. What may come as a surprise is that the calligraphers who produced masterpieces that drew worldwide admiration were not all men. Women played a very significant role in the growth of Islamic culture.

WOMEN'S OCCUPATIONS: CALLIGRAPHY

Reading and writing helped women acquire a variety of cultural qualifications that enabled them to become scientists, writers, and poets. Furthermore, it prepared them to assume responsible positions in the state and to work in the courts (*dīwāns*) of the caliphs helping in the facilitation of all kinds of transactions. As far back as the third/ninth century, al-Jāḥiẓ described these active women by saying: "The kings and nobility had bondswomen who undertook all kinds of daily responsibilities joining the workforce or staff of the *dīwāns*. There were women who attended to the affairs of people, such as Khāliṣah, the maid of al-Khayzurān; and ʿUtbah, the maid of Rīṭah, daughter of Abū al-ʿAbbās al-Saffāḥ; and Sukkar and Turkīyah, the maids of Umm Jaʿfar. Furthermore, women appeared in public stylishly dressed and nobody decried that or reproached it."[5]

Sitt Nasīm, one of the favorites (*ḥaẓīyah*) at the end of the Abbasid period, played an important role during the caliphate of al-Nāṣir li-Dīn Allah (d. 622/1225). The Caliph taught her calligraphy so she was able to write almost beautifully as he did. When, in his old age, his eyesight weakened and senility overtook him, and he became unable to attend to the affairs of the people, he asked her to respond, as she saw fit, to all the written requests addressed to him. She performed that task for a long time.[6]

Some of the poets and learned men had educated women to assist them. Abū al-ʿAtāhiyah, the famous poet, had a bondswoman to whom he dictated his poetry, and she copied it down very well. Muḥammad ibn al-ʿAbbās ibn al-Furāt (d. 384/994), the ḥadīth compiler and *ḥāfiẓ* who authored one hundred commentaries on the Koran and one hundred history books, had a bondswoman who check what he copied from other books to make sure that there were no discrepancies. This is not as simple as it seems; it requires a high degree of education.

In the palaces of the caliphs in Spain, al-Nuḍḍār (d. 374/984), a favorite of Caliph al-Ḥakam ibn ʿAbd al-Nāṣir the Umayyad (d. 362/972), distinguished herself. She was not only a poet, but also knoweldgeable in mathematics, and was involved in all aspects of learning and in calligraphy.[7] Lubná (d. 394/1003), the secretary of al-Mustanṣir (d. 366/976), was a poetess who excelled in grammar, rhetoric, and mathematics. She produced a variety of fine calligraphic works.[8] And there was Muznah (d. 358/968), the secretary of the Andalusian caliph Nāṣir al-Dīn. She was one of the most distinguished calligraphers.[9]

Many women, in fact, distinguished themselves in calligraphy, acquiring rank and importance as a result. Such was the case with Fāṭimah, the daughter of al-Ḥasan al-Aqraʿ. She wrote in *mansūb* style, follwing the manner of the great calligrapher Ibn al-Bawwāb. Calligraphers all over the Islamic world imitated her.[10] One day, she wrote a note to Muḥammad ibn Manṣūr al-Kandarī, the vizier of Tughril Beg and the first Saljuqi vizier. He was so impressed with her writing style and her eloquence that he presented her with one thousand dinars.[11] When the caliph al-Muqtadir (d. 932) sent the Byzantine emperor a letter declaring a truce between Byzantium and Baghdad, he asked Fāṭimah to pen it in her beautiful handwriting.[12]

WOMEN SCHOLARS AND CALLIGRAPHY

Women's concern for copying religious and scientific books as well as poetical anthologies grew as time went by. Their undertakings combined scholarship and beauty. Mention is to be made here of Fāṭimah (d. 966/1558), the daughter of ʿAbd al-Qādir, better known as Bint Quraymazan. She was a scholar in her own right, and a principal of the ʿĀdiliyah *khānqāh* (a school for Sufis) in Aleppo. She copied, by her own hand, a great number of books.[13]

Another woman scholar was Sayyidah (d. 647/1249), the daughter of ʿAbd al-Ghanī al-ʿAbdarīyah of Granada, Spain, who knew the Koran by heart and was well known for her philanthropic work and for ransoming prisoners. She copied, by her own hand, the whole of al-Ghazzālī's *Ihyā' ʿulūm al-dīn* (The Revival of Religious Sciences).[14] al-Riḍā, the daughter of al-Fatḥ, was a well known writer in Baghdad. She was a prolific writer and copier, and copied the *dīwān* of Ibn al-Hajjāj, a copy of which the historian al-Ṣafaḍī saw. Another well known woman in Baghdad was Shuhdah bint al-Ubrī. Nicknamed "the glory of womanhood," she was a *muḥaddithah*, a compiler of the ḥadīth, who knew by heart the Traditions of the Messenger of God. She was also called *musnidat al-ʿIrāq*, the Iraqi authority. She penned beautiful calligraphy in the fashion of Fāṭimah bint al-Aqraʿ. There was none like her at the time. When she died in 574/1178, the Caliph himself presided over her funeral.[15]

WOMEN EXCEL IN THE COPYING OF KORANS

The core of our subject is women's role in the copying of Korans. Women calligraphers practiced this art all over the Islamic world, from Spain to Syria, Iraq, Persia, and India. They even competed with each other in the copying of wonderful Korans.

Historians mention that in the eastern quarters of Cordova there were one hundred and seventy women copying Korans in the Kufi script. They worked day and night by candlelight which illuminated the streets along three parasangs (*farsakhs*).[16] One woman who copied Korans was the Cordovan ʿĀʾishah, the daughter of Aḥmad (d. 400/1009). She was a good poet and calligrapher, and also a bibliophile who collected a great number of books. She was respected and loved by kings.[17]

During the Sanhājī rule in Tunisia, Durrah al-Katibah, the writer, one of the secretaries in the Sanhājī court, acquired great fame. One of her unparalleled works is the Ḥāḍinah (The Nursemaid) Koran. In the court of Banū Zīrī there were several foreign bondsmaids, one of whom was from Byzantium. She was captured by pirates during the reign of the Sannājī prince al-Manṣūr, and taken first to Mahdiyah and later to Qayrawān. al-Manṣūr bought her and changed her name to Fāṭimah. She was very intelligent, so al-Manṣūr entrusted her with the nursing of his son, Bādis. This is why she came to be known as Fāṭimah al-Ḥāḍinah, that is, the nursemaid. When al-Muʿizz ibn Bādis consolidated his power, he raised her position, thus raising the prestige of and respect for his father's nurse and teacher. Fāṭimah endowed the mosque of ʿUqbah in Qayrawān with valuable books, rare works, and gilded Korans, some of which still exist in the old library. Some of the Korans are written with smelted gold in the old Kufi scripts. One of the endowed Korans was copied by a certain Durrah. On the last page is written, "In the Name of God the Merciful, the Compassionate, Fatimah the Nursemaid, the nursemaid of Abū Manād Bādis. I endowed (*ḥabastu*) this Koran to the Mosque of the City of Qayrawān in the month of Ramadan 410 A.H. (1019 C.E.)." And on the other side of the paper is written, "This Koran was copied, diacritically marked, decorated, gilded, and bound by ʿĀlī ibn Aḥmad al-Warrāq for the honorable Nursemaid. May God protect her, at the hand of Durrah, the calligrapher, may God keep her." Fāṭimah died in 420/1029, but her Koran remains with us.[18]

WOMEN CALLIGRAPHERS IN THE OTTOMAN PERIOD

During the Ottoman period, calligraphry gained a very high standing in society. Several women calligraphers flourished. Among them were ʿIbrat; Zāhidah Salmá Khanum; Sharīfah ʿĀʾishah Khanum; Silfinaz Khanum; Farīdah Khanum, the Qastumonian; Khadījah Kuzaydah Khanum Çelebi; and Nukhah Khanum.

Many of the Ottoman sultans were themselves calligraphers, as were their mothers. Durrah Khanum, the mother of Sultan Maḥmūd Khān, copied a Koran in the year 1172/1758. This Koran was held by the Maḥmūdīyah Library in Medina. It is said that it was carried away by the Ottoman Turks to Istanbul when they left the Hijaz.[19] The mother of Sultan ʿAbd al-Majīd Khān, who ascended to the throne in 1255/1839, penned a copy of *Dalāʾil al-khayrāt*, which was also among the holdings of the Maḥmūdīyah Library in Medina.

Among the most splendid works of the Turkish women calligraphers is a Koran copied by *al-sharīfah* and *ḥāfiẓah* Zulaykhah Khātimī al-Saʿdī, the daughter of al-Ḥajj ʿAbd al-Karīm Zādah Bisār-i Yārī, in 1276/1859. "*al-Sharīfah*" indicates that she was a descendant of the family of the Prophet, and "*ḥāfiẓah*" indicates that she was one of those who knew the Koran by heart. The calligrapher who knew the Koran by heart, whether man or woman, was thought to be more trustworthy.

The first two pages of this Koran are splendidly illuminated. Within "The Opening" (*al-Fātiḥah*) and the beginning of "The Cow" (*al-Baqarah*), several *āyāt* (verses) are decorated with very colorful folial and floral designs on a gilded background. Though I have seen many gilded Korans, I don't believe I have seen anything as beautiful as these two pages. The other pages of this Koran have wide, gilded border surrounded by a fine blue line. The verses are separated by gilded circular designs filled with variated ornamentations. The titles of the surahs are placed within gilded panels, within which the number of the surah is written in white. In the margins, the *aḥzāb* (60th part) and *ajzā'* (30th part) are indicated by circular designs within which the word *ḥizb* or *juz'* is inscribed. The designs have a head and a tail similar, in a way, to a colored spike, and one of them is differently shaped. The script is in beautiful Naskhi script, the binding is leather filigreed in gold. A Jeddah scholar owns this Koran.

It is believed that there exists a spiritual and mystical bond between women and the letters of the alphabet. One writer described a woman calligrapher by saying: "Her ink was like the blackness of her hair, her paper was like the tanned skin of her face, her pen was like one of her delicate fingers, and her knife was like the penetrating sword of her sweet looks." The eyebrows of a beautiful woman have been compared to the Arabic letter *nūn*, her eye to an *ʿayn*, her temple to a *wāw*, her mouth to a *mīm*, and her braided hair to a *shīn*. For a woman to be considered really beautiful, one of the qualifications was good penmanship. It was said that a lucky woman was one who combined the beauty of body and face with that of character and penmanship.

NOTES

1. The Holy Koran, 68:1.

2. Ibid., 96:1–4.

3. Ibid., 2:282.

4. Ibid., 29:48.

5. ʿAmr ibn Baḥr al-Jāḥiẓ, *Rasā'il*, 2 vols., ed. A.M. Hārūn (Cairo, 1964), 2:156.

6. Khalīl ibn Aybak al-Ṣafadī, *al-Wāfī bi-al wafayāt*, ed. Wadād al-Qāḍī (Wiesbaden, 1982), 16:239.

7. al-Suyūṭī, *Bughyat al-Wū'āt*, 2 vols., ed. M. Abū al-Faḍl Ibrāhīm (Cairo, 1965), 2:269.

8. Loc. cit.

9. 'Umar Riḍā Kahhālah, *A'lām al-nisā'*, 3rd. ed., 5 vols. (Beirut, 1977), 5:49.

10. 'Abd al-Ḥayy ibn Aḥmad ibn al-'Imād, *Shadharāt al-dhahab fī akhbār man dhahab*, 8 vols. in 4 (Beirut, 1966), 4:365.

11. Loc. cit.

12. Yaqūt al-Ḥamawī, *Mu'jam al-udabā'*, 7 vols., ed. D.S. Margoliouth, E.J.W. Gibb Memorial (London, 1923–27), 6:113; 'Abd al-Raḥmān ibn al-Jawzī, *al-Muntaẓam fī tārīkh al-umam*, 10 vols. (Hyderabad, 1359/1940), 9:40.

13. Ibn al-'Imād, *Shadharāt*, 8:347.

14. al-Ṣafadī, *al-Wāfī*, 16:65.

15. Ibid., 14:128, ed. by S. Dedering.

16. Muḥammad Kurd 'Alī, "*Ghābir al-Andalus wa-ḥāḍiruhā*," *Majallat al-Majma' al-'Ilmī bi-Dimashq* 2 (1922), p. 265.

17. Kahhālah, *A'lām al-nisā'*, 3:6.

18. Ḥasan Ḥusni 'Abd al-Wahhāb, *Waraqāt Tūnisīyah*, 3 vols. (Tunis,1964), 1:345; *Shahīrāt al-Tūnisīyāt*, 2nd ed. (Tunis, 1966), pp. 80–82.

19. Muḥammad Ṭāhir al-Kurdī, *Tārīkh al-khaṭṭ al-'Arabī wa-adabuh* (Cairo, 1936), p. 340.

9

Some Illustrations in Islamic Scientific Manuscripts and Their Secrets

David A. King

An estimated 10,000 Islamic scientific manuscripts survive in libraries around the world. Although many were copied after the creative period of Islamic science, they bear witness to a scientific tradition which knew no rival from the eighth to the fifteenth centuries. While many of these manuscripts are illustrated, the illustrations have received scant attention from historians. For example, even though some manuscripts of al-Ṣufi's *Book on Constellations* have been studied by art historians, neither a critical study of the available manuscripts nor a comparative study of the various traditions of illustration has been conducted. Moreover, there are other treatises in which constellation figures occur, and other astrological treatises in which there are illustrations that should be of interest to art historians.

Some attention has been paid to the diagrams in works on engineering (see figure 9.1), and scholars have labored over geometrical diagrams to understand the accompanying mathematical procedures (see figure 9.2). Islamic maps have also fared quite well at the hands of historians, and the state of our present knowledge of Islamic cartography is reasonably advanced. Investigations of diagrams of geometrical planetary models led, in the 1950s, to the discovery of a tradition lasting several centuries of Islamic modifications to Ptolemaic planetary theory (see figure 9.3).

My present purpose is to demonstrate the significance of various other categories of illustrations which I have worked on recently and which open up new chapters in the field of Islamic science.

SOME ILLUSTRATIONS IN TREATISES ON ASTRONOMICAL INSTRUMENTS

Before mentioning some illustrations in Islamic texts on astronomical instruments, let us look at figure 9.4, from the *Shāhinshāhnāme*, which shows the scene at the Ottoman Observatory in Istanbul. The observatory was built in 1577 and demolished in 1580, and we are lucky indeed to have this miniature.

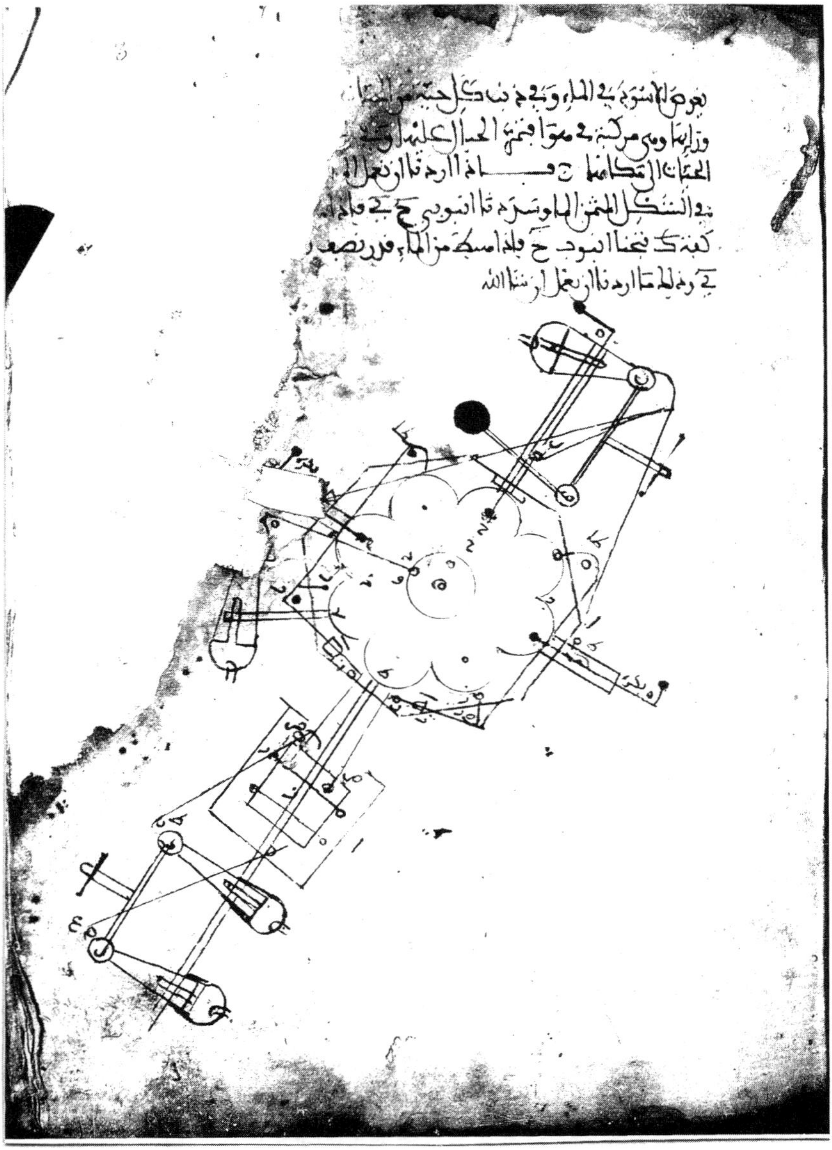

Fig. 9.1. Numerous mechanical devices are illustrated and described in this eleventh-century Andalusian treasure, discovered less than twenty years ago. (MS Florence Bibliotheca Medicea-Laurenziana Or. 152.)

ارتفاع نصف النهار وكشر جيبه و شقو حس نقامه اعنی حس ما بینه وبن
سمتالرواس وتقع ساوی حس سعه المشرق للمدار لموارکدط ه ج وبکون
قطر نامًا علی سطح الافق فهونام علی حططح علی نقطه ضر منه اعنی النقطه
التی یفصله بصفنه محور سقی یقطعه علی ج ع مرکزالدوایر المنواره کلها
بکون علی المحور کا بان ز کا ب الاکر یلمر من قطر المدار فهو سهمه الطا هر
ولا یقع فی سطح المدارو سطح دایره نصف النهار فهو نام علی المحور یقع جیب
نام میل المدار وعقر حس بیله و عقر حس زیاده النصف الطا هر من
المدار علی اربعه و هو حس نصف فصل نهاره وذک بس ما ذکرناه فی یفضل
الحبوب وتقر کقر فی سطح تقو بمنوازین یفضلها سطح نام علیها فهما
منوازیان ان کابان ذک فی اصولا یلدسا عزاوده تقر الما خله بمساویه لزاوا

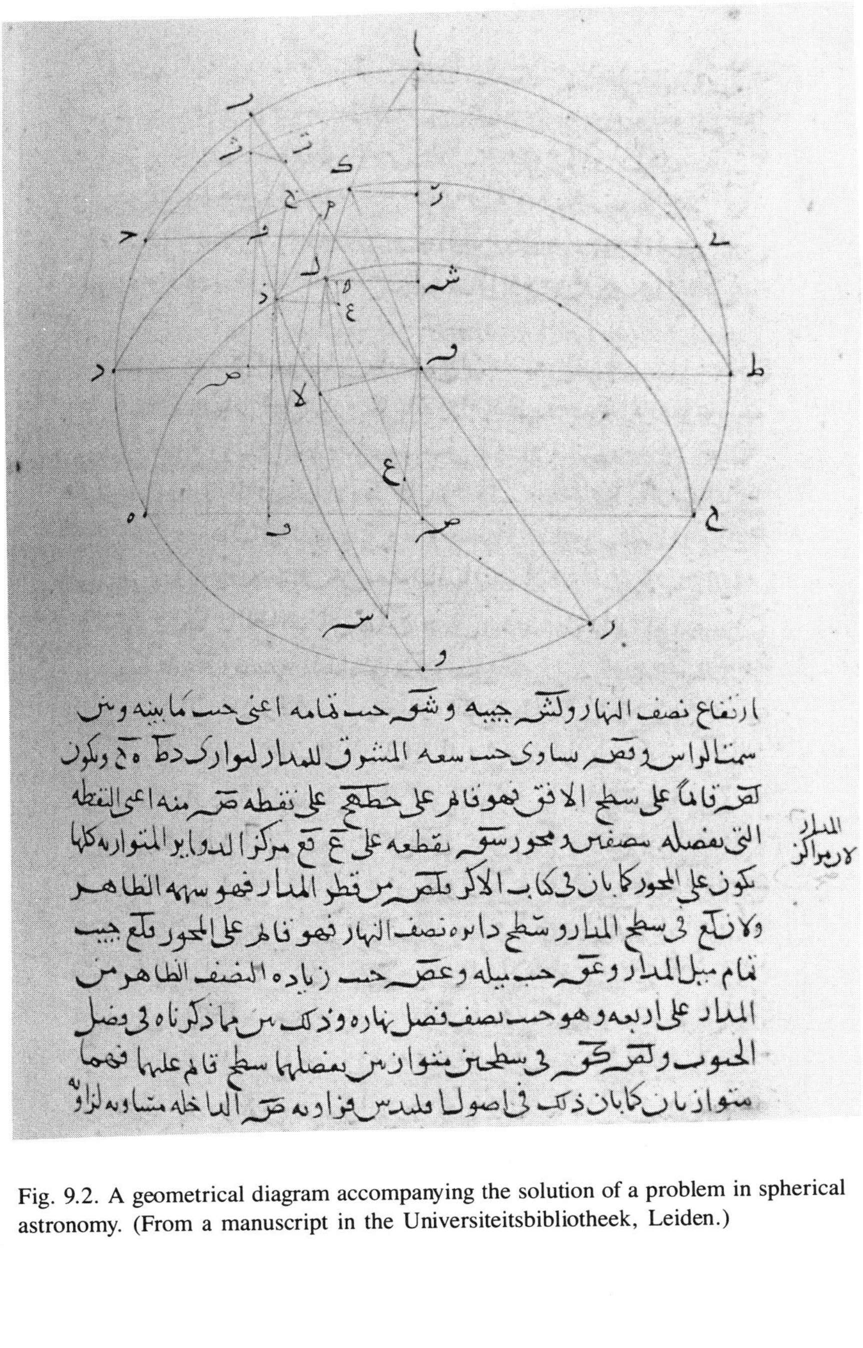

Fig. 9.2. A geometrical diagram accompanying the solution of a problem in spherical astronomy. (From a manuscript in the Universiteitsbibliotheek, Leiden.)

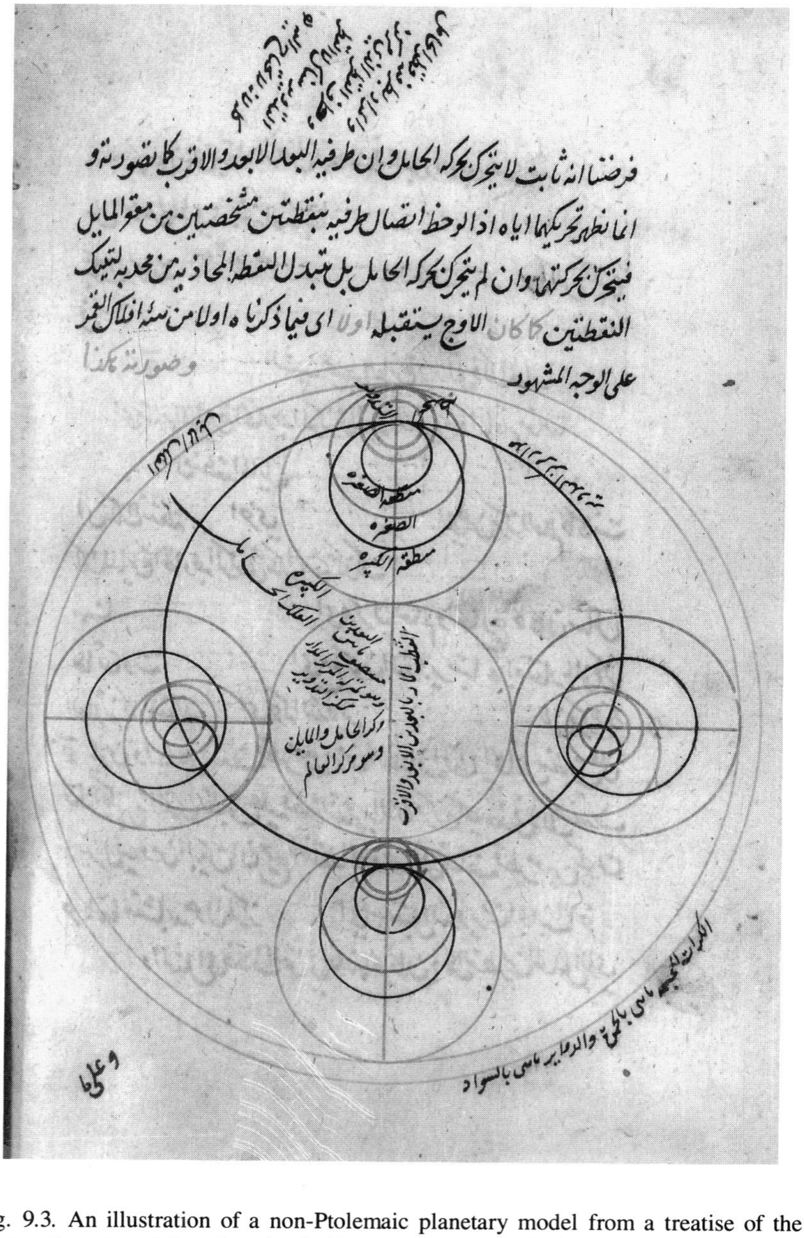

Fig. 9.3. An illustration of a non-Ptolemaic planetary model from a treatise of the thirteenth-century Maragha school. (From a manuscript in the Dār al-Kutub, Cairo.)

Fig. 9.4. The astronomers of the Istanbul Observatory with some of their instruments. This miniature is a veritable gold-mine of information which has yet to be fully exploited. (MS Istanbul University Library Yildiz 1404.)

The director, Taqī al-Dīn, is one of the two men contemplating the astrolabe. Some of the books behind him are now in the University Library in Leiden; his mark of ownership is found on several manuscripts in that library. Taqī al-Dīn himself wrote a treatise on mechanical clocks, and one such clock is featured here. Most of the instruments, notably the astrolabe and two quadrants, and various observational instruments, are of Islamic provenance; one, the terrestrial globe, is European. A terrestrial globe from the workshop of Mercator, with a dedication to Sultan Murād III dated 1579, was auctioned at Christie's of London in 1991; could this be the one illustrated here?

A project currently in progress in Frankfurt aims to catalogue all of the historically significant, surviving Islamic astronomical instruments (as well as European to ca. 1550). As many of the instruments as possible are being examined at first hand, and the relevant manuscript sources are also being exploited for information. Sometimes, manuscripts constitute the only available source of information on certain classes of instruments of which no examples have survived.

Figure 9.5 shows some of the illustrations of unusual astrolabe retia in a treatise on the astrolabe by al-Bīrūnī. These variatons on the standard astrolabe are of considerable historical interest, not least because we now know al-Bīrūnī's source for his information on them. His predecessor, al-Sijzī, actually mentions the astronomers who devised them and the patrons to whom they dedicated examples of them. Alas, all such instruments have disappeared without a trace, and it is left to the modern historian to piece together the details. Dr. Richard Lorch of Munich is currently preparing a critical analysis of all of the related textual material. Sometimes we are more fortunate in having both text and instrument, although in the following examples the instruments were known to modern scholarship before the texts.

An astrolabe in the Metropolitan Museum of Art in New York bears the signature of the Yemeni Rasulid Sultan al-Ashraf and is dated 690/1291 (see figure 9.6). A few decades ago, it was pronounced a fake: no Yemeni sultan could have made such an astrolabe. Perhaps, it was speculated, the astrolabe was made for him in Cairo, because the Yemen is a backwater, and no serious astronomy could have been practiced there. We now know of *over one hundred Yemeni astronomical manuscripts* attesting to an active tradition of astronomy in the Yemen from the tenth century to the twentieth. One of these, preserved in the Egyptian National Library, is an illustrated treatise by al-Ashraf on the construction of the astrolabe and sundial (see figure 9.7). Appended to the text, which may well be in the Sultan's own hand, is a set of *ijāzah*s by two of his teachers approving six astrolabes which he made and mentioning various features of each. One of these is clearly the New York instrument.

Another case is an astrolabe in the Benaki Museum in Athens which was made by Ibn al-Sarrāj in Aleppo in 729/1328 or 1329. It is the most sophisticated

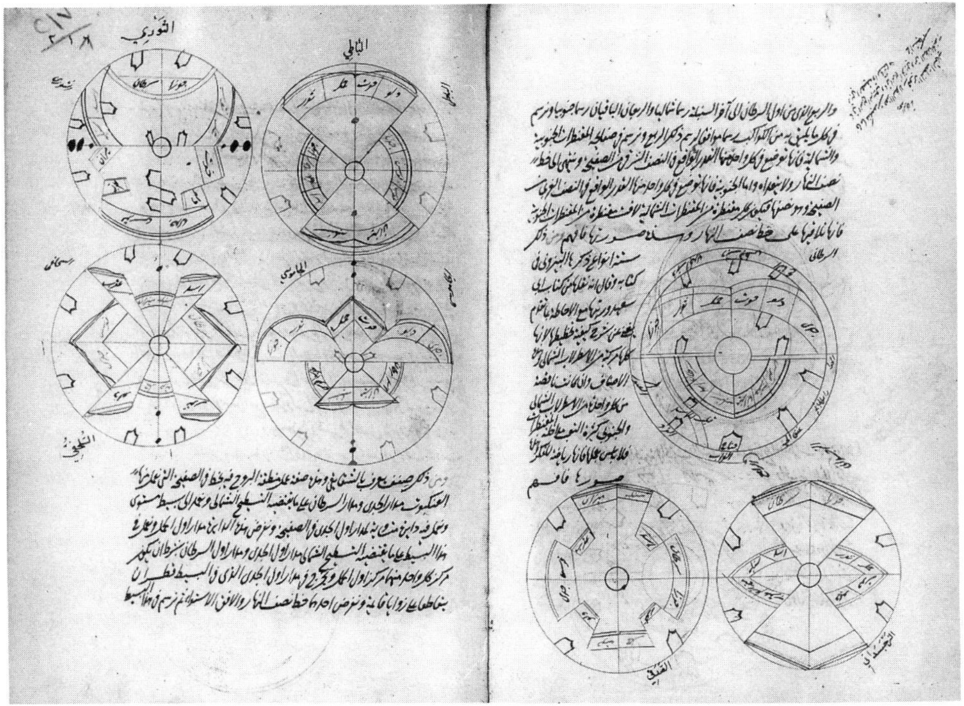

Fig. 9.5. Non-standard astrolabes illustrated in the treatise on astronomical instruments by al-Marrākushī (Cairo, ca. 1280). The text is based on al-Bīrūnī (Central Asia, ca. 1025), who abridged the discussion of them by al-Sijzī (E. Iran, ca. 1000). (MS Cairo Dār al-Kutub K 3821.)

Fig. 9.6. The back of the astrolabe of the Yemeni Sultan al-Ashraf, dated 690/1291. This is the only known Islamic astrolabe on which the back is devoted to astrological information and also one of the few on which the sun, moon, and five planets are indicated by their symbols. The very same peculiarities are featured in an illustration found in al-Ashraf's treatise on astrolabe construction (see figure 8.7). (Metropolitan Museum of Art, New York, inv. no. 91.1.535.)

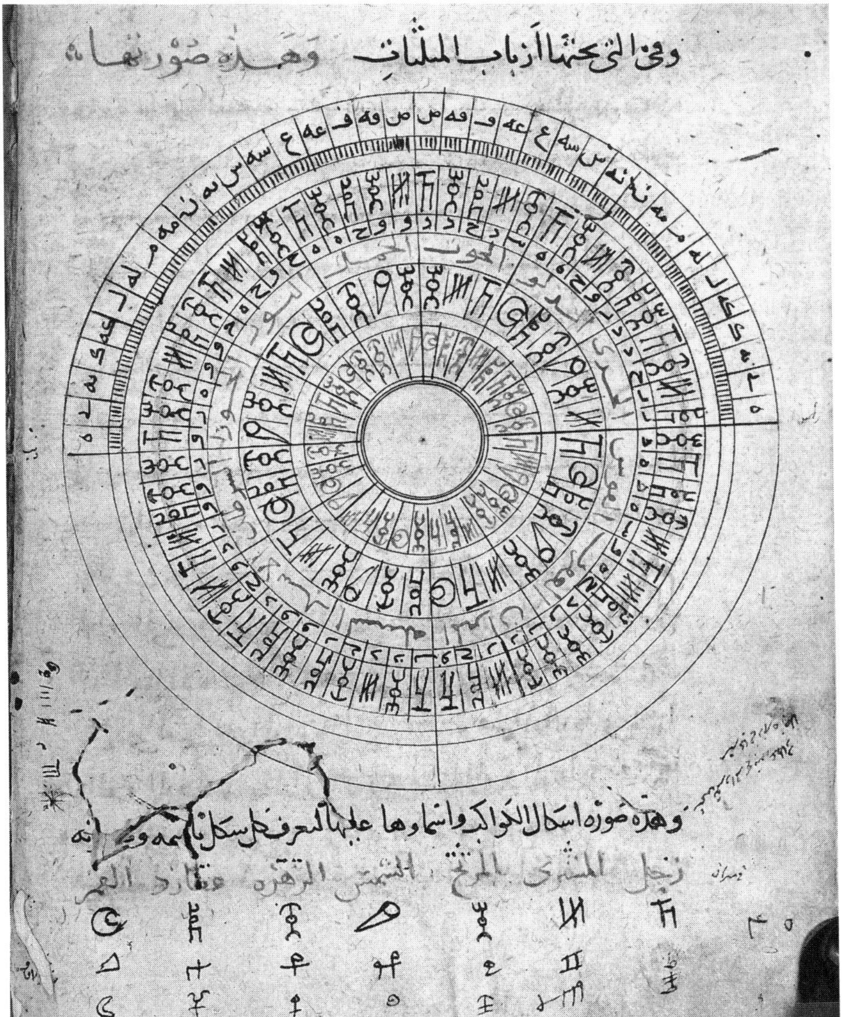

Fig. 9.7. One of numerous illustrations in al-Ashraf's treatise on astrolabe construction. If any proof were needed that the New York astrolabe was indeed due to al-Ashraf. . . but none is. The treatise also deals with sundial construction (no medieval sundials are known from the Yemen) and contains the earliest known description of a magnetic compass in any astronomical text.

astrolabe ever constructed, being universal in five different ways (see figure 9.8). (Most astrolabes have plates serving a series of latitudes; the universal astrolabe with a single plate serving all latitudes was invented in Andalusia in the eleventh century.) A manuscript in Princeton contains an account by the fifteenth-century Egyptian astronomer ʿAbd al-ʿAzīz al-Wafāʾī of the use of Ibn al-Sarrāj's remarkable instrument. (al-Wafāʾī actually owned the astrolabe; his name is engraved on the edge of the rim.) In his treatise, al-Wafāʾī complained that Ibn al-Sarrāj had not explained its use, and so he undertook to do this himself. It is fortunate that he did, because the use of some of the parts is not at all obvious. Ibn al-Sarrāj emerges as a genius. But who was he? We knew

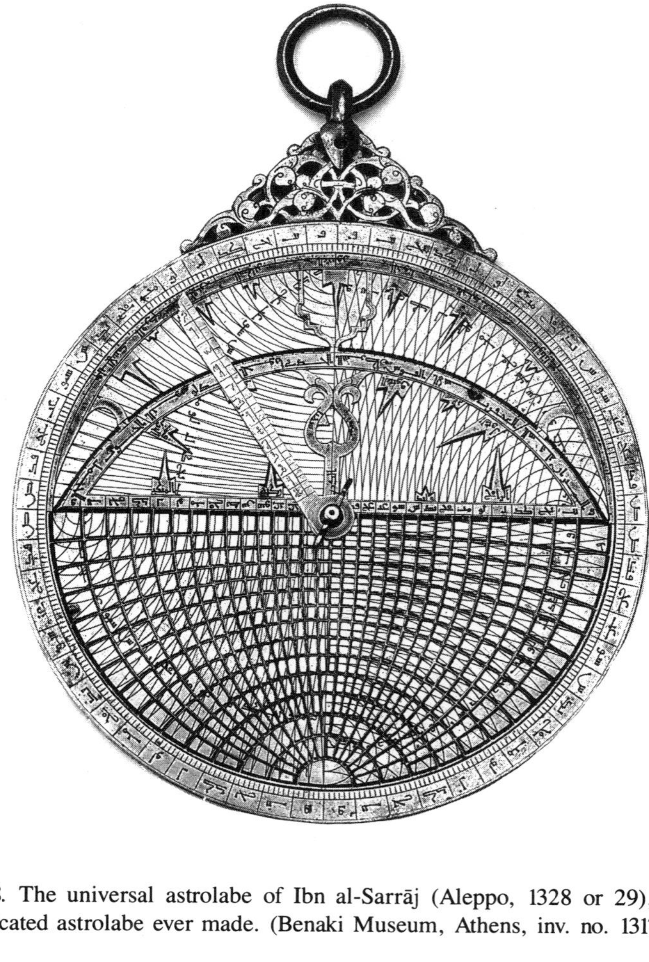

Fig. 9.8. The universal astrolabe of Ibn al-Sarrāj (Aleppo, 1328 or 29), the most sophisticated astrolabe ever made. (Benaki Museum, Athens, inv. no. 13178.)

but little about him until 1983, when a richly illustrated manuscript was discovered in the Chester Beatty Library in Dublin (miscataloged as a Persian work on the astrolabe). It turned out to be a treatise by Ibn al-Sarrāj, probably in his own hand, describing all of the different varieties of instruments known to him, and all those invented by him (see figure 9.9). Although this treatise was clearly written before he developed his quintuply-universal masterpiece, it provides ample evidence of his background and has yet to be exploited for the historical information that it contains.

QIBLAH MAPS

Another genre of illustration serves to display the sacred direction (*qiblah*) of localities in the Muslim world. The map in figure 9.10 (l.h.s), found in an eighteenth-century Egyptian treatise, is a crude cartographic attempt to demonstrate the *qiblah* in various localities, which are roughly displayed on an orthogonal latitude and longitude grid. Such maps were prepared already in the ninth century, and later others were with a more sophisticated projection of the parallels of latitude and meridians such that the former are straight lines and the latter ellipses. However, most Muslim cartographers, and surely all scientists, knew that one could not merely read the *qiblah* off a map by simply joining a locality to Mecca and measuring the direction of the line-segment. The scientists knew that the problem had to be solved on a sphere or on a mathematically acceptable two-dimensional representation thereof. Although very few such maps with orthogonal grids specifically designed to find the *qiblah* are known, in 1989 there appeared at Sotheby's in London a cartographic representation of a much more sophisticated kind, on which the meridians are no longer equally spaced, and the parallels of latitude are no longer parallel (see figure 9.11). The combination is so devised as to enable the user to read off the *qiblah* on the circular scale and to read off the distance from Mecca on the diametral rule. The instrument was clearly made in Isfahan around 1710. It is not too much to hope that somewhere in the vast manuscript sources available for further study of Islamic science, a treatise on the construction of such an instrument might one day be found. In April 1994 it was discovered that the Isfahan world-map represents a cartographic tradition that goes back at least to al-Bīrūnī (ca. 1025), who authored a dozen works on mathematical cartography, only two of which are known to have survived. A series of Islamic geographical tables from the fifteenth, fourteenth, and twelfth centuries give, in addition to the usual longitudes and latitudes, here based on al-Bīrūnī's distinctive values, the *qiblah*-values for 250 localities from Spain to China. The *qiblah*-values are given to the nearest ten minutes, and it has been shown that they can only have been derived from a world-map centered on Mecca, such as is found on the Isfahan instrument. A preliminary notice of this remarkable cartographic tradition will appear in the article "Samt" in *The Encyclopedia of Islam*, new edition.

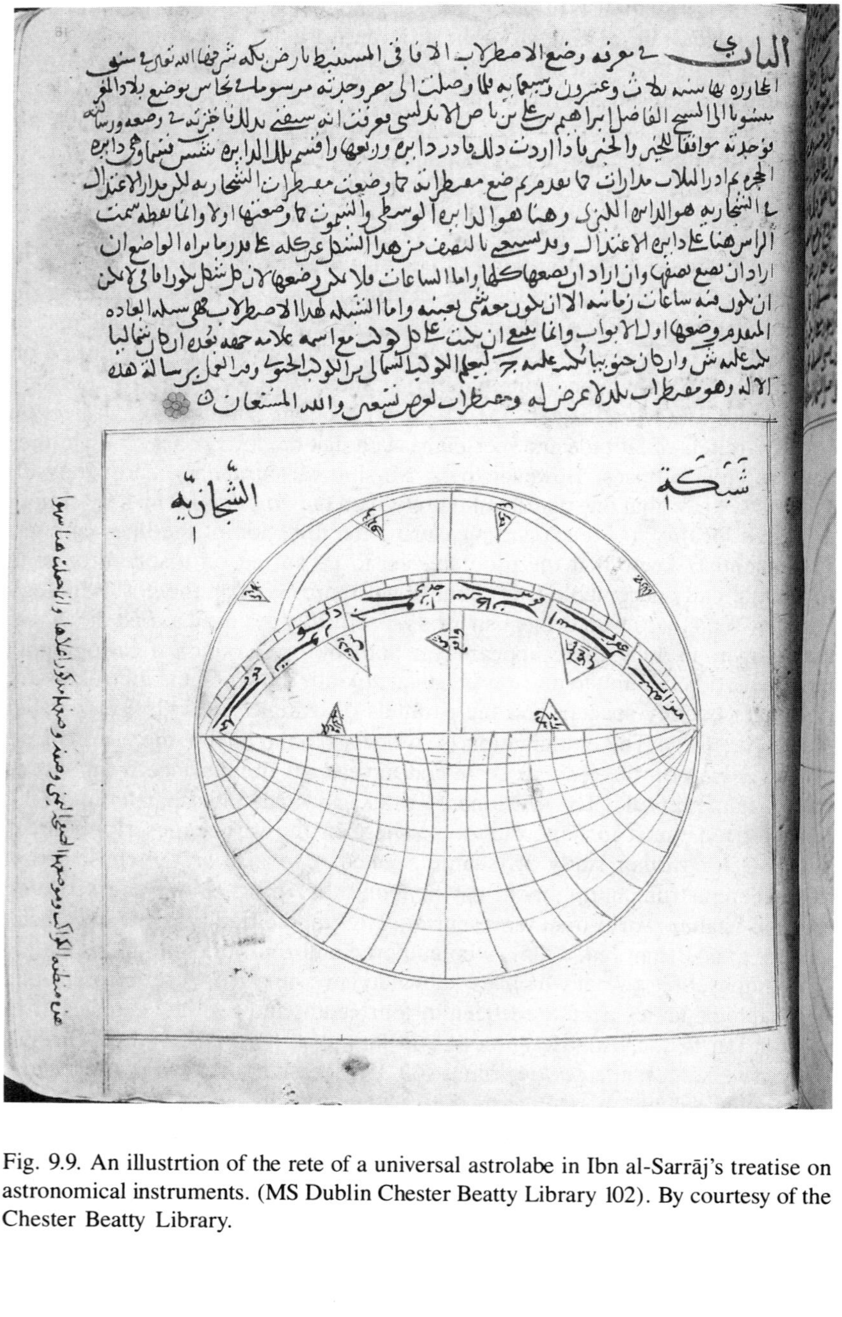

Fig. 9.9. An illustrtion of the rete of a universal astrolabe in Ibn al-Sarrāj's treatise on astronomical instruments. (MS Dublin Chester Beatty Library 102). By courtesy of the Chester Beatty Library.

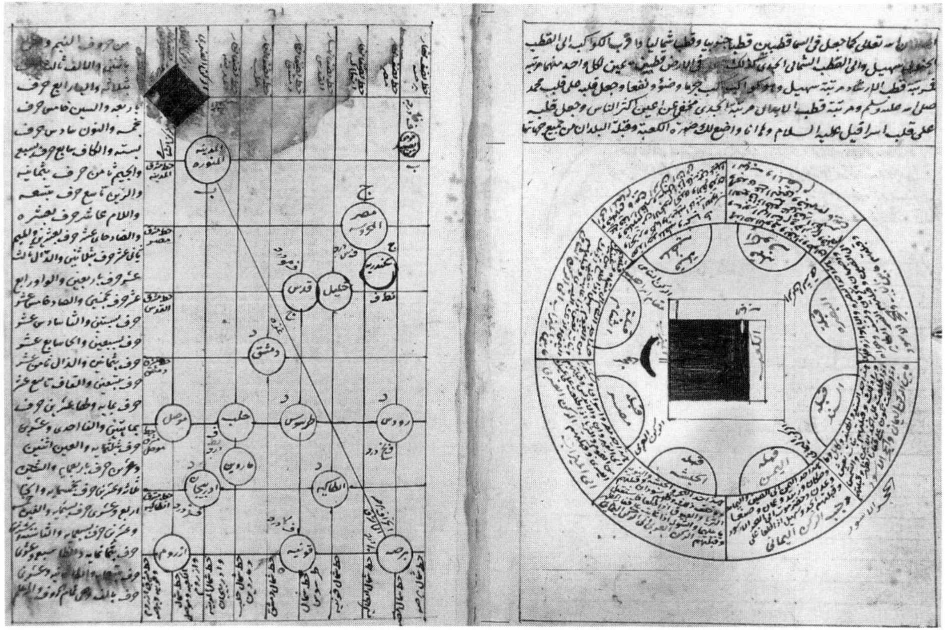

Fig. 9.10. On the left, the Kaʿbah is depicted—appropriately inclined to the meridian—on a crude cartographic grid from which one can determine the *qiblah* very approximately by joining one's city to the Kaʿbah (here Bursa is shown connected to the Kaʿbah [via Medina]). On the right is a diagram of sacred geography showing various areas around the Kaʿbah and indicating the astronomical horizon phenomena which define their *qiblah*s. (MS CAiro Dār al-Kutub Talʿat *majāmiʿ* 811.)

Fig. 9.11. A *qiblah*-indicator from Isfahan, ca. 1710, unique of its genre. The *qiblah*s and distances from Mecca of 150 localities marked on the cartographic grid—which can be read from the circumferential scale when the diametral rule, center at Mecca, is laid on the marker for the locality in question—are given accurately for all practical purposes. (Private collection, photograph from the Museum of the History of Science, Oxford.)

DIAGRAMS REPRESENTING THE SACRED GEOGRAPHY OF ISLAM

In various Islamic sources, by no means restricted to scientific texts but including also treatises on the sacred law of Islam and encyclopedias, there are found illustrations of the divisions of the world around the Kaʿbah. The diagrams of this kind with twelve divisions of the world around the Kaʿbah in the treatises of Yāqūt and al-Qazwīnī are well known (see figure 9.12). Their purpose is to identify regions of the world which have the same *qiblah*. But these diagrams are secondary, that is, they were based on more elaborate prototypes, in which the way to find the *qiblah* in each sector was described in detail. The instructions were not to use the *qiblah*s found by the astronomers using mathematical

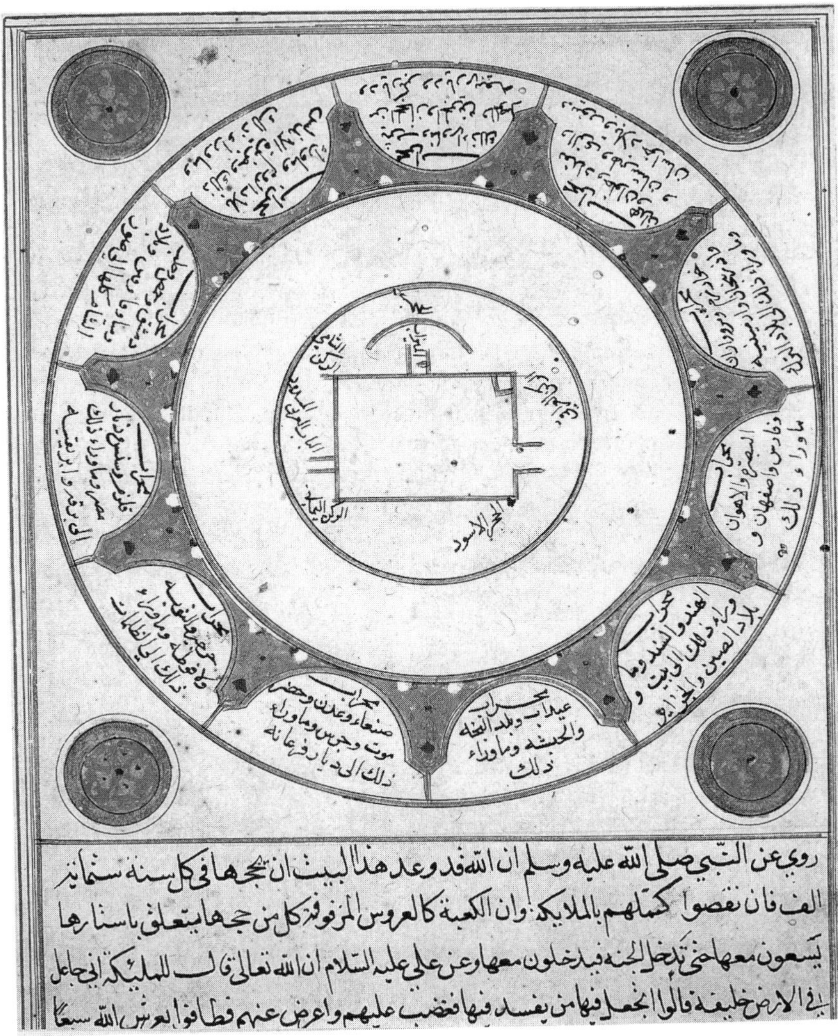

Fig. 9.12. An eleven-sector scheme of sacred geography from a manuscript of al-Qazwīnī's *Āthār al-bilād* (Iraq and Syria, ca. 1250). The information on the *qiblah* in each sector has been suppressed. Also one of the sectors in the original scheme has been ommitted by mistake (MS Dublin Chester Beatty 4163). By courtesy of the Chester Beatty Library.

formulae applied to geographical data, but rather to face the risings and settings of particular fixed stars or of the sun at various times of the year. We now know that schemes for finding the *qiblah* in different regions by such procedures were advocated from the tenth century onward, and that over the centuries some twenty different schemes of what I call "sacred geography" were formulated. Many of these were illustrated in the manuscripts (see figures 9.10 [r.h.s.] and 9.13–9.15); others were recorded only in words; and some were used on astronomical instruments (see figure 9.16). These popular methods for finding the *qiblah* were advocated by the legal scholars of Islam, who had little time for the opinions of the scientists. Their authority lay in the fact that such procedures had been used by the *ṣaḥābah* for laying out some of the earliest mosques. But why had the *ṣaḥābah* used such procedures?

The earliest Muslims knew that when they were standing in front of the walls of the Kaʿbah they were facing significant astronomical directions. Also, the four corners of the Kaʿbah were associated with different regions of the world, and intermediate regions with particular segments of the perimeter of the edifice. Thus, when Muslims in those regions wanted to face the appropriate part of the Kaʿbah, they should face those very same directions. (This means of facing a distant object is quite reasonable if one bears in mind that the direction of a distant locality is to some extent arbitrary, let alone the direction of a particular part of a distant edifice.) The diagrams were intended to serve as *aides-memoires* to the faithful, as well as to provide pictorial representations of the entire world and the relation of its regions to the physical focus of Islamic worship, the Kaʿbah.

A DIAGRAM FOR LAYING OUT THE FOUNDATIONS OF A VENTILATOR

Another remarkable diagram in Ibn al-Sarrāj's treatises on instruments purports to display the orientation of the ventilators that were a distinctive feature of the skyline of medieval Cairo (see figures 9.17 and 9.18). Why would such a diagram feature in a treatise on astronomical instruments? Since the 1970s, we have known that in the corpus of astronomical tables that was used in medieval Cairo for timekeeping and regulating the times of prayer, one table enabled the user to find by means of the sun the orientation of the ventilator (*bādahanj*), namely, winter sunrise (ca. 27° S. of E.). Inspection of the sole surviving ventilator of any consequence in modern Cairo reveals that it is aligned with the foundations of the house (the Musāfirkhāne) on whose roof it stands. Indeed, the house and the whole of the medieval city of Cairo are aligned in this direction, the major thoroughfare of the city being in the perpendicular direction.

The fact is that the entire medieval city of Cairo was oriented in the *qiblah* of the *ṣaḥābah*, towards winter sunrise. Now, the city was built alongside the old Pharaonic/Roman Canal from the Nile to the Red Sea, which at that point flowed perpendicular to that direction, so either the orientation of Cairo is

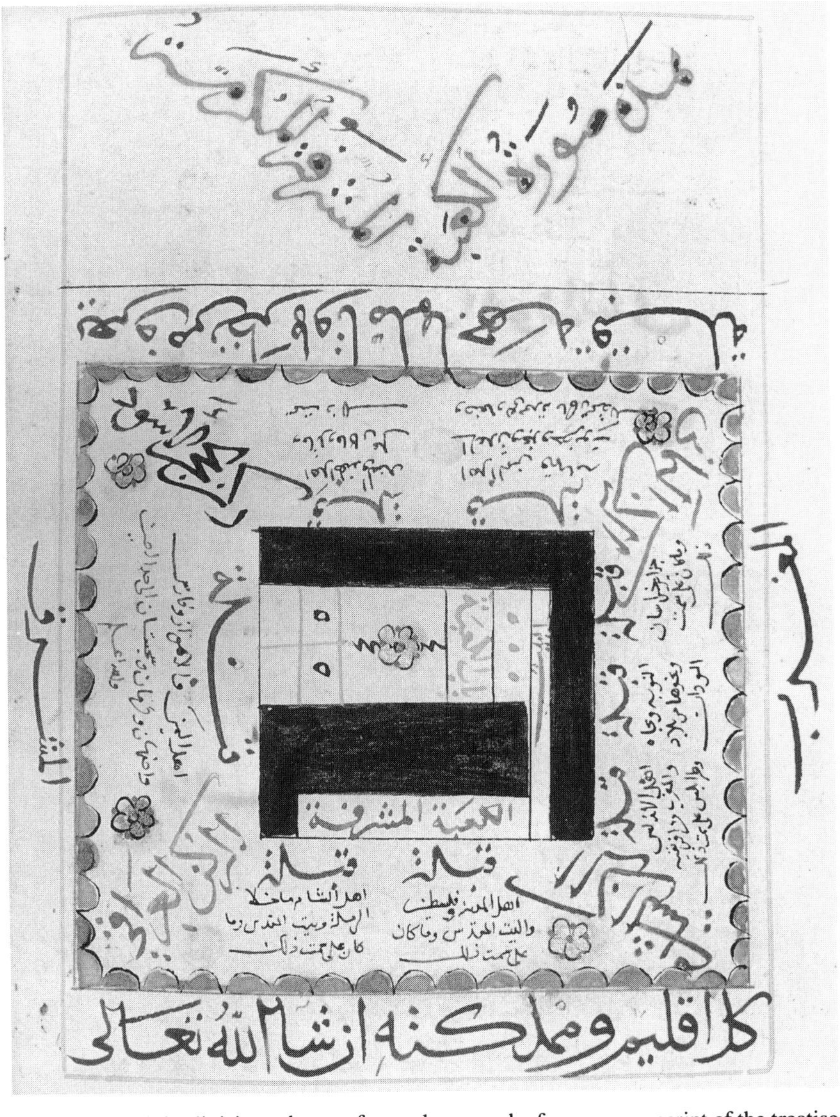

Fig. 9.13. An eight-division scheme of sacred geography from a manuscript of the treatise on cosmography by Pseudo-Ibn al-Wardī (Aleppo, ca. 1420). There are several different traditions of sacred geography in the numerous manuscripts of his treatise; the illustration in the published text shows two of these but are hopelessly corrupt. (MS Topkapi Sarayi Müzesi Kütüphanesi A 3025.)

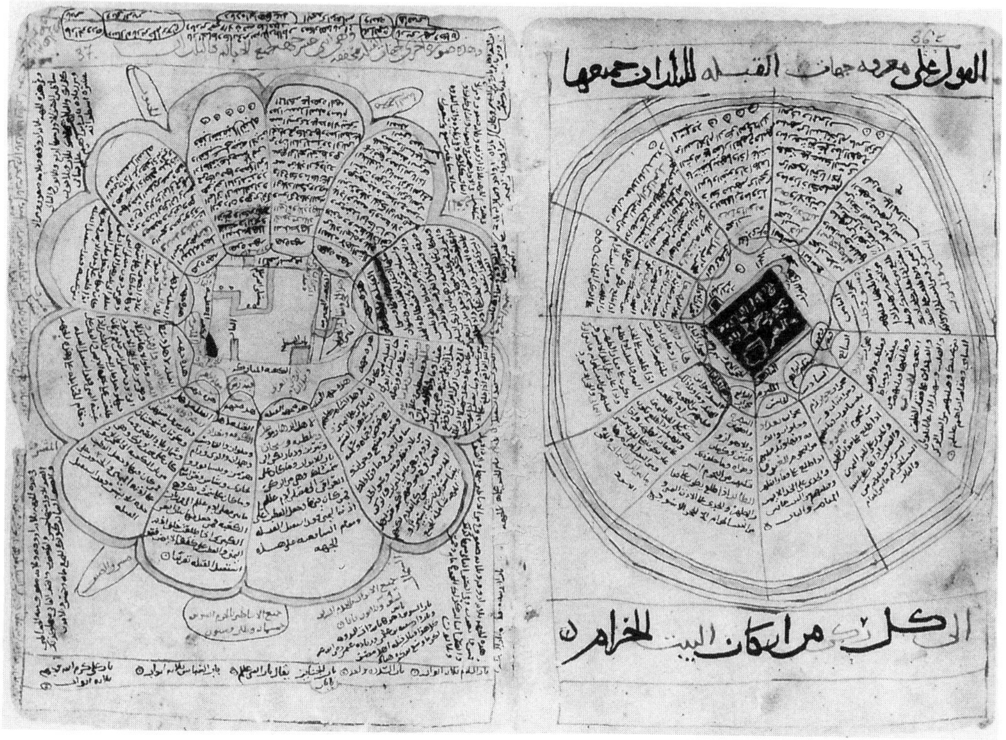

Fig. 9.14. Two different twelve-sector schemes of sacred geography with associated astronomical horizon phenomena for finding the *qiblah*, as found in a manuscript of a thirteenth-century Yemeni treatise on folk astronomy. (MS Milan Biblioteca Ambrosiana Supp. 73.)

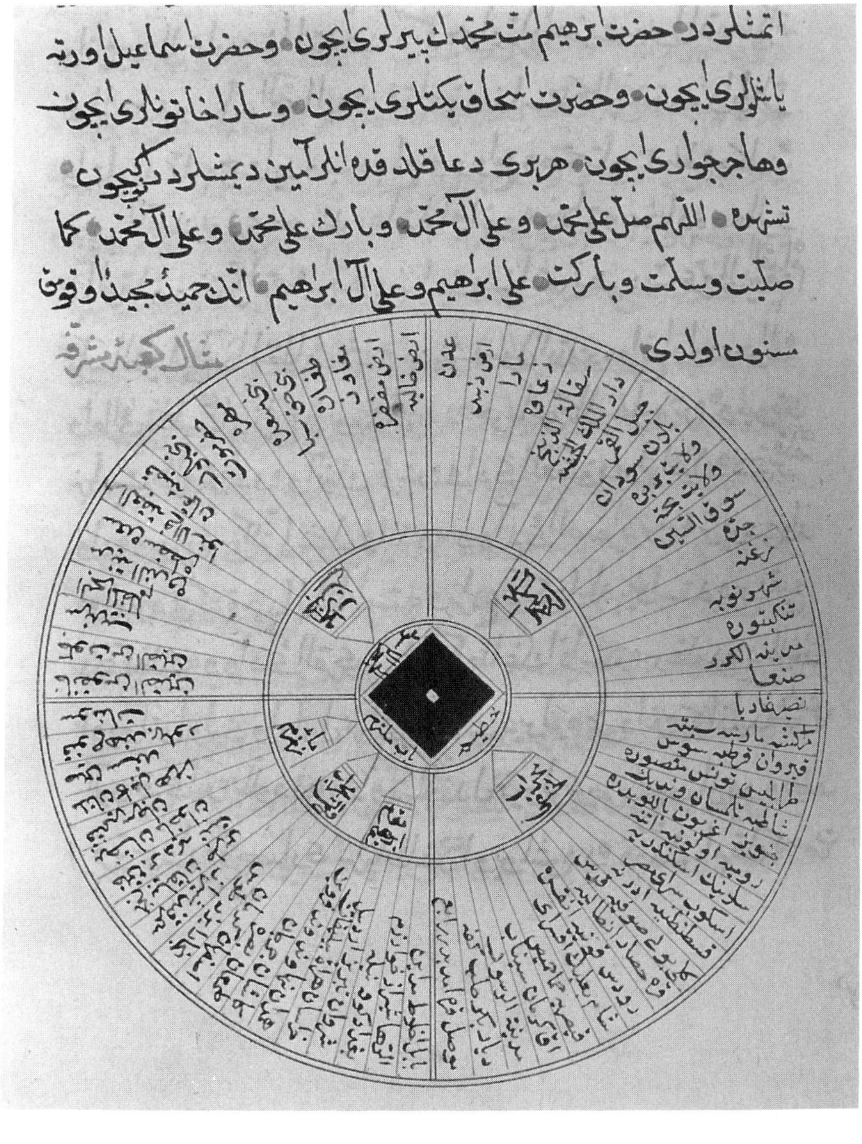

Fig. 9.15. An Ottoman scheme of sacred geography with 72 divisions of the world around the Kaʿbah, suitable for marking on a horizontal *qiblah*-indicator (see figure 9.17). (MS Topkapi Sarayı Müzesi Kütüphanesi B 179.)

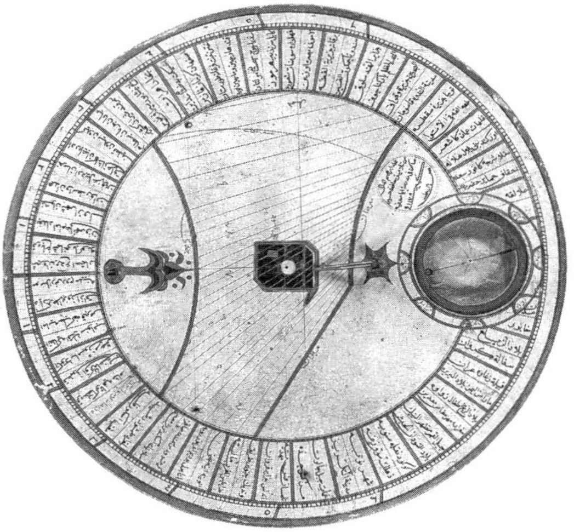

Fig. 9.16. An Ottoman sundial cum *qiblah*-indicator on which a scheme of sacred geography has been included on the circular base. (Berlin Deutsche Staatsbibliothek, Sprenger 2048.)

Fig. 9.17. The imposing ventilator on the Musāfirkhāne in Cairo, one of the few surviving examples. In medieval times, most buildings in Cairo were fitted with such ventilators, all astronomically oriented (Photo Abū Max.)

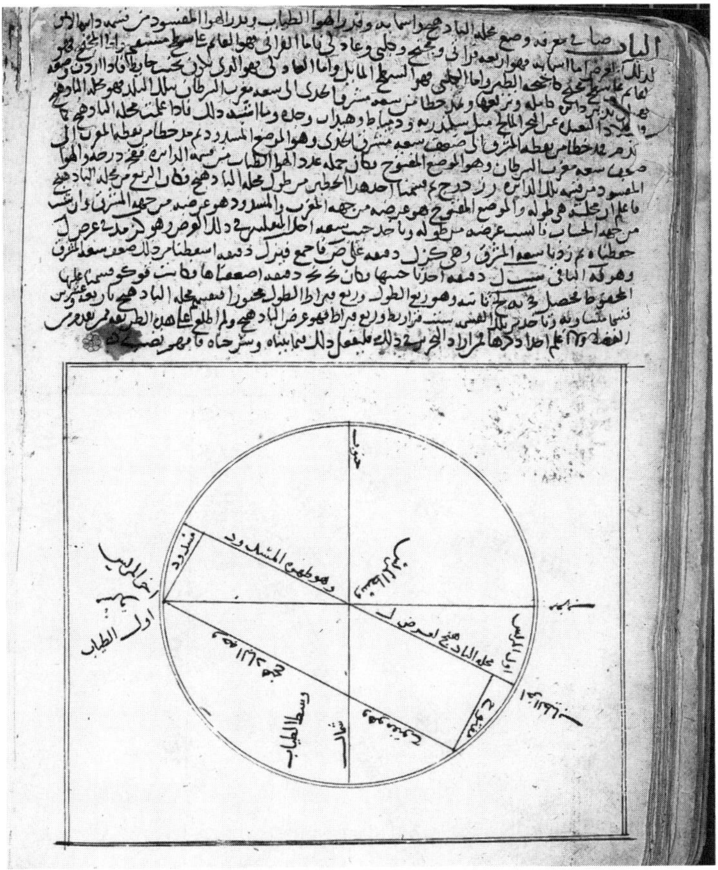

Fig. 9.18. A diagram showing the orientation of ventilators in medieval Cairo, found in the treatise on astronomical instruments of Ibn al-Sarrāj (Aleppo, ca. 1325) (MS Dublin Chester Beatty Library 102). By courtesy of the Chester Beatty Library.

fortuitous, or—and there is no evidence whatsoever for this—the site was chosen because the rectangular street pattern would be *qiblah*-oriented. A few years after the city was built, the astronomer Ibn Yūnus computed the *qiblah* in Cairo to be 37° S. of E., 10° to the south of the *qiblah* of the *ṣaḥābah*, and the Azhar and al-Ḥākim Mosques were erected 10° askew to the city-plan. Many of the religious edifices in Cairo constructed by the Mamluks have their outside walls oriented with the city plan and their inside walls and *miḥrāb*s aligned with the *qiblah* of the astronomers. The City of the Dead outside Cairo is aligned with its main axis perpendicular to the *qiblah* of the astronomers; architecture in al-Qarāfah is oriented due south, in keeping with the *qiblah* favored by the Shāfiʿī school. The different *qiblah*s accepted in medieval Cairo are shown in figure 9.19. Thus, a diagram of a ventilator in an astronomical text led to the discovery of the basic orientations underlying one of the most important Islamic cities.

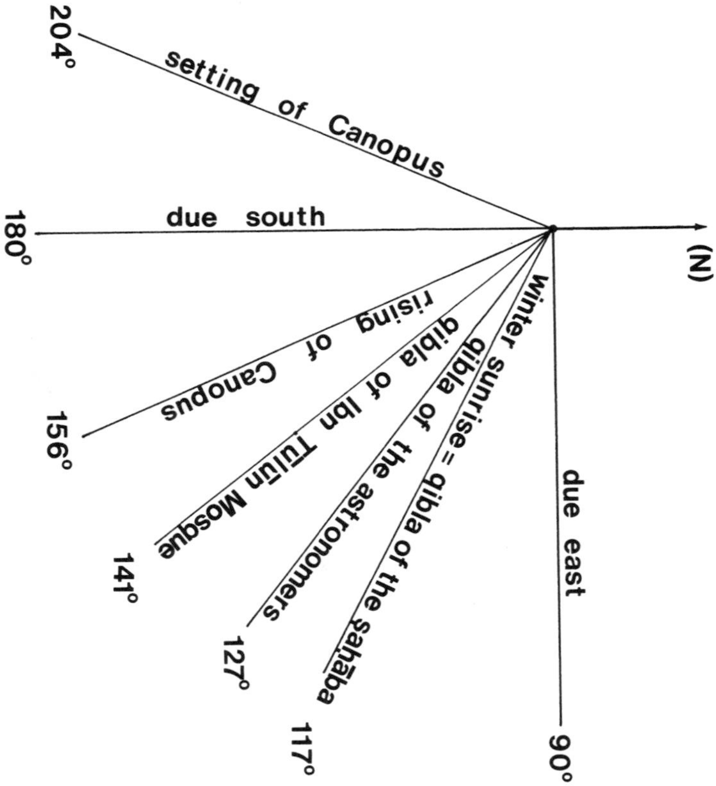

Fig. 9.19. The different *qiblahs* accepted in medieval Cairo. In the case of the southerly *qiblahs*, any direction between the rising and setting of Canopus would have been considered acceptable.

AN ILLUSTRATION OF THE SIGNIFICANCE OF THE KA'BAH

A series of Arabic texts, mostly not illustrated and all recently investigated for the first time, discuss the orientation of the Ka'bah itself. The base is rectangular (not square, as is often stated). See figure 9.20 [l.h.s.], with its major axis pointing toward the rising of Canopus, the brightest star in the southern sky, and its minor axis pointing toward the setting of the sun at the midwinter solstice. (At Mecca, these directions are indeed roughly perpendicular.) Thus, admonitions to face the rising of Canopus as the *qiblah* are common in Andalusia and Egypt; winter sunset in Iraq and Iran; and summer sunrise in the Sudan and Ethiopia. But there was no unity of opinion about the orientation of the Ka'bah, let alone about the *qiblahs* in the different regions.

One notion which is *not* illustrated in any medieval Arabic text, but which is explicit in various wind-schemes described in the manuscript sources, and which underlies the very origin of the word *qiblah*, is the following (see figure 9.21). If one stands in front of (*istaqbala*) the southwest wall of the Ka'bah (facing summer sunrise), one is facing the east (*qabūl*) wind. The north (*shamāl*) wind is on one's left (*shamāl*), blowing from Syria (*al-Shām*), and the South (*janūb*) wind on one's right (*yamīn*), blowing from the Yemen (*al-Yaman*). The west wind (*dabūr*) blows on one's back (*dabr*). This is evidence enough (and there is more) that the sacred direction (*qiblah*) of the Arabs in the pre-Islamic period was towards the east. But there are further meteorological and meteoric associations of the Ka'bah, not the least the "Black Stone" embedded in the southeastern corner. While the diagram of the Ka'bah shown in figure 9.20 (r.h.s.) and interpreted in figure 9.22 was taken from an eighteenth-century Egyptian manuscript, its conception was at least half a millennium older; the diagram recaptures some of these associations of the edifice. Note that the Ka'bah is even correctly shown inclined to the meridian. The Aristotelian overtones—the elements and their qualities—are not attested elsewhere, but the geographical features and the association with the winds are. I have argued elsewhere that these pre-Islamic associations of the Ka'bah lend credence to the Islamic belief that the Ka'bah is a copy of a celestial counterpart, *al-bayt al-ma'mūr*. In modern terms, I suggest that this implies that it was built as an architectural representation of a pre-Islamic cosmology, featuring the sun and stars in its alignment and the winds and rains in its attributions.

CONCLUDING REMARKS

In brief, there are numerous illustrations in the Islamic scientific sources which can further our understanding of different aspects of Islamic science and even aspects of Islamic institutions. One should never rely solely on the illustrations if there is an accompanying text. But the need for facsimile editions of important manuscripts and of comparative studies of illustrated texts should be obvious.

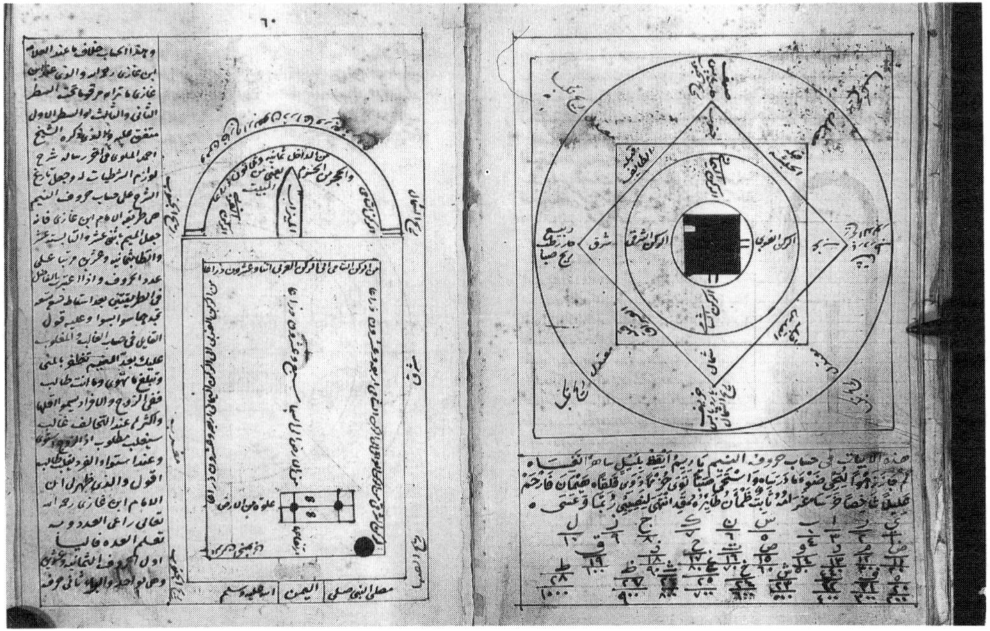

Fig. 9.20. On the left is a ground-plan of the Ka'bah (the rectangular shape is here exaggerated) and on the right a diagram which associates the edifice—incorrectly oriented—with the cardinal directions and their intermediaries, the winds, and the *qiblah*s of various localities. (MS Cairo Dār al-Kutub' Ṭal'at *majāmi'* 811.)

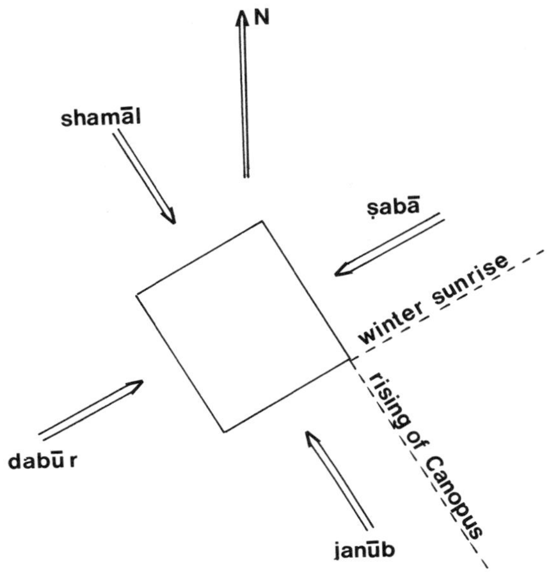

Fig. 9.21. The basic orientation of the Kaʿbah and the directions of the four "cardinal" winds as recorded in various medieval texts. Actually, the minor axis is aligned with the most southerly setting point of the moon.

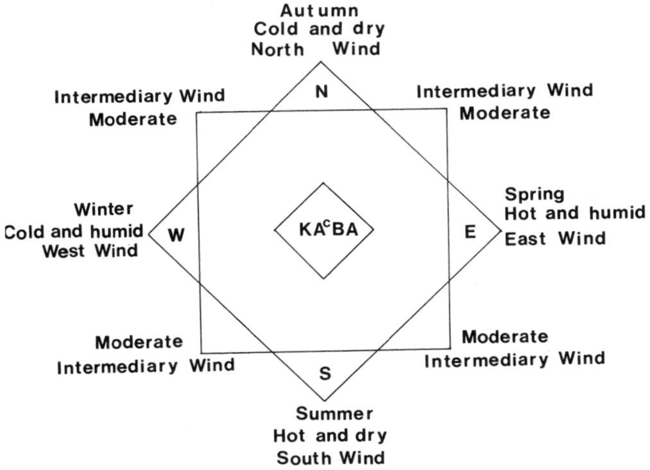

Fig. 9.22. The basic information on the Kaʿbah contained in figure 9.20 (r.h.s.). The orientation of the Kaʿbah has been "corrected"; in fact (see figure 9.10 [l.h.s.] and figure 9.21), its major axis is at about 30° E. of S.

One just has to compare the variety of representations of sacred geography in a few manuscripts of texts that are well known and that have already been published, but not in critical editions (for example, al-Qazwīnī, Yāqūt, and Ibn al-Wardī), to recognize the need for such studies.

In 1986, I was in the Bibliotheca Palatina Exhibition in Heidelberg, looking at a manuscript of Abū al-Fidā''s geography from the Bibliotheca Vaticana. The manuscript was opened to an illustration of the names of various regions of the world arranged in twenty-eight sectors of a circle (see figure 9.23). The diagram was quite different from any that I had ever seen, yet I knew that there was no such diagram in the 1840 published edition of that text. When I got home, I checked the appropriate place in the text and found a footnote by the editor at the place where Abū al-Fidā' wrote: "I have made a diagram (*zā'iraja*) from which can be found the position of every traditional climate and this is it. . ." The footnote read: "La figure qui se trouve ici dans l'original a été placée sous forme d'index à la fin du volume." In fact, the place names in the diagram have been swallowed up in the index and are no longer identifiable.

When preparing facsimile editions of manuscripts, strict guidelines must be followed, otherwise the result can be useless. Tampering with words that have been partially devoured by worms, removing original folio numbers, reshuffling folios without comment, and merging fragments from different copies of the same work without indication, all these contravene the most basic academic standards. Alas, they are features of the facsimile series published in recent years in Frankfurt, which has already been devastated by one reviewer who is a leading specialist on Arabic manuscripts. But the series has problems other than those which were noted by that reviewer, namely, the meddling with illustrations.

Two examples must suffice here. Firstly, the constellation figures and stars in the illustrations of a fine manuscript of al-Ṣūfī's *Kitāb ṣuwar al-kawākib* have been altered: the result is thus more suited for the proverbial coffee-table than for the next generation of art historians, who will still have to consult the original manuscript for the illustrations. Secondly, on a diagram of sacred geography in the Istanbul manuscript of the second volume of the encyclopedia entitled *Masālik al-abṣār fī mamālik al-amṣār*, by the early fourteenth-century Mamluk administrator Ibn Faḍlallāh al-ʿUmarī, the Qur'ānic verse (3: 97), *wa-man dakhalahu kāna āmin*^{an}, "whoever enters (the Kaʿbah) will be safe," has been written in gold ink on the representation of the Kaʿbah. Now, the modern scribe who "fixed up" the photos of the various manuscripts for the Frankfurt facsimile "edition" erased this inscription to insert another one more bold, and wrote *āmin*^{an} with two *alifs* at the beginning. The illustrations in medieval manuscripts deserve more respect than this.

I hope to have shown how manuscripts in general and illustrations in particular can further our understanding of Islamic heritage. Libraries have

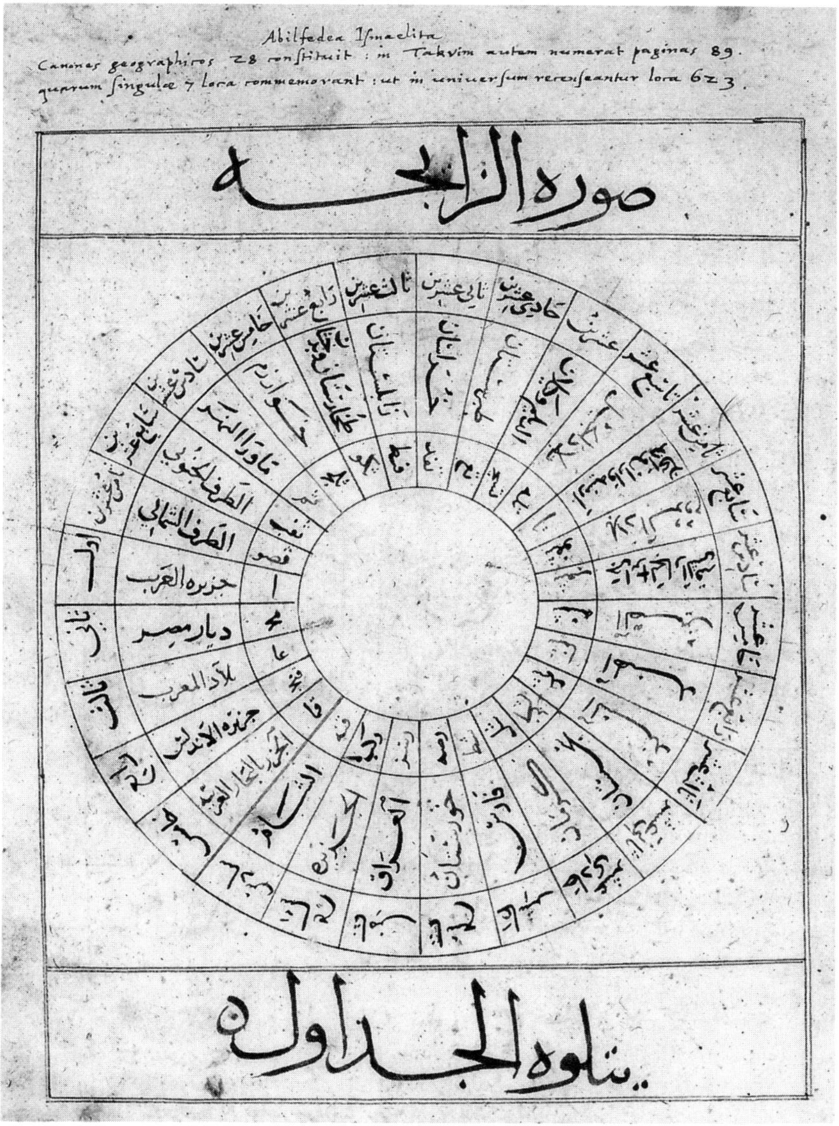

Fig. 9.23. A diagram showing 28 traditional divisions of the world, from a manuscript of the geographical treatise of Abū al-Fidā' (Hama, ca. 1320) which never made it into the published text. (MS Vatican arabo 266.)

these sources in trust and should treat them with the respect they deserve, which means cataloging them and making them available to scholars. We investigators should also treat them with respect, for they hold the key to many a mystery.

BIBLIOGRAPHICAL NOTES

Many illustrations for Islamic scientific manuscripts, some rather spectacular, are reproduced in S.H. Nasr, *Islamic Science: An Illustrated Study* (London: World of Islam Publishing Co. Ltd., 1976). Some 240 extracts from Islamic scientific manuscripts, many of them illustrated, are to be found in D.A. King, *A Survey of the Scientific Manuscripts in the Egyptian National Library* (Winona Lake, IN: Eisenbrauns, 1986). See also John E. Murdoch, *Album of Science: Antiquity and the Middle Ages* (New York: Charles Scribner's Sons, 1984), for various illustrations from Islamic scientific manuscripts.

On the activities of Taqī al-Dīn, see A. Sayılı, *The Observatory in Islam*, Publications of the Turkish Historical Society, series VII, no. 38 (Ankara: Türk Tarih Kurumu Basımevi, 1960), pp. 289–305; and A.S. Ünver, *Istanbul Rasathanesi*, Türk Tarih Kurumu Yayınlarından, V. Seri, Sayı 54 (Ankara: Türk Tarih Kurumu Basımevi, 1969).

On illustrations of constellation figures, see, for example, the works by J. Upton and E. Wellesz cited in the bibliography to the article, "al-Ṣūfī," by Paul Kunitzsch, in *The Dictionary of Scientific Biography*, 16 vols. (New York: Charles Scribner's Sons, 1970–78), 8:149–50.

On illustrations in astrological texts, see, for example, Zeren Tanındı (Akalay), "Astrological Illustrations in Islamic Manuscripts," *Proceedings of the I. International Congress on the History of Turkish-Islamic Science and Technology, Istanbul, 14–18 September 1981*, pp. 71–90; idem, "An Illustrated Astrologicai Work of the Period of Iskandar Sultan," *Akten des VII, Internationalen Kongresses für Iranische Kunst und Archäologie, München, 17–20 September 1976* (Berlin: Dietrich Relmer Verlag, 1979), pp. 418–25; and Stefano Carboni, "Two Fragments of a Jalayrid Astrological Treatise in the Keir Collection and in the Oriental Institute in Sarajevo," *Islamic Art* 2 (1987), pp. 149–86.

On non-Ptolemaic planetary theory in Islamic astronomy, see G. Saliba, "The Astronomical Tradition of Maragha: A Historical Survey and Prospects for Future Research," *Arabic Sciences and Philosophy* 1 (1991), pp. 67–99, and the works there cited.

On illustrations in treatises on engineering, see A.K. Coomaraswamy, *The Treatise of al-Jazarī on Automata* (Boston: Museum of Fine Arts, 1924); Donald R. Hill, *The Book of Knowledge and Ingenious Mechanical Devices* (Dordrecht (NL) and Boston: Dr. Reidel Publishing Company, 1974); and numerous other writings by Hill. See also Ahmad Y. al-Hasan and Donald R. Hill, *Islamic Technology: An Illustrated History* (Cambridge: Cambridge University Press;

and Paris: UNESCO, 1986). On the independent Andalusian tradition, see the chapter, "Technologia andalusi," by Donald R. Hill, in Juan Vernet, Julio Samso, et al., *El Legado Científico Andalusi* (Madrid: Ministerio de Cultura, 1992), pp. 157–72.

On Islamic cartography, see the article, "*Kharīṭa*" (Map), by S. Maqbul Ahmad, in *Encyclopedia of Islam*, new edition (Leiden: E.J. Brill, 1960–) (hereafter *EI*[2]); and various chapters in *The Historv of Cartography*, eds. J.B. Harley and David Woodward (Chicago; London: The University of Chicago Press, 1992), vol. 2, book 1: *Cartography in the Traditional Islamic and South Asian Societies*.

On al-Ashraf and his astrolabe, see D.A. King, "The Medieval Yemeni Astrolabe in the Metropolitan Museum of Art in New York," *Zeitschrift für Geschichte der arabisch-islamischen Wissenschaften* 2 (1985), pp. 99–122, repr. in *idem*, *Islamic Astronomical Instruments* (London: Variorum Reprints, 1987), 2; and on Ibn al-Sarrāj and his astrolabe, see ibid., 9. Numerous illustrations of other instruments and extracts from treatises on instrumentation are found in idem, "Strumentazione astronomica nel mondo medieval e islamico," a chapter in *Gli strumenti*, ed. Gerard Turner (Milan: Electa, 1990), pp. 154–89 and 580–85, the first of a series of richly illustrated volumes on the history of sciences, Paolo Galluzzi, general editor. An abridgement of the English original is published as "Some Remarks on Islamic Astronomical Instruments," *Scientiarum Historia* 18 (1992), pp. 5–23. On the Frankfurt project to catalogue medieval instruments, see my "Medieval Astronomical Instruments: A Catalogue in Preparation," *Bulletin of the Scientific Instrument Society* 31 (December 1991), pp. 3–7; and also no. 36 (March 1993), pp. 17–18.

On Islamic sacred geography, see my study in *Islamic Art*; a survey is in the article, "Makka: As Centre of the World," in *EI*[2]. See also D.A. King and G.S. Hawkins, "On the Orientation of the Kaʿba," *Journal for History of Astronomy* 13 (1982), pp. 102–9, repr. in King, *Astronomy in the Service of Islam* (Aldershot, UK: Variorum Reprints, 1993); idem, "Architecture and Astronomy: The Ventilators of Medieval Cairo and Their Secrets," *Journal of the American Oriental Society* 104 (1984), pp. 97–133; and idem, Richard Lorch, "Qibla Charts, Qibla Maps, and Related Instruments," in *History of Cartography* 2:1, pp. 189–205.

On facsimile editions of manuscripts and how they should not be prepared, see J.J. Witkam, "Arabic Manuscripts in Distress: The Frankfurt Facsimile Series," *Manuscripts of the Middle East* 4 (1989), pp. 175–80. For some suggestions concerning facsimile editions of Islamic scientific manuscripts which would be of use to scholars, see my paper, "Some Remarks on Islamic Scientific Manuscripts and Instrument, and Past, Present and Future Research," in *The Significance of Arabic Manuscripts*, ed. John Cooper (London: Al-Furqān Heritage Foundation, 1992), pp. 115–43 (some of the illustrations have been shuffled and no longer correspond to the captions).

10

A Royal Manuscript and Its Transformation: The Life History of a Book

Priscilla P. Soucek and Filiz Çağman

The focus of this essay is a single volume now in the Topkapı Sarayı Library, Istanbul, Hazine 1510.[1] The importance of this book derives both from its intrinsic quality and from the way in which its life history can be reconstructed on the basis of physical and historical evidence. Despite or perhaps because of its checkered career, this book sheds light on a little studied dimension of Islamic manuscripts—the way they have been transformed from the moment of their initial creation until the present day.

Recent studies have stressed how the rulers of Iran during the fourteenth through sixteenth centuries employed calligraphers, painters, illuminators, and binders to produce sumptuous volumes for their personal libraries. Indeed, the commissioning of books bearing royal names and titles appears to have become an attribute of princely status and power.[2] The special prestige attached to books with a royal or princely provenance appears to have encouraged another method of book collection used by rulers, that of appropriating volumes from each other's libraries.[3] Although there are few documentary records of these transactions, the transfer of books from one owner to another has often left physical traces in the manuscripts which can be used to reconstruct the history of a book.

Elements in a manuscript indicating a change of ownership include repainted dedication pages, altered colophons, and the addition or deletion of library seals. In case of illustrated manuscripts, paintings are not infrequently different in date and provenance from the manuscript's text itself. Sometimes illustrations were added over the text, or even over earlier paintings. The motives which led to the alteration of manuscripts undoubtedly varied, but in some cases a group of manuscripts display similarities in the way they were altered; this makes it possible to speculate about the reasons for such changes.

Hazine 1510 is notable for the variety of transformations it has undergone. It contains evidence that it was originally produced for a royal owner and that it was subsequently seized by a rival ruler. It also has both paintings connected with its original patron and others added at a later date. Some of the later paintings obscure earlier ones, others are added directly over the text. These physical changes were accompanied by efforts to conceal the book's original provenance and date. The technique and style of the later paintings link Hazine 1510 with a group of manuscripts some of which also have colophons giving similar falsified dates and provenance.

Evidence suggests that Hazine 1510 has had a long and complicated life. Various components of it can be dated over a hundred and fifty year period during which the manuscript probably traveled from Shiraz to Herat and finally to Istanbul. An identification of these phases demands a knowledge of manuscript production under the Muzaffarid, Timurid, Safavid, and Ottoman dynasties. It also can be linked with three rulers: the Muzaffarid Shāh Shujā', and the Timurids Shāh Rukh and Sulṭān Ḥusayn Bāyqarā. What is perhaps even more intriguing is that one of its transformations involved more than a hint of fraud; although, who defrauded whom remains a mystery.

Before turning to the various transformations to which Hazine 1510 has been subjected, it is necessary to examine its contents. The text of 760 folios has three distinct components: a *Shāh-nāmah* of Firdawsī (fols. 2b–484b), a dictionary by Asadī Tūsī entitled *Lughat al-Furs* (fols. 485b–498a), and a *Khamsah* of Niẓāmī (fols. 499a–775b). The manuscript also contains three dated colophons (fols. 7a, 484b, 775b), two dedication pages (fols. 1a, 499a), and what appears to be a portion of a chancery document (fol. 498a). Another important component is the manuscript's battered but once splendid binding with lacquer painting on the exterior and filigree and molded ornament on the interior. There are poetic inscriptions on the binding's doublure and the exterior of its flap.[4]

This essay on Hazine 1510 attempts to reconstruct the history and evolution of its component parts—the *Shāh-nāmah* and its associated text *Lughat al-Furs*, the *Khamsah* of Niẓāmī and the binding, and to consider how and when they were joined to form the present manuscript. The primary evidence for this study comes from internal evidence in the Hazine 1510 itself and from its comparison to other manuscripts. This analysis will be divided into several sections. First, the text's provenance and the date of its component parts will be established; then its links with the Timurid rulers Shāh Rukh and Ḥusayn Bāyqarā will be studied; and the binding's importance will also be analyzed.

Only the late Ivan Stchoukine has published comments on the artistic character of this manuscript. He refers to Hazine 1510 in three publications, an article and two monographs: one on Turkish painting, and a second on illustrated copies of Niẓāmī's *Khamsah*.[5] His analysis of Hazine 1510 focused exclusively on its illustrations and was based on the information in F. E. Karatay's catalogue of Persian manuscripts in the Topkapı Sarayı Library, namely that the *Shāh-nāmah* and *Lughat al-furs* were copied by Manṣūr ibn Muḥammad ibn Warqah ibn ʿUmar Bakhtiyār in 903/1498 and that the *Khamsah* was completed in 906/1501 by Luṭf Allāh ibn Yaḥyā ibn Muḥammad al-Tabrīzī.[6] Karatay makes no mention of the manuscript's dedicatory medallions, nor does he raise any questions about the veracity of information contained in its colophons.

Stchoukine concluded that paintings in the *Shāh-nāmah* portion of Hazine 1510 were added in the Safavid period, circa 1520–25, and that those in the *Khamsah* portion were added in Turkey circa 1570. He finds specific Turkish parallels for both the painting's landscape and figural elements.[7] This position led him to assume that very similar landscape paintings in an often published *Anthology* dated to 801/1398 were also executed in Istanbul circa 1570.[8] This manuscript is now in the museum of Turkish and Islamic Art, Istanbul, T. 1950.

Recently three Persian scholars have published comments about the character of Hazine 1510's text. The most extensive description is that by J. Khāliqī-Muṭlaq in his analytical articles discussing the manuscripts of Firdawsī's *Shāh-nāmah* which he has been using to prepare his edition of that text. In them he describes both the physical characteristics of Hazine 1510 and the importance of its text recension. His description of Hazine 1510 is more precise than that of F. E. Karatay, as he mentions the *Shāh-nāmah*'s two colophons, in addition to its initial medallion and the document on folio 498a. Although he appears somewhat puzzled by its putative date of 903/1498, J. Khāliqī-Muṭlaq stresses the archaic features of Hazine 1510's text and its close kinship with the Florence manuscript dated to 614/1217.[9] He also brought the *Lughat al-Furs* portion of this manuscript to the attention of F. A. Mujtabā'ī and A. A. Sādiqī, who were preparing a new edition of that work. In their preface these authors mention that Hazine 1510's version of the *Lughat al-Furs* differs in significant respects from the other manuscripts which they used to prepare their edition. They were not able, however, to evaluate the importance of its idiosyncracies.[10] These Persian scholars, who worked from microfilms, assume the *Shāh-nāmah*'s present colophon date of 903/1498 to be correct.

Despite the attention which has been given to both Hazine 1510's illustrations and to portions of its text no analysis has yet been made of its calligraphy, illumination, or binding, nor of their importance for the manuscript's history. Hence, it is necessary to establish the date and place of the manuscript's origin through an examination of its calligraphy and illumination and by subjecting its colophons to a critical analysis before considering Stchoukine's views on the paintings of Hazine 1510, and those of Khāliqī-Muṭlaq about its *Shāh-nāmah* text. A physical examination of Hazine 1510 shows that the two main components of its text, the *Shāh-nāmah* and the *Khamsah*, although distinct in their features, are closely related in execution. Both have the same page size (26.1 by 16.3 cm), but they differ in their written surfaces. The *Shāh-nāmah* has twenty-seven lines spaced over 19.2 cm, whereas the *Khamsah* has twenty-five lines in 17.5 cm.

Despite the fact that both portions of Hazine 1510 have colophon dates from the tenth Hegira century, the character of their illumination and calligraphy connects them with fourteenth-century Shiraz, a city that was a center of both literary culture and manuscript production. Both portions can be proven to belong firmly to that tradition, although at some later moment these connections were intentionally obscured. The affinity of Hazine 1510 with the manuscript tradition of Muzaffarid Shiraz as well as the later deliberate obfuscation of that connection can be documented through a study of its colophons.

The most direct evidence for Hazine 1510's link with Shiraz comes in the *Khamsah* colophon, folio 775b (figure 10.1). There the calligrapher Luṭf Allāh al-Tabrīzī describes himself as both the manuscript's scribe and illuminator (*katabahu wa dhahhabahu*) and gives its place of production as *Dār al-mulk Shīrāz*.[11] He also gives his *laqab*, or honorific epithet, as "Kamāl al-Jalālī," which probably links him to the last important Muzaffarid ruler, Jalāl al-dīn Shāh Shujāʻ (ruled 765/1357–786/1384). An examination of the colophon also shows tnat its present date, *Rajab* 906/January–February 1501, is not the original one. Only the terminal element *sitt* (six) is untouched: the number giving the decade has been virtually erased, and the century was modified so that *sabʻa miyah* (700) has become *tisʻa miyah* (900). The original date contained the numbers 7__6; since remaining traces suggest the missing decade was *sabʻīn* (seventy), the original date was probably *Rajab* 776/December 1374 - January 1375.

An examination of the *Shāh-nāmah* portion of Hazine 1510 shows that its colophon date of 5 Dhū' al-Ḥijjah 903 has been altered, in a similar fashion, by erasing the decade and changing *sabʻa miyah* (700) to *tisʻa miyah* (900) (figure 10.2). In this case the erased decade appears to be *thamanin* (80) which means that the original date must have been 783/1382, thus also within the reign of Shāh Shujāʻ.

A further confirmation of the Muzaffarid origin of this manuscript is offered by the identity of its scribe who gives his lineage for five generations: Manṣūr ibn Muḥammad ibn Warqah ibn ʻUmar b. Bakhtiyār, and adds a *nisbah*, "al-Bihbihānī," followed by a geographical gloss: *min aʻmāl Jabal Jilūyah* (figure 10.2). The same scribe has used a virtually identical signature formula in the well-known *Anthology* now in the museum of Turkish and Islamic Art (T. 1950) dated to *Muḥarram* 801/September–October 1398 mentioned above[12] (figure 10.3).

The geographical references in this signature draw attention to Manṣūr's link with the village of Bihbihān in the region of Kūh Gilūyeh situated northwest of Shiraz. Little is known about Bihbihān, which appears to have been a small settlement in a fertile valley, but it was the successor to a much more important town, Arrajan or Kūrat Qubād, which had been situated at the juncture of roads

Fig. 10.1. Topkapı Sarayı Müzesi, Hazine 1510, fol. 775b, Colophon of Niẓāmī *Khamsah*

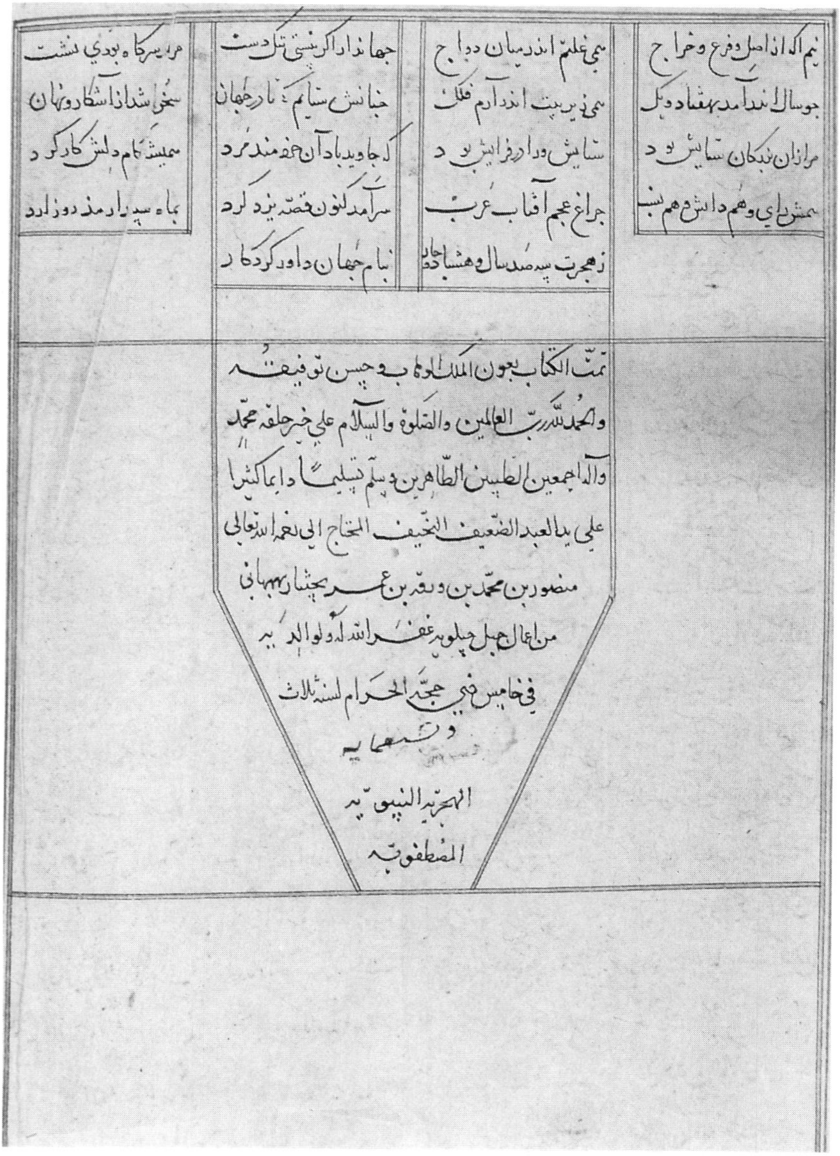

نیم اکه از اصل و فرع و خراج
همی غلتم اندر میان دواج
جهاندار اگر نیستی تنگ دست
مرا بر سر گاه بودی نشست

جو سال اندر آمد به هشتاد و یک
همی زیر بیت اندر آرم فلک
جهانش ستایم که تا در جهان
سخن شد از آشکار و نهان

مرا زان نیکان ستایش بود
ستایش و دار و فرایش بود
که جاوید باد آن خردمند مرد
همیشه کام دلش کار کرد

همش رای و هم دانش و هم نسب
چراغ عجم آفتاب عرب
سر آمد کنون قصه یزدگرد
بماه سپندارمذ روز ارد

ز هجرت سه صد سال و هشتاد و چار
بنام جهان داور کردگار

تمت الكتاب بعون الملك الوهاب وحسن توفيقه
والحمد لله رب العالمين والصلوة والسلام على خير خلقه محمد
وآله اجمعين الطيبين الطاهرين وسلم تسليما دائما كثيرا
على يد العبد الضعيف النحيف المحتاج الى رحمة الله تعالى
منصور بن محمد بن ورقة بن عمر بن بختيار بهبهاني
من اعمال جبل جيلويه غفر الله له ولوالديه
في خامس في حجة الحرام لسنة ثلاث
وتسعمايه
الهجرية النبوية
المصطفوية

Fig. 10.2. Topkapı Sarayı Müzesi, Hazine 1510, fol. 484b, Colophon of Firdawsi *Shāh-nāmah*.

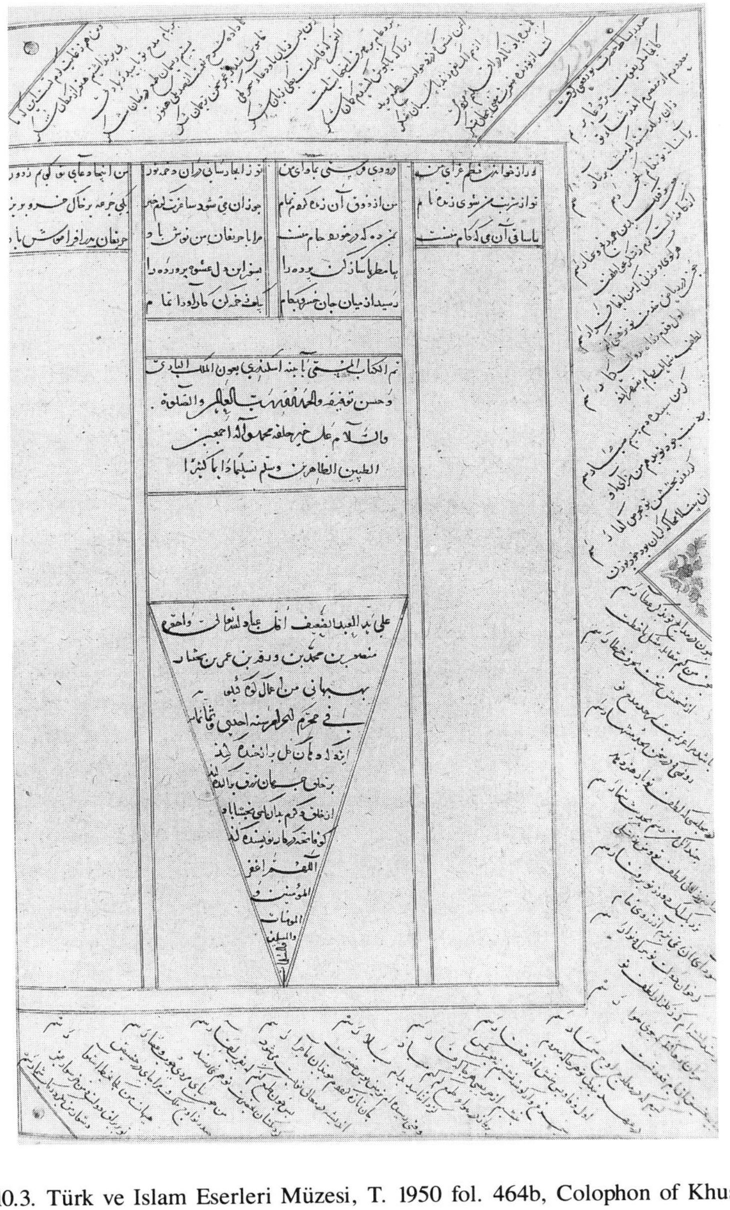

Fig. 10.3. Türk ve Islam Eserleri Müzesi, T. 1950 fol. 464b, Colophon of Khusraw Dihlavi, ʿĀīnah-i Iskandarī.

linking Isfahan and Shiraz with Ahwāz, Basrah, and Baghdad. Arrajan was ruined by invasions and conflict between the Isma'ilis and various rulers during the eleventh and twelfth centuries. Before its devastation the area was noted for its fertility and abundant water. The dates and pomegranates of Arrajan were especially prized.[13] It is most unlikely, however, that Bihbihān was a center of manuscript production.[14]

A Shiraz provenance for both the *Shāh-nāmah* portion of Hazine 1510 and the *Anthology*, T. 1950 is also suggested by the illumination used in both manuscripts which contains dense gold vegetal scrolls silhouetted against blue, black, white, or green fields.[15] This style of illumination was widely used in Shiraz manuscripts from circa 1370 to circa 1430.[16] As befits a royal commission, the headings of various books in the Hazine 1510 *Khamsah* are executed with more intense colors and heavier gold pigments than are most Shiraz manuscripts.

The *Shāh-nāmah* portion of Hazine 1510 also contains two more colophons, one without a signature or date on folio 6b at the conclusion of the text's preface, and another one on folio 7a (figure 10.4). The latter, written on paper that differs

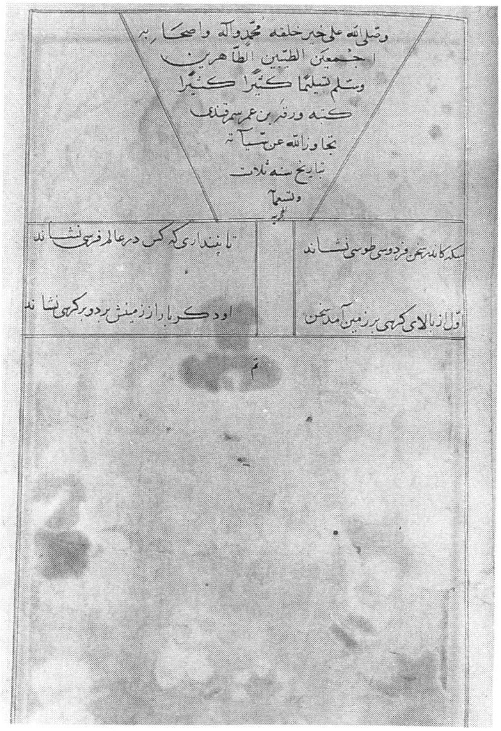

Fig. 10.4. Topkapı Sarayı Müzesi, Hazine 1510, fol. 7a, "Colopon Signed by Warqah ibn 'Umar Samarqandī."

in color and texture from that of the original manuscript, contains the "signature" of one "Warqah ibn ʿUmar Samarqandī," and is dated 903 A.H./1498.[17] It seems probable that this name was chosen both to mimic that of the original *Shāh-nāmah* scribe Manṣūr al-Bihbihānī by using part of his name, "Warqah ibn ʿUmar," and to harmonize with information contained in the Ḥusayn Bāyqarā *firmān* now affixed to folio 484a, where the scribe of a *Shāh-nāmah* manuscript is listed as "Warqah ibn ʿUmar Samarqandī" (figures 10.2, 10.5).

The insertion of this superfluous colophon appears connected with other changes made to Hazine 1510, such as the alteration of colophon dates, all of which had as an aim the deliberate transformation of a Muzaffarid manuscript into one linked with eastern Iran and the Timurid Sulṭān Ḥusayn Bāyqarā. Possible motives for these changes will be considered below.

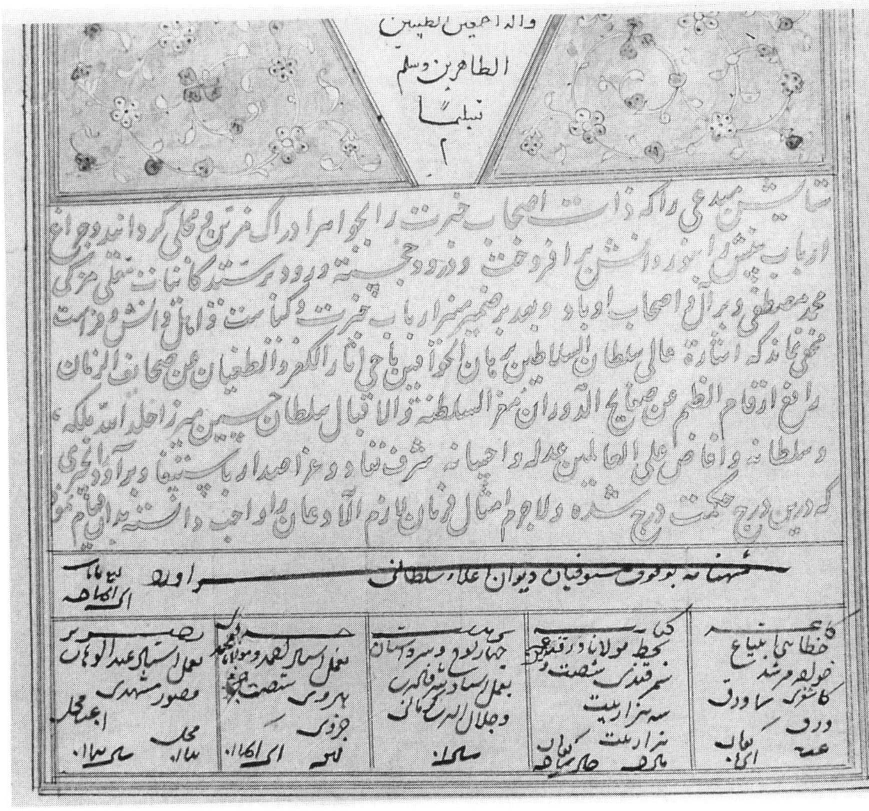

Fig. 10.5. Topkapı Sarayı Müzesi, Hazine 1510, fol. 498a, "Firmān in the Name of Ḥusayn Bāyqarā."

Although the illumination and calligraphy of this *Shāh-nāmah* are of high quality, the manuscript carries no direct indication of the patron's identity. It does, however, open with a roundel illuminated in a Muzaffarid style which may have once contained the name of its owner. At present this roundel contains the name and titles of the Timurid Ḥusayn Bāyqarā, who ruled in Herat from 1468 to 1506, written on a heavy gold ground which may well conceal an inscription giving the name of the manuscript's original owner (figure 10.6).

A scrutiny of the *Shāh-nāmah* section of Hazine 1510 shows, however, that Ḥusayn Bāyqarā was not the first Timurid to be connected with it. Three folios bear the library seal of Timur's son Shāh Rukh who ruled from Herat from 1405 to 1447.[18] His name also appears in a dedicatory medallion which has been glued onto the initial page of the manuscript's *Khamsah* portion[19] (figure 10.7).

Shāh Rukh is less known as a patron of calligraphers and painters than his nephew Iskandar Sulṭān ibn ʿUmar Shaykh or his sons Bāysunghur and Ibrāhīm Sulṭān, but he appears to have been a particularly assiduous collector of manuscripts. Another specimen bearing the imprint of his library seal is a very early copy of Khusraw Dihlavī's *Khamsah* dated to 756/1355 which was used by Soviet scholars as the basis for a critical edition. This manuscript was copied in Shiraz and one of its two scribes was Muḥammad ibn Muḥammad ibn Muḥammad known as "Shams al-Ḥāfiẓ al-Shīrāzī," who is most probably the poet Ḥāfiẓ.[20]

Shāh Rukh could have acquired his stock of Shiraz manuscripts in a variety of ways. His long struggle with the sons of his brother ʿUmar Shaykh, including his defeat of Iskandar Sulṭān at Isfahan in Mugarram 817/March–April 1415, and his defeat of Bāyqarā in Shiraz one year later in the spring of 818/1416, provided him with several opportunities to seize manuscripts.[21]

No attempt has yet been made to compile information about the contents of Shāh Rukh's library, but from published data it appears that his books retained their original colophons or illustrations. The use of his seal or the affixing of a medallion containing his name and titles mark manuscripts as his property, but do not present a claim that the books were originally prepared for him.

As was noted above, the *Shāh-nāmah* portion of Hazine 1510 opens with a similar medallion proclaiming Sulṭān Ḥusayn Bāyqarā as its owner. His name and titles are also included in a *firmān* which has been glued to onto folio 498a below the unsigned colophon of *Lughat al-Furs*, the text of which follows the *Shāh-nāmah* (fols. 485b–498a) (figure 10.5). Although undated, the *Lughat al-Furs* manuscript appears to be contemporary with the *Shāh-nāmah*, thus circa 1382, and was perhaps also copied by Manṣūr al-Bihbihānī. The *firmān* below the colophon on folio 498a makes reference to the cost of a *Shāh-nāmah* manuscript. Before considering this document, however, it is useful to examine the illustrations and binding of Hazine 1510.

It is now appropriate to consider Stchoukine's views that both landscape and figural elements of its *Khamsah* illustrations were Turkish.[22] This position

Fig. 10.6. Topkapı Sarayı Müzesi, Hazine 1510, fol. 1a, Dedication Medallion in the name of Ḥusayn Bāyqarā.

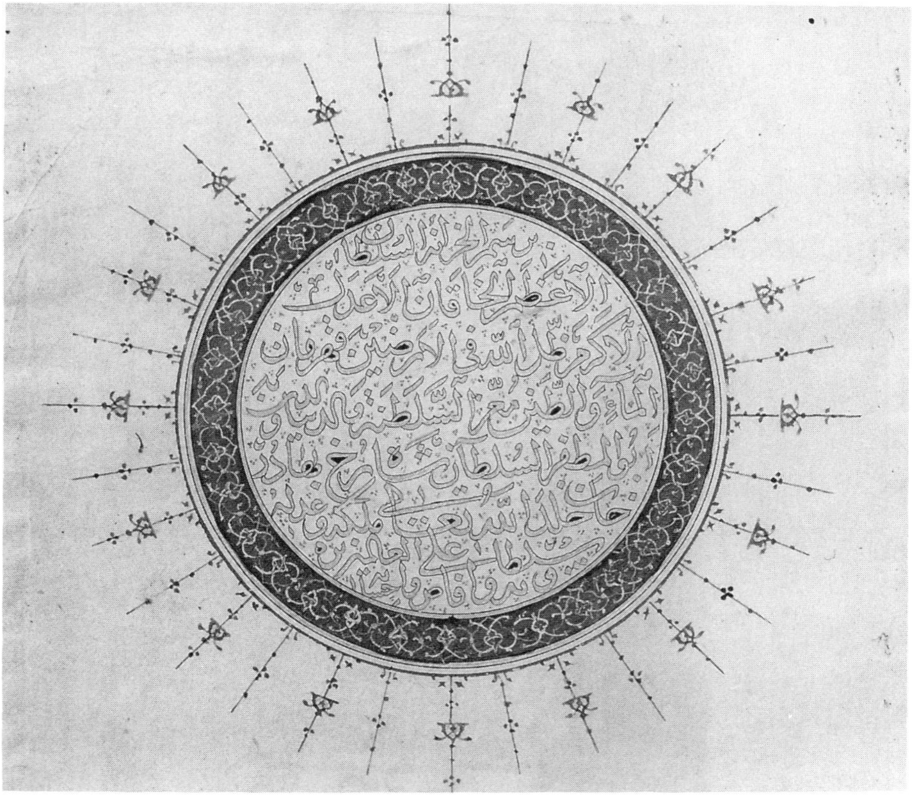

Fig. 10.7. Topkapı Sarayı Müzesi, Hazine 1510, fol. 499a, Dedication medallion in the name of Shāh Rukh.

led him to assume that very similar landscape paintings in an often published *Anthology* dated to 801/1398, T. 1950, mentioned above, were also executed in Istanbul circa 1570.[23]

Despite flaws in his analysis, Stchoukine did draw attention to two significant aspects of the Hazine 1510 *Khamsah* illustrations: that they contain figures painted in a style often associated with Ottoman Turkey, and that some of them depict landscapes reminiscent of the well-known examples from the 1398 *Anthology.* What Stchoukine does not seem to have realized is that landscape and figural components of the *Khamsah* paintings belong to two distinct phases of its creation, and that the later figural compositions now obscure the earlier landscape paintings.

The presence of landscape paintings under *Khamsah* figural compositions is sometimes evident only from the back of a painted page where metallic pigments have stained the paper. These stains reveal the presence of trees, mountains, streams, and rocks which are hidden by the later compositions.[24] In other cases, portions of the original landscapes serve as a background to the later figural paintings,[25] and in one case the original landscape scene was never overpainted[26] (figure 10.8).

Stchoukine's conflation of two stages in the Hazine 1510 *Khamsah* illustrations led him in turn to the wrong conclusion about the connection of its landscape scenes with similar paintings in the *Anthology* of 1398. Ironically, his conclusion that both were Ottoman Turkish led him to publish repeatedly those paintings in Hazine 1510 in which the late-fourteenth-century compositions were the most visible.[27]

The only one of the fifteen *Khamsah* paintings in its original condition is a landscape located in the *Sharaf-nāmah* folio 682b (figure 10.8). The landscape consists of two ranges of hills, each outlined by a heavy black line. One is highlighted in gold, the other in red. A stream, once silver-colored, arises on the right and flows toward the bottom of the painting, where it is bordered by strongly colored rocks highlighted with gold.

Although similar landscape elements are also prominent in the paintings of the 1398 *Anthology* copied by Manṣūr al-Bihbihānī, there are important differences between the two groups of paintings. The first is visual; some of the *Anthology* paintings are more complex with up to four ranges of hills one behind the other.[28] The second distinction is functional; all of the *Anthology* paintings occupy the spaces left between the colophons and headings of its sections. Thus, they function as end-papers providing visual interest where otherwise there would have been a blank space or an empty page. In Hazine 1510, however, all the paintings are placed *within* Niẓāmī's text.

The scene on folio 682b, for instance, is in a passage describing a spring garden, which may explain why it was not repainted (figure 10.8). Several other paintings in Hazine 1510 are also located in passages which describe a setting rather than a dramatic moment. Most of the paintings in Hazine 1510 make extensive use of gold and silver pigments, which are often still visible under the later additions, or which can be seen on the backs of those pages. For example a row of golden hills appears along the top of the scene of Khusraw's Lion combat, and a purple landscape highlighted by gold and silver is visible under the later figural composition of Farhād carrying Shīrīn.[29] From these indications it appears that the original paintings in the *Khamsah* portion of Hazine 1510 were landscapes in rich hues enlivened with gold and silver but without the addition of any human figures.

Stchoukine's claim that the landscapes from Hazine 1510 and T. 1950 have an Ottoman Turkish character is contradicted by both documentary and visual

Fig. 10.8. Topkapı Sarayı Müzesi, Hazine 1510, fol. 682b, "In Praise of Spring."

evidence. The stylistic features of the Hazine 1510 *Khamsah* landscape paintings are also paralleled in Muzaffarid manuscripts with figural painting. Tapestry-like settings, the use of rich colors highlighted with gold and silver, as well as a similar treatment of individual motifs are evident in the paintings of a *Shāh-nāmah*, also in the Topkapı Palace Library, Istanbul, which is dated to 772/1370.[30]

Thus an examination of the text and illumination of Hazine 1510 makes clear that both are of Muzaffarid date, and the same can be said with confidence about the landscape paintings which originally illustrated its *Khamsah* portion. The questions of when and for what reason figural compositions were added over those landscapes are more difficult to answer. First, however, the date and origin of the *Shāh-nāmah* illustrations must be established.

A close inspection of the *Shāh-nāmah* portion of Hazine 1510 suggests that it too has been subjected to considerable alteration. It presently has one double-page illustration (fols. 7b–8a) located between the preface's spurious colophon (fol. 7a) and the opening of the *Shāh-nāmah* text (fol. 8b). There are also twenty-one paintings of modest size within the text itself. Although there are no traces of Muzaffarid illustrations, the *Shāh-nāmah* paintings appear to have been executed over the manuscript's text.

I. Stchoukine has made a sharp distinction between the *Khamsah* and *Shāh-nāmah* paintings, calling the former high quality Ottoman work of circa 1570, and the latter mediocre Safavid examples from 1510–20.[31] There are certainly differences of scale and execution between the two groups of paintings: those in the *Khamsah* are larger and contain more golden highlights, but these distinctions are counter-balanced by numerous similarities. A comparison of "Ḍahhāk enthroned" from the *Shāh-nāmah* (fol. 13b) with the enthroned prince from the *Khamsah* (fol. 502b) reveals considerable affinities of the two paintings in compositional structure, coloring, and figural type.

The only major difference between the scenes is that figures in the *Shāh-nāmah* wear Safavid turbans and *kulāhs*, whereas those in the *Khamsah* scene have a turban shape closely paralleled in some early Ottoman manuscripts such as the *Selim-nāmah* of Shukrī executed in the 1520s.[32] Even this distinction may be moot because flaking paint reveals that the Safavid turbans of the *Shāh-nāmah* illustration cover others similar in shape to those in the *Khamsah* (figures 10.9 and 10.10).

The difficulties which Stchoukine encountered in evaluating the date and provenance of the figural compositions in Hazine 1510 are understandable. The style of their paintings links each with a period of artistic and historical change during the first decades of the sixteenth century which coincided with the formation of the Safavid state, in particular Shāh Ismāʿīl's campaigns in Khurasan during 1510, as well as his defeat by the Ottomans under Suṭān Selim in 1514.

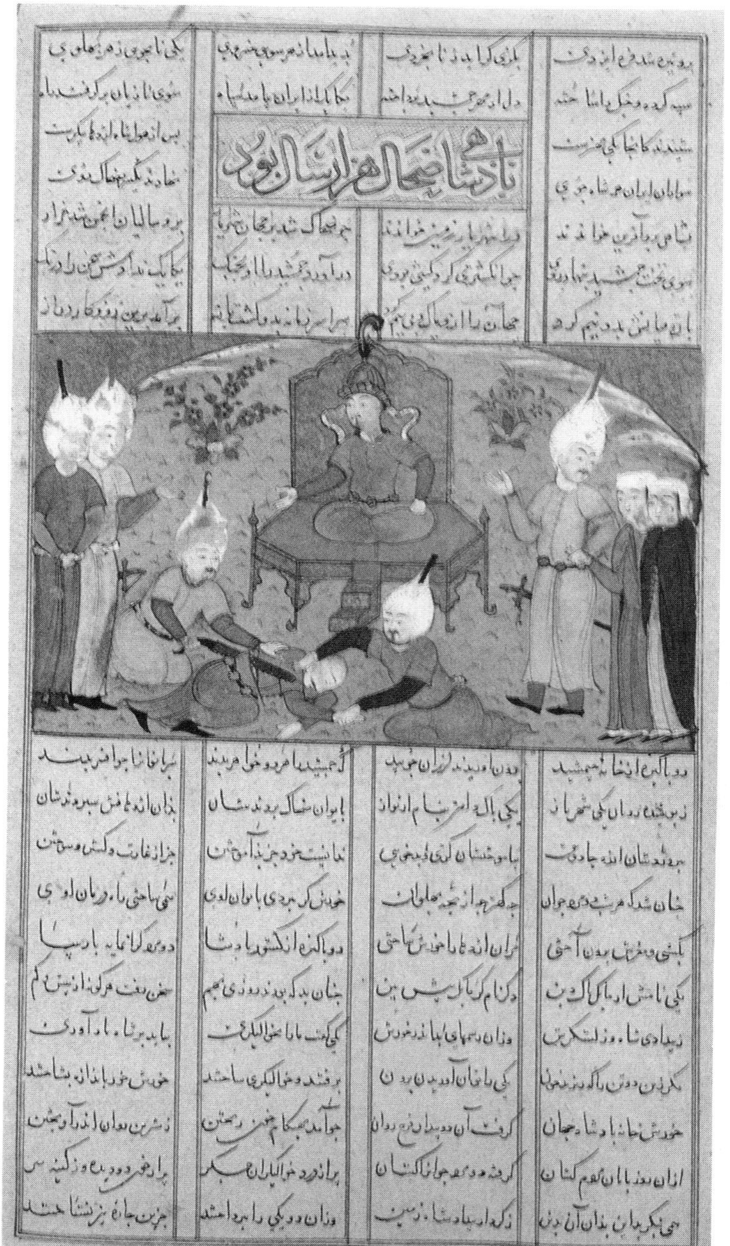

Fig. 10.9. Topkapı Sarayı Müzesi, Hazine 1510, fol. 13b, "Ḍaḥḥāk Enthroned."

Fig. 10.10. Topkapī Sarayī Muzesi, Hazine 1510, fol. 502b, "In Praise of His Patron: A Prince Enthroned."

Sulṭān Ḥusayn Bāyqarā's son, Badīʿ al-Zamān Mīrzā, was a witness to these events; he was taken to Tabriz by Shāh Ismāʿīl in 1510 and then to Istanbul in 1514 by Sulṭān Selim. The victorious Ottoman army returned to Istanbul laden with booty that included manuscripts from Shāh Ismāʿīl's library, some of which had probably been taken by the Safavids from the Timurid libraries of Herat only a few years earlier. Scribes, illuminators, and painters dislocated by these historical events also moved between Herat, Tabriz, and Istanbul.[33]

These momentous changes are also reflected in the illustrated manuscripts of the period. Traits commonly associated with one center, such as Herat or Tabriz, can be found side by side with others which have clear links to Ottoman patronage. It is against this rather confused background that figural illustrations in both the *Shāh-nāmah* and *Khamsah* sections of Hazine 1510 must be studied. Some of the manuscripts with comparable paintings also have colophons linking them to Herat or to the Timurids, but others have a Safavid or Ottoman provenance. Many questions surrounding the place of Hazine 1510 among these manuscripts are beyond the scope of this essay. Here attention will be focused on a reconstruction of that manuscript's history.

Although the two groups of illustrations have much in common, details of each find their closest comparisons in different manuscripts. Thus the *Shāh-nāmah* illustrations are most comparable to paintings with a clear Safavid pedigree such as those in another *Shāh-nāmah* copy, Hazine 1499[34] and in a copy of Navāʾī's *Khamsah*, Revan 810.[35] Manuscripts with the closest artistic ties to the *Khamsah* paintings can be linked to Ottoman court patronage. They include a copy of ʿAlī Shīr Navāʾī's *Gharāʾib al-Sighar* now in the Egyptian National Library Cairo, copied in 935/1531–32 by Ḥājj Muhḥmmad al-Tabrīzī ibn Mālik Aḥmad, a calligrapher known to have been employed at the Ottoman court,[36] and a second manuscript of Navāʾī's poetry copied by the same calligrapher in 937/1530–31 now in Oxford.[37]

A group of manuscripts which deserves special scrutiny for its connections to the *Khamsah* paintings of Hazine 1510 are other examples where paintings have been added over the manuscript's text or inserted into odd spaces in an earlier manuscript. This group includes Hazine 987, a copy of Jāmī's *Dīvān*, and on of Navāʾī's *Navādir al-Shabāb*, Revan 805.[38] These manuscripts are illustrated in a style very similar to that used in late-fifteenth-century Iranian manuscripts; this style, however, is also connected with paintings in the *Selim-nāmah* of Shukrī and thus, was probably current in Istanbul during the 1520s and 1530s. Another link between the illustrative style of *Khamsah* portion of Hazine 1510 and Ottoman painting is provided by a *Dīvān* of Kamāl Khūjandī in Vienna, A.F. 92. This manuscript, copied in western Iran circa 1480, was later illustrated with three large paintings and 1,196 vignettes inserted into gaps in the text. Since in execution illustrations are comparable to ones in the manuscripts copied by Ḥājj Muḥammad al-Tabrīzī mentioned above, it is likely that they were added in Istanbul.[39]

This preliminary survey has suggested a connection between the figural illustrations of Hazine 1510 and artistic currents in Tabriz and Istanbul during the early sixteenth century. Yet, as was demonstrated above, Hazine 1510 was certainly in Herat during the latter decades of the fifteenth century. Evidence concerning the manuscript's historical evolution is also provided by its binding and by its *firmān* in the name of Sulṭān Ḥusayn Bāyqarā.

Despite its poor state of preservation, the binding of Hazine 1510 adds an important dimension to the manuscript's history. The lacquer painted outer covers are divided into an inner zone consisting of a field broken by a recessed central medallion with quarter medallions in the corners, and a border zone of four-lobed and oblong cartouches. Except for their recessed medallions, the covers are decorated with gold painting on a black ground. The medallions were painted in red and other colors, and are rimmed by small silver-gilt nails which probably once supported metal filigree ornaments.

The binding's doublure has a central field with black and gilt leather filigree ornament silhouetted against a blue paper ground. The outer zone has four-lobed and oblong gilded cartouches flanked by narrow gold bands. The larger oblong fields contain stamped inscriptions.

The back covers of Islamic bindings generally have an attached flap which can be folded under the front cover. Between the flap and the back cover is a rectangular zone which protects the book's outer margin. Naturally the dimensions of the connecting area should be equivalent to the height of the manuscript to be covered.

An examination of the binding of Hazine 1510 reveals a curious feature. The panel between the back cover and its flap carries two zones of ornament on both the interior and exterior. The flap's internal decoration is identical to that of the covers—a central zone of leather filigree and a frame of gilt and molded cartouches. On this zone's lacquer painted exterior ten inscribed cartouches are arranged in two horizontal rows.

These exterior cartouches contain verses describing the book for which the binding was made. The first two refer to Firdawsī's *Shāh-nāmah*, the second pair speak of Niẓāmī and his poetry, and the third group, unfortunately damaged, mention the verses of ʿAlī Shīr Navāʾī. The final couplet praises the book as a whole and reiterates its contents. The concluding hemistich reads: *Shāh-nāmah va Khamsah va Dīvān-i Amīr*. Thus it would appear that the binding of Hazine 1510 was made to contain three texts: the *Shāh-nāmah* of Firdawsī, the *Khamsah* of Niẓāmī, and an undetermined portion of the *Dīvān of* ʿAlī Shīr Navāʾī. Perhaps more careful reading of the couplet concerning Navāʾī's poetry will yield clues as to which portion might have been included. The binding would accommodate forty or fifty more folios. The missing *Dīvān* and the absence of a reference to *Lughat al-Furs* do, however, raise the question of whether this binding was originally made for the manuscripts of Hazine 1510. Before considering this question further it is necessary to discuss other aspects of the binding.

Verses inscribed on cartouches framing both covers and flap of the doublure consist of three *rubāʿ*īs or quatrains composed by the Timurid poet ʿAbd al-Raḥmān Jāmī.[40] Two of them are particularly appropriate for their location, for they describe a book and its binding. One quatrain praises the beauty of the book's pages, using the metaphor of a flowery meadow. Its pages are compared with rose-petals and its calligraphy with basil.[41] Another quatrain extols the book's pages because they have given fresh life to ages past and describes the dazzling beauty of the book's cover, stating that its cover has transformed leather into the turquoise sphere of the sky and that its spine is made from braided sunbeams.[42]

These verses by Jāmī have a significance which goes beyond the history of Hazine 1510. The second quatrain is of particular interest. Its language about renewing the past, and its metaphors of sun and sky for a book binding appear at first fanciful but may in fact be quite literal descriptions of a special book. These terms could describe a *muraqqaʿ* or album consisting of choice specimens of calligraphy from various periods and bound with a golden, jeweled cover.

Jāmī's comparisons of its cover to the turquoise sky and of its spine to braided sunbeams provide a surprisingly accurate decription of some extant bindings. These have covers and flap adorned with *fīrūzekārī*, a technique in which thin slices of turquoise are inlaid into a metal, usually gold, frame. One binding with *fīrūzekārī* panels on its covers and flap has a spine of braided gold wire which it is tempting to equate with Jāmī's "braided sunbeams."[43]

Extant bindings with *fīrūzekārī*-decorated covers are of Ottoman court manufacture. The binding mentioned above, for example, is dated 997/1588–89 by the Koran which it contains. The taste for turqoise and gold bindings, however, appears to be of Iranian origin, and the Istanbul examples are often attributed to Persian goldsmiths employed at the Ottoman court.[44] Ottoman court records also mention jeweled bindings sent as gifts by Safavid rulers, although none seem to have survived.[45] Jāmī's verse suggests that *fīrūzekārī* bindings were also produced in Timurid Herat.

Jāmī's verses do not reveal the identity of the *muraqqaʿ* for which they were composed, but they may be linked with the most famous Timurid album—one arranged in 879/1474–75 for Sulṭān Ḥusayn Bāyqarā. Compiled by royal order, it evidently contained choice specimens of calligaphy and painting donated by persons of culture and learning. Although the album itself is lost, its preface survives in the *inshā'* manual of a high Timurid official, ʿAbdallāh Marvarīd.[46]

If Jāmī's verses were composed to praise an album compiled for Ḥusayn Bāyqarā, their later circulation confirms the broader popularity of Timurid culture. In addition to stamped inscriptions on Hazine 1510, Jāmī's quatrain about rose-petals and basil is impressed on the doublure of a richly ornamented

Safavid binding.[47] A variant of the second quatrain describing the album's contents and its dazzling binding is inscribed on the lacquer-painted binding of a 1544 copy of Jāmī's *Khamsah*.[48] These examples raise the question of whether there is any particular significance to the use of Jāmī's poetry on the binding of Hazine 1510.

It is evident that Jāmī's verses were not composed specifically for the binding of Hazine 1510, but his quatrain about a book with a golden jeweled binding appears particularly apposite for it. Although this binding did not have a spine of braided gold or a cover of turquoises set in gold, it is likely that some kind of metal fittings once covered the medallions on the binding's cover and flap now ringed by gilded silver nails.

Some Ottoman bindings combine lacquer-painted covers with jeweled ornament. One in the Istanbul University Library with the customary gold over black lacquer field, has jewel-encrusted filigree medallions attached to its cover.[49] The practice of inlaying leather or lacquer bindings with jewels creates an effect reminiscent of both Safavid and Ottoman metalwork where a dark ground is enlivened with gold and jewel inlays or medallions. Some of the finest examples of such metalwork preserved in Istanbul are thought to be of Iranian origin and may even have formed part of the booty from the Ottoman victory of 1514.[50]

The history of lacquer-painted bindings has yet to be written but the technique was used in Herat from the middle of the fifteenth century onward, particularly on a book's exterior. An early example inscribed with the name of the Timurid prince Bābur ibn Bāysunghur (d. 861/1457) has exterior covers painted in gold on a black ground and doublures with leather filigree medallions.[51] One of the most splendid Timurid lacquer bindings is on a manuscript of the *Hasht Bihisht* copied for one of Sulṭān Ḥusayn Bāyqarā's sons, Sulṭān Muḥammad Muḥsin in 902/1496–97 by Sulṭān ʿAlī Mashhadī. All surfaces of its binding are lacquer-painted. The front cover has a medallion scheme, and the back a field of interlocking lobed medallions.[52]

Another lacquer binding connected with Timurid Herat is that on a copy Sulṭān Ḥusayn Bāyqarā's *Dīvān* in the Topkapı Museum, E.H. 1636.[53] Its scheme follows a traditional pattern with a central medallion and four quarter medallions in the corners. These units are filled with floral scrolls and cloud-bands executed in two tones of gold over a black ground.

In the Hazine 1510 binding, these same motifs are used to fill its field and border cartouches. Indeed, this style of painting appears to have had a considerable vogue and is found on bindings probably produced in both Safavid Iran and Ottoman Turkey. At present, it is often difficult to establish the provenance and date of such bindings probably because of the mobility of craftsmen in this period.

Provisionally, however, the binding of Hazine 1510 seems to have closer links with Iranian than Ottoman examples in the design and execution of its doublure as well as in its use of border cartouches.[54] Sometimes in Safavid bindings a lacquer painted field with scroll and cloud-band designs is paired with both stamped and gilded medallions and similarly ornamented border cartouches.[55] In other cases the external cartouche frame is painted in the fashion seen in Hazine 1510. One binding of this type even has a doublure scheme with a filigree field and border cartouches which is also closely analagous in design to that of Hazine 1510. It is attached to a manuscript dated to 965/1557–58.[56] The doublure of this latter manuscript is, however, also similar in design to that of the Oxford *Lisān al-Ṭayr* copied by Ḥājj Muḥammad al-Tabrīzī in 937/1530–31 mentioned earlier.[57]

These comparisons highlight one of the key problems facing anyone who wishes to study the history of bindings. It is at present difficult to distinguish between similarites due to conservatism in the artistic and technical traditions of bindings and chronological ambiguities created by transferring bindings from one manuscript to another. Redecoration or repair of bindings also adds an element of confusion to their chronology.

At present what can be established is that Hazine 1510's binding was probably made by an Iranian craftsman during the first decades of the sixteenth century in either Iran or Turkey. If it was originally created to house the manuscripts it now contains, it may be contemporary with the insertion of the *firmān* and the changes made to the manuscript's colophons, that is, sometime after 906/1503.

Now that the contents and binding of Hazine 1510 have been analyzed, it is appropriate to examine the text with the name of Ḥusayn Bāyqarā mentioned above. This document is written on another piece of paper which has been pasted over the fourteenth-century page (figure 9.5). Although portions of the paper are abraded as though some of the text had been erased and then rewritten,[58] in the main the document appears to be authentic, if truncated. It lacks headings, seals, colophons, and endorsem ents.[59]

The document is written in two different scripts, and has two sections: an upper one in one in black-outlined gold script which contains invocations, the titles and epithets of Ḥusayn Bāyqarā and the royal decree, and a lower portion in black labeled as a *bar-āvard*, or estimate of expenses, for the production of a *Shāh-nāmah* manuscript. The text specifies that the manuscript in question is being forwarded to the accountants (*mustawfiyān*) of the royal *Dīvān* along with the *firmān* proper. The firman requests that individuals listed in the *bar-āvard* be recompensed for the expenses and labor involved in the production a manuscript which must have been presented (unsolicited?) to Sulṭān Ḥusayn Bāyqarā. Those named in the *bar-āvard* are probably to be identified with the "skilled men" (*asḥāb-i khibrat*) and the "learned" (*ahl-i dānish*) praised in the opening invocation.

The *bar-āvard* also has two sections: an upper one that gives the total cost of the manuscript, four *tūmāns*, 2,450 *dīnārs*, and a lower one arranged in five columns, that lists the amounts to be paid to specified individuals. The five columns are labeled (from right to left): *kāghaz* (paper), *kitābat* (copying), *tazhīb* (gilding), *jadval* (margination), and *taṣvīr* (painting).

For each category, the column lists the person(s) to be paid, the cost per item, and the number of items involved. Thus, under paper we see mention of the purchase of *kāghaz-i hiṭāyī*, or Chinese paper, the name Khwāja Murshīd-i Kāshgarī, the quantity of 600 pages (*awrāq*), and the unit price of twenty dinars a page (*waraq*) for a total of 12,000 dinars. In the second column, copying, the calligrapher is identified as Mawlānā Warqah ibn ʻUmar Samarqandī, who copied 63,000 *bayts* at 250 dinars per thousand *bayts* for a total of 15,750 *dīnārs*. In the third column under illumination the craftsmen are listed as Sharaf al-Dīn and Jalāl al-Dīn Kirmānī, and they are to be given a total of 6,000 *dīnārs* for executing four illuminated pages. The two marginators, Ustād Aḥmad and Mawlānā Muḥammad Haravī completed sixty *juz'* at the price of forty dinars a *juz'* for a total of 2,400 *dīnārs*. Last comes the painter, ʻAbd-ul-Wahhāb Muṣavvir-i Mashhadī, who executed twenty-one scenes at 300 *dīnārs* apiece for a total of 6,300 *dīnārs*. When added together these sums equal 42,450 *dīnārs*, or 4 *tūmāns*, 2,450 *dīnārs*.[60]

Various aspects of this text are worthy of closer study, but here the focus will be on its significance for the history of Hazine 1510. This *bar-āvard* describes the cost of a *Shāh-nāmah* manuscript consisting of 600 leaves, or 60 gatherings, containing 63,000 verses with 4 illuminated headings or pages and 21 paintings. When these numbers are compared to the *Shāh-nāmah* of Hazine 1510 questions arise. The most difficult to reconcile are the figures concerning the manuscript's length—63,000 verses on 600 folios or 60 *juz'*.

The Hazine 1510 *Shāh-nāmah*, however, has only 484 folios, and approximately 52,000 verses.[61] The relative brevity of this *Shāh-nāmah* copy has been interpreted by J. Khāliqī-Muṭlaq as a sign of its unusual conservatism and fidelity to Firdawsī's original text.[62] Now that Hazine 1510 has been identified as a Muzaffarid manuscript that probably was copied in 783/1382, its relationship to other early, accurate copies of the *Shāh-nāmah* should receive even greater attention, especially in connection with efforts to reconstruct Firdawsi's original text.[63]

The *firmān*'s data on illuminations and paintings is more compatible than its text description with the present condition of Hazine 1510. The *Shāh-nāmah* could be described as having four illuminations, namely an initial medallion, folio 1a, two illuminated pages at the opening of the preface, folios 2b–3a, and a fourth page at the beginning of the poem itself, folio 8b. The listing of twenty-one paintings is also accurate if the double page painting situated between the preface and the body of the poem is excluded. The *Shāh-nāmah* of Hazine 1510 now has twenty-three paintings, but two of them added on blank pages between the preface and body of the *Shāh-nāmah* may well have been added to the manuscript at a later date (fols. 7b–8a).

Although it is logical to assume that this document describes the manuscript to which it is affixed, such a conclusion leaves major questions unanswered. The basic discrepancy between the *firmān* and Hazine 1510 lies not in the inconsistency of its numbers but rather stems from its implicit origin and purpose. The document appears to describe a routine court transaction in which Sulṭān Ḥusayn Bāyqarā accepted a manuscript presented to him by its makers and ordered them to be recompensed for their efforts. The document's stress on "people of learning" suggests that some of those involved were scholars, and the relatively small sum to be expended for paintings may imply that they were of modest size and quality. Finally, it does not seem probable that the treasury of Ḥusayn Bāyqarā would have expended the considerable sums listed here for paper, copying, illumination, and margination if it had been suspected that the manuscript in question had been written, illuminated, and marginated more than a hundred years earlier.

If the *firmān* and Hazine 1510 had separate origins, what is the significance of their present juncture? Here only a provisional answer to this question can be given. It seems probable that the insertion of this document into Hazine 1510 is connected with alterations in its colophon dates: from 783 to 903 in the *Shāh-nāmah* and from 776 to 906 in the *Khamsah* and with the addition of a superflous colophon dated to 903 in the name of "Warqah ibn ʿUmar Samarqandī." This scribal name, chosen to harmonize with that of the original *Shāh-nāmah* calligrapher, was then inserted into the *firmān* after the name of its original scribe had been erased. The superflous colophon's use of the *nisbah* "Samarqandī" buttressed "Warqah's" credentials as a Timurid calligrapher and strengthened Hazine 1510's connection with Sulṭān Ḥusayn Bāyqarā's *firmān*. A desire to provide a Herat pedigree for Hazine 1510, and to harmonize it with the *Shāh-nāmah* manuscript described in the *firmān* may also have stimulated the addition of twenty-one paintings to its previously unillustrated *Shāh-nāmah* text. It is even possible that the addition of Sulṭān Ḥusayn Bāyqarā's name to the *Shāh-nāmah*'s initial medallion had the same goal.

The changes suggested above seem to have had a related aim and purpose: to transform a manuscript from Muzaffarid Shiraz that had belonged to Shāh Rukh into one from Timurid Herat which was linked with the patronage of Sulṭān Ḥusayn Bāyqarā. The addition of the now missing *Dīvān* by ʿAlī Shīr Navā'ī could also have formed part of the same goal and given Hazine 1510 yet another connection with Timurid Herat. A new binding inscribed with the verses of Jāmī and embellished with jewels may have completed this process of transformation.

In order to examine the plausibility of these hypotheses, the questions surrounding Hazine 1510 must be considered in the larger context of its time. It seems unlikely that these changes antedate the death of Ḥusayn Bāyqarā in 912/1506, or the end of his dynasty the following year. The pillaging of Herat by the Safavids in 1510 must have put both Timurid documents and manuscripts into wider circulation and may provide the *terminus ante quem* for various changes made to Hazine 1510.

If the transformation of Hazine 1510 occurred after the end of the Timurid dynasty, with the goal of "Timuridizing" a Muzaffarid manuscript, it must have been done in a place where things Timurid had a high prestige. Three possible locations come to mind: the Uzbek domains of Khurasan and Transoxiana, Safavid Tabriz, and Ottoman Istanbul. Further investigation is needed before a definite conclusion can be reached, but stylistic features of the paintings added to the *Shāh-nāmah* and of the manuscript's binding point to Tabriz, whereas the *Khamsah* paintings suggest a link to Istanbul. Perhaps both features can be explained by the well-documented presence of Iranian craftsmen at the Ottoman court and the high prestige which Timurid culture and art enjoyed in sixteenth-century Istanbul.

NOTES

1. F. E. Karatay, *Topkapı Sarayı Müzesi Kütüphanesi Farsça Yazmalar Kataloğu*, [hereafter *FYK*] (Istanbul, 1961), no. 348, p. 131.

2. Thomas W. Lentz and Glenn D. Lowry, *Timur and the Princely Vision* (Los Angeles, 1989).

3. The history of another Topkapı manuscript, Hazine 762, is a good example of the transfer of a book from one royal owner to another. See Ivan Stchoukine (*Les Peintures des manuscrits de la "Khamseh" de Niẓâmî au Topkapı Sarayı Müzesi d'Istanbul* (Paris, 1966), ms. no. 13, pp. 71–81).

4. The authors would like to thank A.H. Morton of the University of London for his transcription of numbers contained in the *firmān*, and K. Eslami of Princeton University for assistance in interpreting the *firmān*'s text. They also benefited from discussing the binding's inscriptions with F. Bagherzadeh of Paris and A.-M. Schimmel of Harvard University.

5. I. Stchoukine, "Origine turque des peintures d'une Anthologie persane de 801/1398," *Syria* 42 (1965), pp. 139–40, pl. 11; idem, *La Peinture turque d'après les manuscrits illustrés Ier partie; de Sulayman Ier à Osman II: 1520–1622* (Paris, 1966), pp. 64, 111, pl. 25a & b; idem, *Les Peintures des manuscrits*, ms. no. 65, pp. 150–51, pls. 79,80.

6. Karatay, *FYK*, no. 348, p. 131.

7. Stchoukine, *Peinture turque*, pp. 64, 111.

8. M. Aga-Oglu, "The Landscape Miniatures of an Anthology of the year 1398," *Ars Islamica* 3 (1936), pp. 77–98; Stchoukine, "Origine Turque," pp. 137–39.

9. Jalāl Khāliqī-Muṭlaq, "Mu'arrifī wa 'arẓyābī-yi barkhī āz dastnavīshā-yī Shāh-nāmah," (2), *Irān-nāmah*, 4:1 (1364/1985), 30–31, 35–36; (3), *Irān-nāmah*, 4:2 (1364/1985) 248, 250–53. The authors would like to thank Mr. K. Eslami for bringing these references to their attention.

10. Asadī Tūsī, *Lughat-i Furs*, ed. Fatḥ Allāh Mujtabā'ī, 'Alı Ashraf Sādiqī, (Tehran, 1365/1986), p. 13. The authors would like to thank Mr. K. Eslami for bringing this publication to their attention.

11. Luṭf Allāh also copied a manuscript of Firdawsī's *Shāh-nāmah* now in the Egyptian National Library, Cairo, which is dated to 796/1392–94 (I. Stchoukine, "Les Manuscrits illustrés musulmans de la bibliothèque du Caire," *Gazette des Beaux Arts* 77, no. 3 (January–June 1935), p. 141).

12. The principal difference between the T. 1950 (fol. 464b) colophon and that of Hazine 1510 (fol. 484b) is that the former uses a Persian form for this gloss: *min a'mal kūt gilūyeh*.

13. Heinz Gaube, *Die südpersische Provinz Arragan/Kuh-Giluyeh von der arabischen Eroberung bis zur Safawidenzeit* (Vienna, 1973), pp. 15, 25, 72–77.

14. As suggested by A. Sarkisian, *La Miniature persane du XIIe au XVIIe siècle* (Paris, 1929), p. 33.

15. Hazine 1510, fol. 1b, 2a; T. 1950, fol. 1b, 2a.

16. For an early example see M. Lings, *The Quranic Art of Calligraphy and Illumination* (Westerham, Kent, 1976), p. 119, pl. 60, and for a late one see ibid., p. 172, pls. 82–83.

17. The page appears to have been inserted after the manuscript had been written.

18. Hazine 1510, fols. 6a, 222a, 377a.

19. Hazine 1510, fol. 499a.

20. Manuscript no. 2179, Tashkent, Institute of Oriental Sciences of the Uzbek Academy of Sciences, *Miniatures Illuminations of Amir Hosrov Dehlevi's*

Works, ed. H. Suleimanov, pls. 87, 88; Amir Husraw Dikhlavi, *Maṭla' al-anwār*, ed. T.A-O. Magerramov (Muharramov) (Moscow, 1975), pp. 74–76; another manuscript of probable Shiraz origin once in the library of Shāh Rukh is a copy of Farīd al-Dīn 'Aṭṭār's *Jawhar al-zāt* now in the Österreichische Nationalbibliothek, Vienna, A. F. 384. This manuscript also contains the seal of the Ottoman ruler Beyazit II. (D. Duda, *Islamische Handscriften: I Persische Handschriften*, 2 vols. (Vienna, 1983), vol. 1, pp. 52–53; vol. 2, figs. 8–9.).

21. 'Abd al-Razzāq Samarqandī, *Maṭla' al-Sa'dayn*, ed. M. Shafī' (Lahore, 1946), vol. II:1, pp. 162, 164–66.

22. Stchoukine, *Peinture turque*, pp. 64, 111.

23. M. Aga-Oglu, "The Landscape Minniatures," pp. 77–98; Stchoukine, "Origine turque," pp. 137–39.

24. Hazine 1510, fols. 540a, 545b, 566a, 636b, 675b, 713a, 775b.

25. Hazine 1510, fols. 502b, 512b, 547b, 563a.

26. Hazine 1510, fol. 682b.

27. Stchoukine, *Peintures des manuscrits*, pls. 79a, 80. See note 4 above.

28. Some of these lush settings containing palm trees and pomegranates may depict the calligrapher's native region of Kūh Gilūyeh.

29. Hazine 1510, fols. 547b, 563a; see Stchoukine, *Peintures des manuscrits*, pls. 79a, 80.

30. Hazine 1511; B. Gray, "The School of Shiraz from 1392 to 1453," in *The Arts of the Book in Central Asia: 14th–16th Centuries* (Paris, 1979), pl. 34, fig. 71.

31. Stchoukine, *Peinture turque*, pp. 64, 111.

32. Ibid., no. 8, p. 51, pls. 6–7.

33. F. Çağman, "The Miniatures of the Divan-i Hüsayni and the Influence of Their Style," in *Fifth International Congress of Turkish Art*, ed. G. Fehér (Budapest, 1978), pp. 231–59, esp. 241–42.

34. Stchoukine, *Peinture turque*, no. 20, pp. 58–59; E. Atil, *Turkish Art* (Washington, DC, 1980), pl. 18.

35. A. S. Levend, *Ali Sir Nevai: III: Hamse* (Ankara, 1967), illus. between pp. 16–17, 152–53, 215–17, 264–65.

36. Ibid., pp. 237–38; I. Stchoukine, "Les Manuscrits illustrés musulmans de la bibliothèque du Caire," *Gazette des Beaux Arts* 77 (January–June 1935), pp. 151–52; L. Binyon, J.V.S. Wilkinson, B. Gray, *Persian Miniature Painting* (London, 1933), no. 140, p. 133, pl. 90b.

37. Oxford, Bodleian Library, Or. 195, Navā'ī, *Lisān al-Ṭayr*, in *Miniatures Illustrations of Alisher Navoi's Works*, pls. 182–91.

38. Çağman, "Miniatures of the Divan-i Hüseyni," pp. 229–30, figs. 22–23.

39. Duda, *Islamische Handschriften* I, vol. I, pp. 30–33, Abb. 333–37; see above, notes 33 and 34.

40. ['Abd al-Raḥmān Jāmī], *Dīvan-i kāmil-i Jāmī*, ed. H. Raḍī (Tehran, 1341s/1962), [n.p.], "*Rubā'īyāt*," nos. 48, 77, 213, pp. 815, 818, 835.

41. Ibid., no. 48, p. 815.

42. Ibid., no. 213, p. 835.

43. Topkapı Palace Museum 2/2132, in *The Anatolian Civilisations III*, "Ottoman" (Istanbul, 1983), no. E 199, pp. 229–30.

44. See also C. Köseoğlu, *The Topkapı Saray Museum: The Treasury* (New York, 1980), pl. 81, p. 202.

45. F. Çağman, "Serzergerân Mehmet Usta ve Eserleri, in *Kemal Çig'a Armağan* (Istanbul, 1984), p. 54, esp. notes 13, 15.

46. ['Abdallāh Marvarīd], *Staatsschreiben der Timuridenzeit*, ed. and trans. H. Roemer (Wiesbaden, 1952), no. 74, pp. 131–34, 199–200, facsimile fols. 74a–76a; for a transcription of the text, see M. Haravī, "Muraqqa'-sāzī dar dawrah-i Tīmūrīyān," *Hunar va Mardum*, no. 143, 1305s, pp. 34–36.

47. An unidentified binding illustrated on the cover of the first volume of *Türkiye Yazmaları Toplu Katalogu* (Istanbul, 1982).

48. A. F. 66, Österreichische Nationalbibliothek, Vienna (D. Duda, *Islamische Handschriften: I Persische Handschriften* [Vienna, 1983] vol. II, Abb. 35.)

49. Çağman, "Serzergerăn Mehmet Usta," p. 54, note 14.; Istanbul University Library, A. 6546, a Qur'han copied by Yedikulī Sayyid ʿAbdallāh in 1127/1715. The binding may be earlier than the text it encompasses.

50. Köseoğlu, *The Treasury* nos. 74–76, p. 200.

51. Duda, *Islamische Handschsriften*, vol. I, 71–72; vol. II, Abb. 18–20.

52. Aslanapa, "Art of Bookbinding," p. 64, pls. 17–18.

53. Ibid., p. 63, ill. 29; Çağmen, "Miniatures of the Divan-i Hüseyni," pp. 231–33.

54. For examples with a clear Ottoman provenance, see Z. Tanındı, "Rûganî Türk Kitap Kaplarinin Erken Örnekleri," in *Kemal Çığ'a Armağan*, pp. 223, 226–32, figs. 1, 5–11, 13–21; *Soliman le Magnifique* (Paris, 1990), no. 130; M. Rogers and R. Ward, *Süleyman the Magnificent* (London, 1988), no. 24a–b, pp. 80–81.

55. ʿAlī Shīr Navā'ī, *Khamsa*, Dorn 560, Leningrad State Public Library, in *Miniatures Illustrations*, pls. 43–58. This manuscript appears to be of sixteenth-century western Iranian origin, although it has a colophon which alleges that it was copied in Timurid Herat in 898/1492–93.

56. Haldane, *Islamic Bookbindings*, pl. 83, p. 82.

57. *Miniatures Illustrations*, pl. 183.

58. The most abraded section contains the calligrapher's name, "Warqah b. ʿUmar," however, his *nisbah* "al-Samarqandī," appears to be original.

59. Concerning the form of *firmāns* see *Tadhkirat al-mulūk: a manual of Safavid Administration*, ed. trans. V. Minorsky, appendix 4b, pp. 199–200.

60. The authors would like to thank Prof. A. H. Morton for assistance in reading this document.

61. Manuscripts of Firdawsī's *Shāh-nāmah* vary considerably in length, but a length of 63,000 verses would be compatible with a manuscript of 600 folios copied with four text columns of twenty-seven lines to the page, a common page length. See, for example, Hazine 1515 with 622 folios and twenty-three lines per page (F. Karatay, *Farsça Yazmalar*, no. 334, p. 127).

62. Khāliqī-Muṭlaq, "Mu'arrifi. . .*Shāh-nāmah*," (3), *IN*, vol. 4:2, pp. 240, 250–53.

63. This new date would appear to move Hazine 1510 from its current position as number forty-five to number eight in his list of *Shāh-nāmah* manuscripts arranged by date, and from number fifteen to number six in his listing of complete copies of the text (J. Khāliqī-Muṭlaq, "Mu'arrifī. . .*Shāh-nāma*" (1), *IN*, vol. 3:3, 1364/1985, pp, 386–387; Ibid., (2), *IN*, vol. 4:1, pp. 30–31; Ibid., (3), *IN*, vol. 4:2, pp. 231, 248).

11

Fāris al-Shidyāq and the Transition from Scribal to Print Culture in the Middle East

Geoffrey Roper

It is well known that printing came late to the Arab and Muslim Middle East; it is also well known that when it did become established, it had significant effects on the intellectual and social development of the area. These have become truisms, because historians have routinely acknowledged and paid lip-service to their importance. However, what they have not done, by and large, is to analyze, or even to spell out, the progress and consequences of this major transformation of social communication, and the changes in human relationships within Middle Eastern society which flowed from it. Such an undertaking, indeed, has not been possible, even for those few historians who are conscious of the need for it, because the materials for such a study have yet to be assembled. Nevertheless, it is possible to draw attention here briefly to a few general points about the nature of the transition from scribal culture to print culture, before illustrating that transition in the career and writings of one leading figure involved in it.

Although block-printing was practiced in the medieval Muslim Middle East, long before in Europe, the technique does not seem to have developed there beyond the printing of single-leaf amulets and talismans: it was apparently never used for the production of books, which remained entirely in the hands of scribes until the eighteenth century, and predominantly so until well into the nineteenth century, despite the widespread adoption of printing elsewhere. This reflects the maintenance of a monopoly of knowledge by a traditional elite group—the *'ulamā'*—whose control over the scribal transmission and dissemination of texts served to reinforce established patterns of authority in Muslim society. It has been pointed out, moreover, that, especially towards the end of the scribal era, "knowledge" often tended to be regarded as a mystical and secret entity, and writers tended accordingly to prefer an obscure style of expression; this in turn encouraged what has been called a "magic garden" mentality, promoting esotericism at the expense of both lucidity and rationality.[1]

Printing eventually served to break this monopoly by creating a new culture based not only on a new means of transmitting texts, but also on a new approach to selecting, writing, and presenting them, aimed at a new kind of reader. In the process, it contributed to a demystification of language and literature, a revival of the classical heritage, and a new self-awareness. These led in turn both to a cultural revival (*nahḍah*) and to political movements of a nationalist character. Although it started, among Muslims, as a means for modernizing rulers to educate, communicate with, and influence a new elite of their own creation, it eventually, as in early modern Europe, penetrated much further into society and into the consciousness of significant sections of the population. In doing so, it helped to redefine peoples' relations with the sacred, with power and authority, and with the community.[2] Moreover, although the technology of printing came to the Middle East from Europe, it was not, as some historians have assumed, just a manifestation of, and vehicle for, Westernization: it had its own direct effects, which operated both on the cognitive plane and on the socioeconomic plane.

In the forefront of this process, which amounted to nothing less than the modernization and renewal of the literary and intellectual culture of the Middle East, were certain litterateurs—*udabā'*— who, as Carter Findley has pointed out, came from the old literary scribal elite, but evolved into the vanguard of the new culture.[3] It is on one of the most celebrated of these that I now wish to focus, and to try to trace in him and through him the emergence of that new, print-based culture and the transformations that it brought.

Fāris al-Shidyāq, later Aḥmad Fāris Efendi, was very much a product of the old scribal culture—not just in a passive sense, but as an active and enthusiastic practitioner and connoisseur of it. Born in Lebanon in the first decade of the nineteenth century into a Maronite family which had traditionally provided clerks, scribes, and tutors for feudal lords,[4] he grew up in a literary household. His father had collected books on a variety of subjects, which the young Fāris avidly read, especially literary works and poetry.[5] These books were, of course, all manuscripts: although Arabic printing had been introduced into Lebanon in 1734,[6] and Arabic printed books had also been imported from Europe since the 16th century,[7] they were restricted to Christian religious and liturgical books, produced in quite small quantities for the use of the clergy: literary and educational books were available only in handwritten copies. Following the family tradition, Fāris himself became at an early age a professional copyist, and was employed, among other assignments, to copy the registers and chronicles of the amir Haydar al-Shihābī in connection with the compilation of the latter's composite history of Lebanon and neighboring countries.[8] He also produced, for Christian patrons, numerous copies of other works, in both Arabic and Syriac, some of which survived in ecclesiastical and private collections in Lebanon.[9]

al-Shidyāq from the outset strove for high technical and aesthetic standards in his copying. In later years, he remarked, for instance, on the necessity of using the correct implements for writing Arabic—reed pens, not quills;[10] he also recalled that in his youth he had enthusiastically cultivated excellence in handwriting (*jūdat* or *tajwīd al-khaṭṭ*), and whenever he saw fine script, devoted himself to imitating it.[11] During his stay in Egypt between 1828 and 1835, he continued to copy books for his own use, and possibly for others (although we cannot be certain of this). A copy of Zawzanī's commentary on the *Muʿallaqāt*, for instance, made by him in Cairo in 1833, is extant,[12] and it bears a note that it was still in his possession in 1855/56.[13] He also made notebooks (*kurrāsah*) of extracts of manuscript works that he thought would later be of use to him, such as Damīrī's zoological encyclopedia, *Ḥayāt al-ḥayawān*, which he later used when translating an English natural history textbook for publication.[14] Throughout his later life he continued to copy books, and assembled such a large collection of manuscript volumes by this means that he used to worry, so it is said, about what would happen to them after his death.[15] He also made careful copies—often more than one—of his own works, some of which survive in this form.[16]

As well as being a scribe, Fāris was an avid reader and collector of manuscripts. During his stay in Egypt, he seems to have immersed himself in classical Arabic literature, most of which at that time was still unpublished, and acquired some manuscripts there.[17] Later, when he went to Europe, he made a point of visiting the great libraries of Paris, London, Cambridge, and Oxford, and reading important works in their collections of Arabic manuscripts.[18] He described in some detail his visit to the British Museum Library (now the British Library) and mentioned some of the works of Arabic literature that he read there—almost certainly, in some cases, for the first, and perhaps the only, time: Ibn Quṭaybah, al-Zamakhsharī, al-Jāḥiẓ, Abū Tammām, and al-Mutanabbī.[19] He noted ruefully that he was not allowed to copy works in their entirety when there, but only to make extracts or summaries.[20] During the last thirty years of his life, when he was living in Istanbul, he frequented the manuscript collections there also, and wrote articles in his newspaper, *al-Jawā'ib*, enumerating the libraries and their contents, and complaining about the restricted access and poor working conditions in them.[21] Evidence of his love of fine calligraphy and illumination emerges from some of his descriptions of the manuscripts which he had seen, such as the sumptuous copy of Fīrūzābādī's *al-Qāmūs* in the Koprülü Library.[22]

But al-Shidyāq's main concern when studying manuscripts, especially in this latter period, was always to establish accurate texts that faithfully reflected what the classical authors had written. To this end, he made detailed comparisons and evaluations of the manuscript copies he encountered,[23] and as he did so, he became acutely aware of how some of these texts had become subject to corruption (*al-taḥrīf wa-al-taṣḥīf*) in the process of copying, because of the ignorance and negligence of scribes.[24] He noted that manuscript copies were often defective,[25] that is, lacking part or parts of the text; and he was furthermore aware that much Arabic literature had been lost altogether through the destruction of unique or rare manuscript texts.[26] Moreover, even many of those texts that survived were scarce and hard to locate or obtain, as he had discovered, for instance, when trying to find copies of the *dīwān*s of the great classical Arabic poets in Cairo when he was a young man.[27]

So al-Shidyāq was well aware that the revival of Arabic literature and culture depended on bypassing the old scribal tradition, much as he revered it and was a part of it, and finding a new means of transmitting and preserving both classical texts and new writing. Fortunately, the development of his own life and work had shown him that just such a means was now available, that could and should be widely adopted in the service of Arabic learning and letters. From the time that he left his native land in 1826, his career was inextricably bound up with, and dependent on, the use of the printing press. At the beginning of that career, it was still a suspect novelty in the Arab and Muslim Middle East; by the time of his death sixty years later, it had become the normal and accepted method of producing and transmitting Arabic texts.

The first press with which al-Shidyāq was involved was that run by the English Church Missionary Society (CMS) in Malta. He spent about eighteen months there in 1827–28, helping to prepare Christian religious texts—commentaries on the parables of Jesus and a new metrical translation of some of the Psalms[28]—for printing and distribution mainly in Lebanon and Egypt. However, ill health caused him to leave Malta for Egypt, where he spent the next seven years. During this time, he worked for a while on the newspaper *al-Waqā'i' al-Miṣrīyah*—the first Arabic newspaper to be published anywhere—and was therefore one of the first Arabs, if not the very first, to practice the craft of journalism.[29] While thus engaged, he no doubt became familiar with the operations of the state press of Muḥammad ʿAlī at Būlāq, where the newspaper was produced. However, it seems that he soon became disillusioned with Egyptian government service, mainly because of delays in payment of his salary,[30] and by 1832 he was again working for the missionaries in Cairo.

At the end of 1835, al-Shidyāq went back to Malta, and over the next six years again helped to prepare and edit translations of a number of Christian religious books; but in addition to these, he also published at the CMS press a series of secular didactic works on geography, natural history, and language. Three of these were written or compiled by him, being his first published works; another was carefully translated by him from English. He also prepared and produced the *editio princeps* of an earlier Arabic grammar, the *Baḥth al-maṭālib* of Jibrīl Farḥāt (Malta, 1836). This was the first of many manuscript works which were to be published at his hands over the next fifty years.

al-Shidyāq's role at the Malta Arabic press in the 1830s and 1840s was such as to make him fully conscious of all that was involved in this new method of book production and of its potentialities. Not only did he prepare copy for the press, he also acted as a proof reader and corrector, becoming acutely aware of the importance of vigilance and meticulousness in these tasks. At the end of his own Arabic grammar and reader, *al-Lafīf fī kull maʿná ṭarīf*, he refers specifically to his own role in its printing and asks the reader's forgiveness for any typographical errors remaining.[31] By that time he had already raised the typographical standards of the Malta press to a much higher level than had existed there previously. Not only Arabic, but also Ottoman Turkish texts were checked and proofread by him. Nor was his work confined to textual editing and correction—he also had a hand in designing and preparing the punches for a new Arabic typeface, in three sizes, which was brought into use in 1838, and which has been admired for its beauty and excellence.[32]

The Arabic press in Malta was closed down in 1842, and for the next fifteen years al-Shidyāq's work in the field of editing and publishing bore fruit not in the Arab world, but in Europe. He translated the whole of the Bible into Arabic and saw it through the press in England—a major undertaking which must have made him fully acquainted with established printing and publishing practices at a large-scale scholarly press, in this case William Watts in London.[33] He also had published in Paris in 1855 his own extensive autobiographical and literary work, *al-Sāq ʿalá al-sāq*, for which a special, new Arabic typeface was prepared and cast[34]—again he corrected all the proofs himself.[35] He also became interested again in journalism and newspaper publishing: a prospectus for a new political journal under his editorship was issued in France in 1858.[36]

In 1857, al-Shidyāq was invited to Tunis to apply his knowledge of publishing and journalism to the foundation of a new state press and newspaper there.[37] Before this came to fruition, however, certain intrigues at the Tunisian court caused the task to be assigned to someone else.[38] But his brief stay in Tunis was nevertheless of great importance to the development of his subsequent career. For it was there that he embraced Islam, and by doing so qualified himself for a new and more influential role in the renewal of Arab and Muslim culture in the second half of the nineteenth century.

In 1859 or 1860, al-Shidyāq went to Istanbul, where he lived for the rest of his life. He seems to have been appointed in the first place as Chief Corrector (*Ra'īs al-muṣaḥḥiḥīn*) at the Imperial Press (*al-Maṭbaʿah al-Sulṭānīyah*),[39] but his first major task was to launch a new Arabic newspaper called *al-Jawā'ib*, which started in 1861 and continued, with two short interruptions, until 1884. It was this newspaper that brought al-Shidyāq his greatest fame, because it was widely distributed, carrying his name, his writing, and his ideas all over the Arab and Muslim worlds. But although al-Shidyāq had now achieved his long-standing ambition to edit and publish an Arabic newspaper, journalism by no means displaced book publishing in his career. In 1868, he published his own large-scale treatise on Arabic etymology, *Sirr al-layāl fī al-qalb wa-al-ibdāl*, at the Imperial Press. Then, in 1870, he established the Jawā'ib Press (*Maṭbaʿat al-Jawā'ib*) with new equipment, and not only did this take over the printing of the newspaper after which it was named, it also published a long series of books, mostly in Arabic but also some in Turkish. These have teen collected, studied, and enumerated by the eminent al-Shidyāq scholar Mohammed Alwan[40] and it is not necessary to go over that ground here except to note his finding that the number of publications totalled 75, and that they fell into essentially four categories: classical Arabic literature; al-Shidyāq's own works; works by other contemporary authors, mostly his friends, supporters, or patrons; and miscellaneous semi-official Ottoman publications. By the time of al-Shidyāq's death in 1887, he could truly be said to have been not just one of the greatest Arabic writers of the age, but also one of its foremost editors and publishers.

al-Shidyāq did not just passively accept and make use of the printing press in the furtherance of his own career and reputation: he was also an active protagonist and propagandist of the print revolution. "In truth," he wrote, "all the crafts that have been invented in this world are inferior to the craft of printing. To be sure, the ancients built pyramids, set up monuments, erected statues, fortified strongholds, dug canals and water conduits, and paved military roads; however, those crafts, compared with the craft of printing, are but one degree above savagery. After printing became widespread, there was no longer any likelihood of the disappearance of knowledge which had been disseminated and made public, or the loss of books, as was the case when they were written with the pen."[41] It was, perhaps, because he had been precipitated early in his career into the print-oriented world of Malta and Europe that he did not share the antagonism towards printing and the mass production of books that was felt by many of his contemporaries among the educated Arab elite. The latter were no doubt motivated by their instinctive awareness of the threat that it posed to their monopoly of knowledge and authority. On the contrary al-Shidyāq recognized the undesirability of that restrictive monopoly: "Much of our literature," he complained, "is possessed by a few individuals who do not think it in their interest to give it a wider spread among the people."[42] Printing was the way to break out of this situation. Not only would it help preserve literature that would otherwise be lost, something to which he attached immense importance, as the previously quoted passage indicates,[43] but it would also make books much easier for everyone to obtain, read, and collect.[44] Printing establishments would even themselves become centers of culture, places for educated people to make for when visiting a country or locality.[45]

al-Shidyāq was aware that the Arabs and Muslims were backward in this matter, because he had studied the history of printing in China and the West, and devoted a substantial section of his book on Europe to it,[46] as well as articles in *al-Jawā'ib*;[47] he also described a copy of the Gutenberg Bible of 1455, which he saw in the British Museum, and other early European printed books.[48] But what really impressed him was the sheer volume of book and newspaper publishing in contemporary Europe: in several of his books and articles, he treats the matter at length, giving detailed statistics.[49] This, he considered, was an important cause of Europe's ascendancy, and the lack of printing an equally important cause of ignorance and decline among the Arabs and Muslims.[50] What were needed, he wrote, were presses "to print. . .books useful for men, women, and children, and for every single class of people, so that they know what their rights and obligations are (*mā lahum wa-mā 'alayhim min al-ḥuqūq*)."[51] He was thus suggesting that the printed word could bring about social and political, as well as intellectual, emancipation and advancement.

I have sought to demonstrate that al-Shidyāq was both a major participant in and a protagonist of the print revolution in the Middle East. It remains to consider the effects that his activities, and the products of his endeavors, actually had in bringing about the shift from scribal to print culture in the Arab and Muslim Worlds. In discussing the equivalent shift in early modern Europe, the historian Elizabeth Eisenstein has identified three fundamental changes, or rather "clusters of changes," which printing brought to the processes of communication and transmission by the written word: the much wider dissemination of texts in all fields; their standardization; and their preservation for posterity. Each of these had far-reaching effects, not only on intellectual, but also on social and economic, development.[52] It may be useful, therefore, to apply this conceptual framework to the effects of the print revolution in the nineteenth-century Middle East, and to al-Shidyāq's part in it.

One of al-Shidyāq's biographers has made the point that his role in editing books for the press was really a continuation of his former trade as a copyist of manuscripts;[53] this is true up to a point, but it ignores the quite different effects which his new activities had. The Arabic tracts and textbooks which he edited and published in Malta were distributed on a large scale throughout the Middle East and were widely used in schools. al-Shidyāq enumerated some of the earlier Malta books which he himself used when a teacher in Cairo,[54] and these missionary publications were also widely disseminated amongst the Christian populations of Egypt, Lebanon, Palestine, Syria, and Iraq, as well as finding their way into the hands of some Muslims and, in some cases, into Muslim state schools.[55] The traditional *kuttābs*, whether Muslim or Christian, had not taught even the Arabic language, still less other subjects, in a systematic, graded manner, and had therefore tended to produce "functional illiterates."[56] The use of these Malta textbooks, as well as locally produced ones which followed their example, and some which al-Shidyāq later published in Istanbul for the Ottoman state schools,[57] helped to extend basic literacy. Moreover, the provision of instructional books to large numbers of individual pupils, which only printing made possible, encouraged them, at the outset of their education, to regard reading and studying from books as an individual and private activity, and one that was potentially within the reach of all. It is at least possible that some of the changes in perceived relationships between the individual and society, which became apparent among some intellectuals in the Middle East in the latter part of the nineteenth century, may have owed something to this new factor in their earliest childhood intellectual experience.

al-Shidyāq also played a pioneering role in disseminating the means for Arabs to learn European languages. In the scribal era, textbooks for this purpose were to all intents and purposes nonexistent. But al-Shidyāq's first published work was an English grammar for the use of Arabs,[58] which was distributed along with other Malta books in the Middle East, and of which a second edition was published at the Jawā'ib Press in Istanbul.[59] He also produced a book of grammatical exercises and dialogues[60] and later, in Paris, a grammar of French in Arabic.[61] Without such aids, the possibilities of Arab intellectuals of that era becoming acquainted with Western knowledge and culture directly through the medium of print would have been much more restricted than they were.

al-Shidyāq's activities as a journalist and newspaper publisher were, of course, even more crucial in bringing the printed word to a large Arab and Muslim readership. The role of newspapers and periodicals in creating a new reading public and a new social and political awareness in the nineteenth-century Middle East is, I think, generally appreciated, and this is not the place to consider it in detail. But two points can be mentioned which perhaps are not sufficiently recognized. The impact of journals like *al-Jawā'ib* went beyond the literate classes, because the reading of them was likely in many situations to have been a group activity. In coffee-houses and other places where people gathered, the illiterate and poorly educated also imbibed the printed word through the reading of extracts and passages out loud by their more literate companions. This applied also to some printed books, especially works of classical literature, such as the *Maqāmāt* of Hamadhānī, printed at al-Shidyāq's Jawā'ib Press in 1880 in an edition which was specifically intended to "please the reader and the listener" (*al-qāri' wa-al-sāmi'*).[62] al-Shidyāq also had a policy of serializing some classical works in *al-Jawā'ib* before publishing them separately, such as al-Amidī's *al-Muwāzanah bayna Abī Tammām wa-al-Buḥturī*.[63] Even those that were not serialized were always heavily advertised in the newspaper and distributed by its agents in Tunis,[64] Alexandria,[65] Beirut,[66] and elsewhere, as well as by post from Istanbul.

Nor were al-Shidyāq's activities as a disseminator confined to his own publications: he also acted as an agent and distributor for contemporary Arabic printed books from other publishers, including those in Tunisia and Lebanon.[67] *al-Jawā'ib* also carried many notices of newly published Arabic books from a variety of sources, including especially the Būlāq Press in Egypt. This was all in keeping with al-Shidyāq's mission to spread the benefits of the print revolution as widely as possible (see figure 11.1).

The standardization of texts and of their physical presentation was another important aspect of the print revolution in which al-Shidyāq was fully involved. Unlike most of his predecessors and contemporaries who prepared editions of classical Arabic works, he went to great trouble to establish sound texts by comparing and collating as many manuscript copies as he could find and noting their differences; and he encouraged others who edited texts for the Jawā'ib Press to do likewise.[68] Only in this way could a worthwhile and authoritative *editio princeps* be created. But he was well aware that compositors and editors, too, could make errors, and caveats to this effect were included in several of his books,[69] as well as, often, errata lists.[70] The correction of such errors, however, as well as additions and improvements to the texts themselves, could be incorporated into new, revised editions of books—a characteristic feature of the print era, in contrast to the progressive corruption of text in manuscript copies. This applied, of course, equally to new works, such as al-Shidyāq's own: five of his books were issued in revised editions under his supervision.[71] The awareness that printing could enable standard, corrected, and authoritative texts to become widely available for reference also made it particularly suitable for the promulgation of laws and state regulations, and al-Shidyāq was involved in this also: with Jawā'ib Press published a number of Ottoman legal codes and enactments in both Arabic and Turkish.[72]

The standardization of language itself was another of the effects of printing enumerated by Eisenstein. In the case of Arabic, this was less marked than in Europe, since strict classical norms applied to the written language, and the literary development of the vernaculars was ruled out. But the publications of al-Shidyāq's grammars, reading book, and textbooks in Malta did play a part in improving the written Arabic used by Arab Christians, which by the early nineteenth century had in many cases deteriorated into something akin to Middle Arabic, or into what he scathingly called *rakākah* (feebleness or poverty of style).[73] He also introduced into his publications, especially his translations, many newly coined words for new and alien objects and concepts, "for which," as he pointed out, "no equivalents could be discovered in classical Arabic. . .and that," he went on, "is to provoke the Arabs into putting into circulation new post-classical (*nuwallad*) expressions which will save them from choking on foreign jargon and protect them from an inundation of it."[74] Some of these neologisms found a permanent place in the language, and are still in use.[75] It was of course the power of print to circulate and reinforce the new usages that gave al-Shidyāq this seminal role in creating new lexical standards and norms for the Arabic language.

It is appropriate to remark here also that not only new vocabulary, but a whole new style of Arabic prose emerged at this time, and al-Shidyāq was

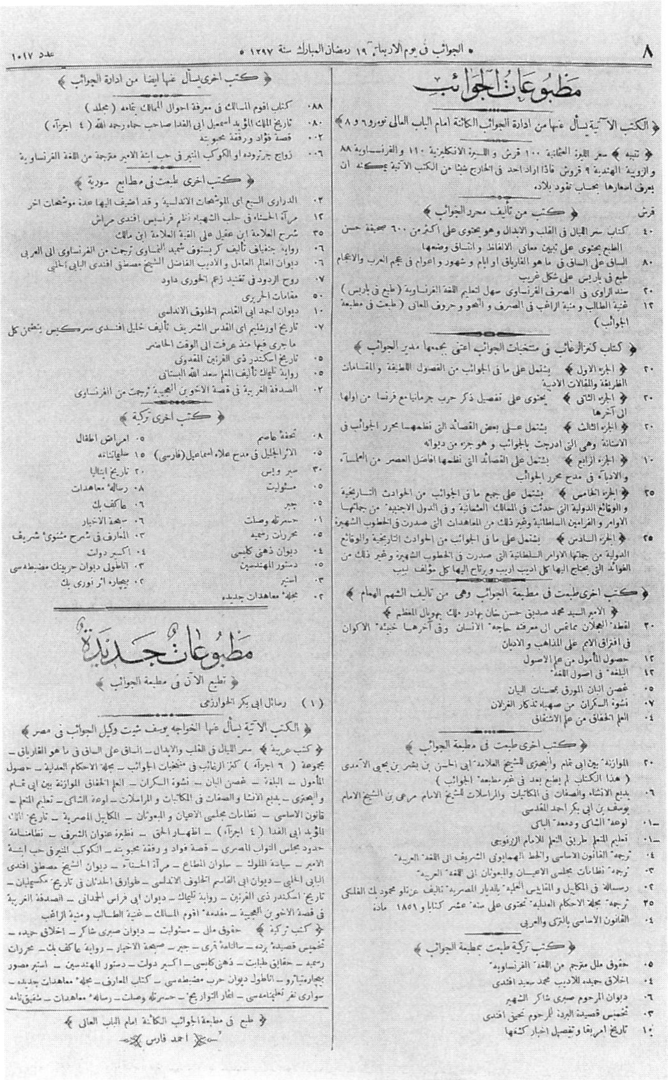
الجوائب في يوم الاربعاء ١٩ رمضان المبارك سنة ١٢٩٧ — عدد ١٠١٧ — ٨

مطبوعات الجوائب

الكتب الآتية يسأل عنها من ادارة الجوائب الكائنة امام الباب العالي

كتب من تأليف محرر الجوائب

كتاب كنز الرغائب في منتخبات الجوائب اعتنى بجمعها مدير الجوائب

كتب اخرى طبعت في مطبعة الجوائب وهي من تأليف الشهم الهمام

كتب اخرى طبعت في مطبعة الجوائب

كتب تركية طبعت بمطبعة الجوائب

كتب اخرى يسأل عنها ايضا من ادارة الجوائب

كتب اخرى طبعت في مطابع سورية

كتب اخرى تركية

مطبوعات جديدة

تطبع الآن في مطبعة الجوائب

طبع في مطبعة الجوائب الكائنة امام الباب العالي

احمد فارس

Fig. 11.1. The back page of al-Shidyāq'a newspaper *al-Jawā'ib*, no. 1017, Istanbul, 19 Ramaḍān 1298/25 August 1880. The right-hand column gives a price list of al-Jawā'ib Press books available from the newspaper offices, starting with al-Shidyāq's own works, including the original Paris edition of his *al-Sāq alá al-sāq*—"of alien appearance" (*'alá shakl gharib*). On the left are other Arabic and Turkish books which can be supplied, including some from "Syrian," that is Lebanese, presses, followed by a list of those available from the Egyptian agent of *al-Jawā'ib*. (Cambridge University Library, NPR. B. 411.)

one of the prime movers in this development. There is no doubt that he was steeped in the old classical norms and usages, and he also showed himself to be, in many of his writings, quite fond of obscurity and recondite verbiage. But he nevertheless realized that the new patterns of readership created by the print revolution necessitated a new, simpler, and more direct style, geared primarily to the communication of knowledge and ideas rather than to preserving the mystique of a literary elite. This was equally true when he was writing school textbooks for the Malta press, and when he was deploying the new medium of journalism later in Istanbul. To this print-based creativity of al-Shidyāq, and some of his contemporaries, can perhaps be traced the origins of the modern standard Arabic written language.

But if the advent of printing can be held partly responsible for new linguistic and literary standards, the new ways of presenting and packaging texts, to ease the task of the reader, are wholly due to it. In this development, too, al-Shidyāq played an active role. On the one hand, with his background as a scribe and calligrapher, he was keen to ensure that type styles reflected the best scribal norms. As already mentioned, he accordingly helped to design a new typeface for the Malta Arabic press in the 1830s; later, when he set up his own Jawā'ib Press in Istanbul, he ensured that its types followed the established Ottoman Arabic tradition, unlike the "alien form" (*shakl gharīb*) of the typeface with which his autobiography had previously been printed in Paris.[76] On the other hand, he made a determined, even if only partly successful, attempt to improve and regularize other typographical and design features of the books for which he was responsible: some of these features, as Eisenstein has demonstrated in the case of European printed books, can be of crucial importance in determining their impact on readers. The books produced at the early Turkish and Egyptian presses were usually modelled quite closely on traditional manuscript layouts and styles of presentation. al-Shidyāq's books, however, both those from Malta and those of the Jawā'ib Press, look different. For the most part he abandoned the marginal commentaries and glosses with which earlier books were often festooned. In some cases running heads were introduced, repeating the title or number of the chapter or section at the top of each page as an aid to those referring to the book.[77] Nearly all al-Shidyāq's books have title pages, setting out clearly and systematically not only the title itself, but also the name of the author, the name of the press, the place and date of publication, and whether it is a first or later edition. This was an important innovation of the print era, to which al-Shidyāq became accustomed in Malta and later adopted at his press in Istanbul, one of the first in the Middle East which consistently did this. This practice, as Eisenstein has pointed out, engendered "new habits of placing and dating," as well as helping the subsequent development of more precise cataloging and enumerative bibliography.[78] Another new feature of the print era to be found in most of al-Shidyāq's publications is a table of contents, with page numbers, likewise enabling the reader to make more systematic use of the book.

Page layouts, under al-Shidyq̄'s guidance, also set new standards, being generally more spacious and easier on the eye than most ordinary manuscripts or earlier printed books from the Middle East. Margins are reasonably wide, and, as already mentioned, unencumbered by glosses or commentaries. The spacing between words tends also to be more generous, leaving a better overall ratio between black and white than on most pages of Būlāq or early Turkish printed books. These were features of the Malta Arabic books on which al-Shidyāq worked early in his career, and they later appeared in the products of his Istanbul press, making them easier to read and therefore more accessible to a wider public. Some of them can be considered as forerunners of twentieth-century Arabic book design.[79]

Another feature of the modern Arabic printed book which differentiates it markedly from its manuscript forebears is the use of punctuation. al-Shidyāq's attempts in this field, though, were a failure. By the late 1830s, he had become familiar with European books and literature, and had observed the usefulness of punctuation marks in clarifying the structure and meaning of passages of prose. In 1839 he published at Malta his primer and, reading book of literary Arabic, *al-Lafīf fī kull maʿná ṭarīf*, and boldly decided to introduce Western punctuation into it, using commas, dashes, colons, exclamation marks, question marks, quotation marks, and full stops (see figure 11.2). He set them out in his introduction, explained their use, and urged that they should be generally adopted in Arabic, "since," he wrote, "that would save the perpetration of much [error] on the paths of exegesis, and safeguard the reader in reading, and the traverser of the pitfalls of delusion. If this is necessary," he went on, "in Frankish languages, then it is even more necessary in Arabic, because of. . .the ramification of clauses (*tafrīʿ al-jumal*) one upon another."[80] This remarkable proposal was, however, far ahead of its time. Although all these punctuation marks appear throughout the first edition of *al-Lafīf*, they were—apart from the full stop—very seldom used even in other Malta books for which al-Shidyāq was responsible. In the second edition of *al-Lafīf*, published in Istanbul at his Jawā'ib Press in 1881, all the punctuation marks were omitted, as well as the relevant section of the introduction from which I have quoted. Not until the twentieth century was full punctuation widely adopted in Arabic.

The bindings of books, as well as their contents, were another field for standardization. Whereas manuscripts were generally bound individually by or for their owners, mass-produced printed books could have standard bindings issued by their publishers. Generally, these were printed wrappers or boards (sometimes cloth-backed)—such were the standard bindings, for instance, of al-Shidyāq's Malta books. His Jawā'ib Press in Istanbul continued this practice; but it also issued many of its books in cloth or roan bindings, with titles

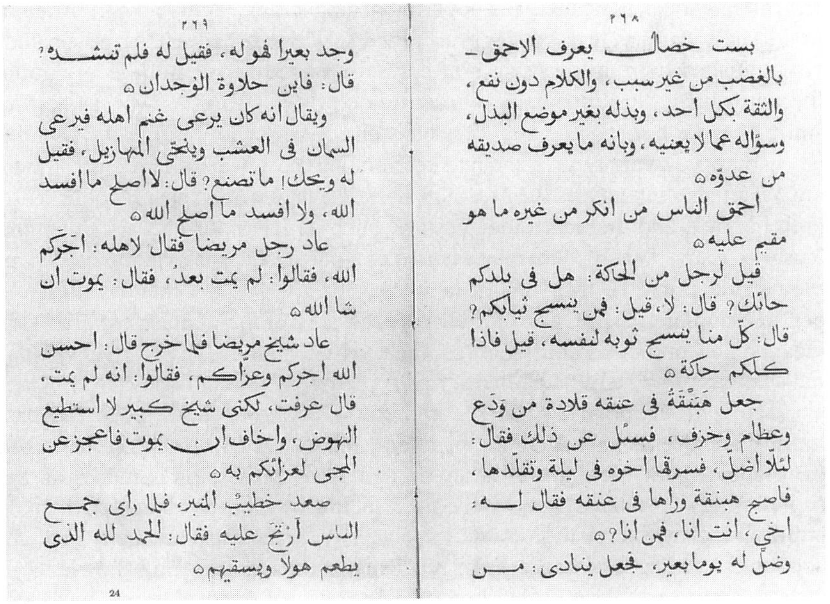

٢٦٨

بست خصال يعرف الاحمق ـ
بالغضب من غير سبب، والكلام دون نفع،
والثقة بكل احد، وبذله بغير موضع البذل،
وسؤاله عما لا يعنيه، وبانه ما يعرف صديقه
من عدوه ٥

احمق الناس من انكر من غيره ما هو
مقيم عليه ٥

قيل لرجل من الحاكة: هل فى بلدكم
حائك؟ قال: لا، قيل: فمن ينسج ثيابكم؟
قال: كلّ منا ينسج ثوبه لنفسه، قيل فاذا
كلكم حاكة ٥

جعل هَبَنّقَةُ فى عنقه قلادة من وَدَع
وعظام وخزف، فسئل عن ذلك فقال:
لئلّا اضلّ، فسرقها اخوه فى ليلة وتقلّدها،
فاصبح هبنقة وراها فى عنقه فقال له:
اخي، انت انا، فمن انا؟ ٥
وضلّ له يوما بعير، فجعل ينادى: من

٢٦٩

وجد بعيرا فهو له، فقيل له فلم تنشده؟
قال: فاين حلاوة الوجدان ٥

ويقال انه كان يرعى غنم اهله فيرعى
السمان فى العشب وينحّى المهازيل، فقيل
له ويحك! ما تصنع؟ قال: لا اصلح ما افسد
الله، ولا افسد ما اصلح الله ٥

عاد رجل مريضا فقال لاهله: اَجَرَكم
الله، فقالوا: لم يمت بعدُ، فقال: يموت ان
شا الله ٥

عاد شيخ مريضا فلما خرج قال: احسن
الله اجركم وعزّاكم، فقالوا: انه لم يمت،
قال عرفت، لكنى شيخ كبير لا استطيع
النهوض، واخاف ان يموت فاعجز عن
المجى لعزائكم به ٥

صعد خطيبُ المنبر، فلما راى جمع
الناس آُرْتِجَ عليه فقال: الحمد لله الذى
يطعم هولا ويسقيهم ٥

24

Fig. 11.2. Two pages from al-Shidyāq's *al-Lafīf fī kull maʿná ṭarīf*, Malta, 1839, showing his use of punctuation marks: dash, comma, question mark, and colon. The typeface, which has been admired for its beauty, was specially cut and cast in Malta, almost certainly to his designs. The only incongruous feature is the use of Western numerals for the page signature. (Cambridge University Library, Moh.315.d.18 sel.)

embossed in gilt on the front and the insignia of the press on the back.[81] They thus became homogenized. mass-produced consumer durables, complete with trade marks—harbingers of a new uniform commodity culture.

All these elements of standardization which printing brought to the form and content of books contributed to what Eisenstein has called a new "esprit de système" and served to "reorder the thought of readers."[82] It seems reasonable, therefore, to claim that pioneering print-oriented authors and publishers like al-Shidyāq contributed significantly in this way to the emergence of new modes of thought and patterns of consciousness in the modern Middle East.

Along with increased dissemination and standardization of tests, the third "cluster of changes" associated with the print revolution, according to Eisenstein, was their preservation. al-Shidyq's views on the loss and corruption of Arabic texts in the scribal era, and the potential role of printing in preserving them, have already been indicated. His book-publishing activity at his press in Istanbul was largely dedicated to putting into practice what he had earlier advocated. He published there a long series of carefully edited texts of classical Arabic literature, including especially works of poetry and *adab*. As well as editing some of them himself, he also created a circle or "school" of editors whom he encouraged to apply similar standards: among those whose names are known are Yūsuf al-Nabhānī and Rasūl al-Najjārī.[83] The new works that he published—both his own and those of other writers, such as Khayr al-Dīn al-Tūnisī and Yūsuf al-Asīr—were also thereby assured of a permanent place in the literature: their works might be forgotten or neglected for a while, but they would never perish completely like many of their predecessors of the manuscript era. This meant a new and more confident response to the challenge of creative writing; for whereas previously much literary effort had gone into the task of retrieving, encapsulating, summarizing, and commenting upon past knowledge and past literary achievement, now, in the print era, this could all, in a sense, be taken for granted. New ideas and original thoughts and expression could claim the full energies of writers, who were now secure in the knowledge that, once published, they too, would be safe for posterity. What this eventually brought about was nothing less than a major reorientation of literature and knowledge—instead of always looking backwards, it could now look forward to new horizons.

This in turn meant a new role for the author, and a new sense of self-awareness and autonomy for writers. al-Shidyāq himself provides a good example of the new role model. Throughout his published works can be sensed a vibrant individualism, even egotism—much of his writing is indeed directly about himself.[84] He also assumes in many places a direct relationship with his readers, addressing them and even suggesting that he is confiding secrets to them.[85] This has been recognized in several studies of European literary history as a feature of the new role of writers in the print era: instead of transmitting texts to present and future audiences or imagined assemblies of fellow scholars, the writer was addressing a large number of persons "who were not gathered together in one place but were scattered in separate dwellings and who, as solitary individuals with divergent interests, were more receptive to intimate interchanges than to broad-gauged rhetorical effects."[86] Hence, authors emerged who aimed to suggest an intimate relationship with their many unknown readers, while in the process developing their own cult of self: Montaigne is the example often cited in the case of the European Renaissance[87]—in the Arab renaissance (*nahḍah*) of the nineteenth century, al-Shidyāq can perhaps be seen as a similar phenomenon. This new individualism of the print era also found a manifestation in the conduct of protracted and often vituperative literary disputes between al-Shidyāq and contemporary authors such as Ibrāhīm al-Yāzijī and Rizqallāh Ḥassūn.[88] While such contentions were by no means unknown in literary circles in earlier periods of Arabic literature, the possibilities of print gave them a new potency and currency, encouraging them to be transmitted rapidly across long distances (Ḥassūn lived and published in London, al-Yāzijī in Beirut, while exchanging literary squibs with al-Shidyāq in Istanbul), and bringing them immediately before a wide readership.

But the new authorial assertiveness of al-Shidyāq owed most of all to the fact that printing enabled him to earn his living from writing and publishing. Unlike most of his scribal predecessors, he was not a priest nor an imām nor a legal scholar nor a courtier nor, except for a brief period, a teacher. He was a professional author and editor—an almost completely new phenomenon in the Middle East and the Muslim world. At times, he wrote, translated, and edited for a salary, as in Malta and Egypt and during part of his stay in England; at other times, he wrote speculatively, aiming to sell the printed editions of his works, such as his travelogues, autobiography, and grammars of French and Arabic. In Istanbul, he became an entrepreneurial author-publisher and newspaper editor.

al-Shidyāq's independence, however, was not so absolute that he could dispense entirely with patronage. In the Arab and Muslim worlds, as elsewhere, there had always been, among the rich and powerful, those who had attracted and rewarded writers, especially if the writers provided them with pleasing entertainment or gratified their vanity. al-Shidyāq occasionally played this traditional role, especially when seeking preferment or sponsorship: he wrote a number of odes in praise of the Bey of Tunis and other Tunisian notables, for instance, some of which were printed.[89] But the power of the press offered scope for a new kind of patronage: it could provide literature and information not just to gratify a ruler, but to be disseminated on his behalf, to promote his wider aims and interests—in other words, propaganda. al-Shidyāq became aware of this at an early stage in his career, when he worked for the official Egyptian gazette, *al-Waqā'i' al-Miṣrīyah*, which promoted the policies of the Egyptian ruler Muḥammad 'Alī, and which he later sarcastically dubbed a *mamdaḥ*, or praise-factory.[90] When he had his own newspaper in Istanbul, he was under the patronage of the Ottoman Sultan and generally supported his interests, particularly his pan-Islamic pretensions; but he also received, for much of that time, subventions from the Bey of Tunis, the Khedive of Egypt, and the Nawāb of Bhopal.[91] Sometimes, of course, these interests came into conflict, and on two occasions this led to the temporary closure of the newspaper on the Sultan's orders.[92] Not only the paper, but some of the Jawā'ib Press books, also, were designed, and subsidized, to support these interests, including books written by the reformist Tunisian chief minister Khayr al-Dīn and the Nawāb of Bhopal, and semi-official pro-Ottoman publications, such as the lavish album of portraits of the sultans edited by al-Shidyāq's son, Salīm Fāris.[93]

al-Shidyāq was generally able to balance these sources of patronage in such a way as to preserve a fair degree of independence for himself, and this was all the easier because the power of print, coupled with his unprecedented and unique skills in using it, made him indispensable to his patrons to an extent that court writers of the scribal era never were.

In conclusion, we can perhaps reiterate that al-Shidyāq personified, both in his career and in his attitudes, the dawn of a new cultural era for the Arab and Muslim worlds, in which the communications revolution caused by the printing press brought radical changes in the intellectual, political, and social life of the area. No historical account of the Middle East in the nineteenth and twentieth centuries can be adequate unless it takes into account the causes, stages, and consequences of these changes. But for this to be possible, much more must be known about the history of the presses, and the nature of what they produced, than is the case at present. The printing history and historical bibliography of the Middle East has been a shamefully neglected subject, both in comparison with equivalent studies in relation to early modern Europe, and in comparison with the study of Islamic manuscripts. The profile of the subject therefore needs to be raised, and historians, bibliographers, and librarians alike must work to rectify what remains a serious defect in our understanding of a vital aspect of the history of Muslim and Middle Eastern civilization.

NOTES

1. C.V. Findley, "Knowledge and Education in the Modern Middle East: A Comparative View," in *The Modern Economic History of the Middle East in Its World Context*, ed. G. Sabagh (Georgio Levi Della Vida Conferences, 10) (Cambridge, 1989), p. 132.

2. Cf. R. Chartier, "General Introduction: Print Culture," in *The Culture of Print: Power and the Uses of Print in Early Modern Europe*, ed. R. Chartier, trans. L.G. Cochrane (Cambridge; Oxford, 1989), p. 1.

3. Findley, op. cit., p. 132.

4. K.S. Salibi, "The Traditional Historiography of the Maronites," in *Historians of the Middle East*, ed. B. Lewis and P.M. Holt (London, 1962), p. 223.

5. Fāris al-Shidyāq, *al-Sāq ʿalā al-sāq fī-mā hūwa al-fāriyāq* (Paris, 1855), p. 22.

6. Wahid Gdoura, *Le début de l'imprimerie arabe à Istanbul et en Syrie: Évolution de l'environnement culturel (1706–1787)* (Tunis, 1985), passim.

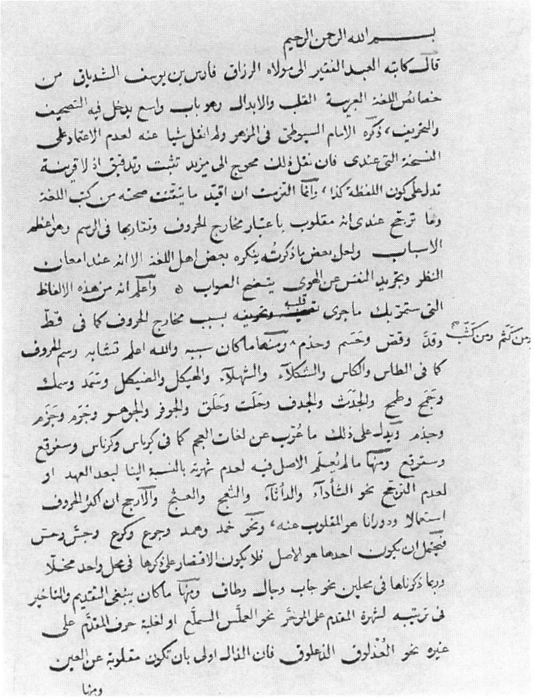

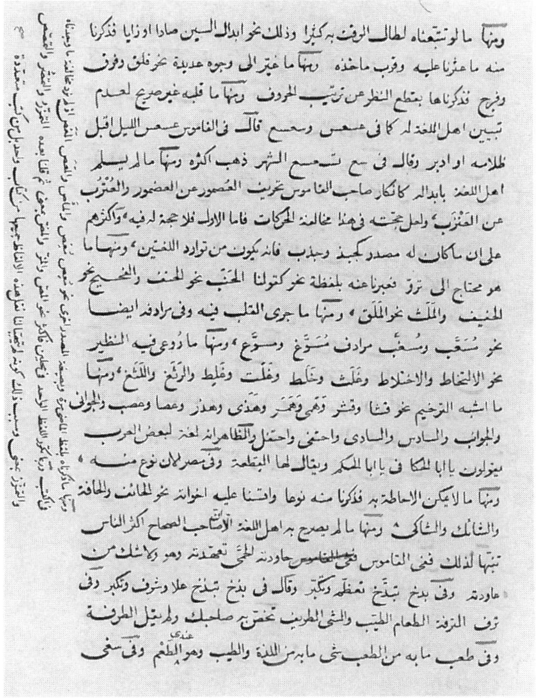

Fig. 11.3. A-B (together). Autographed manuscript, dated 1850, of an appendix on *qalb* and *ibdāl* in an early draft of al-Shidyāq's *Kitāb al-jāsūs ʿalá al-qāmūs*. The text differs from his later published work on the subject (*Sirr al-layāl fī al-qalb wa-al-ibdāl*, Istanbul, 1284/1868). (Cambridge University Library, MS Or. 1446, fols. 81v–82r.)

7. G. Roper, "The Export of Arabic Books from Europe to the Middle East in the 18th Century," in *BRISMES: Proceedings of the 1989 International Conference on Europe and the Middle East* (Durham; Oxford, 1989), pp. 233–66.

8. al-Shidyāq, *al-Sāq*, p. 34; A.H. Hourani, "Historians of Lebanon," in *Historians of the Middle East*, ed. B. Lewis and P.M. Holt (London, 1962), pp. 230–32.

9. Fīlīb dī Tarrāzī, *Aṣdaq mā kān*, 3 vols. (Beirut, 1948), 2:192–93; Muḥammad ʿAbd al-Ghanī Ḥasan, *Aḥmad Fāris al-Shidyāq* (Cairo, 1966), p. 33.

10. [G.P. Badger and Fāris al-Shidyāq], *Kitāb al-muḥāwarah al-unsīyah fī al-lughatayn al-Inkilizīyah wa-al-ʿArabīyah* (Malta, 1840), p. 134.

11. al-Shidyāq, *al-Sāq*, p.34; idem, *Muqaddimat dīwān Aḥmad Fāris Efendi* (Istanbul, n.d.), p. 2.

12. J. Macdonald, University of Leeds, Department of Semitic Languages & Literatures [now Department of Modern Arabic Studies], *Catalogue of Oriental Manuscripts, III: Arabic Mss 101-150* (Leeds, [1959]), p. 28, no. 128.

13. Top of first page, before the *Bismillāh*.

14. [W.F. Mavor], *Sharḥ ṭabāʾiʿ al-ḥayawān*, trans. Fāris al-Shidyāq (Malta, 1841), pp. 3–4.

15. Ḥasan, op. cit., p. 34.

16. M.B. Alwan, "Aḥmad Fāris ash-Shidyāq and the West," Ph.D. dissertation, University of Indiana, 1970, pp. 28–29, no. 85, and pp. 226–27, nos. 13–16; ʿImād al-Sulḥ, *Aḥmad Fāris al-Shidyāq: athāruhu waʿaṣruhu*, 2nd ed. (Beirut, 1987), pp. 251–52; A.J. Arberry, "Fresh Light on Ahmad Faris al-Shidyaq," *Islamic Culture* 26/1 (1952), pp. 156–64; A. Gacek, *Catalogue of the Arabic Manuscripts in the Library of the School of Oriental and African Studies, University of London* (London, 1981), p. 183, no. 303.

17. al-Shidyāq, *Muqaddimah*, p. 4.

18. Aḥmad Fāris al-Shidyāq, *Kitāb al-riḥlah al-mawsūmah bi-al-wasīṭah ilá maʿrifat Māliṭā wa-kashf al-mukhabbaʾ ʿan funūn Awrubbā* (Tunis, 1238/1867), pp. 128, 338; Ibrahim Abu-Lughod, *The Arab Rediscovery of Europe:*

A Study in Cultural Encounters (Princeton, 1963), p. 121; Alwan, *Aḥmad Fāris*, pp. 52, 59, 79.

19. al-Shidyāq, *al-Riḥlah*, p. 338.

20. Ibid., p. 337.

21. Aḥmad Fāris al-Shidyāq, *Kanz al-raghā'ib fī muntakhabāt al-jawā'ib*, 7 vols. (Istanbul, 1288–99/1871–81), 1:154–55, 5:184–85; al-Sulh, op. cit., pp. 130, and 241, no. 1.

22. Aḥmad Fāris al-Shidyāq, *al-Jāsūs ʿalá al-qāmūs* (Istanbul, 1299/1881), pp. 93–94.

23. al-Sulḥ, op. cit., p. 132.

24. al-Shidyāq, *Muqaddimah*, pp. 4, 16–17; al-Sulḥ, op. cit., p. 241, no. 4.

25. al-Shidyāq, *Muqaddimah*, p. 4.

26. Badger and al-Shidyāq, *al-Muḥāwarah*, p. 103; al-Shidyāq, *al-Riḥlah*, p. 382; al-Sulḥ, op. cit., p. 130.

27. al-Shidyāq, *Muqaddimah*, p. 4.

28. Details of these and other activities of al-Shidyāq in Malta and Egypt are drawn from the archives of the Church Missionary Society now kept at the University of Birmingham.

29. al-Sulḥ, op. cit., p. 34.

30. al-Shidyāq, *al-Sāq*, p. 337.

31. Fāris al-Shidyāq, *al-Lafīf fī kull maʿná ṭarīf* (Malta, 1839), pp. 298–99.

32. Abū al-Futūḥ Raḍwān, *Tārīkh Maṭbaʿat Būlāq* (Cairo, 1953), p. 25, "*huwa ghāyah fī jamāl al-khaṭṭ wa-jūdat al-ṭabʿ*," referring to the 1840 edition of *Kitāb al-zāriʿ, aw, amthāl Rabbinā Yasūʿ al-Masīḥ wa-tafsīruhā*, which was set in these types.

33. *al-Kutub al-Muqaddasah* (London, 1857).

34. al-Shidyāq, *al-Riḥlah*, pp. 306, 309; al-Sulḥ, op. cit., p. 73.

35. al-Shidyāq, *al-Riḥlah*, p. 309.

36. *Iʿlām*, Marseilles (1858). Cf. Bibliothèque Nationale, *Catalogue général des livres imprimés de la Bibliothèque Nationale* (Paris, 1912), 49: col. 930.

37. See A. Ameuney's (Antūniyūs al-Amyūnī) preface to Fāris al-Shidyāq's *Poems/Qaṣā'id* (London, 1857), p. (2).

38. al-Sulḥ, op. cit., pp. 77–83.

39. al-Shidyāq, *al-Riḥlah*, p. 6.

40. Mohammed B. Alwan, "The History and Publications of al-Jawā'ib Press," *MELA Notes* 11 (1977), pp. 4–7. Unfortunately, the detailed bibliography of the Press's publications, referred to in this article, does not seem to have been published.

41. al-Shidyāq, *al-Riḥlah*, p. 382.

42. Badger and al-Shidyāq, *al-Muḥāwarah*, p. 103.

43. See also *al-Jawā'ib* 614, quoted in al-Sulḥ, op. cit., p. 130.

44. Badger and al-Shidyāq, *al-Muḥāwarah*, pp. 132–133.9.

45. al-Shidyāq, *al-Sāq*, p. 515.

46. al-Shidyāq, *al-Riḥlah*, pp. 375–82.

47. al-Shidyāq, *Kanz*, 1:157–60.

48. al-Shidyāq, *al-Riḥlah*, p. 337.

49. Badger and al-Shidyāq, *al-Muḥāwarah*, pp. 99, 102, 132; al-Shidyāq, *al-Riḥlah*, pp. 337–78; idem, *Kanz*, 1:157–60.

50. al-Shidyāq, *Kanz*, 1:161.

51. al-Shidyāq, *al-Sāq*, p. 516.

52. E.L. Eisenstein, *The Printing Press as an Agent of Change: Communications and Cultural Transformations in Early Modern Europe* (Cambridge, 1979), passim.

53. Muḥammad Aḥmad Khalaf Allāh, *Aḥmad Fāris al-Shidyāq wa-ārā'uhu al-lughawīyah wa-al-adabīyah* (Cairo, 1955), p. 84.

54. "Fares Eshediak's remarks concerning the children in the School at Cairo, of the year 1932," *CMS Archives*: CM/073/61.

55. Cf. numerous reports in the *CMS Archives*, and in *Missionary Register*, 1826–53.

56. Findley, op. cit., p. 133.

57. al-Sulḥ, op. cit., pp. 132, and 241, no. 7.

58. Fāris al-Shidyāq, *al-Bākūrah al-shahīyah fī naḥw al-lughah al-Inkilizīyah* (Malta, 1836).

59. M. Orhan Durusoy, *Istanbul Belediye Kütüphanesi alfabetik katalog, II: Belediye ve M. Cevdet kitaplar, Arapça ve Farsça basma eserler* (Istanbul, 1954), p. 14, no. 2073.

60. Badger and al-Shidyāq, *Kitāb al-muḥāwarah al-unsiyah* (Malta, 1840).

61. Fares Echckidiak and G. Dugat, *Sanad al-rāwī fī al-ṣarf al-Faransāwī* (Paris, 1854).

62. Badīʿ al-Zamān al-Hamadhānī, *Maqāmāt* (Istanbul, 1298/1880), p. 100, colophon.

63. Istanbul, 1287/1870. Cf. Alwan, "History," p. 5

64. See, for example, *al-Jawā'ib* 872 (1.7.1877), p. 4, col. 2.

65. See, for example, ibid. 932 (11.7.1878), p. 4, col. 3.

66. See, for example, ibid. 1009 (10.6.1880), p. 4, col. 2.

67. See price list in *al-Jawā'ib* 1017 (25.8.1880), p. 8, col. 2. Cf. Alwan, "History," p. 6.

68. See, for instance, Hamadhānī, *op. cit.*, p. 100; idem, *Rasā'il* (Istanbul, 1298/[1880]), p. 238; Abū Muḥammad al-Qāsim ibn ʿAlī al-Harīrī, *Kitāb durrat al-ghawwāṣ fī awhām al-khawāṣṣ* (Istanbul, 1299/1881), p. 257, where Ms copies are identified and differences mentioned. Cf. al-Sulḥ, op. cit., p. 132.

69. E.g., *al-Lafīf*, p. 299; *al-Sāq*, p. vii.

70. E.g., Farhāt, op. cit. (the list is not present in all copies); al-Shidyāq, *al-Riḥlah*, pp. 387–88; Mikhā'īl ʻAbd al-Sayyid al-Miṣrī, *Sulwān al-shājī fī al-radd ʻalá Ibrāhīm al-Yāzijī* (Istanbul, 1289/1872), after p. 110.

71. *al-Bākūrah* (Malta, 1836; Istanbul, 1881); *al-Lafīf* (Malta, 1839; Istanbul, 1881); *Kitāb al-ṣalawāt al-ʻāmmah* (Book of Common Prayer) (Malta, 1840; London, 1850); *al-Riḥlah* (Tunis, 1867; Istanbul, 1881); *Ghunyat al-ṭālib wa-munyat al-rāghib* (Istanbul, 1872/1888).

72. Cf. lists and announcements in *al-Jawā'ib.*

73. al-Shidyāq, *al-Sāq*, book 2, ch. 3.

74. Badger and al-Shidyāq, *al-Muḥāwarah*, pp. 3–4.

75. Muṣṭafā al-Shihābī, *al-Muṣṭalaḥāt al-ʻilmīyah fī al-lughah al-ʻArabīyah*, 2nd ed. (Damascus, 1965), p. 50; Ḥasan, op. cit., p. 144; Alwan, "Aḥmad Fāris," 210–11.

76. List of publications available inside front wrapper of Abū Muḥammad Jaʻfar al-Sarrāj's *Kitāb maṣāriʻ al-ʻushshāq* (Istanbul, 1301/1883).

77. E.g., al-Shidyāq, *al-Jāsūs*.

78. Eisenstein, op. cit., p. 106.

79. E.g., Hamadhānī, *Rasā'il*, 1880.

80. al-Shidyāq, *al-Lafīf*, pp. 4–5.

81. Alwan, "History," p. 7.

82. Eisenstein, op. cit., p. 105.

83. al-Sulḥ, op. cit., p. 131.

84. J.A. Haywood, *Modern Arabic Literature, 1800–1970* (London, 1971), p. 53.

85. E.g., in *al-Sāq*, pp. 75, 230, etc.

86. Eisenstein, op. cit., p. 230.

87. Cf. ibid., and references there cited.

88. Alwan, "Aḥmad Fāris," pp. 64–65.

89. Fāris al-Shidyāq, *Qaṣīdah yumdaḥ fīhā Aḥmad Bāshā Wālī Mamlakat Tūnis* (Paris,1851); idem, Poems/*Qaṣā'id*.

90. al-Shidyāq, *al-Sāq*, p. 255. Cf. Alwan, "Aḥmad Fāris," p. 41.

91. Alwan, "Aḥmad Fāris," pp. 64–65.

92. G.P. Badger, "Arabic Journalism," *The Academy* 20/497 (1881), p. 366; idem, "The Press of *al-Jawāīb*," ibid. 20/503 (1881), p. 473; Alwan, "History," p. 5.

93. *Abdaʿ mā kān fī ṣuwar Salāṭīn Āl ʿUthmān/Album des souverains ottomans*, ed. Salīm Fāris (Istanbul, [1885?]).

12

The Book in the Modern Arab World: The Cases of Lebanon and Egypt

George N. Atiyeh

The book is not only a vehicle of communication, it is first and foremost the outstanding expression and reflection of a culture. The role and position of the book in a society is bound to the nature, historical circumstances, and psychological configurations of that society. In fact, there is no single pattern that applies to all societies outside the common elements that characterize the human race as a whole, and books are no exception. When one considers the role and position of the book in the Arab world, one needs to take into account the above factors, and bear in mind the basic differences that exist between Western and Arab circumstances and the different forces that have gone into play in the Arab world during the modern and contemporary periods. These forces, different in strength and orientation, while bringing the West closer to the Arab world in certain respects, have been unable to eliminate the basic differences between the two. I do not agree with the racist slogan of Kipling that West is West and East is East and the twain will never meet; I believe that there is a continuous and fundamental attraction between the two, regardless of their differences. The story of the book in the Arab world is an expression of this attraction.

In the Arab world, the art of printing, publishing, and distribution of books on a large scale among all classes and among young and old approached the European level and acquired some semblance of maturity almost four centuries after Gutenberg's invention. Part of the gap created by time and technology has been filled in some Arab countries, yet there is still a long way to go to bridge the gap completely. Unfortunately many of those, who deal with the book have not always been able to keep what was good in the manuscript era, in terms of scholarship, and take full advantage of what is good in the printing age.

Historically speaking, the Arabic printed book appeared first in Europe, in Italy.[1] Other European countries soon followed suit, such as Holland, France, England, and Germany. The Arabic printed book did not see the light of day in the Arab world until 1706. With this in mind, I will try to survey the development of book production and dissemination, and to examine the role played by books in the renaissance of the Arab world, singling out some outstanding examples that were signs of or landmarks in the generation of new trends or cultural orientations.

The Arab world covers four great geographic regions, North Africa and the Nile Valley on the African continent, and the Arabian peninsula and the Fertile Crescent in Western Asia. This being a large area to cover in a short essay, I will limit myself to surveying the two countries that were and remain pioneers in book production, namely, Lebanon and Egypt. Although in the recent past and at present other Arab countries have been playing an increasingly important role, the roles of Lebanon and Egypt were and remain seminal as far as printed books are concerned.

Intellectually, the modern era in the Arab world experienced, in its early stages, the rise of a number of religious, cultural, and political movements directed at the regeneration of Islam, and also aiming at social and political reforms. Some were fundamentalist, although not radical, in approach, such as the Wahhabi movement in the Arabian Peninsula, and the Senusiyah in Libya. Others were less fundamentalist but still religiously inspired, such as the reformist movement of Khayr al-Dīn in Tunis, and the Salafīyah in Morocco. The common denominator among these movements was regeneration or reform, yet the movements took different forms, approaches, speeds, and goals. In Lebanon and Egypt, contact with the West brought with it a variety of movements, a search for new identities, nationalism, rationalism, and secularism, which grew up side by side with religious and conservative traditionalism.

Lebanon and Egypt had something in common that provided them with certain advantages over other Arab countries. Both had continuous early contact with the West, and during Ottoman rule they shared a certain freedom due to the absence or relaxation of Ottoman control. The Ottoman colonial power, which began in 1516—more or less at the same time as the first Arabic book was printed in Fano, Italy, in 1514—was weakened when Muḥammad ʿĀlī (1805–49) assumed power in Egypt in 1805, and Mount Lebanon assumed certain autonomy under Bashīr II (1789–1840). Lebanese autonomy grew under the Mutaṣarrifīyah (1864–1914), and provided the Lebanese with more freedom to run their own affairs.

Variation in the degree of control from province to province in the Ottoman Empire and the extent of contact with the West favored some areas above others in providing an environment favorable to cultural growth and the development of particular modernizing situations. Lebanon and Egypt were thus favored. Among the elements that went into the making of modernity were the influence of Western education on literary, political, and social life; the liberation of man's mind to pursue the truth on his own advocated by a number of progressive intellectuals; and a new world outlook. The role of the book in this development was crucial. In fact, the book helped loosen the strangle-hold of the *'ulamā'*, the religious learned men, over education. In most of the Ottoman Empire, including the Arab world, the *'ulamā'* opposed the introduction of printing. It was only in 1727 that the use of the printing press for printing in Arabic script was permitted, and that was only for the production of non-religious materials. Belief in Islam's superiority over other religions, because the Koran is God's eternal word, and veneration of the Arabic language as the medium for revealing the word of God, made the *'ulamā'*, the Sultan, and others oppose the use of a metal object, coming from Christendom, to reproduce the honored language of revelation. There were certainly other reasons for this opposition, but those listed above were the weightiest ones. Here one wonders if the absence of printing was not an important element in the late arrival of modernism and modern technology to the Empire. Most of the Empire was rather slower in the assimilation and circulation of the new learning, leaving the Arab world far behind the West in terms of progress. Lebanon and Egypt were the first to realize this and to take advantage of the printing press.

Lebanese commercial and educational relations with the West began in the late sixteenth century, yet the printing of books, first introduced by the Christians of Lebanon and Syria, took until the nineteenth century to achieve significant consequences, inasmuch as most of what was printed early on were religious texts meant to teach, mainly to strengthen and defend the faith. One can easily state that the printing of books in that early period had little effect on the modernization process or on raising the level of culture on a large scale. The seeds of progress, however, were planted.

In an era when the manuscript was the main carrier of information and ideas, one needed to be wealthy in order to afford books. The shop of the *warrāq* (a man who made a profession of transcribing books) became rare, and those few restless spirits who seek knowledge in every age had only church or mosque libraries to resort to. Knowledge had a mystique of its own, and people who possessed it, or owned the tools to acquire it, did not let it go out except sparingly, or often not at all. The dissemination of books on a wide scale did not prevail until the later decades of the nineteenth century when printing with movable type had reached most of the Arab countries and a large reading public became attracted to books. Iraq, for example, had its first movable type press only in 1860, Tunis in 1861, and Morocco in 1912.[2]

It is obvious that there is a symbiotic relationship between books and education. The spread of schools and education in the nineteenth century was accompanied by the development of book production. Like education, book production started hesitantly in the eighteenth century and then began working its way steadily through stages of adaptation and translation, into a stage of more creativity, independence, variation, and much wider influence. Let us look at this process by focusing on the two countries that are most representative of this phenomenon. But before we do that, it should be noted that when we talk about the private publishing that became common at the end of the nineteenth century, we don't mean publishing houses in the Western sense. Publishing was done either by printing presses that were established primarily for printing books, or by bookstores that were established exclusively for selling books then added publishing and distribution to their activities. What they published, they did, most of the time, at the expense of the author, with little or no control over quality of scholarship or organization of the materials. The gradual move from *maṭbaʿah* (press) and *maktabah* (bookstore) to *dār* (publishing house) was to become fully fledged only in the twentieth century.

LEBANON AND THE BOOK

Printing in Arabic movable type was introduced into Lebanon[3] as early as 1610, in the Maronite monastery of St. Anthony, located in Quzhayyā, in North Lebanon, not far from the famous cedars of Lebanon. Only one book was produced in the short life of this pioneering endeavor. It was an Arabic language Psalter, but in a Karshūnī[4] typeface. Lebanon had to wait until 1734 for a second and more lasting venture.

During the seventeenth century, the light of learning was kept dimly burning mostly by a group of Maronite clergy who had received education in the Maronite College in Rome. Having developed there a greater sense for scholarship, they were able to inject a new vitality into their church and environment. Outside the Maronite community, there were also glimmers of intellectual and literary life, reflected in a weak but persistent manuscript tradition. Copying of books and calligraphy were very much present among Muslim scholars in different parts of what is now Lebanon, such as in Tripoli and Jabal ʿĀmil,[5] as well as in the monasteries, where bishops and patriarchs encouraged their monks to copy books carefully and beautifully. Books were treated, by those who could afford them, judiciously and with the full respect usually afforded to precious things.

During the eighteenth century, education and books received a boost from the establishment of new schools. The French Jesuits established a school in ʿAyn Ṭūrā (1728), and Maronite colleges were established in Zgharta (1735), and ʿAyn Warqā (1789), which played a prominent role in advancing education and scholarship. The growing need for books was satisfied by publishing them in Europe. They were mostly books in liturgy, teaching language, some classics, and anthologies of pious and ascetic works.

The first printing press that advanced the cause of book production in the Arab world was the one set up by ʿAbdallāh Zākhir (1684–1748). Zākhir came to Lebanon from Aleppo, Syria, after the split within the Antiochian Orthodox

Church (ca. 1724) and his becoming an advocate of Greek Catholicism. In Aleppo, Zākhir had worked for Patriarch Athanathios Dabbās (1685–1724), who was the first in the Arab world to establish a press with Arabic movable type (1706). In 1723, Zākhir, a skilled artisan and intellectual, established his own press at the monastery of Yuḥannā al-Sābigh, in the town of Shuwayr, in the Kisrwan district. The setting up of this press met the needs of a growing number of readers and of Maronite Christians who began replacing the Syriac language used in their speech, liturgy, and writing with Arabic.

Because of its clear and beautiful type, Zākhir's press became a model for the St. George Orthodox Press, established in Beirut in 1751. Zākhir himself had cut two new typefaces, both more elegant and closer to the rounder and lighter Naskhi style of writing. In fact, by adopting Arabic type and improving the typeface, Zākhir broadened the horizons for the book in the Arab world. The intellectual content of the books produced by these two pioneering presses was mainly theological and devotional in nature. Neither the worldly literature of Europe nor its political and artistic ideas seem to have had any great impact on the subjects of the books. Almost all had either a religious or a linguistic theme. Both the Shuwayr and St. George presses printed the Psalms, which were used not only as a prayer book to be recited during liturgy, but also as a textbook for learning Arabic. The fact that the Psalms were printed fifteen times between 1610 and 1776 was a sign of the growing interest of the Christian population of Lebanon in the Arabic language.[6]

The dissemination of books was confined to religious groups, or among rich and powerful individuals who were fond of books and were attracted by the prestige that goes with amassing books in private libraries. Among the well known libraries were the Arslān family library in ʿUbay, Jirjīs Ṣafā's in Dayr al-Qamar, and the libraries of Dayr al-Sharfeh, Dayr al-Mukhalliṣ, and Dayr al-Balamand.[7]

The first half of the nineteenth century saw important political, social, and educational developments take place. The Egyptian Ibrāhīm Pāshā, who occupied Syria between 1831 and 1840, started several schools. This gave a powerful impulse to national education. American missionaries set up a press in Beirut. Before moving to Beirut in 1834, the American Press was first established in Malta, where Fāris al-Shidyāq, a key figure in the renaissance of Arabic books and literature, was instrumental in improving its typography by designing an attractive new Arabic typeface and by introducing many of the organizational aspects of modern book production.

The American Press of Beirut probably reached the widest audience of any nineteenth-century press in the Arab world by publishing for writers who were in the forefront of the surging literary revival, like Naṣīf al-Yazījī (1800–71) and Butrus al-Bustānī as well as for the professors at the Syrian Protestant College (now the American University of Beirut).

The American missionaries, particularly those of the American Board of Commissioners for Foreign Missions, were able to attract many Lebanese and Syrians, converting them to Protestantism through their new, attractive, and serious publications. This prompted the Jesuits to counter the evangelizing activities of the Protestant missionaries by setting up their own press in 1848. In a very short time, and using new equipment, the Jesuit press was able to produce thirty books in 350 thousand copies.[8]

A look at publishing around the middle of the century would show that religious works explaining the principles of religion or dealing with spiritual contemplation were the dominant category. *al-Iqtidā' bi-al-Masīḥ* (Imitation of Christ), which was first printed by Zākhir in 1739, went into several printings. There were also many works of polemics among Catholics, Protestants, and Orthodox. Wortabet's *Dalīl al-ṣawāb ilá ṣidq al-Kitāb* (The True Guide to the Veracity of the Book), published in 1851, was one of them, as was *al-Hudá al-amīn fī daḥḍ arā' al-brutastantīyīn* (The Faithful Guide to Refuting the Opinions of the Protestants), by the Jesuit fathers.

Language textbooks were numerous, the most important of which were *Baḥth al-maṭālib fī 'ilm al-'arabīyah* (A Study of What is Needed to Learn the Arabic Language), which was first printed by the American Press in 1827, then went into several editions, and *Majma' al-baḥrayn* (The Meeting of the Two Seas), by Naṣīf al-Yazījī. In history, we find Tannūs al-Shidyāq's *Akhbār al-a'yān fī jabal Lubnān* (The History of the Notables of Mount Lebanon) (1859), and *Tārīkh Salāṭīn Bānū 'Uthmān* (History of the Ottoman Sultans) (1858), by Ibrāhīm al-Najjār. In geography, Cornelius van Dyke's *al-Mir'at al-wāḍiyah fī al-kūrah al-arḍīyah* (The Bright Mirror of the Terrestrial Globe) (1852) was one of several works published by the American Press. Van Dyke also published works in mathematics and geometry. It was at about this time that translations of Western novels, such as *Paul et Virginie*, by Bernardin de Saint-Pierre, began to appear.

This is only a sample of the books that were read or discussed in schools or in the cultural circles and societies that began to form. The book was able to improve the application of grammatical rules, set new directions for the writing of history, cultivate the mind, and bring to the fore new genres in Arabic literature.

The second half of the nineteenth century saw the extension and expansion of education and the modernization of the Arabic language. The revival of the national language inaugurated a literary renaissance which indirectly produced a nationalist consciousness and a feeling of cultural distinction between what was Arabic or Syrian and what was Ottoman. This was also reflected in the rise of non-missionary, or national, schools, colleges, and associations that invigorated cultural consciousness and national feeling.

With the progress of publishing, both of books and of serials, and a growing desire for more knowledge, the intellectual contents of books became varied and wide in scope. Gradually, the subjects turned away from the religiously didactic and language-related, to books dealing with all fields of human knowledge, inaugurating new trends in literature, politics, and the sciences. As advances in book production and the diversification of subjects and levels of scholarship took place, individually owned and run presses were sprouting up all over the place. The outstanding impact, however, came from the establishment of institutions of higher education to which presses were attached or related, and which undertook publishing and editorial programs. First came the Syrian Protestant College (now the American University of Beirut) in 1866, and then the Catholic St. Joseph University in 1874. Both competed for the minds and souls of Christians and Muslims alike. The competition was not necessarily negative in that it encouraged plurality and coexistence. Each wanted to define itself by excelling in certain specific areas. Up to the end of the century, the Catholic Press focused on the production of language and literary works, grammars, dictionaries, and chrestomathies of current and classical works. Many of these early publications are, until today, still widely used, for example, the dictionary *al-Munjid*.

The American University, on the other hand, took a different direction, that of the sciences. It produced books in medicine, natural sciences, astronomy, and also dictionaries. The two presses, however, were guided by strict moral and religious norms, as well as by a high standard of scholarship. They did not publish any work they thought to be of doubtful value. Furthermore, whatever was published was carefully edited and checked for correctness and presentation. In the two translations made of the Bible by the American and Catholic Presses, there was the belief that the exact and correct translation from Hebrew and Greek was not enough unless it were eloquently and clearly expressed and presented. Translation of the Bible had a considerable impact on Arab culture by making it available to the general reading public. Familiarity with the Bible was instrumental in introducing a variety of motifs and notions into modern Arabic literature.

Alongside these venerable presses, there mushroomed a number of presses that were not restrained by the above norms nor by the promptings of the state or religious institutions. Addressing themselves to a new kind of secular readership, they turned to the translation and adaptation of texts for their literary or entertainment value alone. Driven by a desire to sustain and profit from their presses and publishing activities, the many periodicals and journals that began to proliferate serialized original and translated novels, stories, and plays. These were new genres of literature, unlike what had existed previously in popular and classical Arabic works. They catered to the new crop of literate public, mostly for entertainment.[9] Some were written with a didactic purpose behind them, and most had weak plots and were full of interpolations.

The increase in the number of printing presses was due to several causes. The reading public increased greatly with the spread of education; the government was, relatively speaking, tolerant, especially when it did not feel politically threatened; and the growing number of newspapers and periodicals encouraged reading. A lurking desire for greater and surer information led to the publication of reference tools, such as encyclopedias, dictionaries, and almanacs.

The awakening of the national consciousness translated itself into editions of what were and still are called "heritage" books. This contributed not only to the emergence of modern styles in prose and poetry, but also to energizing the desire to learn more about the history of the country and its ancient cultures. In 1881, Jurjī Yannī (1856–1941) published a history of greater Syria (*Tārīkh Sūrīyā*), which included Lebanon. Some learned people, such as Nawfal Elias Nawfal (1812–87), began to build their own libraries of classical and other Arabic works and to publish on the history of religions and the sciences.[10]

This cultural awakening, one should emphasize, was not limited to the Christian community, but was shared by their Muslim compatriots. The most eminent expression of the awakening among the Muslims was the creation of al-Maqāsid Benevolent Society, which sponsored the establishment of schools in Beirut and the surrounding areas. Among the most distinguished authors and scholars who played a role in its foundation and development was al-Shaykh Yūsūf al-Asīr (1815–89),[11] a judge who authored many books and articles on jurisprudence and languages.[12] Because of his great linguistic expertise, he was called upon to help in the translation of the Bible into Arabic. There was also al-Shaykh Ibrāhīm al-Aḥdab (1826–91), another judge and great linguist, and ʿAbd al-Qādir al-Qabbānī (1847–1935), the founder of the newspaper *Thamarāt al-funūn*, and a member of al-Funūn Society, which should be given credit for buying a press and sponsoring the publication of many books.

By the end of the nineteenth century, Beirut and the rest of Lebanon had more than twenty presses, in addition to the American and Catholic presses. Their output reached several thousand titles and covered all branches of human knowledge. Subject-wise, the end of the century saw the prevalence of humanistic over religious topics; nonetheless, the diversity of subjects was surprising. Topics included the principles of logic, philosophy, literature, natural sciences, history, geography, religious dogma, spiritual readings, rituals, ethics, popular literature, and the newly introduced genres of literature, the novel and the play.

Unlike other Arab countries, the growth of the book industry and the development of printing were carried out by private individuals and institutions, and not by the government. The Lebanese were able to create new fonts, and improve the quality of books and printing in general. Yet books were not always up to good standards in terms of indexing, annotations, structure of the contents, and extent of typographical errors.

The dissemination of books outside the schools was not highly organized. The most common way to advertise a new book, or books in general, was on the book's own cover or last page.[13] In fact, books were sold in general stores, or by the authors themselves. Financing was provided by the author, and at times was subsidized by an association, such as the Muslim al-Funūn Society or by a friend of the author.[14]

To publish books, newspapers, and periodicals, one needed to get a permit from the government, especially in Beirut. Because of its growing commercial and educational importance, Beirut was the capital of an Ottoman province (*wilāyah*) in 1888. Until then it had been subordinate to the province of Damascus. The first Ottoman printing law was decreed on 6 January 1857. It was guided by two principles: licensing to publish and prior censorship of all publications. In Lebanon, the effects of this law were slight at first. The presses operated by the various Christian sects were virtually the only ones until the 1870s. The Ottoman authorities did not see a great need to censor their publications because they did not present any challenge to the authorities. As of 1871, the position of the *maktubji*[15] was given greater authority. The occupant of this position was the editor of the official gazette and other government publications, as well as being the censor. In 1885, when exercise of censorship became stricter, books were required to be sent to Istanbul for approval before publication. This prompted many authors to send their books to Cairo for publication, instead. Many of the authors and intellectuals themselves began to move to Egypt during ʿAbd al-Ḥamīd the Second's (1876–1908) rule, as it became difficult to publish under the stricter governmental censorship. There were other causes why Syrian and Lebanese authors, journalists, and political activists moved to the Egyptian cities of Cairo and Alexandria.[16] Publishing in the Arab world was greatly invigorated through many decades by this convergence of Syrians and Egyptians. The interaction between Lebanese and Syrian expatriates or immigrants and Egyptian intellectuals produced exciting and trend-setting publications in which the overriding passions expressed by the intellectuals and political activists was the challenge of modernity, that is, the transformation of a "backward" Arab world into a modern one. As an example, one can give the publications of Fārah Antūn's *Ibn Rushd wa-falsafatuh* (Averroes and His Philosophy) (Alexandria,1903), in which he advocated rationalism and secularism, and seemingly implied that Islam checked all rational inquiry and all science. These were views that contrasted sharply with the prevalent intellectual and religious atmosphere in Egypt. A controversy between Antūn and one of the most enlightened Muslim scholars, Muḥammad ʿAbduh, ensued. ʿAbduh, in his work *al-Islām wa-al-Naṣrānīyah maʿa al-ʿilm wa-al-madanīyah* (Islam and Christianity on Science and Civilization) (Cairo, 1902), defended Islam and maintained that Christianity was intolerant by nature and that modern European civilization developed when Europe liberated itself from Christianity. At the end of the century, the endeavors of both the Syrians and the Egyptians converged together to give a great boost to book publishing.

The Young Turk revolution of 1908 broadened for a short period the horizon of freedom. All kinds of associations and political clubs were formed and the number of presses increased. With the growth of higher education at all levels and greater communication with the West, Lebanon entered the first decade of the twentieth century with ample freedom and a greater acceptance of scientific values. But no sooner did Turkey enter the First World War than Mount Lebanon lost its autonomy as well as its intellectual vitality. In 1920, under the French occupation which followed the departure of the Turks, Lebanon regained a great deal of its publishing vitality. The American and Catholic presses reequipped themselves with modern machines from Europe and the United States. In 1927, the Catholic Press began the publication of the monumental series *Bibliotheca Arabica Scholasticorum*, in addition to its many religious and educational publications. Throughout the following decades, it remained one of the most important publishers. It published books not only for Lebanese authors, but also for scholars and institutions around the world, including such prestigious institutions as L'École des Langues Orientales, of Paris, and the Warburg Institute, of London. Likewise, its publications were disseminated all over the Arab world, Europe, and the Americas. The dictionary of Father Maʿlūf, *al-Munjid*, the grammar of Rashīd al-Sharṭūnī, *Mabādi' al-ʿArabīyah*, and the literary chrestomathy of Luis Cheikho, *Majānī al-adab* were sent by the thousands to Cairo, the great marketplace for Arabic books.

The American Press alone published 462 books in 143,073 volumes in 1922, these included Bibles in all sizes and formats, religious, educational, and literary works, as well as series in archaeology, the natural sciences, and oriental studies. Its books were disseminated worldwide.[17]

The 1940s saw the rise of individually owned and run publishing houses. The age of *dār*, a publishing house that finances its own publications and launches them into the marketplace, arrived in Lebanon. Several such houses were established, among which Dār al-Makshūf published mostly in literature, and Dār Ṣadir-Rīḥānī diversified its publications into the fields of law, sociology, history, and the classics. Dār al-ʿIlm lil-Malāyīn (Knowledge for the Millions Publishing House) was another publisher of works on varying topics. Its English-Arabic dictionary, *al-Mawrid*, is one of the most widely circulated.

Not all the publishers were in Beirut; there were several outside that belonged to religious congregations and played an important role in the history of the book in Lebanon. They were, in a way, heirs to the scholarly traditions of the Lebanese monasteries. The most important ones were al-Maṭbaʿah al-Būlīsīyah, al-Mukhallişīyah Press, and the press of the Lebanese Mission.

The publishing of books and serials reached its peak after the Egyptian Revolution of 1952. The nationalization of the book industry in Egypt, the greater, sometimes chaotic, freedom in Lebanon, and the long tradidion in printing turned Beirut into the Mecca of publishing in and for the Arab world.

In fact, the Arab, and not the Lebanese market, became the main factor in the growth of the book industry. With the opening of the rich markets in the Arabian peninsula, the focus of interest became set on that part of the world, with its high demand for textbooks, children's books, and religious works. During the 1970s, the number of publishing houses increased tremendously. Most specialized in social, political, or religious publications, and supported the ideological position of one group or another. Beirut became the publishing capital for dissident groups, which flocked to it from all over the Arab world. Books on socialism, nationalism, and secularism were produced for the educated class by these ideological publishers. A great many titles dealt with the Palestine question and the Arab-Israeli conflict, as well as with solutions to the economic and social problems of the region. Literary works, whether creative, such as poetry or fiction, or literary criticism, equaled all other classes in number. Some poets, such as Nizār Qabbānī, and novelists, such Ghādah al-Sammān, established publishing houses exclusively for publishing their own works, which were popular all over the Arab world.

Scholarly publishing did not suffer greatly as a result of the changes in interests and directions. New universities, such as the Lebanese, Arab, and Holy Spirit (Kaslik) Universities, had successful publications, though they were limited in scope.

Production of new dictionaries and reprinting of old ones became a major industry, but also a source of confusion regarding new terminology in the sciences. Authors who could not publish in their own countries, and those who wanted good production and wide distribution, relied on Lebanese publishers. The ease and convenience of publishing in Lebanon attracted even the most eminent writers in the Arab world. They contracted with Lebanese publishers to reprint and distribute their works. Najīb Maḥfūẓ's *Awlād ḥāratinā* was serialized in Egypt, but was printed in book form only in Lebanon, because its publication in book form was prohibited in Egypt. It presented the Prophet Muḥammad and other prophets in a manner unacceptable to the *'ulamā'*. Even during its civil war of 1975–91, Lebanon remained a major center of publishing, although several other Arab countries established their own publishing houses. Lebanon was also among the first to mount book fairs, now a popular phenomenon in all Arab countries. A sobering fact about Lebanon, however, is that it is common to find there pirated books, and unscholarly editions and reprints of the classics, often with the critical apparatus removed, along with the claim that these are new editions.

THE BOOK IN EGYPT

The decisive events in the modern and contemporary history of Egypt are the French occupation in 1798; the rise of Muḥammad 'Ālī (1805); the British occupation and the 'Urābī revolution (1882); the 1919 revolution and the struggle for independence (this is a period historians like to refer to as the liberal era); the 1952 revolution; and the Camp David agreement (1979). Each of these events had a great impact on the book in Egypt.

The first printing presses with movable type came to Egypt in 1798, brought by Napoleon Bonaparte during his invasion of Egypt. Accompanied by fifty savants, historians, geographers, engineers, linguists, and physicians, Napoleon claimed that the presses he brought were to help in making available the books describing Egypt, which his scholars were supposed to and did write. However, the first book printed was not written by the scholars; it was *Amthāl Luqmān al-ḥakīm* (The Proverbs of Luqman), published by the Orientalist Jean Joseph Marcel. *La Déscription de l'Égypt*, the result of the investigations of the scholars brought by Napoleon, was printed long after his armies had left Egypt in 1801. In fact, his publication program was aimed at trying to identify the principles of the French Revolution with Islam. A few Egyptian scholars, their curiosity aroused, visited the press and asked questions on how it could affect culture, but the French impact on Egypt as a whole was only gradually and indirectly felt after the French departure.

The manuscript era did not begin to cede ground until Muḥammad ʻĀlī established, in or about 1822, the famous Būlāq Press.[18] Directed first by Nicholas al-Masābkī (d. 1830), who was of Lebanese origin, the press soon became the symbol of modernization in the Arab world. After taking office, Muḥammad ʻĀlī realized that the key to successfully opposing the might of the Ottoman Empire and aggressive Europeans like Napoleon lay in education along Western lines, particularly in practical, technical subjects. Between 1822 and 1842, the press at Būlāq published 243 titles in Arabic, Turkish, and Persian. A glance at the titles shows clearly where Muḥammad ʻĀlī's interest was: forty-eight were on military and naval subjects. He had seen and noted how successful the modern arms of the French had been against the antiquated arms and methods of the Mamluks. It should be noted, however, that the books published in Egypt during the first half of the century were not all in military or applied sciences; 55.7 percent were in the humanities, the pure and applied sciences constituted only 27.7 percent, and the social sciences 25.1 percent.[19]

In order to prepare Egyptians for professional schools, and to train officials and translators, Muḥammad ʻĀlī sent students to Europe to study typography, among other things. He also opened several schools, the most famous of which was the school of languages (Madrasat al-alsun), opened in 1836. In 1837 he appointed as its head Rifāʻah Rāfiʻ al-Ṭahṭāwī (1801–73). Over the next twenty years, al-Ṭahṭāwī wrote or translated thirty-eight books in different subjects, including geography, history, Greek philosophy, as well as military science. Most of these were published by the Būlāq Press. al-Ṭahṭāwī had lived in Paris for five years. His book, *Takhlīs al-Ibrīz ilá talkhīs Bārīz*, contains many observations on the manners and customs of the French. The importance of this work, published by Būlāq, resides in telling us how the men who took part in the early modernization of Egypt under Muḥammad ʿĀlī thought and felt, and the impact of nineteenth-century Europe on a traditionally educated Muslim. The French, al-Ṭahṭāwī states in his book, compose books on all subjects, even on such subjects as cooking, which means that even craftsmen must know how to read in order to acquire a complete knowledge of their craft.

Aware that the system of schools he had established could not function without books, Muḥammad ʿĀlī bought several presses and attached them to the schools he had founded, such as the Abū Ziʿbil Press, attached to the school of medicine.

Būlāq books are sought after now and valued as important early imprints. There were, however, criticisms leveled against their production. The title pages were not independently presented (they were crammed with long introductions inside of which the title and author's name were inserted without distinguishing them visibly from the rest of the text) and the beginnings of new chapters were often not distinguished by larger or different types, scripts, or colors. It was similar, in these respects, to the way manuscripts were produced. Apparently, it was difficult to jump from the manuscript age to the age of printing all at once. The Būlāq printed books, nonetheless, were clear and easy to read, and they had hardly any typographical errors.

Unlike in Lebanon, the early presses in Egypt were owned and run by the government. Private presses hardly existed in Egypt. We know of an ʿAbd al-Rāziq press established in 1837,[20] but there is no evidence that it contributed to book publishing. The role of the private sector was to come later. The social and cultural situation in Egypt around 1840 was not ready yet for the development of private publishing, especially in light of the fact that the Būlāq Press welcomed the printing of non-governmental books at the expense of their authors for reasonable prices,[21] and that the general public was not yet enlightened enough on the value of books.

The original commitment of the Būlāq Press was to government publications, such as annual reports and the official gazette, *al-Waqāʾiʿ al-Miṣrīyah*. It nevertheless published a huge number of books in all fields, but mostly in those that conformed or coincided with the ideas of Muḥammad ʿĀlī for the revival of Egypt. They included books in the military sciences, textbooks, and books on religious and literary subjects, as well as dictionaries. In fact, the first book ever printed there was an Italian-Arabic dictionary. There were also books that might be considered encyclopedias, such as *Maʿrifatnāmeh*, in Turkish, and popular works, such as the *One Thousand and One Nights* and *Laṭāʾif Naṣr al-Dīn Khōjā* (The Witty Jokes of Naṣr al-Din Khoja).

Būlāq books were often given as gifts by Muḥammad ʿĀlī to European royalty or to friends and visitors. They were, in fact, read more outside than inside of Egypt. Apparently, the press did not have a bookstore attached to it. Edward Lane, who visited Egypt between 1833 and 1835 and wrote a detailed account of his stay there, does not mention that he himself had seen one.[22] We know, however, that there were a few bookstores in different parts of the city.[23] A bookstore for Būlāq books was established around 1836, yet the dissemination of books among the population was extremely limited.

The fortunes of the Būlāq Press fluctuated after the death of Muḥammad ʿĀlī. In 1862, Saʿīd Pāshā (1854–63), the ruler of Egypt, realizing that the press had fallen on hard times, donated it to ʿAbd al-Raḥmān Rushdī on the condition that he would keep printing the laws and the forms needed for government operations. Twenty years later, the press reverted to the government and several enhancements were introduced in equipment and typefaces to make it one of the best in Egypt. In spite of its heavy emphasis on military sciences and textbooks, the influence of the Būlāq Press was great in that it represented a leap from the Middle Ages into the modern age. In the first place, it transformed the way books were produced, making them available cheaply, on a large scale, and in solid and adequate binding. In addition to its service to education, it encouraged more people to read and own books. Likewise, it encouraged more people to publish, thus setting in motion the renaissance of Egypt. As was the case in Lebanon, the translation of books from Western languages enriched the Arabic language by the coining of new words and the resuscitation of others. More importantly, it was the carrier of new ideas and methodologies. In a way, it upset the traditional trend then represented by al-Azhar. The books published by that old institution were not only limited in scope, they were rife with glosses and convoluted language full of rhetoric.

The expansion of book publishing after Muḥammad ʿĀlī continued to advance as the private sector, especially bookstores, began to assume the initiative, and the educated public increased in number, particularly during the rule of Ismāʿīl (1863–79). Book shops becoming publishers is a pattern that remains alive until now. It was during Ismāʿīl's rule that the Egyptian National Library was established. There was a hiatus when the number and type of books published was reduced, during the rule of Tawfīq (1879–92), due to a new law restricting publications. As for scholarly publishing, which began to pick up during the second half of the century, special mention should be made of the Institut Français de l'Archéologie Orientale du Caire, founded in 1881 by Gaston Masparo. Since 1900, the Institut has been its own publisher, and also acted for several decades as publisher to the Egyptian Antiquities Service, the Coptic Archaeological Society, the Egyptian Geographical Society, and the illustrious Institut d'Egypte.[24]

With the growth of the newspaper and periodical publishing, the printing presses were improved, especially at the beginning of the British occupation and during the rise of the nationalist movement that sought independence for Egypt. The British occupation, in certain ways, provided more freedom of expression, as long as it did not conflict with Britain's imperial policies. Egypt was set on its way to becoming the intellectual and publishing leader of the Arab world. This was done with some significant assistance from the Lebanese and Syrian intellectuals and entrepreneurs who began to immigrate to Cairo and Alexandria.

The role played by the Syrians (*al-Shawām*) in the book and publishing industries was a major one. One of the earliest private publishing houses was established by an Egyptianized Syrian, Aḥmad al-Bābī al-Ḥalabī, in 1859. In 1894, al-Hilāl Bookstore, later called Dār al-Hilāl, was established, shortly after the founding of *al-Hilāl* magazine (1892) by Jurjī Zaydān. Dār al-Hilāl issued hundreds of books by famous Arab and non-Arab authors in all subjects, and they were distributed all over the world, wherever there were Arabic readers or institutions with Arab studies. One of the most influential presses, Najīb Mitrī's Dār al-Ma'ārif, played a leading role, together with al-Manār Press, founded by Rashīd Riḍā, the editor and publisher of *al-Manār* magazine. Another important bookstore and publisher was Yūsuf Tūmā al-Bustānī's The Arab Bookstore. These presses and bookstores published many books by the Lebanese and Syrian intellectuals who emigrated to Egypt and got involved with their Egyptian counterparts in the reform movements that were characteristic of the Arab awakening. In addition to making available to a wide readership the ideas and methods of the West, they wrote and published on subjects not tackled before, such as Jurjī Zaydān's book on *Tārīkh al-lughah al-'arabīyah* (History of the Arabic Language); Ibrāhīm al-Yazījī's *Taqwīm al-lisān al-'arabī* (Rectification of the Arabic Tongue); Sulaymān al-Bustānī's translation of Homer's *Iliad*, with an introduction that remains until now a source of inspiration for many literary critics; and Khalīl Muṭrān, who introduced dialogue and unity of structure into Arabic poetry.

By the end of the nineteenth century, Egyptian book production had increased tenfold. In her bibliography on books published in Egypt during the nineteenth century, 'Āyidah Nuṣayr (Nossair) lists 9,782 works under 107 subject headings. Among them are 2,762 titles dealing with religious subjects, 2,015 in literature, 1,372 in social sciences, 1,092 in history, 705 in philosophy, and only 242 in the natural sciences. Textbooks numbered 372.

Cairo, with its cosmopolitan environment and high rate of literacy compared to most Arab cities, grew into a giant book market and intellectual center. The period between the 1920s and 1952 is dubbed correctly by many scholars as the liberal age in Egypt. It was a period in which the great writers, such as Ṭaha Hussein, Aḥmad Luṭfī al-Sayyīd, Maḥmūd 'Abbās al-'Aqqād, Tawfīq al-Ḥakim, and Aḥmad Amīn, among others, wrote, theorized on literary criticism, and proposed new orientations for social development in a flowing and elegant language. This was the period that saw the publication of two of the most controversial works in the contemporary history of the Arab world.

In his *Fī al-shiʿr al-jāhilī* (On Pre-Islamic Poetry), Ṭaha Hussein, while trying to prove that pre-Islamic poetry was really non pre-Islamic, but had been forged in the post-Islamic period, advocated the use of Cartesian methodology, a method that, if applied to the texts of religion, might cast doubt on their authenticity. In *al-Islām wa-uṣūl al-ḥukm* (Islam and the Principles of Government), ʿĀlī ʿAbd al-Rāziq advocated the idea that the caliphate is not a necessary part of Islam. The implication of this was to sanctify the establishment of a secular state. Rebuttal of these two books was so intense that an entire bibliography could be devoted to the topic.

This period also saw new endeavors to improve the quality of books. One of the most significant enterprises was the non-profit organization Lajnat al-Ta'līf wa-al-Tarjamah wa-al-Nashr (The Committee for Writing, Translation, and Publishing), directed by a number of eminent intellectuals who felt the need to compensate for the low cultural level of commerciai publishing. The private sector was motivated mostly by profit, which publishers found highly accessible by issuing books of religious nature or pulp fiction. The prominence of religious and heritage books was strengthened by the establishment of the Dār al-ʿUlūm Faculty at al-Azhar University, and by an increasing number of Islamic associations advocating religion as the best defense against colonialism, political as well as cultural. Islamic heritage books and religious pamphleteering became strongly represented on the book publishing scene and so remain until the present time.

With the coming of the 1952 revolution, the scene changed dramatically. Nasser's *Philosophy of the Revolution* and *al-Mithāq* (Charter) of the Arab Socialist Union (the party of the government), set in motion (and turmoil) the nationalization of the publishing industry, in order to help the society transform itself rapidly into a socialist one. Dār al-Hilāl, Dār al-Ahrām, and Dār al-Maʿārif were taken over by the government, but were given semi-autonomous status. A massive publishing organization was created, al-Mu'assasah al-ʿĀmmah lil-Ta'līf wa-al-Nashr (the General Authority for Writing and Publishing), and a governmental plan was drawn. The plan consisted of publishing books and periodicals that it was thought would meet the cultural, literary, political, social, scientific, and religious needs of Egypt. Publishing was to deal with social questions and the Arab revolution, and also with providing Arab libraries with the best in Arab and world heritage. Translations of the best works in world literature were to be undertaken (the One Thousand Books Project), but would not be limited to Western works; African, Asiatic, and Latin American titles would also be included.[24]

In 1972, al-Hay'ah al-Miṣrīyah al-ʿĀmmah lil-Kitāb (the General Egyptian Book Organization, or GEBO) replaced the General Authority for Writing and Publishing. It was defined as a non-profit enterprise. All book-related activities, including the National Library and the National Archives, were consolidated and placed under its wings. Among the many activities GEBO now sponsors is an annual international book fair during the last week of January.

At present, the Egyptian government, through GEBO and the semi-autonomous publishing giants of Dār al-Ahrām, Dār al-Hilāl, and Dār al-Ma'ārif, remains the largest publisher, in spite of the fact that there is little intervention in the publishing plans of these institutions and the fact that commercial private publishing has been on the increase since President Sadāt's open-door policy was established.

THE AGONIES OF THE ARABIC BOOK

I would have liked to talk about the ecstatic pleasure one derives from the many good works published all over the Arab world, but given the overwhelming number of problems that afflict the Arabic book, one cannot gloss over the glaring reality. Although I will deal mostly with the Egyptian book, the problems are not limited to that country; they apply to most Arab countries, in varying degrees.

The problems facing the book in Egypt may be described as technological, economic, political, and organizational. The four are naturally interrelated and need to be looked at jointly. While struggling with its Arab socialism experiment, Egypt sought and was able to raise the standard of living of its masses. The book was considered one of the basic tools for cultural, economic, and social development. Because of several factors, however, the book suffered on many fronts in terms of quality and dissemination. Tharwat 'Ukāshah, the minister of culture, in a statement made in 1967 stated that, "We find it [the book), dangerously behind in spite of the many efforts, forces, allocated funds. and material and moral encouragement."[26]

Its new socialized structure alienated Egypt from other Arab countries culturally, and from the technological revolution in printing that was taking place in the 1970s. The decline of book publishing in Cairo took place at the same time as Lebanese publishers were modernizing their equipment and becoming big and efficient distributors of books all over the Arab world. Beirut became the Arab publishing capital, replacing Cairo. The absence of clear copyright laws, and the inconsistent implementation thereof, contributed to the problems in Cairo. Beirut became the beneficiary and the culprit in most cases of copyright violations. Several of Beirut's publishers excelled in book piracy, a matter morally reprehensible, but hailed by many as making available, and cheaply, works that would not have been available otherwise.

Politics was another factor that influenced the relative decline in book production. Egypt was alienated during the time of the Nasser regime from Saudi Arabia and Tunisia, both big markets for Egyptian books, and from the rest of the Arab world after the Camp David Agreement (1979), when it was boycotted by the members of the League of Arab States. Furthermore, government intervention, which supported only the public sector, created a discouraging atmosphere for authors and publishers.

In 1972, the UNESCO-sponsored Year of the Book, the Arab League Educational, Cultural and Scientific Organization (ALECSO) held a conference in Doha, Qatar (4–10 December) on the dissemination and distribution of the Arabic book. Mr. Bahīj ʿUthmān, then the president of the Lebanese Union of Publishers, reported on the difficulties in disseminating Arabic books. According to his account, books coming out in one Arab country and going to other countries, like Iraq, Saudi Arabia, Libya, and others, have to receive the imprimatur of a censor before distribution. In some other countries, all imported books have to be distributed by the public sector distribution agencies, which leads to the same kind of restrictions on access. In fact, most of the present distribution companies prefer to distribute newspapers and magazines because it is less risky and more profitable. Smuggling of books by secondary exporters is also a common phenomenon. Reading habits are still not well developed, and with competition from audio-visual media, this situation is not likely to improve. Illiteracy rates are still high. Most works are printed in editions of less than five thousand copies, for an Arab population of 180 million. Moreover, most Arab countries have not yet developed adequately their national libraries or national bibliographies.

Probably the greatest agonies come from an indirect pressure, the control exercised by religious authorities over the doctrinal purity of any book that might be construed as having even an indirect bearing upon the tenets of Islam, and in some cases Christianity. Notwithstanding the sophistication of many Arab writers and their concerns for scholarly research methods and presentation, many are the books that still lack precision in the texts, and suffer from typographical errors, and many are the publishers who seek the least expensive printing and paper, are negligent in placing footnotes, making indexes, ensuring correct and exact citations, and including all the bibliographic information needed on the title page. In conclusion, the Arabic book, in spite of the many and great strides taken towards better, more beautiful presentation, advanced scholarly approaches, and sophisticated language during two centuries of expansion, still has a long way to go. Furthermore, in my opinion, the abundance of religious tracts and belles-lettres has not served to produce a more coherent and cohesive society especially when one considers the many problems and conflicts that trouble the Arab world today.

NOTES

1. The earliest Arabic work that has reached us is a book of Christian prayer, *Kitāb ṣalāt al-sawāʿī* (Horlogium breve), which was printed in Fano in 1514. The first Koran printed was one printed around 1537 in Venice by Alessandro

de Paganino. See Angela Nuovo, "El Corano arabe ritrovato," *La Bibliofilia* 89, no. 3 (1987), pp. 237–71. Books in Arabic were produced in Italy by *Typographia Medicea*, established in 1585 at the advice of Pope Gregory XIII. In addition to the Bible, the press published Avicenna's *Canon Medicinae* and al-Idrīsī's *Kitab Nuzhat al Mushtāq*. See Josée Balagna, *L'imprimerie Arabe en Occident* (XVIe, XVIIe, et XVIII siècle) (Paris, 1984).

2. See, on the history of printing in Arab countries, Khalīl Sabāt, *Tārīkh al-ṭibā'ah fī al-sharq al-'arabī*, 2nd ed. (Cairo, 1966); see also the dissertations of Moncef Chenoufi, "Le problème des origines de l'imprimerie et de la presse arabe en Tunisie dans sa relation avec la Renaissance (*Nahda*) 1847–1887," Université de Paris IV, 1970; Fawzi Abdulrazak, "The Kingdom of the Book: The History of Printing as an Agent of Change in Morocco between 1865 and 1912," Harvard University, 1989; and Wahid Ghdoura, *Le début de l'imprimerie, arabe à Istanbul et en Syrie (1706–1787)* (Tunis, 1985).

3. The reference to Lebanon in this article does not take into account the historical difference between Mount Lebanon, which did not include Beirut, Tripoli, Sidon, and other areas, and Greater Lebanon, which was proclaimed by General Gouraud, High Commissioner of the French Republic. Lebanon became a republic in 1926, and gained its independence from the French in 1943.

4. *Karshūnī* is Arabic in Syriac script.

5. Jabal 'Āmil is in southern Lebanon and is inhabited mostly by Shi'ite Muslims. See Muḥammad Khalīl al-Murādī, *Silk al-durar fī a'yān al-qarn al-thānī 'ashar*, 4 vols. (Cairo, 1301/1883; repr. Baghdad, 1968), 1:7.

6. See Basile Aggoula, "Le livre libanais," in *Exposition le livre et le Liban jusqu'a 1900* (Paris, 1982), p. 308.

7. See Muḥammad Kurd 'Akī, *Khuṭaṭ al-Shām*, 6 vols. in 3, 3rd ed. (Damascus, 1983), 6:197.

8. Khalīl Sabāt, *Tārīkh al-ṭibā'ah fī al-sharq al-'arabī*, 2nd ed. (Cairo, 1966), p. 52.

9. Sixteen of Alexander Dumas' (*père*) novels were translated, including such works as *The Count of Monte Christo, The Three Musketeers*, etc. See M. Yūsūf Najm, *al-Qiṣṣah fī al-adab al-'arabī al-ḥadīth*, 3rd ed. (Beirut, 1966), pp. 21–31.

10. The private library of Nawfal was sold to the American University of Beirut.

11. For more information on al-Asīr and al-Aḥdab, see Mārūn ʿAbbūd, *Ruwwād al-nahḍah al-ḥadīthah* (Beirut, 1952), pp. 72–77.

12. Several books of polemical emendations or corrections of linguistic errors were produced as the language was being transformed from ornate and verbose to a more direct and substantial style. Saʿīd al-Sharṭūnī published *al-Sahm al-ṣā'ib fī takhti'āt ghunyat al-ṭālib* (The Correctly Hitting Arrow in Faulting Ghunyat al-Ṭālib), a criticism of A. Fāris al-Shidyāq's *Ghunyat al-ṭālib*, a grammar book promoting the new style advocated by al-Shidyāq. Both al-Aḥdab and Al-Asīr in turn published rebuttals of *al-Sahm*.

13. An example of such advertisement reads: "This book is sold in Beirut by Messrs Karulla, Fatḥallah Tājir and Yūsuf Kāmid." See *Le livre et le Liban*, p. 309. Dr. Yusuf Khoury of The American University of Beirut called my attention to al-Maktabah al-Jāmiʿah, a bookstore established by Khalīl and Amīn al-Khoury in 1877 in Beirut. The 1888/89 catalog of the bookstore lists titles published by the bookstore, and religious, scientific, medical, and literary works sold there, including titles from Turkey, Egypt, Mosul (Iraq), and Germany.

14. See the title page of Yūsūf al-Dibs' book, *Mughnī al-mutaʿallim* (The Enricher of the Learned) (Beirut, 1869), where it says, "It was printed at the expense of the author and his friend Rizqallah Khadra."

15. See ʿAbd al-ʿAzīz ʿAwād, *al-Id*ārah al-ʿ*Uthmānīyah fī wilāyat Sūrīyā, 1864–1914* (Cairo, 1969), p. 91.

16. On the Syrians and Lebanese in Egypt, see the chapter on this subject in Albert Hourani, *The Emergence of the Modern Middle East* (Berkeley, 1981), pp. 103–23; also, Thomas Philipp, *The Syrians in Egypt* (Stuttgart, 1985).

17. Nasrallah, op. cit., p. 91.

18. On the Bulāq Press, known later as al-Maṭbaʿah al-Amīrīyah, see the excellent work of Abū al-Futūḥ Raḍwān, *Tārīkh Maṭbaʿat Būlāq* (Cairo, 1953).

19. See the English language introduction in ʿĀyidah Nuṣayr (Aida I. Nossair), *Arabic Books Published in Egypt in the Nineteenth Century* (Cairo, 1990). The percentages total more than one hundred because some titles' subjects overlap categories.

20. Sabāt, op. cit., p. 175.

21. Raḍwān, op cit., p. 260.

22. Edward Lane, *An Account of the Manners and Customs of Modern Egyptians Written in Egypt During the Years 1833–35*, (London, 1836), p. 190, "The booksellers in Cairo are, I am informed, only eight in number and their shops are but ill stocked."

23. Michaud et Poujoulat, *Correspondence d'Orient*, 8 vols. in 4, 6:299, Letter 112, Cairo, April, 1831; cited in Raḍwān, op. cit., p. 300.

24. John Rodenbeck, "A Scholarly Publisher in Egypt," *Scholarly Publishing* (July 1985), p. 320.

25. Sha'bān Khalīfah, *Dār al-Kutub al-Qawmīyah* (Cairo, 1991), pp. 267–68.

26. Government of Egypt, Ministry of Culture, "*al-Kitāb al-'arabī*," in *Arba'at mu'tamarāt* (Cairo, 1917), p. 209.

13

Mass Higher Education and the Religious Imagination in Contemporary Arab Societies

Dale F. Eickelman

Mass higher education in the Arab and Muslim worlds is reshaping conceptions of self, religion, nation, and politics. It is as basic to reconfiguring notions of self and society in the Arab world of the late twentieth century as was the introduction of printed books in sixteenth-century rural France.[1] Ironically, however, we know more about the uses of literacy in medieval and premodern Europe than in the contemporary Muslim and Arab worlds. Many scholars have noted linkages between advanced education and religious activists, or "fundamentalists," that they are reinstituting older forms of religious understanding and action rather than creating, even if inadvertently, new ones. The result is to deflect attention from both conceptual innovations and emerging networks for communication and action that affect virtually all Muslims and profoundly shape the direction of contemporary Muslim thought. Fundamentalism, the claims of its adherents notwithstanding, is a distinctly modern phenomenon.[2]

In this article I examine the "objectification" of the religious imagination in the Muslim Middle East, the process by which three kinds of questions come to be foregrounded in the consciousness of large numbers of believers: "What is my religion?" "Why is it important to my life?," and "How do my beliefs guide my conduct?" Objectification does not mean seeing religion as a uniform or monolithic entity, although it is precisely that for some thinkers. I argue that these explicit and "objective" questions are distinctively modern ones that increasingly shape the discourse and practice of all Muslims, even as some legitimize their practices and beliefs by asserting a return to authentic established traditions. I focus on *how*, at this time in history and in certain contexts, religions have been objectified in the consciousness of many people. In part, this issue is easier to address than *why*, but it is also more neglected. For something like religion to be objectified in people's consciousness, it must be discussed, and this entails discourse. If, for reasons of political intimidation or social deference, people do not discuss it directly, then it is discussed publicly *for* them by "experts" with whom they may or may not agree.

Distinctive to the modern era, this discourse and debate about tradition involve large numbers of people. They also necessarily involve an awareness of other Muslim and non-Muslim traditions, even if understandings of these other traditions are often distorted. Mass education and mass communication facilitate such awareness and, in changing the style and scale of possible discourse, reconfigure the nature of religious thought and action and encourage explicit debate over meaning. Although both mass education and mass communication are important in all contemporary world religions, the full effects of mass education, especially higher education, are just beginning to be felt in much of the Muslim world.

My approach in this article is not linear and evolutionary—in this respect it differs from Habermas',[3] although it is inspired by his emphasis upon forms of communicative action in other respects—but contextual; I seek to describe the salient characteristics of an integrated cultural transformation. Bourdieu's[4] studies of higher education, which explore correspondences and affinities among status, authority, and the "ways of knowing" inculcated by various educational institutions, can serve as a point of departure for understanding the dramatic transformations of religious authority that are occurring in much of the Muslim world today. Bourdieu is most effective in suggesting how the complex practices of educational institutions reproduce unequal relations of wealth and authority in society, but less so in showing how even repressive political systems leave room for contestation.[5] Indeed, some form of resistance to a society's central institutions would appear critical for sustaining the cultural construction of authoritative discourse, if only to coopt sources of possible opposition and dissent. In this respect, Gramsci[6] serves as a useful complement to Bourdieu, who emphasizes the reproduction of existing social arrangements. Although conceptually less tidy, Gramsci suggests that intellectuals and their discourse, although constrained by the established social order, never just reproduce it but create, even if inadvertently, the seeds of resistance and contestation. In order to focus on the development of new "authoritative" discourses and resistance to them, I seek to place such discourses in their specific historical and political contexts.

Some elements of contemporary Islamic ideologies deflect attention away from such specific contexts. Muslims conventionally represent themselves as "People of the Book," yet until recently most Muslims—and certainly those in the Middle East—were not sufficiently literate to read or comprehend directly the Qur'ān or other religious texts. Nonetheless, the idea of the book and the text has long pervaded many social contexts. In this respect, the uses of literacy and of the spoken and written word in the Arab "core" of the Muslim world strongly resemble those in the so-called Muslim "periphery."[7] Even where texts are not present, people behave as if they are. The idea of the Book, by analogy with the divine text of the Qur'ān,[8] conveys for many Muslims the idea that valued knowledge is fixed and memorizable. In Morocco, the cognitive style associated with Islamic knowledge remains closely tied to popular understandings of Islam and has important analogies in nonreligious spheres of knowledge.[9]

Memorization of the Qur'ān continues to be a virtually unquestioned form of cultural capital for Moroccans, although few still memorize it in its entirety, as was common for an earlier generation. Qur'ānic memorization served as a paradigm for subsequent learning in the religious sciences as well as in other fields of knowledge; ideally, texts were mnemonically "possessed." Beginning in the 1920s and 1930s, the Moroccan elite began to send their sons to the schools of the French protectorate. As this occurred, the prestige of Islamic higher education, left increasingly to students from rural regions, suffered a rapid decline, although the popular idea of knowledge as fixed and memorizable still prevailed.[10] The advent of mass higher education since the 1970s, however, challenges this paradigm and offers an alternative cognitive style.

RELIGIOSITY AND MASS HIGHER EDUCATION

Major changes in basic religious or political perceptions often occur incrementally and are not perceived as significant at the time. Only in retrospect are they recognized as sharp breaks with the past. Discussing ties of dependence in feudal Europe, Marc Bloch[11] wrote that successive generations did not consciously create new social forms but instead gave rise to them "in the process of trying to adapt the old." Much the same can be said of mass higher education. Even when mass higher education is used to sustain old patterns of belief and authority, its very structure engenders new "authoritative" ways of thinking about self, religion, and politics.

For the most part, mass higher education is a recent phenomenon in the Middle East. It began in earnest only in the 1950s. Fifteen to twenty years later, that is, by 1975 or 1980, after large numbers of students began to complete its advanced cycles, its consequences could be more clearly discerned. In Egypt, the number of primary school pupils more than doubled in the decade following the 1952 revolution. Corresponding increases in secondary and university education began in the mid-1960s (see fig. 13.1). The timing of educational expansion varies for other parts of the Middle East. Major educational expansion in Morocco began in the 1960s.[12] In Oman, a case to be considered in detail here, educational opportunities began to expand significantly only in the 1970s. In 1972–73, there were 25,000 students at all levels in Oman. By 1982–83, there were 142,000, and by 1987–88, 276,000. In 1975–76, a mere 22 students were enrolled in secondary education within Oman. By 1987–88, this number had risen to 13,500. In postsecondary education, a critical mass among Omanis emerged only in the late 1980s.[13]

A complementary measure of change is book production. As of 1982, the Arab world was producing 40 books per million inhabitants, far below the world

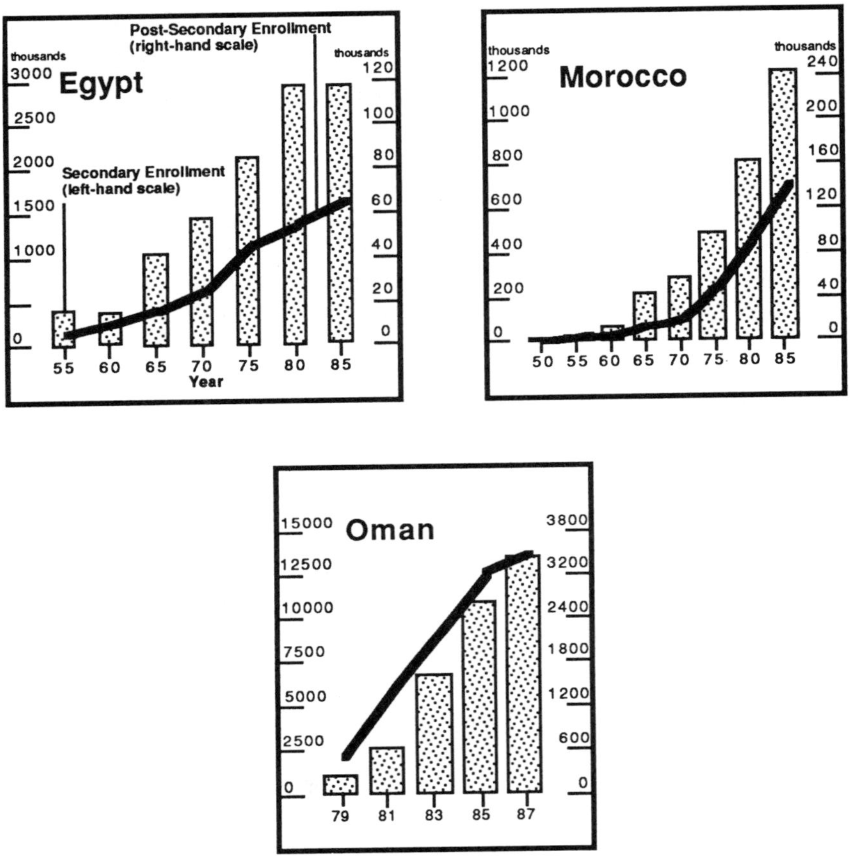

Fig. 13.1. Statistics on secondary education in Egypt, Morocco, and Oman.

average of 162 titles per million. Although more recent figures are unavailable, the gap appears to be closing rapidly.[14] Likewise, the first cohort of Moroccans to benefit from mass higher education in Arabic, as opposed to French, and to have acquired their pervasive "habits of thought"[15] in the country's national language, is creating a demand for the "re-imagining"[16] of Islam and national identity. Only in the last few years has a significant readership for "quality" books in Arabic developed in Morocco.[17] For the increasingly influential cohort of university graduates, reading is a means of "appropriating,"[18] organizing, and making objective ideas of society, religion, and self.

Authoritative Discourse

With the spread of mass higher education in the Muslim world, access to the Qur'ān as well as to other books and the ways of knowing inculcated by them, has shifted in form. Religious authority in earlier generations derived from the mastery of authoritative texts studied under recognized scholars. Mass education fosters a direct, albeit selective, access to the printed word and a break with earlier traditions of authority. As Hassan al-Turabi, the Sorbonne-educated leader of the Muslim Brothers in the Sudan and a former attorney-general, has said, "Because all knowledge is divine and religious, a chemist, an engineer, an economist, [and] a jurist are all *'ulamā'* [religious scholars]."[19] Thus, the privileged position of traditionally educated religious scholars has eroded. Although religious activism has many sources, it appeals mainly to those who have benefited from modern education. In 1953, for example, only 22 percent of the Egyptian Muslim Brothers were *not* of the educated urban middle classes.[20] In the occupied West Bank after 1967, the occupying authorities encouraged religious activism in order to counter secular nationalism; belatedly, they discovered that popular religious protest offered an equally if not more tenacious opposition to their authority. As early as 1979, a poll at one West Bank university indicated that 43 percent of the students identified themselves with fundamentalist rather than with secular nationalist organizations. Throughout the occupied territories, youths "with a relatively high educational level" are the core of these groups.[21] Muslim fundamentalist discourse, such as that of Morocco's 'Abd al-Salām Yāsīn,[22] assumes a familiarity with the language of Marxist and other "Western" discourses, against which it confidently reacts. Belief and practice are now expressed in public and explicit forms and are more directly related to political action than they previously were.

Sayyid Quṭb's *Ma'ālim fī al-ṭarīq* (Signposts),[23] said to be the most widely read book among younger Muslims worldwide, would never have had the impact it did without the spread of mass education and the access to analytical and exegetical texts that such education provides. In Iran, the Friday sermon has become *the* focal political event; in it, government speakers explain policies, problems, and events of the week to audiences much wider than any assembled during the Shah's regime, notwithstanding the Pahlavi state's full control over mass communications. These sermons often refer to published sources and arguments for authority, implying an audience familiar with texts and the principles of citation. Not all of the audience can follow such arguments in detail, but they recognize the forms of authority. Even the nonreligious and the antireligious are obliged to follow the sermons to remain abreast of political developments, and the sermons themselves presume an awareness of world events and an ability to understand policy.

Religion as System and Object

A second consequence of mass higher education is perhaps most evident from contemporary fundamentalist discourse, in which religious beliefs are seen as *systems* to be distinguished from one another. The fundamentalist thinker Sayyid Quṭb, executed by Nasser in 1966, described Islam as a "system" (*minhaj*) of beliefs and doctrines. Quṭb saw Islam as self-contained, yet thinking of religion in this way makes it possible to borrow from other systems and to incorporate changes,[24] thereby increasing the system's viability. When fundamentalists declare that they are engaged in the "Islamization" of their society, they make explicit their sense of religious beliefs as an objective system. Thus, since the 1980s, Moroccans have commonly referred to activists as "the Muslims" (*al-muslimūn*). Irony is far from absent, since all but about 20,000 of Morocco's 26 million citizens are Muslim.

Language and Community

Finally, the standardized language of mass higher education encourages new senses of community and affinity. Anderson[25] argues, for example, that the rise of written vernacular languages in Europe since the sixteeth century and the spread of print technology have created language communities wider than those of face-to-face interactions yet narrower than the communities created by shared sacred languages. With modifications, this premise can be transposed to many Islamic contexts.

One indication of shifts in the religious imagination of a younger, educated generation in many parts of the Middle East is the effort of the state to coopt fundamentalist discourse. In Morocco in the 1960s and early 1970s, both the monarchy and its political opposition employed a "developmentalist" idiom in which "religious" issues were separated from "political" ones. By the late 1970s, the public language of the monarchy's supporters was much more religiously oriented, and the monarch asserted that he was developing a cadre of Ministry of the Interior officials trained in administration and Islamic thought. He claimed that his political actions were modeled upon those of the Prophet Muḥammad:

> In all modesty, Ḥassan's school is the school of Muḥammad V. . .and the school of Muḥammad V is that of the Prophet. . . . Most of us know the Prophet only as messenger of God. . . . His political and diplomatic life remain unknown and we await the day when someone firmly attached to his religion and proud of its teachings will write on this subject.[26]

From North Africa to Jordan, Egypt, and Turkey, the impact of modern mass education is pervasive. In the context of a set national curriculum in which Islamic studies is one subject among many, students are taught about the unity of Muslim thought and practice. An impersonal relation between students and curriculum is stressed, and matters of controversy among Muslims are excluded. Even while teaching that Islam permeates all aspects of life, the formal principles of Islamic doctrine and practice are compartmentalized and made an object of study. As mentioned earlier, Sayyid Quṭb employed terms such as "curriculum" (*minhaj*) to describe Muslim doctrine as a system of closely related beliefs and principles. This pervasive notion of system is a profoundly new element in modern religious thought, as are the catechisms that are now becoming common for many Muslims, including Ibāḍī Muslims who, together with the better known and more numerous Sunnī and Shī'ah, form the third major doctrinal cluster (*madhhah*) in the wider Islamic community. Such catechisms help their schooled users to understand the key thinkers of their tradition and to explain doctrinal tenets to other Muslims.[27]

RELIGION AND EDUCATION IN OMAN

The adoption of mass higher education in Oman[28] is sufficiently recent that I was able to witness its beginning in the late 1970s. Schooling became widely available after the 1970 palace coup in which Qābūs ibn Sa'īd replaced his father, Sa'īd ibn Taymūr (1932–70), as ruler. By the early 1980s, Oman had a sufficient number of secondary school graduates, members of the armed services and civilian government with in-service training, and university students abroad (and, since the opening of Sultan Qaboos University in 1986, in Oman itself) to engender a transformation in what constitutes authoritative religious discourse. The shift to a print- and cassette-based religiosity and the exposure of large numbers of young Omanis to a written, formal, "modern standard" Arabic through schooling and the mass media have altered the style and content of authoritative religious discourse and the role it plays in shaping and constraining domestic and regional politics.[29]

The overall trend has been one of turning away from ritual and symbolic contexts in which—to cite an account of a contemporary Mayan community in Guatemala—"meaning comes to rest more on usage than on referentiality; learning consists of improvisation rather than rationalization; and mastery of form ultimately takes precedence over understanding of context,"[30] and toward intellectualism and an explicit statement of belief inseparable from the study of texts, or at least an invocation of them. Because the discourse of Oman's mufti, Shaykh Aḥmad ibn Ḥamad al-Khalīlī, is authorized, frequent, and publicly accessible, it provides an accurate reading of contemporary religious trends even as it reflects and responds to competing Muslim voices.

For example, when in 1986 a senior religious authority in Saudi Arabia issued a *fatwá* (authoritative religious interpretation) that was interpreted as hostile to the Ibāḍīyah, al-Khalīlī, who is Ibāḍī, responded in a nationally televised address by invoking specific texts and thinkers as his authorities. Indeed, the perceived attack from an unsympathetic Muslim authority was part of an overall pattern of competing Muslim discourses shaped by discursive texts.[31] The major difference between the Ibāḍīyah of Oman and their counterparts in Algeria and Libya is that modern educational opportunities came last to Oman. Students and other Omanis looked to the mufti to formulate appropriate ways of explaining Ibāḍī interpretations of Islam to other Muslims. These students constitute the development of explicit statements of belief and practice. Indeed, Oman's mufti rarely puts his ideas in writing himself, but they are frequently promulgated through cassettes and public addresses that are later transcribed (and occasionally translated) for use in discussing Islam with other Muslims or representing Omani religious traditions to outsiders.[32] One cassette, for example, responds to a letter from an Omani student in the United States who had written the mufti that some of his "Sunnī brothers" had warned against allowing Ibāḍīs to lead prayers or participate "in the administration of our mosques and Islamic Centers in this place on the claim that they are a section of the Khawārij," an early Islamic revolutionary sect that advocated death for Muslims not adhering strictly to its tenets. The student had asked for guidance in responding to such claims and "the reason for not circulating [Ibāḍī] books and references in the libraries and in the Muslim Universities."[33]

Religiously minded younger Omanis, especially those who take seriously the critiques of contemporary Arab and Muslim fundamentalist and radical thinkers, such as the late Sayyid Quṭb, find Shaykh al-Khalīlī's arguments persuasive. The mufti, despite the fact that he holds a government sinecure, cites with approval books banned in Oman, giving the appearance of autonomy from state censorship and control. As in Egypt,[34] state authorities, by "authorizing" some radical discourse, encompass and control it. Omanis harbor few illusions that Shaykh al-Khalīlī's invocation of prohibited literature will have any effect on its continued interdiction. The mufti's discourse shows how a spokesperson for the ruling elite can coopt discourse of the opposition, including Marxism, and integrate some traditional practices, such as the *dars*, into modern contexts in order to sustain authority. Some of the mufti's most biting critiques are offered as quotations or paraphrases from other writers, which distances him from formulations he nonetheless offers with approval. Shaykh al-Khalīlī is careful to specify authors, titles, page numbers, and often even publishers—a form of citation familiar to members of his audience with a modern education but absent from traditional religious discourse.

Shaykh al-Khalīlī's discourse is almost exclusively oral, so that even newspaper summaries of his views are edited by others.[35] He regularly travels throughout the Sultanate, meeting with religious notables, and draws large crowds for his public lessons. When the ruler ordered special prayers in support of the Palestinian people in March 1988, the mufti led the congregation in one of Oman's largest mosques. Through regular radio programs and a weekly newspaper column, he offers *fatwás* in response to queries from Omanis. Shaykh al-Khalīlī's frequent participation in international Islamic conferences—in Jidda, in Cairo, and at Sultan Qaboos University in February and March 1988 alone—is extensively reported. In addition to undertaking this heavy schedule of speaking, the mufti plays a pivotal role in committees that shape public religious expression in schools, the media, and the "suggested" texts for Friday sermons. Again, however, these sermons are in formal Arabic, and thus their specific content is understood only by traditionally educated religious scholars and those who have received a modern education.

Shaykh al-Khalīlī's articulation of Islamic issues contrasts sharply with the pattern that prevailed in Oman until the 1970s. For the Ibāḍīyah, the older pattern was sustained by an interlocking universe of religious notables whose literary output centered on poetry and tribal histories that were circulated largely in manuscript form among the educated elite.[36] Alternative constructions of Islam and of Muslim identity were marginal concerns. Textual references were primarily to Omani scholars and did not reflect debate or confrontation with the wider Muslim community. For instance, in Oman of the 1920s and 1930s, the presence of the prominent Tripolitanian Ibāḍī writer and Arab nationalist Sulaymān al-Bārūnī (1870–1940) had no significant influence on the form of religious discourse.[37] In many parts of Oman, Sunnī, Shīʿī, and Ibāḍī communities were closely intertwined, but their relations were of juxtaposition rather than of dialogue and interaction. Members of each community were aware of the religious practices of the others, but this awareness did not engender a systematic formulation of sectarian distinctions. This awareness came to the forefront with the introduction of modern education.

Until the last two decades, Ibāḍī, Sunnī, and Shīʿī doctrines and practices were not explicitly thought of as systems that could be compared and contrasted. What was practiced was assumed to be Islamic, pure and simple. Omanis were, of course, aware of other Muslim communities, some very close at hand, but the other communities and their interpretations of doctrine and practice were at the periphery of the moral imagination of religious intellectuals and others.

The intensification of government services, education, and control since 1970 has heightened people's imagination of Oman as a political community,[38] with territorial limits and spheres of authority accepted by both the ruler's supporters and his opponents. Although this transformation was accelerated after 1970, it was well under way before then. Sultan Saʿīd may have been a reactionary in the last decades of his rule, but his repressive actions brought a new unity to Oman's diverse sectarian and ethnic population; their dislike of him engendered a sense of unity that could not be broken even by enticements from neighboring countries then opposed to Oman.[39] The government of Sultan Saʿīd may have been weak in scale, scope, and services, but it provided a clearly defined center against which its opponents united as *Omanis*. In 1965, a United Nations team that had conducted extensive interviews with Omani exiles in Saudi Arabia, Cairo, and elsewhere concluded:

> Most persons interviewed made it clear that they would perfer to see Oman united as one country. Some had in mind the unification of the territories previously controlled by the Sultan and the Imam, while others wished to see the Trucial Sheikhdoms also included as part of the future Oman. One person said that there was no Muscat, only Oman. Another said that people from Oman and from Muscat were all Omanis. . . .Oman had been one country before its division and it should be one country again.[40]

In post-1970 Oman, the state has heightened the sense of national identity by vastly expanding education, the bureaucracy, the police, military and security services, business opportunities, and by providing infrastructure and communication facilities. In textbooks and formal discourse, Omanis are treated as "citizens" (*al-muwāṭinūn*), a role with implied obligations to and reciprocal expectations of the state, the ruler, and his close associates. "Nation" (*waṭan*) in the northern Oman interior no longer primarily means one's community or tribal territory, but Oman itself. Many young Omanis perceive the obligations and expectations framed by the state's new rhetoric as hypocritical, but this rhetoric nonetheless forms the articulated standard by which policies and decisions are justified. Indeed, requesting the government to adhere to its stated principles is a tolerated form of dissent.

Mass education has had a major impact on the style of religiosity of younger Omanis, even as state authorities seek to use education to preserve "traditional" values and to distance religion from the political sphere. At its most basic, the style of intellectual technology introduced by modern schooling constitutes a significant break with the earlier emphasis upon the written word, mediated by an oral tradition and oriented toward a mastery of accepted religious texts acquired through study under religious scholars recognized by the wider community. At least in formal terms, a curriculum of specifically delineated subjects and prescribed texts is taught by a changing array of teachers, and competence is measured by examination. Nonetheless, as seen in the iconic value of the mufti among Omanis who cannot follow his lessons in formal Arabic, replete with spoken references and page citations, the older style of religiosity exists alongside the new one and is selectively incorporated into contemporary dominant discourse.

The prescribed curriculum has made Islamic studies a nonsectarian subject. This "generic" Islam includes such topics as the life of the Prophet Muḥammad and those of his sayings (ḥadīth) that Sunnī, Ibāḍī, and Shī'ī Muslims all accept as authentic. As a consequence, the curriculum includes no discussion of the development of Ibāḍism or of major doctrinal divisions within the Muslim community. The same "generic" Islam is propagated in Omani newspapers and periodicals and in the Friday sermons carried on Oman radio and television.

An unintended consequence of making Islam a part of the curriculum is to make it a subject that must be "explained" and "understood." Yet treating

Islam as a system of beliefs and practices implicitly highlights differences within the Muslim community. Thus one Omani from the interior, now a police official, recalled his experiences as a boarder at a secondary school in the late 1970s, his first close association with Omanis from sects other than his own:

> In religion classes, the teachers, who were mostly Egyptian, were careful to cite only sayings of the Prophet that were accepted by all the sects [*madhāhib*]. Once, when a teacher quoted one not accepted as authentic by the Shīʿah, they walked out of class and staged a protest. We never discussed sectarian matters in class; that was forbidden. In the dormitories, our discussions were often intense. Our purpose wasn't to convince others to change their sect [*madhhab*], but to make the best argument possible for our side [*ṭarafinā*]. (Interview, New York, 20 May 1985)

Such discussion requires participants to emphasize the distinctive features of their beliefs. The previously cited letter from a student to Shaykh al-Khalīlī indicates that the awareness of sectarian differences is further accentuated when Omanis participate in religious activities with their counterparts, sometimes perceived as hostile or misinformed, from Muslim groups outside Oman.

Participation in Muslim associations and study groups, as well as exposure to video and audio cassettes and the literature of various groups, also shifts shared perceptions of Islamic thought and the context in which it is shaped. Ready access to the printed word and to expositions of Islamic doctrine in transnational Arabic (as opposed to regional and local dialects) largely derives from modern mass education, radio, television, and cassettes and is fairly recent for most Omanis. The state creates and sustains a communications network that touches the lives of most citizens. In other cases, the state interdicts certain communications or expressions of opinion.

The movement to institute Friday sermons at mosques throughout Oman in the 1980s constituted a subtle challenge to state authority. At the same time, it illustrated the importance of the shift from ritual to explicit statements of belief. Among the Ibāḍīyah of Oman's northern interior, only the imām in Nizwa offered Friday sermons prior the the "new era." As young Omanis became educated, however, many of them led movements to have Friday sermons read in mosques throughout the interior, as is now done. One of Oman's first generation of village schoolteachers observed of the northern Oman interior, "People here do not know Islam; they pray and sacrifice, but they do not know why" (interview, Nizwa region, 9 March 1988). Before the mid-1970s, statements such as this would have been almost incomprehensible in most towns and villages, but by the late 1980s they had become so common that older persons, who disagreed with the notion that "being Muslim" entailed an ability to articulate a credo, could "interpret" such comments for me and could identify the characteristics of those most likely to share them: younger, educated Omanis.

This nascent intelligentsia is independent of state authority and often skeptical of it, pointing out discrepancies between what they see as the law of the Sultanate and the prescriptions of Islamic law (*sharīʻah*). Yet these same critics are products of the modern state, educated and employed by it, and they concur with the state, at least for the present, on the limits of public discourse. The mufti's allusions to earlier forms of—and deviations from—Islamic rule are applied by some of his audience to contemporary local situations. At the same time, however, the mufti is the Omani representative to the Islamic Conference Organization and other international religious bodies. Even arrangements for the *ḥājj* (the pilgrimage to Mecca) pass through governmental organizations and are bound by regulations established by state authorities. In 1987, the minister of justice announced plans to coordinate "objective" programs in religious education, sermons, and media discussion of religious issues to "enlighten the public on religious matters and to urge the believers to fulfill their obligations."[41] It could be misleading to speak of an Omani, Pakistani, Saudi, French, and Moroccan Islam, but the boundaries, administrative and economic ties, and traditions of national entities implicitly shape religious discourse, just as a print-oriented, modernist Islam induces the specific discussion of sectarian divergences. In Oman, as in other countries, much Islamic literature circulates in *samizdat* form, not because it is "subversive" in the sense of attacking the state, but because it has not found explicit approval. For example, one Algerian book[42] provides a catechism of Ibāḍī beliefs and "correct" sources and indicates its "stand-alone" nature by appending a glossary of key historical events, personalities, and theological terms (*kalāmīyah*) so that interested readers can acquire a "proper" understanding without the tutorials of traditional Islamic learning. Such books had no audience in Oman a decade ago and were not in local circulation.

CONCLUSION

Oman provides a recent example of a general shift to a religious activism that marginalized the authority of traditional religious leaders, a trend paralleled elsewhere among both Muslim and non-Muslim populations, including those in Indonesia and India.[43] With this transformation, religious authority shifts from elite specialists recognized as masters of religious texts and often inaccessible rhetorical forms to religious and political activists who seek open religious discussion and action and whose authority is based upon persuasion and the interpretation of accessible texts. This shift reshapes national cultures and politics because it constitutes a critique of arbitrary state authority and questions state efforts, as in Oman and Morocco, to coopt religious activism. While the full political concomitants of the shift are beyond the scope of this article, there are indications among Shīʻī Arab intellectuals in the Gulf, for example, that even the Qur'ān is no longer invoked as an unquestioned source for the legitimization of democratic moves because, as an Arab Gulf businessman put it, "terms such as 'consultation' [*shūrá*] occur only infrequently and do not constitute a fully developed political theory" (interview, Washington, DC, 27 April 1990). Such a statement implies a reading and analysis of the Qur'ān as a text and an explicit notion of theory and interpretation.

The new forms of religious understandings are pervasive but do not inexorably displace older forms. Elements of traditional religious understandings often survive in altered form. Many aspects of *madrasah* (mosque school) education remain significant. In Morocco, for example, the models of peer learning in *madrasah* education and in religious brotherhoods have been taken over by religious activists, who are often obliged to meet surreptitiously because of state sanctions against them.

The monarchy, for its part, uses the Qarawīyīn mosque-university to train senior administrators in the religious sciences in an effort to accord the state greater legitimacy; and religious lessons (*dars*), often with the monarch in attendance, are broadcast nightly throughout Ramaḍān, the Muslim lunar month of fasting.[44] In some parts of rural Morocco, wealthy Muslims sponsor small *madrasahs*, in which men of learning who congregate to study religious texts in the older mnemonic tradition are fed and lodged at the patron's expense. Fanny Colonna (personal communication, 1975) observed that in the Gurara region of southern Algeria, known for its tradition of religious learning, Qur'ānic schooling was considered better adapted to local needs than the schooling provided by the state. Support for Qur'ānic schooling thus also served as a vehicle for contesting state authority.

Madrasahs in Iran now serve as places to train the political elite, a reversal of their role before the 1979 revolution, when many *madrasah* students were drop-outs from secular higher education, which required them to pass entrance examinations.[45] Because they are trained in both traditional and modern schools, young Iranian mullahs are able to "bridge" religious styles, utilizing aspects of both forms of religious expression as circumstances warrant. Text-based religious activism may constitute a new dominant religiosity but this, does not prevent its carriers from selectively incorporating older forms. Elsewhere, as in the Arabian peninsula and in an Islamicizing Pakistan, jurists and teachers of the religious sciences for all levels of state education receive highly modified forms of what is nonetheless called "traditional" Islamic education.

The Prophet Muḥammad's contemporaries, whose lives bridged the pre-Islamic age of ignorance and the age of Islam, were called *mukhaḍrams*. Moroccan intellectuals now in their forties sometimes apply this term to themselves. Many shared the hope of imminent political and economic reform in the heady years after independence. Now they share a disenchantment with the commitment to reform of an earlier generation, having seen that the end of colonial domination, like the enthusiasms for secular ideologies in the 1960s and early 1970s, brought no significant transformations. Some have placed their hopes in the new forms of religiosity with their implicit promise of reform and renewal. Many, however, do so in a way critically different from that of their predecessors. They apply the term *mukhaḍram* to themselves, but also point out how their practical understanding of religion differs from that of their seventh-century counterparts. They are not just conscious of adhering to (or reacting against) innovative forms of religious belief and practice; they also think of these new forms as systems that can be differentiated from others and consciously reworked. This consciousness of form prevents authoritative knowledge from being monolithic and states from coopting an objectified Islam for themselves: alternatives can always be envisaged, even as the determinative power of historical context is recognized. As antipathetic as some contemporary Muslim religious activists say they are to the "West" they nonetheless share with those who live in the West a commitment to texts, analysis, synthesis, and personal authority that draws upon their own traditions and heritage.

NOTES

The author wishes to thank the National Science Foundation, The Fulbright Faculty Research Abroad Program, and the MacArthur Foundation Program for Research for supporting his field research. Thanks also are extended to all those who reviewed this paper, which first appeared in the *American Ethnologist* after its delivery at the conference, *The Book in the Islamic World*, and is reprinted here with kind permission from the American Anthropological Association.

1. See, on the introduction of printed books, Natalie Zemon Davis, "Printing and the People," in *Society and Culture in Early Modern France*, ed. N.Z. Davis (Stanford, CA: Stanford University Press, 1975), pp. 189–226. See also Jack Goody, *The Logic of Writing and the Organization of Society* (Cambridge: Cambridge University Press, 1986); and Brian Stock, *The Implications of Literacy* (Princeton, NJ: Princeton University Press, 1983).

2. See Bruce B. Lawrence, *Defenders of God: Fundamentalist Revolt against the Modern Age* (San Francisco: Harper & Row, 1989).

3. See Jurgen Habermas, *Communication and the Evolution of Society* (Boston: Beacon Press, 1979).

4. See Pierre Bourdieu, *Homo Academicus* (London: Polity Press, 1988).

5. See Jean Comaroff, *Body of Power, Spirit of Resistance: The Culture and History of a South African People* (Chicago: University of Chicago Press, 1985).

6. Antonio Gramsci, "The Intellectuals," in *Selections from the Prison Notebooks*, ed. and trans. Q. Hoare and G.N. Smith (New York: International Publishers, 1971), pp. 3–43.

7. Michael Lambeck, "Certain Knowledge, Contestable Authority: Power and Practice on the Islamic Periphery," *American Ethnologist* 17 (1990), pp. 23–40.

8. Johannes Pederson, *The Arabic Book*, trans. G. French (Princeton, NJ: Princeton University Press, 1984).

9. Dale F. Eickelman, "The Art of Memory: Islamic Education and Its Social Reproduction," *Comparative Studies in Society and History* 20 (1978), pp. 465–516. See also the author's *Knowledge and Power in Morocco* !Princeton, NJ: Princeton University Press, 1985).

10. Ibid. See also Jacques Berque, "Dans le Maroc Nouveau: Le rôle d'une université islamique," *Annales d'histiore économique et sociale* 10 (1938), pp. 193–207; and "Lieus et moments du réformisme islamique," in *Maghreb: Histoire et societés*, ed. J.B. (Paris: Editions J. Duculot, 1974), pp. 162–88.

11. See Marc Bloch, *Feudal Society* (Chicago: University of Chicago Press, 1964 [1939]).

12. World Bank, *World Development Reports*, volumes for 1981–1989 (New York: Oxford University Press, 1981–89).

13. The statistics on which these graphs are based are necessarily approximate, as countries frequently change their classification of educational institutions. In smaller countries such as Oman, students in military and police academies and in specialized courses sponsored by government ministries are excluded from the statistics on secondary and postsecondary education. Further, students whose education is supported by private funds, a significant phenomenon in a state with oil revenues, are underreported. See Sultanate of Oman (Development Council, Technical Secretariat), *Statistical Year Book*, volumes for 1979–1989 (Muscat: Directorate General of National Statistics).

14. Ives Gonzalez-Quijano, "Le livre arabe et l'édition en Egypt," *Bulletin du Centre de Documentation Economiques, Juridiques et Sociales*, Cairo, 25 (1989), special issue, p. 18.

15. See Bourdieu, op. cit., and his *La noblesse d'état* (Paris: Editions de Minuit, 1989). See also M'hammed Sabour, *Homo Academicus Arabicus* (Joensuu, Finland: University of Joensuu Publications in Social Sciences, no. 11, 1988).

16. See Benedict R. Anderson, *Imagined Communities* (London: Verso, 1983).

17. Michael W. Albin, "Moroccan-American Bibliography," in *The Atlantic Connection: 200 Years of Moroccan-American Relations, 1786–1986,* ed. J. Bookin-Weiner and M. El Mansour (Rabat: Edino Press, 1990), pp. 5–18.

18. Roger Chartier, *The Cultural Uses of Print in Early Modern France*, trans. L.G. Chochrane (Princeton, NJ: Princeton University Press, 1987), pp. 6–11.

19. James Piscatori, *Islam in a World of Nation-States* (New York: Cambridge University Press, 1986). See p. 19, where the author cites Hassan al-Turabi.

20. Ibid., p. 29.

21. Jean-François Legrain. "Islamistes et lutte national palestinienne dans les territoires occupes par Israel," *Revue française de science politique* 6 (1986), p. 229.

22. See Abd Assalam Yassine, *La Revolution à l'heure de l'Islam* (Grignac-la-Nerthe, France, 1981).

23. Sayyid Quṭb, *Maʿālim fī al-ṭarīq* [*Signposts*] (Cairo, Dār al-Shurūq, 1981).

24. William E. Shepard, "Islam as a 'System' in the Later Writings of Sayyid Qutb," *Middle Eastern Studies* 25 (1989), pp. 45–46.

25. Anderson, op. cit.

26. Hassan II (King of Morocco), *Discours et interviews* (Rabat: Ministry of Information, 1984), p. 162.

27. See, for example, Bakīr ibn Saʿīd A'washt, *Dirāsāt Islāmīyah fī al-uṣūl al-Ibāḍīyah* (Cairo, 1988). Ibāḍī Muslims constitute just under half of Oman's indigenous population of about 1.1 million. Significant Ibāḍī communities are also found in East Africa, Libya, and southern Algeria. Non-Ibāḍī examples of catechisms include Muhammad Hamidullah's *Introduction to Islam*, 2nd ed. (Gary, IN, 1970), intended as a "correspondence course on Islam" and available in several languages, and Mehmet Soymen's *Concise Islamic*

Catechism, trans. I. Ekmeleddin (Ankara: Directorate of Religious Affairs, 1979), which was translated from Turkish into English as a "manual" for English-speaking Muslims.

28. The country's official name until 1970 was the Sultanate of Muscat and Oman, reflecting a de facto division of the northern half of the country from 1913, following a religious uprising in the northern interior, to 1955 (the coast was controlled by the sultan, the interior by a theocratic Ibāḍī imām). With British support in 1955, the northern interior was assimilated into the sultan's domains and the imām fled into exile in Saudi Arabia. A major uprising two years later required British intervention to suppress. From 1957 to 1970, Arab League supporters of the imām-in-exile urged the United Nations to recognize Oman's northern interior as an independent state.

29. Dale F. Eickelman, "Ibadism and the Sectarian Perspective," in *Oman: Economic, Social and Strategic Developments*, ed. B.R. Pridham (London: Croom Helm, 1987), pp. 31–50; also the author's "National Identity and Religious Discourse in Contemporary Oman," *International Journal of Islamic and Arabic Studies* 6 (1989), pp. 1–20.

30. John Watanabe, *Mayan Saints and Souls in a Changing World* (Austin, TX: University of Texas Press, 1992), p. 99. For Sumatra, see John Bowen, *Sumatran Politics and Poetics: Gayo History, 1900–1989* (New Haven, CT: Yale University Press, 1991).

31. Eickelman, "National Identity," p. 1–20.

32. See Aḥmad ibn Ḥamad al-Khalīlī, *Who Are the Ibadhis?*, trans. Ahmad Hamud Al-Maamiry (Zanzibar: al-Khayirah Press, 1988); also his *The Spread of Ibadhism in North Africa*, trans. A.H. Al-Maamiry (Muscat, 1989).

33. al-Khalīlī, *Who Are the Ibadhis?*, p. 1.

34. See Timothy Mitchell, "L'experience de l'emprisonnement dans le discours islamiste," in *Intellectuels et militants de l'islam contemporain*, ed. G. Kepel and Y. Richard (Paris: Seuil, 1990), pp. 193–212.

35. Sayf ibn Nāṣir al-Kharūṣī, ed. "Muḥāḍarat al-'isrā' wa-al-mi'rāj, yuḥaddithuhā samāḥat al-Shaykh Aḥmad ibn Ḥamad al-Khalīlī" (Speech on Prophet Muḥammad's Night Journey to the Seventh Heaven by His Eminence Shaykh Aḥmad ibn Ḥamad al-Khalīlī), 'Uman, 25 March 1988, p. 11.

36. Dale F. Eickelman, "Religious Knowledge in Inner Qman," *Journal of Oman Studies* 6 (1983), pp. 163–72.

37. John E. Peterson, "Arab Nationalism and the Idealist Politician: The Career of Sulaymān al-Bārūnī," in *Law, Personalities, and Politics of the Middle East: Essays in Honor of Majid Khadduri*, ed. J. Piscatori and G.S. Harris (Washington, DC: The Middle East Institute, 1988), pp. 31–50.

38. Anderson, op. cit., pp. 15–16.

39. United Nations General Assembly, 19th Session, *The Question of Oman: Report of the Ad Hoc Committee on Oman*, A/5846, Annex no. 16, 22 January 1965.

40. Ibid., p. 65.

41. *Times of Oman* (Muscat), 17 December 1987, p. 5.

42. A'washt, op. cit.

43. Bowen, op. cit., pp. 242–57. See also Robert W. Hefner, "The Political Economy of Islamic Conversion of Modern East Java," in *Islam and the Political Economy of Meaning*, ed. W.R. Roff (London: Croom Helm, 1987), pp. 53–78; Trikoli N. Madan, "Secularism in Its Place," *Journal of Asian Studies* 6 (1987), pp. 747–59; and Ananda F. Wood, *Knowledge Before Printing and After: The Indian Tradition in Changing Kerala* (Delhi: Qxford University Press, 1985).

44. Eickelman, "Religion in Polity and Society," in *The Political Economy of Morocco*, ed. I William Zartman (New York, Praeger, 1987), p. 91.

45. Yann Richard, *L'islam chi'ite: Croyances et ideologies* (Paris: Fayard, 1991); and personal communication, 1987.

14

The Book in the Islamic World: A Selective Bibliography

Michael W. Albin

This bibliography aims to provide those interested in studies of the book in the Islamic world with an introductory list of research up to 1990. It is being issued on the occasion of the International Conference on the Book in the Islamic World, held 8–9 November 1990, at the Library of Congress. Although the field of Islamic book studies is of very recent vintage, there is a substantial body of scholarship from as early as the 1940s on relevant topics. Scholars from many countries, working independently, have contributed to this research. Indeed, a comprehensive bibliography would be many times larger than the current list. In order to orient the user to the material selected for inclusion, the bibliography is divided into four broad categories: *General* works, including classics of what has come to be called *histoire du livre*, as well as theoretical works on writing, reading, and liteacy; *The Manuscript Tradition*, under which heading are works concerned with the production and transmission of Islamic piety and learning, and the book arts in the classical age; *Print Culture*, which brings together research on the introduction of the printing press and congeries of effects brought about by printed books and periodicals; and, finally, the *Book and Society*, covering general works on the impact of books on the education and intellectual life of Muslims during the past two centuries.

Although it may not seem proper to single out works for special note, certain writings have become established as classics and must be consulted by specialists in Islamic culture as well as scholars from other disciplines who need general background on the book in Islam. The earliest of these may be F. Rosenthal's *The Technique and Approach of Muslim Scholarship* (1947). T.F. Carter's *The Invention of Printing in China and Its Spread Westward* (1955) has been quoted and debated for what it has to say about the "barriers" to the printing press. The works by Ibn Durustawayh (ed. 1977) and al-Ṣūlī (ed. 1922) represent a larger body of guides for writers and clerks in the age before printing. A. Raḍwān's work (1953) on the Būlāq Press of Cairo is the first and most important work to date on this famous press, and includes many documents affording insights into life in the printshop. Last, but perhaps most important of all, is the work that lay the foundation for Islamic book studies East and West, the *Fihrist* of Ibn al-Nadīm, happily available to us in English translation, thanks to Bayard Dodge.

By way of explanation and apology for the large section on printing history let it be said that this is the result of the special interest of the compiler and the rich holdings of the Library of Congress in this field. The study of the history of the Islamic book being in its infancy, each and every epoch and facet of books, bookmaking, and book use is in need of further research. Of the making of books about books there should be no end.

GENERAL

Aboussouan, Camille, ed. *Exposition Le Livre et le Liban jusqu'à 1900*. Paris: UNESCO, 1982. 408 pp.

Beeston, A.F.L. "The Evolution of the Arabic Language, the Arabic Script. . .and the Arab Books." In *Arabic Literature to the End of the Umayyad Period*, v. 1, pp. 1–26. London: Cambridge University Press, 1983. 547 pp.

Carter, Thomas Francis. *The Invention of Printing in China and its Spread Westward*. 2nd ed. New York: The Ronald Press, 1955. 293 pp.

Chartier, Roger. "Frenchness in the History of the Book: From the History of Publishing to the History of Reading." *American Antiquarian Society Proceedings* 97 (1988), 2: 299–329.

Cole, John Y., ed. *Books in Our Future: Perspectives and Proposals*. Washington, DC: The Library of Congress, 1987. 399 pp.

Einsenstein, Elizabeth L. *The Printing Press as an Agent of Change*. Cambridge: Cambridge University Press, 1979. 2 vols. 784 pp.

Febvre, Lucien, and H.-J. Martin. *The Coming of the Book: The Impact of Printing, 1450–1800*. Trans. by David Gerard. London: N.L.B., 1976. 378 pp.

The Future of the Book. Pt. 1: *The Impact of the New Technologies*, ed. by Priscilla Oakeshott and Clive Bradley; Pt. 2: *The Changing Role of Reading*, by Michel Gault; Pt. 3: *New Technologies in Book Distribution*, by SKP Associates for the Center for the Book, The Library of Congress. Paris: UNESCO, 1982–84.

Goody, Jack. *The Logic of Writing and the Organization of Society*. Cambridge: Cambridge University Press, 1986. 213 pp.

Graham, William A. *Beyond the Written Word: Oral Aspects of Scripture in the History of Religion*. Cambridge: Cambridge University Press, 1987. 306 pp.

Gray, Basil, ed. *The Arts of the Book in Central Asia, 14th–16th Centuries*. By Oleg Akumushkin, et al. Boulder, Colorado: Shambhala, 1979. 314 pp.

Ḥamādah, Muḥammad Māhir. *al-Kitāb al-ʿArabī: makhṭūṭan wa-maṭbūʿan*. Riyadh: Dār al-ʿUlūm, 1984. 315 pp.

Havelock, Eric A. *The Muse Learns to Write: Reflections on Orality and Literacy from Antiquity to the Present*. New Haven: Yale University Press, 1986. 144 pp.

al-Ḥibshī, ʿAbd Allāh. *al-Kitāb fī al-ḥaḍārah al-Islāmīyah*. Kuwait: Sharikat al-Rabīʿān, 1982. 201 pp.

Ibn al-Nad⅔m. *The Fihrist of al-Nadīm, a Tenth-Century Survey of Muslim Culture*. Ed. and trans. by Bayard Dodge. New York: Columbia University Press, 1970. 2 vols.

Kâtib Çelebi. *Kitāb kashf al-ẓunūn ʿan asāmī al-kutub wa-al-funūn*. Ed. by Şeferettin Yaltkaya and Kilisli Rifat Bilge. Istanbul: Milli Egitim Basimevi, 1971. 2 vols.

Losty, Jeremiah P. *The Art of the Book in India*. London: The British Library, 1982. 160 pp.

Mackensen, Ruth S. "Arabic Books and Libraries in the Omayyad Period." *American Journal of Semitic Languages and Literatures* 52 (1935–36): 245–53; 53 (1936–37): 239–50; 54 (1937): 41–61; 56 (1939): 149–57, "Supplement Notes".

Ong, Walter. *Interfaces of the Word: Studies in the Evolution of Consciousness and Culture*. Ithaca: Cornell University Press, 1977. 352 pp.

Pedersen, Johannes. *The Arabic Book*. Trans. by Geoffrey French. Princeton: Princeton University Press, 1984. 175 pp.

La Réforme et le livre: L'Europe de l'imprimé (1517–v. 1570). Compiled by Jean-François Gilmont. Paris: Les Editions du Cerf, 1990. 531 pp.

Rosenthal, Franz. *The Technique and Approach of Muslim Scholarship*. Rome: Pontificum Institutum Biblicum, 1947. 74 pp.

Tsien, Tsuen-Hsuin. *Written on Bamboo and Silk: The Beginnings of Chinese Books and Inscriptions*. Chicago: The University of Chicago Press, 1962. 233 pp.

Turk Kutuphaneciler Dernegi. Basim ve Yayinciligimiain 250, Yili Bilimsel Toplantisi, 10–11 Aralik 1979, Ankara. *Bildiriler*. Ankara: TKD 1980.

Wassef, Amin Sami. *L'Information et la presse officielle en Egypte jusqu'à la fin de l'occupation Française*. Recherches d'archéologie, de phililogie et d'histoire, XVII. Cairo: Institut Français d'Archéologie Orientale du Caire, 1975. 180 pp.

THE MANUSCRIPT TRADITION

Abbott, Nabia. *The Rise of the North Arabic Script and its Ḳur'ānic Development*. Chicago: The University of Chicago Press, Oriental Institute Publication, 1939. 103 pp.

Arnold, Sir T.W., and A. Grohmann. *The Islamic Book: A Contribution to its Art and History from the VII–XVII Century*. New York: Harcourt, Brace and Co., 1929. 130 pp. and plates.

Bosch, Gulnar K., et al. *Islamic Bindings & Bookmaking: A Catalogue of an Exhibition, The Oriental Institute, The University of Chicago, May 18-August 18, 1981*. Chicago: Oriental Institute, University of Chicago, 1981. 235 pp.

Diringer, David. *The Illuminated Book, Its History and Production*. New ed. London: Faber, 1967. 514 pp.

Gratzl, E., K.A.C Creswell, and R. Ettinghausen. "Bibliographie des islamischen Einbandkunst, 1871 bis 1956." In *Ars Orientalis* II (1957): 519–40.

Huart, Clement. *Les calligraphes et les miniaturistes de l'Orient musulman*. Reimpression of the 1908 edition. Osnabrück: Otto Zeller Verlag, 1972.

Ibn Durustawayh, ʿAbdallāh ibn Jaʿfar. *Kitāb al-kuttāb*. Ed. by Ibrāhīm al-Samarrā'ī. Kuwait: Dār al-Kutub al-Thaqāfīyah, 1977. 161 pp.

Inayatullah, S. "Bibliophilism in Medieval Islam." *Islamic Culture* 12 (1938): 155–69.

James, David. *Qur'āns of the Mamluks*. New York: Thames & Hudson, 1988. 270 pp.

al-Khaṭīb al-Baghdādī, Aḥmad ibn ʿAlī. *Taqyīd al-ʿilm*. Ed. by Youssef Eche. Damascus: Dār Iḥyā' al-Sunnah, 1975. 195 pp.

Levey, Martin. "Medieval Arabic Bookmaking and its Relations to Early Chemistry and Pharmacology." *Transactions of the American Philosophical Society* NS 52, no. 4 (1962): 3–79. (Includes translation of al-Sufyānī's work.)

Lings, Martin. *The quranic Art of Calligraphy and Illumination*. London: World of Islam Festival Trust, 1976. 242 pp.

Minorsky, V., ed. and trans. *Calligraphers and Painters: A Treatise by Qadi Ahmad, Son of Mir-Munshi*. Washington, DC: Freer Gallery of Art, 1959.

al-Munajjid, Ṣalāḥ al-Dīn. *Dirāsāt fī tārīkh al-khaṭṭ al-ʿArabī*. Beirut: Dā al-Kitāb al-Jadīd, 1972. 151 pp.

al-Munajjid, Ṣalāh al-Dīn. *al-Kitāb al-ʿArabī al-makhṭūṭ ilá al-qarn al-ʿāshir*. Cairo: League of Arab States, 1960.

Rice, D.S. *The Unique Ibn al-Bawwāb Manuscript in the Chester Beatty Library*. Dublin: E. Walker (Ireland), 1955. 36 pp.

Robinson, Basil W., ed. *Islamic Painting and the Arts of the Book*. London: Faber and Faber, 1976. 322 pp.

Safadi, Yasin H. *Islamic Calligraphy*. London: Thames and Hudson, 1978. 144 pp.

Sarre, Friedrich Paul. *Islamic Bookbindings*. Trans. by F.D. O'Byrne. London: Kegan Paul, 1923. 197 pp.

Schimmel, Annemarie. *Calligraphy and Islamic Culture*. New York: New York University Press, 1984. 264 pp.

al-Sijistānī, ʿAbdallāh ibn al-Ashʿath. *Kitāb al-maṣāḥif*. Cairo: Muʿassasat Qurṭubah, 1986. 223 pp.

al-Sufyānī, Abū al-ʿAbbās. "Sināʿat tafsīr al-kutub wa-ḥall al-dhahab." New ed. by I. al-Samarrā'ī. *Majallat al-Majmaʿ al-ʿIlmī al-ʿIrāqī* 8 (1961): 335–42.

al-Ṣūlī, Muḥammad Ibn Yaḥyā. *Adab al-kuttāb*. Ed. by M. Bahjat al-Atharī. Baghdad: al-Maktabah al-ʻArabīyah, 1922. 272 pp.

Zayn al-Dīn, Nājī. *Muṣawwar al-khaṭṭ al-ʻArabī. Baghdad: al-Majmaʻ al-ʻIrāqī*, 1968. 410 pp.

Zayyāt, H. "al-Wirāqah wa-al-warrāqūn." *al-Mashriq* 47 (1953): 305–50.

THE PRINT CULTURE

ʻAbduh, Ibrāhīm. *Jarīdat al-Ahrām*. Cairo: Dar al-Maʻārif, 1951. 551 pp.

ʻAbduh, Ibrāhīm. *Taṭawwur al-ṣiḥāfah al-Miṣrīyah, 1798–1951.* 3rd ed. Cairo: Maktabat al-Adab bi-al-Jamāmīz, 1951. 322 pp.

Abdulrazak, Fawzi. "The Kingdom of the Book: The History of Printing as an Agent of Change in Morocco between 1865 and 1912." Ph.D. dissertation, Boston University, 1989.

ʻĀd, Yūsuf. "Kayfīyat intāj al-kitāb qabla al-qarn al-tāsiʻ ʻashar." *al-Masarrah* nos. 747–46 (March–April 1988): 231–40; nos. 749–50 (May–June 1988): 330–40.

Albin, Michael W. "The Iranian Publishing Industry: A Preliminary Appraisal." *Libri* 36, no. 1 (1986): 1–23.

ALECSO. *al-Lajnah al-fannīyah li-dirāsat aḥruf al-tibāʻah al-ʻArabīyah*. Cairo: ALECSO, 1971. 173 pp.

ʻĀsim, ʻAlī Ḥusayn. *al-Ṭibāʻah al-ḥādīthah*. 6 vols. Cairo: al-Matābiʻ al-Amīrīyah, 1959–62.

Babinger, Franz. "Die Einführung des Buchdruckes in Persien." *Zeitschrift des Deutschen Vereins für Buchwesen und Schrifttum* 11–12 (1921): 141–42.

Bacel, Paul. "Abdallah Zaher et son imprimerie Arabe." *Echos d'Orient* 11 (1908): 281–87.

Balagna, Josée. *L'Imprimerie arabe en Occident*. Paris: Éditions Maisonneuve & Larose, 1984. 153 pp.

Baysal, Jale. *Müteferrika'dan Birinci Meşrutiyete Kadar Osmanli Turklerinin Bastiklari Kitaplar*. Istanbul: Edebiyat Fakultesi, 1968. 88 pp.

Bulliet, Richard V. "Medieval Arabic *tarsh*: A Forgotten Chapter in the History of Printing." *Journal of the American Oriental Society* 107., no. 3 (July–Sept. 1987): 427–38.

al-Bustānī, Fu'ād Ifrām. "al-Shammās ʿAbdallāh Zākhir." *al-Masarrah* (July 1948), special issue.

Chenoufi, Moncef. "Le Problème des origines de l'imprimerie et de la presse arabes en Tunisie dans sa relation avec la renaissance "Nahda" (1847–1887)." Ph.D. dissertation, University de Lille III, 1974.

Demeerseman, A. "Les données de la controverse autour du probleme de l'imprimerie." *IBLA* 17, nos. 65–66 (1954): 1–48, 113–40.

Demeerseman, A. "Une parente meconnue de l'imprimerie arabe et tunisienne: La lithographie." *IBLA* 16 (1953): 347–88.

Floor, W.M. "The First Printing Press in Iran." *Zeitschrift der Deutschen Morgenländischen Gesellschaft* 130 (1980): 369–71.

Gdoura, Wahid. *Le début de l'imprimerie arabe à Istanbul et en Syrie: Évolution de l'environnement culturel, 1706–1707.* Tunis: University de Tunis, Institut superieur de documentation, 1985. 312 pp.

Gdoura, Wahid. "Le livre arabe imprimé en Europe: Une etape importante dans les relations Orient-Occident (1514–1700). *Revue maghrébine de documentation* 1 (1983): 37–68.

Gerçek, Slim Nüzhet. *Türk matbaaciliği*. Istanbul: al-Diya, 1928. 111 pp.

Groc, G., and I. Caglar. *La presse française de Turquie de 1795 à nos jours: Histoire et catalogue*. Istanbul: ISIS, 1985.

Hamm, Roberto. *Pour une typographie arabe: Contribution technique à la democratisation de la culture arabe*. Paris: Sindbad, 1975. 193 pp.

Hitti, P.K. "The First Book Printed in Arabic." *Princeton University Library Chronicle* 4 (1942): 5–9.

Ihaddaden, Zahir. *Histoire de la presse indigène en Algérie: Des origines jusqu'en 1930.* Algiers: ENAL, 1983. 40 pp.

Ihsanoğlu, Ekmeleddin. *Açiklamalı Türk kimya eserleri bibliyografyası*. Istanbul: IRCICA, 1985. 148 pp.

İşkit, Server. *Türkiyede nesriyat hareketleri tarhinine bir bakış*. Istanbul: Devlet Basımevi, 1939. 484 pp.

Kabacali, Alpay. *Türk kitap tarihi*. Istanbul: Cem Yayinevi, 1989. 158 pp.

al-Kattānī, Zayn al-ʿĀbidīn. *al-Ṣiḥāfah al-Maghribīyah nasha'tuhạ wa-tatawwuruhā, 1820–1966*. 1970? 249 pp.

Khalīfah, Shaʿbān. *Ḥarakāt nashr al-kutub fī Miṣr*. Cairo: Dār al-Thaqāfah, 1974.

Krek, Miroslav. "The Enigma of the First Arabic Printed Book from Movable Type." *Journal of Near Eastern Studies* 38, no. 3 (July 1979): 203–12.

Krek, Miroslav. *A Gazetteer of Arabic Printing*. Weston, MA: The Author, 1977. 138 pp.

"Maṭbaʿa." *Encyclopedia of Islam*. New edition. Vol. 4, pp. 794–807.

Meynet, Roland. *L'Écriture arabe en question: Les projets de l'Academie de Langue Arabe du Caire de 1938 à 1968*. Beirut: Dar al-Mashriq, 1971. 142 pp.

Nasrallah, Joseph. *L'Imprimerie au Liban*. Troisieme conference generale de l'UNESCO. Beirut: Sous la patronage de la Commission Libanaise du Mois de l'UNESCO, Novembre–Decembre 1948. 160 pp.

Nuovo, Angela. "Il Corano Arabo ritrovato." *La Bibliofilia* 89, no. 3 (Sept–Dec. 1987): 247–71.

Raḍwān, Abū al-Futūḥ. *Tārīkh Maṭbaʿat Būlāq*. Cairo: al-Maṭbaʿah al-Amīrīyah, 1953. 523 pp.

Rā'īn, Ismāʿīl. *Avvalīn chāpkhānah-i Īrān*. Tehran: Intishārāt-i Rūznāmah-i "Alik," 1969. 27 pp.

al-Rifāʿī, Shams al-Dīn. *Tārīkh al-ṣiḥāfah al-Sūrīyah*. Cairo: Dār al-Maʿārif, 1969. 2 vols.

Ṣābāt, Khalīl. *Tārīkh al-ṭibāʿah fī al-Sharq al-ʿArabī*. 2nd ed. Cairo: Dār al-Maʿārif, 1966. 378 pp.

Sarkīs, Salīm. *Gharāʾib al-Maktūbjī*. Cairo: al-Mushīr, 1896.

Sarkīs, Yūsuf I. *Muʿjam al-maṭbuʿāt al-ʿArabīyah wa-al-muʿarrabah*. Cairo: Maṭbaʿat Sarkīs, 1928. 2,024 cols. plus indexes.

Stewart, Charles C. "A New Source on the Book Market in Morocco in 1930 and Islamic in West Africa." *Hesperis-Tamdua* 11 (1970): 209–46.

Weisweller, Max. *Der islamische Bucheinband des Mittelalters*. Weisbaden: Harrassowitz, 1962. 193 pp.

THE BOOK AND SOCIETY

ʿAbd al-Karīm, Aḥmad ʿIzzat. *Tārīkh al-taʿlīm fī ʿasr Muḥammad ʿAlī*. Cairo: al-Nahḍah, 1938. 798 pp.

Arasteh, Reza. *Education and Social Awakening in Iran, 1850–1968*. 2nd ed. Leiden: E.J. Brill, 1969. 237 pp.

Berkes, Niyazi. *The Development of Secularism in Turkey*. Montreal: McGill University Press, 1964. 537 pp.

Buheiry, Marwan R., ed. *Intellectual Life in the Arab East, 1890–1939*. Beirut: American University of Beirut, 1981. 192 pp.

Davison, Roderic H. *Reform in the Ottoman Empire, 1856–1876*. Princeton: Princeton University Press, 1963. 479 pp.

Dodge, Bayard. *Muslim Education in Medieval Times*. Washington, DC: Middle East Institute, 1962.

Eche, Youssef. *Les bibliothèques arabes publiques et semi-publiques en Mésopotamie, en Syrie et en Égypte au Moyen Age*. Damascus: Institut Français de Damas, 1967. 447 pp.

Heyworth-Dunne, J. *An Introduction to the History of Education in Modern Egypt*. London: Luzac, 1938. 503 pp.

Hourani, Albert. *Arabic Thought in the Liberal Age, 1798–1939*. London: Oxford University Press, 1962. 403 pp.

Szyliowicz, Joseph S. *Education and Modernization in the Middle East*. Ithaca: Cornell University Press, 1973. 477 pp.

Appendix: Ottoman Imperial Documents Relating to the History of Books and Printing

A COPY OF A DECREE ISSUED BY
HIS IMPERIAL MAJESTY THE PADISHAH MURAD HAN*

Be it hereby known to all governors, sea captains, judges, and other officials stationed in the Imperial domain that two European merchants by the name of Anton and Orasyu [Horatio] Bandini, being bearers of Imperial permission to conduct trade, are buying and selling and doing business by importing certain goods and valuable printed books and pamphlets in Arabic, Persian, and Turkish. Some persons are opening up their shipments by force, and with little or no payment at all are taking their wares and interfering with their trade. It is therefore directed that the said merchants and their agents and employees be allowed to carry on their business in safety and that their merchandise be not seized, and that whosoever disobeys this decree of mine be reported immediately. It is also ordered that their books and goods be purchased in return for the payment of the correct price and that there should no longer be any complaints in this matter. Written in Constantinople on the first of *Zilhicce* in the year of the Hijrah 996.

---

* The Firman (Royal decree) of Sultan Murad III given in October 1588, which allowed European merchants to import books printed in the Arabic script.

AS IT BECOMES NECESSARY IT WILL BE ACCOMPLISHED
(A COPY OF THE IMPERIAL RESCRIPT, A COPY OF THE NOBLE IMPERIAL ORDER)*

This exalted royal order is given to that pinnacle of illustrious persons and notables, the official of the Grand Vezir, Sait, and to that educated select servant of the Palace, İbrahim, may his nobility increase. It is known that upon the establishment of the rising sun of the religion of Muhammad and that with the brightness of the dawn of Ahmed's religious community, may God bless him, and it is understood that since that time the enlightened and meritorious masters of religion, God bless them, wrote books and tracts of science and knowledge in order to protect and conserve the verses of the Koran, the traditions of the Prophet, and the entirety of knowledge. And these words served to maintain the good order of the people, and make known the laws of religion and state, and the organization of the state and community. Editing books and writings and collecting eloquent collections of poetry, they progressed and wrote histories and accounts and worked for the preservation and defense of knowledge and works of culture, facilitating and disseminating sciences and arts. People knowledgeable in Arabic and Persian profited from their explaining and teaching, and organizing the regulations for each of the particular sciences and disciplines. This being proper, in order that they would possess eternal happiness in this world and the next and gain a good reward, they did not cease writing valuable and knowledgeable books and tracts. However, with the passing of days and with the years going by as the Chingizids, created chaotic disturbances and Hulâgu rose to power, and with resplendent Andalusia in the hands of the Europeans, and with the convulsions of wars, killing, and destruction, most literary works have disappeared with their authors. Therefore, today in the Muslim lands the dictionaries of Cevheri and Van Kulu in the Arabic language, and books of history and, copies of scientific works which were burned are rare. Also, people did not give proper care and attention, and lacked concern about copying, so works were not carefully copied. These rare books are an inspiration to students of the arts and sciences and to seekers af knowledge.

Among the technical processes, printing is like coining money and impressing paper with a signet ring. Books produced by printing cause several thousand volumes to be produced from a single volume, all of which are accurate copies. With little effort there is great return, making this a desirable activity to pursue. By virtue of your having composed a learned tract about, and having expertise in, the various above-mentioned activities, you will see to the necessities and expenditures without loss of time, so that on a fortunate day

---

* The Firman of Ahmed III, given in 1139/1727, authorizing Sait Efendi and İbrahim Müteferrika to open a printing house using Arabic script. Authorization was limited to books on practical, that is, secular subjects and excluded those dealing with Islamic sciences.

this Western technique will be unveiled like a bride and will not again be hidden. It will be a reason for Muslims to say prayers for you and praise you to the end of time. Excepting books of religious law, Koranic exegesis, the traditions of the Prophet, and theology, you asked the Padishah's permission in the aforementioned tract to print dictionaries, history books, medical books, astronomy and geography books, travelogues, and books about logic. The aforementioned tract was referred to that very learned religious scholar, that most meritoriously pious mariner on the stormy sea of religious questions, that wellspring of the river of legal opinions, that wearer of the garment of piety, the *Şeyh-ül-İslam* and learned jurisconsult, Mevlana Abdullah, may Almighty God increase his goodness. The question was asked: Zeyd claiming expertise in the science of printing, illuminating, and producing copies of the letters and words of dictionaries, logic, philosophy, and astronomy texts, and like works, thus being able to produce exact copies of these books, is there not permission in the Holy Law for this good work? The one who is an expert at printing seeks a legal opinion because producing an accurate edition of a work in a short time, with no errors and many copies, results in there being an increased number of books, which is a benefit to the community. The answer is: Being able to produce this great benefit, this person receives permission with the condition that several educated persons be appointed as proof readers. Great benefit will come from the order based on that legal opinion, allowing for the exception of the religious subjects mentioned in the tract written with the pearl pen of wisdom. This legal opinion is well prepared and it stands out in a vast ocean as exemplary in the *Şeyh*'s career. What falls from his pen in the form of authoritative opinion is an overflowing garden, a basin of sweet water, a river which waters the desert with springs. The Imperial permission becomes proper on account of this well-explained authoritative declaration, this perfectly eloquent and noble opinion. Copies will be printed of dictionaries, and books about logic, astronomy and similar subjects, and so that the printed books will be free from printing mistakes, the wise, respected and meritorious religious scholar specializing in Islamic Law, the excellent *Kazi* of Istanbul, Mevlana İshak, and Selaniki's *Kazi*, Mevlana Sahib, and Ghalata's *Kazi*, Mevlana Asad, may their merits be increased, and from the illustrious religious orders, the pillar of the righteous religious scholars, the *Şeyh* of the Kasim Paşa Mevlevihane, Mevlana Musa, may his wisdom and knowledge increase, will oversee the proofreading. With the actual setting up of the press, the above-mentioned books in history, astronomy, geography, logic and so forth, after they pass the review of the learned scholars, shall become numerous. However, you will take special care to see that the copies remain free from error and depend on the noble learned men for this. Ordered in the middle of *Zulka'de* in the year 1139 in Istanbul the protected.

IN THE NAME OF GOD, THE MERCIFUL AND COMPASSIONATE, AND BY THAT SEEK GOD'S AID, THE TRACT ENTITLED, "THE USEFULNESS OF PRINTING"*

It is known that it is the inevitable will of God and sovereign divine decree that a community, a society, a people, or an individual, having a desire [to fulfill], becomes successful, blessed, and distinguished if the ruler assents. It is the will of God to arrange everything for the benefit of His servants, who are people of perfect faith, who, by means of His perfect beneficence, unveil the bride of His kindness and expose His hidden desires. This humble, ineloquent person of low endowment, who has need of Almighty God's mercy, in order to become educated, some years ago sought a degree of clear understanding of the glory of ancient peoples and the adventures of the children of Adam. I read a number of histories of ancient nations and works of various religious men; like an ant I industriously studied, but achieved only a poor understanding. There came to me a sudden, clear inspiration, that there are means and instruments that societies and groups of people could use for benefiting the organization of important human matters and for the glory and power of the empire and the state by which the various ancient states mentioned above became well-ordered, powerful, and enlightened, and preserved and perpetuated their religions. And in countries without law or order there was brought into existence order, intelligence, merit, and right guidance. They [the ancients] did not pause for one second in making inventions, artifices, and praiseworthy works. Certainly, modern men follow the path of the ancients; at present in many a state and nation, various educated scholars are producing laws and organizing state and society. This is a means of perpetuating the state organization and of preserving the history of the state and society. It is a means of protection, and a defense against change and alteration on account of falsehoods or untruths according to religion and morals, and a way of creating safety from sudden catastrophes and the changes arising in the poor memory of men caused by the passing of days and years, thus enabling the laws and ordinances of the state and society to be kept correctly, as if they were a compact inscribed in stone, copper, or iron. They have made many books in order to create a means to knowledge and education by open discussion, and they have made an easy road to invention and innovation. If this point is studied intensely, with the aim of one's becoming learned in the goodness of religion and the merits of states, then these books, written as if on a tablet created by strength and purpose from emerald, ruby, gold, and silver, are a means for the religion and state of Islam to continue the glory of the state and the good ordering of

* The essay by İbrahim Müteferrika entitled *Vesiletu-t Tibaa*, on the usefulness of printing, in which he exposes the losses incurred by Islamic learning from the absence of the art of printing and the great benefits its establishment would bring to Muslims in general and Ottomans in particular.

the important affairs of the community. Books are also a tool for perfecting the nation and the state, a method of increasing the majesty of the empire, and of becoming the protector and preserver, until the last day, of arts and sciences and recorded events from the miscalculations of man. And these writings create a solidarity in the community against factions and disorder, and the laws and regulations preserve the good order of the community from change and innovation. Without need for further explanation, it suddenly became very plain that as an aid and help to the general public, the path to follow was to make an effort to publish in the world, in large numbers, books on the necessary arts and sciences, books that are sound and accurate and in every way acceptable. This [printing of books] is a noble profession and beautiful calling. In order to become free from public and private questioning, and in order for him to become responsible for the completion of this important work, and so that it is clear that he is on a true, straight road in this work, a royal indication and command to this servant is necessary.

An Explanation of the Benefits of Printing Books

Being interested in the history of ancient nations, it is not obscured or veiled from the eyes that the *Beni İsrail*, in accordance with the commands of their scriptures, have gained distinction through their preserving of the holy Torah, the preservation and conservation of the scriptures of "the protected peoples" being necessary. For fear of their being miscopied by passing through the hands of numerous copyists, they did not seek to publish widely their religious books and the Torah. The destructive war of Nebuchadnezzar occurred because of their sinfulness in Jerusalem. By this evil fortune of the *Beni İsrail*, Jerusalem was completely conquered, the Ark of the Covenant destroyed, and the copies of the Torah and important books gathered by the people in their homes were thrown into the fire. Therefore, most of the books were lost to posterity. The commands of the Holy Law were the means of education for the *Beni İsrail*, but the true copies and unreliable transmissions thereof became indistinguishable, and the people fell under the authority and leadership of Jesus. When the Christians collected the verses of the noble Gospels, they were heedless of their benefits, and were careless and lazy about preserving them and did not think intelligently about publishing this knowledge among the people. When sainted Jesus, God praise that most illustrious prophet, was taken up to the precincts of heaven, the Christians, falling to quarreling about dogma, splitting into many factions, became followers of false paths and ways of unbelief. Valuing the majesty of the Islamic state and the revealed law of the Prophet, may God strengthen, exalt, and glorify him until the day of judgment, the elders of Islam were not heedless of this abyss of horrors nor were they confused about this source of peril. They shunned and avoided this degree of laziness. With the manifestation of the Koran in great glory, the elders took care that every word of the proclaimed Holy Law, every document or page which had been collected and written down, especially the traditions of the Prophet (that sublime path), they made sure that these original texts and the names of their transmitters were collected and organized into books and collections of wisdom. In this matter they desired to copy and write down without defect their remembrances and the acquired knowledge of the Muslims, preserving it in its details and generality, and they wished to disseminate it and make it available to the general Muslim public. This dissemination was a blessing to the entire community. However, with this community being continuously busy with jihad to the East and West, in a short time the majority of Muslims were confused about the splendid miracles, blessed events, and meritorious, blessed prayers. Learned religious leaders, perfect teachers, and the wisest interpreters of law and religious questions, using the Koran, the traditions, and the consensus of the community, and applying the methodology of analogy, they expended much energy bringing to light accurate interpretations and a sound methodology of interpretation in order to correct false practices and to achieve good. Religious scholars did not cease writing books on various sciences and arts or educating and sending forth students in order to guide the affairs of the people of the community. They produced innovative works, and they knew the blessings of paradise because of the benefit and merit they brought to themselves and their community by this splendid effort. They enabled the struggle for righteousness to continue in this community from its beginning and until the last day. Both the earliest and the latest scholars produced books and compilations which were collected together, but later they were destroyed by war and violence, especially during the evil time of violent confusion caused by the tribulations of the Chingizids when the books of Central Asia were thrown into the Jayhun, leaving no trace behind. When Hulâgu conquered the Abbasids, the books and compositions of the scholars and writers were dumped in the Tigris and their writings washed away, and thus beautiful and intelligent works vanished without leaving a trace. Later, after a long period of the tribulations of this world, the country of Andalusia was torn from the arms of Islam. In the Maghrib, the sun of science set in the oppressive darkness of the Europeans. In former times, the Umayyads conquered the Frankish factions in Andalusia, and by several paths came to great wealth, and they produced many Islamic books. However, now, in the lands of Islam, it is a fact that these books are rare and only a handful remain; throughout all the Islamic domain these books are rare. In the same manner as mentioned above, disturbed conditions, destructive events, and destroying fires each became a terrible malady for books, causing students of the sciences to suffer severe difficulties. The men of the current age, being followers of ease and being exhausted, and having debilitating wealth and ease, ignore beauty; consequently, innovative works are not appreciated or preserved. On one hand, the attitude toward the importance of many works, and of books generally, is laziness and heedlessness, and to a degree learning is despised, so that in this happy place, this mighty city, this vast country, may God preserve it from calamities and evil fortune, in the entire Ottoman domains, dictionaries, like Cevheri and Van Kulu in the Arabic language, and the necessary copies of books on history and biography, and works and volumes on like subjects that are important, are scarce and rare. It goes without saying that these books are brimming with information.

An Explanatory Summation About Printing

Among the arts, the art of printing is a beneficial one; among productive activities, printing is one full of benefits. Printing is a type of inscribing analogous to the action of engraving and writing by the pressing of words and lines on a page, it is like coining money or inscribing walls, or like the impression from a signet ring when pressed down upon a document.

The first benefit among the benefits of printing: This beneficial and innovative art is a clear explainer of the source and wellspring of all the sources, and is an answer to the needs of the people for Islamic books. In order to master Arabic, accurate and comprehensive dictionaries are important. Furthermore, if there are numerous books on history, astronomy, logic, the affairs of the state and nation, and geography, this altogether will create tremendous educational benefits.

The second benefit: From the first appearance of the religion and empire of Islam, in order to well and properly organize and strengthen religion, state, and the important affairs of the community, numbers of interpreters and compilers of nobility and intelligence made compilations and wrote books using the tool of interpretation. The work of the noble compilers and interpreters will become a means of renewal and restoration, because newly printed books, both numerous and accurate, being restored and invigorated as if they had been recently authored, will publish and present to the Muslims all the knowledge of their authors.

The third benefit: With books produced by the art of printing, it is possible to make beautiful calligraphy and splendid specimens of correct composition, eloquent expression, accurate arrangement, and excellent diction, without any mistakes, flaws, or errors. Students of the sciences, in studying and examining such books, are safe from mistakes and are secure from wasting time, because for teaching and learning, accurate texts are a necessity. It becomes unnecessary to compare many texts in order to obtain a correct understanding, and this facilitates learning in the sciences. A peculiarity of books written by pen is that the ink fades due to dampness and drying, and the writing disappears. However, using the methods of printing, its products' ink becomes stable and enduring, and the illustrations and text are not spoiled by water and dampness; they are safe and secure from the misfortune of becoming wet.

The fourth benefit: That printed works become items of commerce is another beneficial result. When a book is printed, there are several thousand exactly identical copies, and printing is a means of producing many clear, excellent, perfect books in a short time. Therefore, books become inexpensive, and students both rich and poor can obtain books and acquire a proper education in the desirable sciences and diplomas in religious studies.

The fifth benefit: With printing, the indexes and tables of contents of books can be made both by summary and in detail. The summary will appear at the beginning of the book, the detailed listing at the end. In the beginning of the books, by means of Indian numerals, will be indicated the proper place of the chapters and sections, thereby organizing the contents of the book so that the sections and chapters are indicated. If it is necessary to refer to the book, its contents and organization are immediately accessible. The second index allows the terms and words used in the book to be found instantly. This index will be placed at the end of the book. This index is to be organized alphabetically and the sought-after information found by this method has its place in the book indicated.

The sixth benefit: With the price of books becoming low, every single person can possess books, and furthermore, the widespread dissemination of books in town and country serves as a means of reducing ignorance.

The seventh benefit: By becoming numerous through the printing process, books become a foundation for the strength of the empire. Spreading throughout the Ottoman domains, the books of noble and desired sciences will become numerous in the cities and towns, and the libraries will become full of books. Furthermore, this country's students will become better educated, and the outlying regions will become more settled and better organized on account of having more books.

The eighth benefit: In the Islamic world the divine duty of jihad has not been abandoned and the warriors are firm. The illustrious Ottoman state, may God preserve it until judgement day, possesses thunderous canons, fierce incendiaries, powerful muskets, and in the activities of the science of war is like the various European masters and its enemies do not pose a difficulty. In the activity of jihad the kings from the Ottoman house, may God support them to the day of judgment, are the leaders and most perfect examples for the Muslims. Because they have attained the perfection of glory and fame among Muslims due to their waging jihad, they will enliven and invigorate the Muslims, and are exalted on account of this. However, it is more worthy to assent to printing, that being a way to make many books exist in the shadow of their royal happiness.

The ninth benefit: All the Christian countries, in making collections in Arabic, Persian, and Turkish, found these books valuable. The aforementioned books, upon being printed, became important and particularly desirable; law, medicine, Euclidean geometry, and other such works were printed in the three languages, and the quality of the books thus produced can clearly be seen. They are full of misspellings and mistakes, and the letters and lines are not easily read. There is no one, finding in his hands a book in Western letters and style, who will see in it any semblance of beauty and decoration or correctness in spelling and orthography. These books are being found in the lands of Islam, having been produced in quantity, and they have become desirable, and are inexpensive. However, their quality and finish is as given above. Those buying and selling books in the Islamic countries are gathering and collecting a benefit, while the Muslims are lower than the unbelievers and polytheists who are taking precedence. In this particular matter, that is, working to make the Muslims take precedence in the book trade, there is a necessary incumbent responsibility, and this gives life to the hope of being allowed to print books.

The tenth benefit: The particularities of this beneficial art's present establishment in the Ottoman state, as mentioned several times in thorough speech and writing, giving an accurate and certain knowledge to all that this is a most useful and beneficial activity, are such that because of its merits several people have become hopeful of establishing this activity and have made applications to do so. If the discussed activity is a desirable activity, but because of many problems is difficult to accomplish, and if on the verge of its occurring a happy fortune does not appear and there is truly delay, the source and reason for these problems exist in the preparation. At the time of consenting by royal order to the completion of this matter, for the strengthening of science, the lord of the fortunate conjunction and of the age, the conqueror of nations of Iran and Turan, the glorious, the noble, the powerful Emperor of the world, may God exalt and strengthen him, with His Majesty's support your servant will overcome doubt and solve the difficulties with God's help, and this Western activity become visible where it was formerly invisible. This art's introduction being arranged, and its appearing on a propitious day because of the Imperial assent, it will cause a glorious exaltation of fortune and unceasing joy. Books, like those mentioned above, coming into being in the Ottoman domains, completely aside from their meeting the needs of the Muslims, is an important event in itself, ennobling Islam and being a means to happiness of the Muslims. The various peoples of the world, that is, the Arabs and foreigners, the people of the Turks, Tatars and Turkmen, Kurds, Uzbeks, Chagatay, Hindi and Sindi, Persians and Maghribis, Yemenis, Greeks, Ethiopians and the Sudanese, all together having been exalted by Islam, they have need of various kinds of books. Therefore, introducing and bringing about this important and great work certainly increases and augments the glory and majesty of the Ottoman state, and is the cause of a glorious victory for the Empire and a splendid preface and a glorious superscription, lasting until the day of judgment. It will be remembered with goodness by the tongues of the world and will bring forth the good prayers of all believers; without dispute, printing is a means to enliven and make happy the Muslims.

Except for those on law, exegesis, traditions, and theology, books will be printed, such as dictionaries, histories, medical texts and science books, philosophy and astronomy books, and information about nature, geography, and travelogues. By its grace and majesty, publication of the glorious royal rescript giving royal permission in this matter from the exalted world-renowned Emperor, defender of the faith's exalted position, is fitting. His support, through his glorious name, for establishing this innovative Western technique in order to produce abundant numbers of books, is an excellent work, making his honor independent of the need of proof. The majestic legal concurrence comprising the Imperial rescript and the legal opinion of the religious authorities is necessary; therefore, this noble and majestic command will be printed at the beginning of the book to be published and will be independent of the text of the book, making it apparent to one and all that printing is desirable and approved. Furthtrmore, his excellency, the *Şeyh-ül-İslām*, that excellent jurisconsult and master of the masters of religion, his approval of this beneficial activity, this source of benefits, and his approval of this great endeavor, this noble striving, and of its being the cause for benefits to one and all, will also be published. In setting about this activity, the pronouncement of royal permission, the indication of noble support from the leaders of the religious scholars, and the other self-apparent merits of printing indicate that in every way printing conforms to the Holy Law. Furthermore, with the pronouncement and statement of support being placed in the beginning of every copy, the doubts of all people will be erased. When the book is printed, in order to be accurate and free of any defect or mistake in respect to the perfection of its composition and language, by our own consent, three or four persons will be employed as proofreaders, with their appointment being included in the royal order which is to be printed in the beginning of the first book from the press; this will act as an assurance to the people. Finally, by way of introduction, a brief summary of the merits and benefits of printing will be presented in a clear, two or three page tract in order to inform the community. All will then become cognizant and all the world will offer her their blessings and prayers.

Translated by
Christopher M. Murphy

Contributors

MICHAEL W. ALBIN is chief of the Order Division at the Library of Congress. From 1976 until 1985, he directed the Library's field office in Cairo, Egypt. His area of scholarly interest is the history of printing in the Islamic World. He is the author of numerous articles on this subject and has been awarded a Fulbright Islamic Civilization grant to pursue research in the archives and libraries of Iraq and Tunisia.

GEORGE N. ATIYEH has been head of the Near East Section at the Library of Congress since 1967. He was educated at the American University of Beirut and the University of Chicago. Before joining the Library, he taught at the University of Puerto Rico and chaired its Department of Humanities. He has authored and edited several books and articles, among which are *al-Kindi: The Philosopher of the Arabs*, *The Contemporary Middle East, 1948–1973: A Bibliography*, and *Arab Civilization: Challenges and Responses*.

RAMZI BAALBAKI is an associate professor of Arabic and director of the Center for Middle Eastern Studies at the American University of Beirut. He is a specialist in Semitic languages and the author of several works on Arabic, including *Semitic Arabic Writing: Studies in the History of Writing and its Semitic Roots*.

JACQUES BERQUE is one of the leading French scholars on the Arab world. He has taught and lectured in many Arab countries and at the prestigious College de France, of which he is an honorary professor. He is the author of more than forty books and articles. His book, *Les Arabes d'hier à demain*, was translated into several languages. He is considered one of the top authorities on North Africa. Professor Berque has recently published a new translation of the Koran into French.

FILIZ ÇAĞMAN is curator of the Topkapi Palace Museum Library. She is a well-known scholar of Islamic art and author of several studies, including *Topkapi Saray Museum: Islamic Miniature Art* and *Etudes Médiévales et Patrimonie Turc*.

DALE F. EICKELMAN is Ralph and Richard Lazarus Professor of Anthropology and Human Relations at Dartmouth College. Since 1968, he has spent over six years in the Middle East, including time devoted to extensive field research in Morocco and the Sultanate of Oman, with shorter stays in Egypt,

Iran, Iraq, and Tunisia. His publications include *Moroccan Islam* (Arabic translation, 1989); *The Middle East: An Anthropological Approach* (Japanese translation, 1988); *Knowledge and Power in Morocco*; and numerous scholarly articles and contributions to edited books. Currently, he is completing a study on changing perceptions of state authority and religious legitimacy in the Arab Gulf. He was president of the Middle East Studies Association of North America.

WADĀD AL-QĀḌĪ is professor of History at the University of Chicago, and taught previously at Yale University and the American University of Beirut. She is the author of a work on the Kisānīyah movement in history and literature, and the editor of *Dirāsāt ʿArabīyah wa-Islāmīyah*, a festschrift in honor of Dr. Iḥsān ʿAbbās. She was awarded the 1993 King Faisal prize for literature.

DAVID A. KING is professor of History of Science at the Institut für Geschichte der Naturwissenschaften, Johann Wolfgang Goethe Universität. He also occupied the same position at New York University. Dr. King is the author of numerous studies on the history of Arabic and Islamic science, and is the compiler of a catalog of scientific manuscripts in the Egyptian National Library.

MUHSIN MAHDI is the Jewett Professor of Arabic Studies at Harvard University. A leading scholar in this country, he is the author, translator, and editor of several philosophical works on Arabic and Islamic philosophy. Among his many works are *Ibn Khaldun's Philosophy of History* and *The Political Orientation of Islamic Philosophy.* He also edited *Medieval Political Philosophy: A Sourcebook*, and *The Thousand and One Nights*, contributing to this edition a thorough and scholarly introduction based on the early Arabic, original sources.

SALĀḤ AL-DĪN AL-MUNAJJID is a well-known scholar in the Arab world, and the author and editor of more than one hundred works. Formerly, he was a counselor at the League of Arab States, in charge of the Institute of Arabic Manuscripts, and the founder of its journal. He is also a member of the prestigious Academy of the Arabic Language in Cairo, and the Arab Academy of Damascus.

SEYYED HOSSEIN NASR is University Professor of Islamic Studies at George Washington University, in Washington, DC. Previously, he was professor of History of Science and Philosophy and Dean of the Faculty of Letters at Teheran University. He was also a visiting professor at Harvard University and professor of Islamic Studies at Temple University. Among his many works are *Three Muslim Sages, Ideals and Realities of Islam, Science and Civilization in Islam*, and *An Introduction to Islamic Cosmological Doctrines.*

GEOFFREY J. ROPER has been Islamic Bibliographer at Cambridge University Library and editor of *Index Islamicus* and *Quarterly Index Islamicus* since 1982. He holds an honours degree in Middle Eastern Studies from the University of Durham and a doctorate from the same university. He has carried out research on Arabic historical bibliography, including a major study of Arabic printing and publishing in nineteenth-century Malta, as well as a number of published articles and reviews.

FRANZ ROSENTHAL was Sterling Professor of Near Eastern Languages at Yale University from 1967 until 1985, when he became professor emeritus. Previously, he had taught at Hebrew Union College and the University of Pennsylvania. Among his publications are *Technique and Approach of Muslim Scholarship, History of Muslim Historiography, The Muslim Concept of Freedom*, and a masterful translation into English of Ibn Khaldūn's *Muqaddimah*.

ANNEMARIE SCHIMMEL was professor of Indo-Muslim Culture at Harvard University. She is the author of more than fifty works in German and English. Among her works are *As Through the Veil: Mystical Poetry in Islam, Calligraphy and Islamic Culture, Mystical Dimensions of Islam, Islam in the Indian Subcontinent*, and *Islamic Names*.

PRISCILLA SOUCEK is Hagop Kevorkian Professor of Islamic Art at the Institute of Art, New York University. She co-authored *The Meeting of Two Worlds: The Crusades and the Mediterranean Context*, and edited *Content and Context of Visual Arts in the World: Papers from a Colloquium in Memory of Richard Ettinghausen*.

Index